D1599158

Paying for the
German Inflation

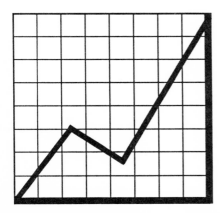

Paying for the German Inflation

Michael L. Hughes

The University of North Carolina Press

Chapel Hill and London

The paper in this book meets the guidelines for

permanence and durability of the Committee on Production Guidelines

for Book Longevity of the Council on Library Resources.

92 91 90 89 88 5 4 3 2 1

Library of Congress Cataloging-in-Publication Data

Hughes, Michael L.

Paying for the German inflation / by Michael L. Hughes.

p. cm.

Bibliography: p.

Includes index.

ISBN 0-8078-1777-5 (alk. paper)

1. Germany—Economic policy—1918–1933. 2. Germany—Economic
conditions—1918–1945. 3. Germany—Politics and
government—1918–1933. 4. National socialism—History. 5. Voting—
Germany—History—20th century. 6. Economic stabilization—
Germany—History—20th century. 7. Inflation (Finance)—Germany—
History—20th century. I. Title.

HC286.3.H84 . 1988   87-24631

332.4′1′0943—dc 19   CIP

TO GLORIA

Contents

Tables

Acknowledgments

In researching and writing this work I have become indebted to many people.

A grant from the German Academic Exchange Service financed my research. I used numerous archives and libraries in Germany, and their staffs were consistently friendly and helpful. I wish in particular to thank Dr. Friedrich Freiherr Hiller von Gaertringen, who allowed me access to the papers of his grandfather, Kuno Graf von Westarp, and who was a most gracious host.

I was fortunate to participate in the project on Inflation and Reconstruction in Germany and Europe, 1914–1929, sponsored by the Volkswagen Foundation, which financed the writing of my dissertation and the initial stages in the writing of this book. The members of the Inflation and Reconstruction project contributed valuable comments from their many perspectives. Dr. Gerald Feldman offered thoughtful, unstinting, and invaluable support from the start. Drs. Larry E. Jones and Claus-Dieter Krohn made many useful suggestions. At the University of California at Berkeley, the Contemporary Western Europe, Law and Society, and Economic History Colloquia listened to and commented on papers on various aspects of the revaluation. Dr. Gunther Teubner and Dr. Richard Buxbaum read earlier versions of the sections on legal developments and provided valuable insights.

Dr. Gloria Fitzgibbon read the entire manuscript carefully and provided substantive suggestions and encouragement beyond anything I can adequately acknowledge.

The journal *Central European History* kindly allowed me to reuse material that appeared in a somewhat different form in Michael L. Hughes, "Private Equity, Social Inequity: German Judges React to Inflation, 1914–1924," *Central European History* 16:1 (Mar. 1983): 76–94.

To all these, and any whom I may inadvertently have omitted, my heartfelt thanks. Any errors, inconsistencies, or omissions are, of course, the responsibility of the author.

Abbreviations

The following abbreviations are used in the text.

BVP   Bayerische Volkspartei

DDP   Deutsche Demokratische Partei

DNVP   Deutschnationale Volkspartei

DVP   Deutsche Volkspartei

GM   gold mark

HG(S)SV   Hypotheken Gläubiger (und Sparer) Schutzverband

KPD   Kommunistische Partei Deutschlands

PM   paper mark

RM   Reichsmark

SPD   Sozialdemokratische Partei Deutschlands

WP   Wirtschaftspartei

Z   Zentrumspartei

For source abbreviations used in the notes, see pages 195–96.

Paying for the
German Inflation

Introduction

Millions of Germans repudiated democracy and voted in the early 1930s for what proved to be the most vicious political movement in twentieth-century Europe. These people were not simply seduced by clever propaganda. They had very real needs—economic, social, political—that the existing democratic order was unable to meet but that the Nazis promised to satisfy.

Among those who voted for Hitler were numerous creditors whose life savings inflation had destroyed. They had paid much of the costs of the German inflation—and they would seek desperately, but not completely successfully, to shift those costs to others. Their experience illuminates both the general problems of dealing with an inflation's aftermath and the Weimar Republic's difficulties in solving those problems. This study will focus on how the Republic's ultimately maladroit efforts to deal with inflation and revaluation made many creditors disillusioned with democracy and susceptible to Nazi rhetoric.

The 100 trillion percent inflation Germany suffered between 1914 and 1923 was a horrific experience for the German people. Although initial increases were modest, by 1923 prices were changing daily and eventually hourly, throwing life into utter chaos. Inflation wiped out savings, made rational investment difficult, and decreased many people's real incomes, often disastrously. It eventually made economic activity so inefficient that stabilizing the currency's value became necessary—at virtually any cost. Like any major inflation, it left behind bitter memories.

Ending a major inflation, stabilizing a currency, can, however, be more painful than inflation itself. Inflation does have certain advantages while it lasts—full employment for workers, increased domestic demand and more favorable access to foreign markets for producers, an easy source of revenue for the government, and the opportunity to pay off debts in depreciated paper for debtors. In order to stabilize, the government must shatter inflationary expectations with a sharp shock and must impose tough policies to force people to reestablish their economic activities on a solid footing. Severe credit restrictions mean unemployment and low wages for employees and, for business and agriculture, reduced income or even bankruptcy. The state's desperate scramble to balance its budget means increased taxes for most or all and drastically decreased expenditures that can devastate those dependent on government programs. And currency stabilization can politically destabilize even a strong state, as people realize how much they stand to lose and how much some lucky individuals stand to gain from government policies.

Germany's experience with stabilization after 1923 illustrates these problems. To stabilize, the government had to impose staggering burdens on a people already reeling from inflation. Many Germans suffered severely. Moreover, because the stabilization was so tenuous, the state argued that it had to spare industry and agriculture from "excessive" burdens—to ensure economic recovery. Most Germans, though, became convinced that the government spared these sectors because economic elites had illegitimate influence with a corrupt system. Many Germans then elaborated alternative ideas of the just society that predisposed them to accept, eventually, Nazi rhetoric. The Weimar Republic and democracy had not yet secured themselves in the hearts of the German people, and the grinding stabilization process eroded the legitimacy of a weak political system. It hence played a crucial role in Weimar's decline and, indirectly, in Hitler's rise, making it a central factor in German history.[1]

Stabilization made explicit how inflation had unfairly expropriated creditors, and it stimulated them to demand redress. Inflation had obliterated the life savings of millions of Germans and had utterly impoverished hundreds of thousands, as debtors were able to pay off their debts in often worthless paper marks. These creditors, mostly individual German savers, had paid much of inflation's costs. They demanded that society compensate them by revaluing debts, that is, by forcing debtors to repay at least partially with gold equivalents. Creditors would then receive some real payment, instead of only worthless paper.[2]

The conflict over revaluation contributed significantly to stabilization's corrosive effects. Providing creditors with anywhere near the recompense they deserved would have destroyed the stabilization, with potentially disastrous consequences. The issue was so complex, though, that most creditors were sincerely convinced the economy could finance full revaluation. Meanwhile, judges, government officials, and politicians set the creditors up for disappointment; out of confusion or expediency, these policymakers periodically raised and dashed creditor hopes by making and breaking unrealistic promises on revaluation. A combination of ignorance, demagoguery, and real moral ambiguity so muddled the issues that many creditors justifiably felt betrayed when the government provided only limited revaluation in 1925. (The Appendix summarizes the provisions of the revaluation legislation.) Convinced that this revaluation did not accord with what a just society should and could provide, they turned against the Weimar Republic and democracy. Their embittered response is important for understanding their eventual swing to Hitler, who claimed to offer a new order similar to their view of the good society. And it is a model for some of the disillusioning experiences that other groups in Germany faced under stabilization's impact.

Stabilization was indispensable, but it contained within it the seeds of future difficulties. Because substantial revaluation would have threatened the credit and competitiveness of producers (usually debtors), the German government had to limit revaluation to provide the necessary economic basis for stabilization. Yet to ensure long-term economic recovery, the government also had to convince its citizens, including creditors, that it was making a good-faith effort to provide the maximum revaluation feasible. Otherwise, Germans might, and in the event did, refuse to save at adequate levels, with serious economic and fiscal consequences. The revaluation struggle hence illuminates the long-term disadvantages of inflation, the favored position of producers in the political process, and the economic constraints that some historians believe foredoomed the Weimar Republic.

The revaluation also decisively influenced German jurisprudence in ways that raised still-controversial questions about the role of the judiciary, the motives of judges, and the extent to which the law can become a force independent of the wishes of politicians. Inflation presented judges with an unprecedented task that the traditional legal order was unequipped to handle. Believing they had to do something, they tacitly redefined the legal order to deal with inflation. But the ways they chose to redefine it radically expanded their own discretion in interpreting the law. When the judges finally dealt with debt revaluation, they shifted from interpreting to making law, at one point openly challenging the constitutional prerogatives of the executive and legislature. And by ruling that "the law" required debt revaluation, they made it a matter of justice, forced politicians to accept some form of it, and decisively influenced its development.

Although Germany's political culture is, of course, unique, its experience with revaluation has current significance. People everywhere try to save for the future, and most depend on some reasonable monetary stability to do so. By destroying such stability, inflation threatens fundamental interests and values and erodes faith in the future. It can evoke vehement demands for relief. Yet every state must reconcile individual demands for equitable treatment with the needs of the economy as a whole.

4 Paying for the German Inflation

The German experience suggests the costs of inflation, the difficulty of providing recompense after inflation, and the political risks involved in trifling with people's sense of equity in these matters. This history cannot offer specific policy alternatives to current policymakers, but it illuminates the factors they must consider in trying to solve the nearly intractable problems of inflation and stabilization.

Inflation and the Creditors

Inflation and the Depreciation of Paper Assets

Early-twentieth-century Germans did not expect prices to rise and had no experience to help them deal with inflation. Prices had been relatively stable in the nineteenth century and had actually fallen between 1873 and 1896. Creeping inflation between 1896 and 1914 had not been striking enough to alter people's assumptions or expectations.[1]

In 1909 Germany had enacted new currency legislation that made paper currency legal tender for all debts. Lawmakers intended to compensate for the relative shortage of gold coins and to provide flexibility in the event of war. The legislation did guarantee individuals the right to convert currency into gold. Most contracts also contained a "gold payment clause" (GM clause), stipulating payment in gold marks (GM) on request. The right to exchange paper currency for gold and to demand GM in payment generally protected creditors against inflation's effects.[2]

The German government promulgated legislation at the outbreak of World War I that opened the way for inflation. On 4 August 1914 the legislature suspended the individual's right to convert bank notes into gold, and it allowed the Reichsbank (central bank) to use government and commercial paper as part of the reserves for issuing new currency. The legislation forestalled any run on the Reichsbank gold reserves, which contemporaries believed guaranteed a currency's value, and allowed the government to print more money. As hopes for a speedy end to the war dwindled, the government issued on 28 September a decree that suspended all GM clauses. Payers could now fulfill their obligations in paper marks (PM). The legislature reserved to itself the right to determine when to repeal these statutes.[3]

The government had asserted that the 28 September decree was "unobjectionable because it does not harm the creditor in any way."[4] Prorevaluation writers later cited this as proof the government did not intend for creditors to suffer from any inflation that might occur. Hence, they argued, creditors could still demand gold-*value* payment, even if the state had had to suspend gold-coin payment temporarily.[5]

Nonetheless, these measures did leave creditors unprotected against inflation's effects. No one in 1914 even vaguely foresaw the inflation's magnitude, but the currency legislation did establish the "mark equals mark principle": for legal purposes a 1915—or 1919 or 1923—paper mark must equal a 1913 gold mark. Creditors must therefore accept any loss of values inflation might entail. And by subsequently forbidding a discount in PM transactions, the government only confirmed the mark equals mark principle—even if this meant losses for creditors.[6]

Even before war's end Germany was in a strongly inflationary situation. The amended currency legislation allowed the government to increase the money supply almost without limit and to finance the war with inflation. For domestic political reasons, the German government feared to raise taxes to pay for World War I. It hence covered only about one-fifth of total government wartime expenditures from normal revenues, the rest (160 billion marks for all levels of government) by loans or treasury bills.[7] Government policies increased the currency supply (*Bargeld*) from 6.9 billion marks in July 1914 to 29.2 billion in November 1918. The domestic price index had risen about 100 percent.[8] And hanging over the economy was a war-debt mountain of 98 billion marks. The debt service alone on this tremendous sum absorbed more than 100 percent of the 1919 Reich (central government) revenue.[9]

Germans generally failed to understand the nature of the price changes. Prevailing monetary theories usually ignored the influence of the quantity of money on price levels, emphasizing instead foreign exchange and supply constraints.[10] During the war, price controls, high war-bond subscriptions, and limited foreign trade hid the effects of the growing money supply. Germans attributed price increases not to "inflation," a fundamental change in the relationship of value between money and goods, but to "*Teuerung*," a temporary dearness of goods resulting from (very real) war-induced scarcity and increased costs. Although the money supply's influence on price levels eventually became obvious, many policymakers—and the vast majority of Germans—long continued to blame the inflation solely on war- and reparations-induced dislocations. They did not realize that the increased money supply implied a permanent increase in PM price levels.[11]

Defeat destroyed the German government's hope that it could shift its war costs to its enemies and aggravated Germany's war-induced economic weakness. The Allies insisted that Germany pay part of *their* war costs through reparations. The Treaty of Versailles deprived Germany of 10 percent of its population, automatically increasing the per capita public-debt and reparations burdens. Germany lost 13 percent of its land area, including important sources of agricultural products and raw materials, as well as extensive manufacturing capacity. The country had to surrender virtually all foreign assets, its entire merchant fleet, and large quantities of rolling stock.

The major cause of inflation, though, was the Reich's continuing budget deficits. Because of inflation and tax avoidance, the new, relatively weak Weimar Republic did not collect enough taxes to cover its expenditures. Even though the real burden of war debt shrank to a mere 0.154 GM by November 1923, the reparations burden remained. Demobilization costs (including long-term charges such as war widows' pensions) were considerable, and political unrest and political philosophy inclined the new regime to expand social programs dramatically. Hence, from 1919 to 1923 taxes never covered more than 35 percent of expenditures and generally covered much less.[12] The Reichsbank covered the deficits by discounting treasury bills, leading to an irregular but continuing increase in the money supply. The note circulation rose from 29.2 billion marks in November 1918 to reach 1.3 trillion in December 1922 and 497×10^{18} (497 quintillion) in November 1923.[13]

The exact motives behind this inflationary fiscal policy are difficult to untangle, but policymakers clearly learned about inflation's causes and possible short-term benefits. At least from 1918 Reichsbank officials told government officials that budget deficits had inflationary implications. In 1919 some government officials noted that inflation would reduce the real cost of the state's debt. And after 1919 many policymakers, industrialists, and union leaders pursued or acquiesced in an inflationary policy because of its short-term advantages. Inflation is a kind of tax, a charge on holders of paper money and paper assets. It provided an indirect and obscure and hence relatively easy method for financing government expenditures. It also temporarily underwrote full employment and an export offensive that allowed German business to recapture many foreign markets. Indeed, some scholars have argued, rather convincingly, that inflationary policies thereby protected the weak Republic from insurrection while it established its authority. Further, after May 1921 some politicians and industrialists talked about inflation as a way to show the Allies that they had to reduce Germany's reparations bill. Finally, civil servants demanded and secured salary increases to maintain their living standards, even though their leaders came to recognize the inflationary implications of the additional government expenditures.[14]

Significantly, policymakers came at least tacitly to accept inflationary policies, even if not all politicians were doing so deliberately to secure specific short-term benefits. On 9 May 1921 the Reichstag (lower house of the legislature) eliminated the requirement that the Reichsbank hold reserves for one-third of the currency issue. Even under prewar monetary theories, removing the reserve requirement was a consciously inflationary policy. Further, the Reichsbank began on 1 June 1921 to purchase gold coins at a premium, acknowledging the paper mark's decline in value; it hence, according to Hjalmar Schacht, "for the first time officially recognized the inflation."[15]

The inflation was not a steady process. Prices occasionally stabilized or even dropped somewhat, and they fluctuated widely in response to foreign speculations and political vagaries. Foreign exchange values, wholesale prices, and the cost of living changed at varying rates.[16] These fluctuations contributed to the creditors' confusion and help to explain the relatively long delay before they began seeking relief.

After 1920 the long-term inflation rate did accelerate, albeit at an irregular pace. By November 1922 the mark had fallen to less than one five-hundredth of its prewar purchasing power, effectively expropriating all but the very richest creditor.[17] When the German government attempted in 1923 to counter France and Belgium by financing passive resistance in the newly occupied Ruhr, it burdened the budget and economy with exorbitant and insupportable costs. The consequent hyperinflation produced a 1,869 million percent rise in the cost of living in 1923.[18]

By September 1923 Germany faced economic and political chaos unless it could end the inflation. The urban economy was dissolving. Farmers would only sell enough of their crop to pay taxes because they saw no sense in accepting paper marks that were depreciating hourly. The agriculture minister feared famine amid plenty.[19] Politicians had earlier argued that the reparations and balance of payments situations would have to improve before Germany could stabilize the mark. Now, however, they felt that Germany *must* attempt to stabilize or face total ruin.

A consensus now existed that the government must stop printing money and create a new currency with some convincing backing. Recognizing the potentially disastrous situation, the Reichstag empowered the government to rule by decree. On 15 October the government established the Rentenbank to issue a new currency, the Rentenmark, secured by a mortgage on all real property in Germany. The Rentenmark was merely an "additional, fixed-value medium of payment," while the virtually worthless paper mark remained legal tender. The government received a limited credit of 1.2 billion Rentenmarks to tide it over while it struggled desperately to balance its budget. The Rentenbank's refusal to extend more credit to the government in December 1923 stabilized the Rentenmark by demonstrating that Germany had indeed stopped the printing presses.[20]

In stabilizing the paper mark at one-trillionth of its prewar value, the state effectively expropriated all holders of paper assets. The government introduced the new currency on 16 November, with one Rentenmark equivalent to one GM, and 4.2 GM equivalent to one U.S. dollar, the prewar rate. When the PM reached 4.2 trillion to the dollar on 20 November, the government established a rate of one Rentenmark to one trillion PM. It chose this rate partly to give the illusion it was reestablishing prewar money values. But the government also deliberately delayed setting the rate in order to reduce the real value of its floating debt from 320 million to 191.6 million Rentenmarks.[21]

Creditors, Debtors, and Revaluation

Maintaining the currency's value was a major responsibility of the nineteenth-century European state. The middle and lower-middle classes depended on a stable currency in daily life and in planning for the future, and they considered this responsibility an essentially moral one. German creditors had saved in the implicit faith the state would preserve the mark upon which those savings were based.

Instead, after 1914 the state debauched the currency. German governments increasingly chose inflation, more or less consciously, as the easiest "tax" for financing the costs of war and defeat. Inflation's most obvious long-term "benefit" was to reduce the real value of Germany's public debt to about two gold pfennigs, less than one cent. It also benefited private debtors by reducing their real burden from about 70 billion marks to less than one gold pfennig. The government had imposed on the creditors much of the cost of World War I and its aftermath.

In considering ways to aid creditors hurt by these developments, Germans generally excluded short-term debts (e.g., demand deposits, commercial credit, treasury bills, consumer credit). Such debts were ephemeral, and creditors ought long since to have recognized inflation's deleterious effects on such PM investments. The debt-revaluation conflict dealt rather with so-called *Vermögensanlagen*: long-term PM investments with the expectation of some reasonable security.

Although the German legal system had recognized the speculative character of all investment under capitalism, the government had endorsed certain assets as *mündelsicher*, as sufficiently secure for investing a ward's capital. Such assets included mortgages within the first 50 percent of assessed value (60 percent in Prussia), savings-bank accounts, mortgage bonds, and government bonds, which were among the most commonly held types of *Vermögensanlagen*. (The other major *Vermögensanlagen* were lower ranking mortgages, industrial obligations [i.e., all long-term, fixed-amount securities issued by any corporation], and life-insurance policies.) In addition, in appealing to the German people to buy war bonds, the government had repeatedly promised that it would faithfully repay the bonds at full value.

Given these assurances, most creditors could not conceive of their assets as speculative investments. Instead, they saw the government's inflationary policies as a base betrayal of explicit and implicit government promises. The German term for revaluation, *Aufwertung*, also implied restoring social and ethical values, and creditors perceived revaluation as a predominantly moral question—they had been swindled and deserved recompense. This moral subtext was a crucial aspect of the creditors' attitude, as was their sense that the government could in fact restore the prewar socioeconomic order.

Creditors, made desperate by their losses, eventually began turning to revaluation. In response to creditor pleas, the courts ruled in November 1923 that the law required "individual" revaluation: judges would revalue each debt individually based on the relative economic situations of creditor and debtor. Because individual revaluation would involve economically deleterious uncertainty, the government rejected it in favor of "schematic" revaluation: the state would legislatively assign each type of debt a fixed revaluation rate (e.g., 25 percent for mortgages). Although fixed rates would reduce uncertainty, the state would have to choose rates low enough to protect weaker debtors, giving stronger debtors a profit. The creditors ultimately demanded instead a revaluation "norm": normal, fixed rates with the right of both parties to sue for an adjustment if circumstances demanded.

The exact number of PM creditors is impossible to establish. Statistics on the total number of PM debts outstanding in 1924 are incomplete. Also, some creditors were credit institutions or other nonphysical persons, and many creditors were creditor to more than one debtor. Some Germans were both creditor and debtor. Probably somewhat over one-fourth but less than one-half of the electorate were, in 1924, net PM creditors.

Although the creditor movement talked as though most voters were creditors, creditor-movement membership was relatively small. Extrapolating from reliable data on local creditor groups in southwest Germany (from December 1925 and January 1926), organized creditors apparently constituted little more than one percent of the electorate. Although obtaining as much as 5 percent of the vote in Land elections, creditor-movement candidates in the 1928 Reichstag election got only 1.6 percent of the vote (part of which may have been noncreditor protest vote).[22]

Revaluation was only one issue among many, and the amount of savings individuals held influenced their perception of it. PM creditors arguably fell into three relatively distinct categories: (1) those opposed or indifferent to revaluation because their savings were minimal; (2) those vehemently favoring revaluation because they had substantial savings or depended on their savings; and (3) a middle group favoring revaluation but ultimately more interested in other issues. Although heuristically useful, these categories were not rigid. Many with meager or modest savings, and even some with no savings, favored revaluation because they were morally indignant at the legal expropriation of the creditors. Conversely, some with large savings opposed revaluation because they feared its economic effects.

Most PM creditors had only meager savings. For them, revaluation was not worth the effort of political agitation, especially compared with more pressing issues such as credit or taxes. More important, Germany could only finance revaluation by transferring funds to creditors from other social groups. Most creditors could lose far more from revaluation-induced higher prices, rents, and taxes than they might gain from any increased value of their meager savings. Basically, only those with above-average savings or who depended on their savings might achieve a net gain. Hence, the creditor movement represented a relatively small minority of the German people.

Most significant for the creditor movement were those who did depend on or had very large PM savings. Approximately 9 percent of the population had lived from pensions or PM assets before the war. Some companies revalued pensions voluntarily, and the government revalued civil-service pensions separately, so that debt revaluation was secondary for an indeterminate number of these pensioners. Many Germans, however, would have been approaching a retirement they had hoped to finance from paper assets, and many voters would have depended on their spouses' assets. Hence those dependent or soon to become dependent on PM pensions or assets, with little other capital to fall back on, presumably made up around 9 to 12 percent of the electorate.[23]

Although the creditor movement was basically an interest group, this category of creditors did constitute a class in one sense. Their relationship to the means of production was not wages, not rents, not profits—but interest payments. With severe monetary dislocation, their economic self-interest became diametrically opposed to that of businessmen and other debtors.[24] They realized this in 1925 and became, paradoxical as it may seem, virulently anticapitalist.

This "class" character of some creditors deserves mention (despite the term's weighty implications) because it illuminates the depth of feeling that motivated the creditor movement. These people's livelihoods were at stake—and they found themselves in a life-and-death battle with the existing capitalist order to recover their lost savings. And their determination, vehemence, and moral indignation, underpinned by their vital economic self-interest, were the motors of the creditor movement.

In an equally important sense, however, such creditors were not a class, indeed they abhorred the very concept of class. They never drew the full implications of their "class" situation as creditors. This situation was, after all, transitory, resulting from inflation and their retirement or imminent retirement. Perhaps more important, they identified themselves as members of a status group, the independent *Mittelstand* of rentiers, artisans, shopkeepers, civil servants, and white-collar workers. This identification ultimately determined the policy goals they pursued: individual revaluation of private debts and full recognition of the GM value of public debts as means to restore their economic independence.

The third group consisted of those with enough PM savings to consider revaluation economically important, even if not decisive, plus those morally indignant enough at creditor losses to support extensive revaluation. Many of the latter were presumably related to creditors whom inflation had deprived of their livelihood. Judges played a vital role in revaluation's development and probably often fell into this category. They had government pensions and so would not have depended on their investments for retirement, but they were relatively well-paid and thrifty and apparently usually had above-average PM savings. Also, the legal expropriation of

PM creditors outraged many judges' sense of equity, not least because of the judiciary's own unwilling role in administering that expropriation before 28 November 1923.

This third group widened the creditor movement's support to include a substantial number of voters, and its sense of the moral need to compensate creditors influenced politicians and the wider society. Once the legislature enacted the revaluation laws, members of this group were presumably less inclined to struggle actively for increased revaluation. But they would sympathize when creditors subsequently attacked the Republic's legitimacy because of its failure to compensate unfairly impoverished savers.

Revaluation supporters were predominantly members of the *Mittelstand*. Table 1 includes the membership by occupation of five local creditor groups (lines 1–5). Often, those most interested in revaluation could not afford the membership dues, and the occupational categories chosen do not correspond exactly to census categories (line 11). Nonetheless, some conclusions about the creditor movement's social origins are possible. Workers were obviously underrepresented, as were farmers (possibly because these creditor groups were in urban areas). Self-supporting individuals (businessmen other than professionals and farmers) were also apparently underrepresented. Most would have been debtors, but some would have depended entirely on their investments for retirement. Civil servants and white-collar workers, on the other hand, made up nearly 38 percent of the membership, but only about 15 percent of the work force. The free professions made up over 14 percent of the membership, but only 1.2 percent of the population. The free professions depended particularly on their savings, because most had no pensions or other social-insurance plans. Also, many lawyers presumably had a professional self-interest in the litigation revaluation could bring.

A sample of 200 letters that creditors sent to government officials (lines 8–10) basically confirms this analysis. Seventy-eight of the letter writers did not give their social status. Of those who did, 61 writers (50 percent) identified themselves as elderly, retired, rentiers, or widows. And surveys of petty rentiers (including owners or former owners of rental property and stocks) showed that they were usually elderly (often widows) or *Haustöchter* (spinsters who lived from an inheritance). Hence the revaluation movement's core was quite probably those dependent on their savings and no longer active in economic life. On the other hand, retirees probably constituted less than 50 percent of all the politically active creditors, because those who depended on their savings would presumably mention their

Table 1. *Social Composition of Creditors (in Percentages)*

Key	Civil Servant	White Collar Worker	Merchant	Manufacturer	Professional	Worker	Farmer
1	16.58	5.71	1.73	0.18	6.30	1.77	0.09
2	25.28	15.52	1.80	—	11.92	2.89	—
3	32.50	13.30	1.42	—	14.25	3.81	4.28
4	29.00	7.11	2.55	0.11	11.79	0.44	0.22
5	13.60	15.63	8.27	1.10	19.48	9.57	7.17
6	23.35	11.45	3.15	0.45	12.74	3.70	2.94
7	25.04	12.89	3.51	0.30	14.31	4.17	3.89
	37.93		3.81				
8	20.00	18.00	21.00		34.40	3.20	3.20
9	9.80	9.00	10.60		17.20	1.60	1.60
10	6.00	5.50	6.50		10.50	1.00	1.00
11	16.04		ca. 17.00		1.20	47.00	6.14

Key:
1–5. These are percentages drawn from 5 local groups of the HGSSV, including (1) Karlsruhe, (2) Mannheim, (3) Ludwigshafen a. Rhine and Schwetzingen, (4) Heidelberg, (5) Worms. They come from G. Winnewisser, *Die Aufwertung der Industrie-Obligationen*, p. 30.
6. The average of all five local groups.
7. The average of all local groups except Karlsruhe, which included the local Rentnerbund.
8. Percentages of those *giving* occupations drawn from a sample of 200 creditor letters.
9. Percentages including those identifying selves either by occupation or as rentier, retired, elderly, or widowed, drawn from the letter sample.
10. Percentages covering all 200 letters, including those who made no identifying comments.
11. Percentage weight of certain groups in German society as a whole, based on the 1925 census and drawn from T. Geiger, *Die Soziale Schichtung des deutschen Volkes*, pp. 20–23, 73. The percentage for the free professions is drawn from the *Grosse Brockhaus*, 1928, article on "Freie Berufen." (These are really only estimates.)

Wife	Widow	Spinster	Privatier	Rentier	Organization	No Occupation Given
2.14	5.80	1.73	1.99	54.13	0.36	1.49
4.69	5.77	10.10	11.91	2.17	0.73	7.22
3.33	6.17	3.33	9.02	—	0.24	8.55
6.00	13.78	15.56	4.33	1.00	—	8.11
—	—	—	11.95	13.23	—	—
4.00	7.87	7.67	7.84	17.63	0.40	6.34
4.67	8.57	9.66	9.30	5.46 14.76	0.48	7.96
—	—	—	—	—	—	—
—	9.80	—	40.10		—	—
—	6.00	—	24.50		—	34.00
—	—	—	9.0		—	—

status in petitioning for relief, whereas those still active in economic life would tend rather to emphasize their moral claim to revaluation. Of the 61 letter writers giving an occupation, nearly 38 percent were civil servants or white-collar workers; 34.4 percent were of the free professions, especially lawyers (who made up 21 percent of those giving an occupation). Self-supporting individuals were well represented in the letters, and evidence from other sources suggests that many older or retired small businessmen favored revaluation because they had invested in *mündelsicher* assets to prepare for old age or disability.[25]

Although no firm data are available, election statistics, the degree of creditor organization, and creditor letters suggest that the movement decisively influenced the political attitudes of only a minority of voters, perhaps less than 20 percent. Many others, though, would have sympathized with the creditors' cause and deplored any failure to treat them fairly. Only about 3 to 5 percent of the electorate were vehement revaluation supporters, although around 9 to 12 percent probably depended or had hoped soon to depend on PM assets for their livelihoods. Perhaps another 7 to 10 percent of voters fell into the middle group of moderate revaluation supporters. These were not insignificant numbers, as creditor success in forcing the government to revise its revaluation policies would show.

Debtors were a variegated group. If most Germans were not substantial creditors, neither were they substantial debtors. Very little mortgage credit was available for wage earners or the salaried, and (short-term) consumer credit was not subject to revaluation. Many businessmen, artisans, farmers, and building owners, however, were still PM debtors and opposed revaluation. Credit institutions, though both creditor and debtor, generally opposed revaluation after February 1924 because of its cost and complexity. Also, the state was the biggest PM debtor, inclining government officials at all levels (and many taxpayers) to oppose revaluation.

Further, many nondebtors came to oppose revaluation, often vehemently. The debtor and banking segments of society, the producer groups, identified themselves as "the economy," as though consumers and creditors deserved short shrift. They convinced themselves and many nondebtors, including many government officials and politicians and some creditors, to oppose revaluation as harmful to producer/debtors and therefore the economy. The creditors, though determined, faced powerful opponents—and a new and confusing situation.

Political Defeat, Legal Victory

The Courts Start Grappling with Inflation

In a capitalist economy, every investment is a speculation. Creditors and debtors must, for example, bear the risk of inflation or deflation. In Germany such "individualistic, capitalistic principles" had the added dignity of being embodied in the late-nineteenth-century Civil Code.[1] Some Germans even considered revaluation immoral because it penalized those investors who had trusted the state not to change the legal rules under which they had invested.[2] The German judiciary, however, eventually came to believe it could not uphold these capitalistic principles—with crucial results.

Legal positivism was the "absolutely ruling legal theory" in Germany before World War I. The state embodied the legislative power and the power to set norms of justice.[3] The judge was only to apply (*anwenden*) the positive, statutory law in the narrowest possible sense. The case-law and equity techniques of Anglo-American jurisprudence had no counterparts in German law.[4]

Although several "general clauses" in the Civil Code seemed to leave scope for judges to interpret private law, the Code's liberal drafters never intended to allow broad judicial discretion. Paragraph 242 of the Code, which states that the "obligor is bound to carry out his performance in the manner required by [equity and] good faith with regard to prevailing usage," was added to assist the judge in clarifying contractual ambiguities, not to encourage judicial activism. Over the last sixty years Paragraph 242 has developed into a central factor in German law, but it was virtually unused before World War I.[5]

Yet prewar jurists were not completely passive. Any judicial ruling requires some interpretation. And German judges gradually began citing earlier court decisions in justifying their own rulings, a prime tool of case-law systems.[6] Also, some jurists (the "free-law school") reacted against the rigidity they perceived in the new code by demanding more scope for judicial interpretation; they touted the general clauses as a firm basis for their proposals.[7]

Nonetheless, most jurists were not yet ready to expand the judiciary's role, and the exact form any expansion might take was far from clear. As the American scholar John Dawson writes, the "revolution in inherited legal tradition" that the courts implemented using Paragraph 242 "surely would not have come so soon or on so great a scale if Germany after losing a war had not been driven to economic catastrophe by . . . inflation of the national currency."[8]

As firm believers in monarchical sovereignty, most German judges had no qualms about submitting themselves to the monarch's will as expressed in legislation, even when that involved recognizing the speculative nature of investment and sustaining the mark equals mark principle during a period of modest wartime inflation. In a 1916 contract case the Reichsgericht even rejected an appeal asserting that Paragraph 242 could overrule that principle. The court argued that the payee had gambled on price changes and must bear the risk. Using Paragraph 242 for relief would create legal uncertainty that would undercut everyone's rights.[9] By 1918 courts were allowing one party to rescind a contract if wartime conditions made fulfilling it extremely burdensome, but higher courts continued to reject price changes per se as adequate grounds to rescind.[10]

Defeat and revolution in 1918 transformed judicial attitudes. The revolution constituted a *Rechtsbruch*, an illegal act and a break in legal continuity. For supporters of monarchical sovereignty, a new constitution based on popular sovereignty could hardly make good this *Rechtsbruch*. Most judges mistrusted the Republic and its parliament and believed they now had a special responsibility for maintaining legality. They obviously wanted to increase their powers at parliament's expense, but the issues they would use to do so remained unclear.[11]

Although inflation accelerated after 1918, wholesale prices fell between March and July 1920. The judiciary therefore only began to erode the mark equals mark principle after mid-1920 when prices began climbing again.

Between June and September 1920, the Reichsgericht's Third Civil Senate reversed itself and ruled a payee could insist on renegotiating a contract. The judges based their decision on (1) [equity and] good faith,

(2) a redefinition of "impossibility of performance" to include the threat of economic ruin from price changes, and (3) *clausula rebus sic stantibus*. This last principle posited that every contract implicitly assumed some preconditions and that the contract would be null if these preconditions ceased to exist. The Civil Code's drafters and the prewar Reichsgericht had both rejected this doctrine because it might endanger *Rechtssicherheit* (legal predictability and security in one's rights).[12]

This case only foreshadowed future developments. As prices stabilized temporarily and open-price contracts became common, the courts allowed only "economic ruin" as sufficient grounds for rescinding contracts. A new jump in prices in autumn 1921, though, apparently convinced the judges that inflation was not merely a temporary effect of war and revolution.[13]

On 3 February 1922 the Reichsgericht's Second Civil Senate accepted the principle that a drastic change in the value of money could by itself nullify a contract by destroying the necessary "equivalence."[14] The judges used a new doctrine formulated by Paul Oertmann, a distinguished legal scholar. He argued that every contract assumed a *Geschäftsgrundlage*, certain unwritten conditions necessary for fulfilling the contract, conditions implicitly or explicitly recognized by both parties. One such condition was a presumption of *equivalence* between the respective performances or actions of the parties to the contract, an equivalence rooted in Paragraph 242. If that equivalence disappeared, the contract was void.[15]

The operating principle in Paragraph 242, *Treu und Glauben*, might more literally be translated as simply "good faith," but "equity and good faith" seems more appropriate in this context. German judges used this principle to establish a jurisprudence somewhat analogous to equity in Anglo-American law. In basing this jurisprudence on a concept of "equivalence," the judges were clearly appealing to considerations of equity as well as of good faith as between the contracting partners. Perhaps most important, the creditors who adopted this phrase often used it as synonymous with equity as well as with good faith. Creditors clearly felt betrayed and robbed by their partners in the debt relationship; but they also believed that equity required that debtors share in the losses Germany had suffered since 1914, rather than shifting the burden entirely to creditors through inflation.

On 27 June 1922 the Reichsgericht's Third Civil Senate, in ruling for adjusting the value of a leased farm, implicitly called the mark equals mark principle into question. In assessing the value of leased property, the PM served solely as a measure of value, not a medium of exchange. The judges observed that the PM was no longer equal in value to the GM in fact, even if it still was in law. The court argued that by destroying the PM's function as a measure of value, the inflation had created conditions unprovided for by statute or private contract, leaving the path open for "free judicial decision."[16] Significantly, by shifting the grounds for invalidating a contract from presumed changes in the goods or performance required (*Teuerung*) to presumed changes in the money, the decision was a major step toward debt revaluation.[17]

By early 1923 the courts had extended revaluation to virtually all reciprocal performances (*gegenseitige Leistungen*). In all cases where one party had to pay money contingent on a second party doing something (e.g., providing goods or services to the first party) or where a personal relationship required some performance expressed in money (e.g., child support payments), the courts had found that the principle of equity and good faith demanded an adjustment of either performance or payment.

Judges based their new activism on *Lückentheorie*, on the idea that a "gap" could exist between a statute and a contract or between two statutes. Rather than continuing to deny that such gaps existed, as legal positivists had, jurists increasingly argued that the judge must occasionally intervene to interpret the will of the parties and the legislature whenever a gap appeared.

In filling such gaps, judges tended to appeal implicitly or explicitly to legal norms or principles of justice *external* to the state and its legal system, in effect to natural law. They thereby inevitably abandoned the old idea of the *Rechtsstaat*, which had rejected natural law as a basis for judicial decision-making because state or judiciary could use such an abstraction capriciously.[18] This idea of the *Rechtsstaat* had presupposed a liberal, laissez-faire state capable of guaranteeing political and monetary stability, so that the legislature could provide explicit statutes presumed to cover all contingencies.[19] Neither the monetary nor the political stability that Germany had enjoyed between 1871 and 1914 existed in the 1920s. Judges faced a new capriciousness: rampant inflation. They seized on Paragraph 242 and the universal concept of equity they said it embodied as a basis for their efforts to deal with inflation's seemingly inequitable effects.

Instead of continuing to allow the parties the option of rescinding or renegotiating a contract, judges eventually began to adjust payment to performance according to their own standards of what was equitable. By their own admission, they were now establishing "economic-legal" and not just "purely legal" principles.[20] They thereby took a direct and potentially crucial role in the German economy—a nearly revolutionary increase in the judiciary's influence on law, such that the judge now "could even circumscribe (*umschreiben*) the tasks of the legislature in such troubled times."[21] This discretion, moreover, would remain long after hyperinflation ended because the rise of the interventionist state has permanently undercut any presumption of policy stability.

The judges' decisions between 1920 and 1922 were quite probably inevitable and met little opposition. Even though Oertmann himself had once warned that broad use of general clauses like 242 might create a "monarchy of judges," the collapse of prewar stability had made legal positivism seem untenable.[22] As one scholar has argued, the war had shown that the free play of social and economic forces could destroy even the strong. This fate could hardly be either the will of the party to a contract who faced destruction or in the interests of the economy.[23] And indeed the government had been contemplating legislative relief for payees shortly before the Reichsgericht acted. So despite some initial expressions of concern, especially about allowing economically unlettered judges to renegotiate contracts, both judges and laymen exhibited a remarkably rapid and uniform metamorphosis in their conception of the *Rechtsstaat*.[24]

Thus far the courts had refused to revalue debts. Even though they had implicitly called into question the mark equals mark principle, jurisprudentially the judges had based their decisions on the performance side of contracts. The only performance in a debt was the money obligation, which judges could not adjust without invalidating the currency legislation. And the Reichsgericht had on 18 December 1920 explicitly rejected debt revaluation as not required even by Paragraph 242.[25]

The courts faced a cruel dilemma. Pre-1914 German law included some protection for certain groups whose weakness under the legal formalism of the old *Rechtsstaat* had been obvious. But the creditors had seemed so strong that special protection for them had seemed unnecessary. In the modest deflation of 1873–96, the mark equals mark principle had actually benefited them slightly at debtor expense. And even many proponents of revaluation accepted that in "normal times"—such as before the war—the creditor had to bear the risk of price shifts.[26] But in a rapid, large-scale inflation, existing law forced the courts to expropriate the creditors (de facto), and the judges had no way *in law* to escape this unfair result.[27]

The Political System Rebuffs the Creditors

While the judiciary was slowly developing legal doctrines on contract revaluation, creditors were rapidly finding themselves reduced to poverty. With the 1921 cost of living 12 times its 1913 level, the inflation had already seriously eroded the ability of petty rentiers (including many who owned stocks or rent-controlled property) to live from their investments. Rentiers who were no longer able to work were often totally impoverished. By March 1921 nearly 75 percent of all petty rentiers earned no more than 20 real marks per month (about $27 in 1987 dollars) from their investments. By the autumn of 1922, investments provided 4,000 of 5,500 members of the Hannover Rentiers Association (Rentnerbund) with less than 63 real marks per *year* (ca. $87 in 1987 dollars).[28]

Although no one seems to have begun preserving creditor letters until late 1922, subsequent letters often told poignantly of the sufferings inflation brought to individual creditors. One 60-year-old man wrote that before the war he could live comfortably on the interest from his assets of 60,000 marks. He had lost all because of the inflation, and he was now working for 15 gold pfennigs an hour (about $10 per week in 1987 dollars) trying to support three children. A 68-year-old man had worked for forty years to build up his business, had sold it in order to retire at age 64, and now found that inflation had destroyed the capital and made him penniless. The orphaned daughter of a civil servant, permanently disabled, had watched her 112,000-mark inheritance turn to worthless paper and had twice attempted suicide.[29] Such tragedies multiplied as millions of creditors suffered the insidious erosion and ultimate annihilation of their savings.

Perhaps the most galling aspect of these creditors' new poverty was that public officials were more interested in giving them charity than in giving them what they considered justice. Some Länder had provided special relief appropriations for petty rentiers in 1920 and 1921. By December 1921 the cost of living was 19 times its prewar level, and the Reich labor minister estimated inflation had driven 400,000–500,000 petty rentiers to depend on public relief. In drawing up guidelines for Reich action, though, the labor minister (who was responsible for the welfare system) argued that "a legal claim by the petty rentier to compensation for the mark's loss of value does not exist; the municipalities [who administered the welfare system] are only obligated for the payment of relief to those investors who no longer have any capital." The government and the Reichstag therefore introduced a special subsidy to municipalities to benefit needy petty rentiers who had capital sufficient to provide an income exceeding 800 PM per year (a modest living in 1914, only about $2 in 1921). In January 1923 the government required municipalities to provide relief for petty rentiers. To compensate the municipalities, the state allowed them to seize beneficiaries' capital on their deaths.[30]

This relief program humiliated creditors. Many municipalities insisted that the rentiers at least provisionally sign over their capital, including in some cases their personal possessions, even though that cast many proud and frugal citizens in the role of charity cases. Although the government claimed such actual seizures as occurred were usually justified and seldom included personal possessions, opposition politicians in the mid-1920s accused the municipalities of hardheartedness in implementing this provision.[31]

In late 1921, as prices reached new heights, the legal community began considering measures to protect creditors' investments from the effects of inflation. In a prestigious legal journal, State Secretary Oskar Mügel (ranking civil servant in the Prussian Justice Ministry) outlined a plan to reintroduce the GM for all new debts and to "recalculate" old debts, including government bonds, into GM based on the PM value the day the law went into effect (equivalent to a 6 percent revaluation in late 1921). Mügel further suggested that mortgage creditors share in mortgaged property's increased PM value. Similarly, mortgage-bond and industrial-obligation creditors would share in any increase in the PM value of the mortgage bank's or company's assets. He rejected face-value repayment in GM because many debtors had suffered losses.[32]

Mügel's plan both stimulated and framed subsequent discussion. He had defined the issue as a legal problem to be solved on a private-law, not an economic or social, basis.[33] His claim that mortgage creditors deserved a share in increased property values struck a responsive chord. Germans had always felt that mortgages were particularly secure, free of any taint of speculation, just because they were connected with a solid object of real value. Up until 1924, Germans concentrated on mortgages in the debt-revaluation struggle, and the perception of mortgages as especially non-speculative may have strengthened the creditors' position.[34]

Although Mügel believed legislative action was necessary for any debt recalculation, he and others suggested that Paragraph 607 of the Civil Code invalidated the mark equals mark principle.[35] According to Paragraph 607, "A person who has received money or other fungible things as a loan is bound to return to the lender what he had received in things of the same kind, quality, and quantity." A 1922 mark did scarcely seem of the same quality as a 1914 mark, but in fact the Code's drafters had intended quality to refer not to money's *value* but to quality as legal tender.[36]

Although the Reichsgericht never depended on Paragraph 607, it had a significant impact.[37] It served as a peg on which judges could hang their suppositions as to the legislature's intentions. More important, to legally untutored creditors it seemed to provide indisputable legal grounds for full revaluation, suggesting that the Republic was blatantly cheating them with its policy of limited revaluation.[38]

On 30 June 1922, with the mark below one-fortieth of its prewar value, the Reich Justice Ministry (under Gustav Radbruch, SPD [*Sozialdemokratische Partei Deutschlands*, social democrats]) suggested making mortgage repayment depend on the creditor's approval. This privilege would have given the creditor leverage to force the debtor to pay a premium in GM if the latter wanted to clear the property of debt.[39] And it would have let creditors keep their assets until the mark rose again (as they wrongly believed it would). Because of wartime economic dislocation, the government had granted various moratoria on debt payment. Creditors hence felt justified in demanding their own moratorium in the face of inflation.[40]

Although government ministers rejected Radbruch's proposal, it almost certainly inspired the widespread rumors that the government was discussing a law to protect creditors. According to the rumors, the government intended to mandate repayment of PM mortgages in GM, presumably at face value. The wartime moratoria for debtors meant most mortgages were now so old that debtors could repay on three months' notice.

Although debtors had for years quietly been repaying their debts in increasingly devalued PM, creditors complained angrily—with some justification—that many debtors were reacting to the rumors by giving the three months' notice. These debtors believed, like the creditors, that the mark might somehow rise again, and they sought to repay their obligations in near worthless paper marks (scarcely 1 percent of prewar purchasing power in August, 0.2 percent in November) before the government could act.[41]

These rumors and the debtor reaction inspired the tentative beginnings of an ultimately militant and politically significant creditor movement. Inflation still seemed an impersonal economic mechanism, almost a natural disaster, most often blamed on foreign reparations demands beyond debtor or perhaps even parliamentary control. But now many creditors faced or had heard of individuals who were "unscrupulously" trying to wiggle out of their moral obligation to repay their debts at full value. Creditors now had someone to blame, someone to get angry at. And because they rejected the laissez-faire capitalist argument that their invest-ments had been a speculation on the currency's stability, they could get morally indignant indeed.[42]

A renewed flurry of activity erupted in late 1922. The Prussian Justice Minister Hugo am Zehnhoff (Z [*Zentrum*, the Catholic Center Party]) supported Mügel's proposal to introduce GM calculation in debts, and his ministry drafted a mortgage-repayment moratorium law.[43] Almost simulta-neously, however, Reich Labor Minister Heinrich Brauns (also Z) decided to deny publicly the rumors of a mortgage-repayment moratorium or similar policy because they were unsettling property and mortgage mar-kets.[44] Meanwhile, petitions were coming in both from creditors demand-ing a moratorium and from economic interest groups and credit institutions who wanted someone to clarify the increasingly confused situation.[45]

Reich Justice Minister Karl Heinze (DVP [*Deutsche Volkspartei*, center-right]) sought to forestall any revaluation. He convened a 28 December meeting at which the Prussian Justice, Finance, and Agriculture ministries favored a repayment moratorium, while the Reich Justice and Economics ministries and Prussian Welfare and Commerce ministries rejected it. Still feeling their way on a difficult issue, both opponents and proponents of revaluation expressed their arguments only inarticulately. Opponents raised economic objections to revaluation—but predominantly in terms of the uncertainty it would create amid hyperinflation. Proponents acknowl-edged revaluation's potential problems but saw it as a risk worth taking on grounds of equity.[46] On 10 January 1923 Heinze urged the cabinet to announce publicly that it planned no repayment moratorium or "any type of valorization [revaluation] measure." With most Reich ministers agree-ing the situation was too chaotic for economic experimentation, the gov-ernment issued such an announcement on 11 January 1923.[47]

After years of tacitly accepting the expropriation of PM creditors, the government had explicitly rejected any steps to preserve creditor assets. It thereby confirmed its acquiescence in the losses that paper-mark creditors were suffering.

The inflation put many credit institutions in an intolerable situation. Both creditor and debtor, they drew their income from the difference in interest rates between their assets and debits. By 1923 their average 0.5 percent interest differential was virtually worthless. Meanwhile, their costs soared as they attempted to cope with inflation's complexities. They reacted with various expedients, but the growing number of mortgage redemption notices threatened to overwhelm all expedients. Because of regional legal and economic conditions, Bavarian mortgage banks in particular faced the possible disappearance of nearly all their reserves and capital.[48]

Hence, in February 1923 some credit institutions began lobbying vigorously for a mortgage-repayment moratorium. Bavarian mortgage banks, in the forefront of this effort, suggested that debt revaluation might eventually be necessary to save them, but in the short run they demanded a five-year repayment moratorium, with a running charge on debtors for administration costs.[49]

To justify demands for special treatment, the banks emphasized their importance to the economy. Once the currency was stabilized, only a working credit system, which the country could not create overnight, could fulfill the need for new credit. Hence, the banks insisted, Germany had to preserve a viable banking sector.[50] Governments were very sensitive to this argument, giving the banks considerable leverage.

On 1 March 1923 Reichstag Deputy Adalbert Düringer (DVP) introduced draft legislation for a mortgage-repayment moratorium.[51] Repayment of all PM mortgages was to depend on the creditor's assent, protecting creditors against losing their entire investment, at least in the short run. If the mark did not rise again, revaluation would be available as an alternative—even though Düringer avoided calling for it. Also, if the debtor wanted to eliminate the debt, the creditor could demand some real premium in return for accepting repayment. Finally, finding some stable measure of value for revaluation would be difficult in a hyperinflation, so that a moratorium seemed more practical and probably stood a greater chance of passage in 1923.

Düringer was a very independent individual. He had left the DNVP (*Deutschnationale Volkspartei*, the conservatives) in mid-1920 over that party's political intransigence and had joined the DVP. A Bavarian mortgage banker had supposedly urged him to introduce his moratorium, but such urgings would have fallen on fertile ground. Long after bankers had decided to side with debtors rather than creditors, Düringer remained with the creditors. Most of his DVP Reichstag colleagues did not accept his moratorium proposal. In the future they would ridicule him because of his preoccupation with revaluation, but he fought resolutely on behalf of impoverished PM creditors. His 1923 struggle for a moratorium helped to publicize the creditors' often deplorable situation, and in 1924 he helped swing the DVP behind proposals for increased revaluation.[52]

The Reichstag Justice Committee considered Düringer's bill eight days after he introduced it, a relatively short period of time. Justice Minister

Heinze, like Düringer a DVP deputy, strongly opposed the bill. He argued that the mark was not going to rise again to any meaningful level. (The cost of living in March 1923 was 2,800 times its 1913 level.) If the mark had not improved when the moratorium ended, the pressure for a revaluation to help creditors would be irresistible. (The hope of eventual revaluation, of course, increasingly motivated supporters of a moratorium.) Revaluation was technically infeasible and economically and fiscally dangerous. The committee accepted Heinze's arguments and overwhelmingly rejected the moratorium.[53]

Meanwhile, an organized creditor movement began developing. In the spring of 1922 an Alliance against Usury and Inflation (*Bund gegen Wucher und Teuerung*) had appeared in Württemberg, but only in late 1922 did creditors found a national Mortgagees Protective Association (*Hypothekengläubiger Schutzverband*: HGSV; later Mortgagees and Savers Protective Association: HGSSV). Düringer helped establish a creditor group in Bavaria in February 1923.[54] These groups were still small and uncertain about what policy to pursue.

Support for revaluation was nonetheless increasing, as inflation turned into hyperinflation. The legal community seemed particularly sympathetic, and by summer most articles in legal journals were prorevaluation.[55] Newspaper articles, Landtag deputies, and some civil servants were discussing ways to aid creditors, including debt revaluation.[56] The apparent mass preference for revaluation is probably illusory: its opponents had little incentive to join in a public debate when the status quo favored them and seemed secure.[57] Nonetheless, the apparent increase in redemption notices, the mark's accelerating collapse, the increasing public debate, and the Düringer bill united to increase creditor and popular awareness of the issue and of possible solutions.

Desperate to bury Düringer's proposal before it built up momentum, the government turned to the Reich Economic Council (*Reichswirtschaftsrat*) for further support. The council included representatives of management and labor from each major branch of the economy plus representatives of the free professions and consumers; it was to provide "expert" advice on the economic implications of proposed legislation. A lengthy discussion on 2 May in a plenary session of the council's economic-policy, fiscal-policy, and housing subcommittees brought the contrasting positions into somewhat clearer focus.[58]

Those favoring the moratorium emphasized the creditors' losses and the need to do *something*: considerations of equity, they argued, demanded action. Although acknowledging that a moratorium might lead to revaluation, proponents emphasized that mortgages were different from other investments because the owner could not easily realize them for cash and because the property that secured them had retained a real value.

Rudolf Hilferding, a SPD economics expert, led the opponents. He argued that the moratorium implied an eventual revaluation. Revaluation, however, was impossible because it could not be limited to mortgages and would end as an attempt to reverse the inflation. Hilferding thought the inflation had actually helped agriculture and industry by wiping out their debt. Germany needed to tap this strength for the common good. Besides, any mortgage revaluation would fall predominantly on urban landlords (because, he said, most farmers had already repaid their mortgages) and could only be financed by transferring the burden to renters.

Agriculture Minister Hans Luther (nonparty), as had Hilferding, emphasized a moratorium's negative effects on new credit. A moratorium would create uncertainty about the burden on mortgaged property and hence about the amount of new credit it could carry. New credit would then be either unavailable until the uncertainty ended or available only at extremely high interest rates. Revaluing old debt would increase the burden on property and make it less able to finance new loans. For the moratorium's opponents, national economic needs outweighed the inequity done to impoverished creditors.

With hyperinflation introducing growing chaos into the economy, even briefly stated economic objections seemed particularly compelling, and revaluation supporters scarcely tried to challenge them. The council voted 38 to 3 to reject a moratorium because it implied revaluation. The "experts" had decisively rejected redress for creditors, a rejection that was well publicized.[59]

When the full Reichstag debated the moratorium bill on 4 July, the discussion proved anticlimactic. Düringer had already admitted a revaluation was impossible, and only he spoke for his own bill. After relatively short debate, the Reichstag sent the bill back to committee for further study.[60] Deputy Erich Emminger (BVP [*Bayerische Volkspartei*, the Bavarian Catholic party]), a revaluation supporter, later suggested that in recommitting the bill the Reichstag was tacitly rejecting any moratorium or revaluation.[61]

While efforts to aid creditors floundered, debtors were redeeming more and more PM debt, leaving many creditors with no legal claims. Mortgage banks were calling in their mortgage bonds, as the law required when their mortgages were paid off. Various private debtors, the Reich, and the cities were offering premiums (usually insignificant in real terms) to induce creditors to allow redemption of debts not yet due.[62]

Meanwhile, the government desperately sought revenues to finance needed housing construction. Already in October 1921 the Labor Ministry had proposed a special levy on landlords to subsidize new housing, lest the profits of inflation flow into the landlords' pockets. And on 22 September 1923, in discussing his plan to use increased real rents (after stabilization) to subsidize new construction, Brauns commented that "prerequisite for that is, however, that a revaluation of old mortgages be excluded once and for all."[63]

Bavaria had proposed a mortgage-repayment moratorium in the Reichsrat (upper house of the legislature, which represented the Länder and had some legislative powers), but on 26 September Reich Justice Minister Radbruch (SPD) rejected it. He argued that one must first decide the revaluation question, which was impossible during the inflation. "On the other hand," he concluded, "a moratorium is unnecessary, for if one subsequently decides on a revaluation, it would naturally have to be given a considerable measure of retroactivity."[64]

Radbruch clearly favored the creditors. The SPD's financial expert, Hilferding, had rejected revaluation and the SPD would oppose revaluation in early 1924, so Radbruch's attitude presumably reflected his personal sympathy for creditors or his ties to the apparently prorevaluation legal community (including the Justice Ministry civil servants). Also, judges were increasingly unhappy at having to implement the currency legislation. Radbruch may have feared a confrontation between government and courts if the government banned revaluation and thereby forced the judges to continue administering the legal expropriation of the creditors.[65]

Agriculture Minister Luther denounced Radbruch's comments sharply. Luther was already obsessed with the need to find tax sources to stabilize the currency. He thought the state would have to tax agriculture heavily, while farmers desperately needed new credit. A revaluation on top of these burdens would bankrupt the agricultural sector. Luther therefore demanded that the government ban revaluation and, as an absolute minimum, repudiate retroactive revaluation.[66]

Hans Luther, who played a major role in German politics from 1916 to 1933, was a central figure in the revaluation conflict. He entered the municipal civil service in 1906, becoming by 1918 the nonpartisan mayor of Essen, a major industrial city. From 1916 he took numerous responsible posts in national affairs, becoming finance minister (1923–24), chancellor (1925–26), president of the Reichsbank (1930–33), and ambassador to the United States (1933–37). His various offices gave him very close ties to and great sympathy for industry and agriculture. Luther believed firmly in the primacy of economic considerations. He accepted implicitly the theory that national well-being depended on freeing the productive sectors of all burdens and constraints so that they could flourish and provide the material bases of national power and welfare. As a nominally nonpartisan civil servant, Luther believed in "administrative" solutions to social problems, in the necessity of eliminating partisan conflict, and in allowing "experts" to determine the most efficient policy. His attitude reflected the mistrust of politics that the prewar Empire had inculcated in its officials. Actually very close politically to the DVP, Luther would favor conservative policies based on supposedly objective considerations. Not apparently ambitious for personal power, he sought control over policy because of an almost arrogant confidence in his ability to determine what Germany needed. His intelligence, diligence, and self-assurance made him an influential if not always well-loved figure.[67]

At a 12 October 1923 meeting, the Agriculture Ministry and the Finance Ministry, which Luther had headed since 6 October, joined the Transport, Reconstruction, and Labor ministries in rejecting debt revaluation. The Economics Ministry agreed but hesitated to support a categorical ban. Although not represented at this meeting, Radbruch on 17 October vigorously rejected the proposed ban.[68]

By himself Radbruch could scarcely have forestalled the revaluation ban the other ministries desired. But he had a powerful ally in Chancellor Gustav Stresemann (DVP), who supported Düringer's moratorium proposal and sympathized strongly with the creditors.[69] On 10 October Stresemann informed Luther by telephone and by letter that he opposed any revaluation ban and intended to discuss the issue at a cabinet meeting. He also wrote to a fellow DVP Reichstag deputy who had requested action on the Düringer bill that "unfortunately I have for the moment been stymied by the opposition of Finance Minister Dr. Luther." In fact, the cabinet neither discussed nor implemented a moratorium or a ban. Stresemann later asserted that he had forestalled Luther's intention of banning revaluation, ensuring that it would remain a live option. But by the same token, Luther had forestalled Stresemann's apparent intention of implementing Düringer's moratorium.[70]

Having failed to settle the revaluation in October, the government faced continuing confusion over the issue in November. Despite its unwillingness to *help* creditors, the cabinet could not bring itself to declare national bankruptcy by repudiating all PM debt. Two Finance Ministry officials even proposed minor government-bond revaluations, one suggesting that doing so might actually forestall excessive Allied reparations demands by increasing the burden on the German economy. The Finance Ministry state secretary, however, countered that despite the (long-term) implications for national credit, the Reich would have to call in its bonds for (short-term) fiscal reasons.[71] Moreover, according to Luther, when he asked one civil servant to draft a ban on private-debt revaluation, the man declared that "he could not formulate this idea of mine legislatively." Luther added that this was not "inability, but rather the wish to distance himself if possible from this measure, which, while absolutely necessary within the larger regulation, was highly unpopular."[72]

In the chaotic conditions of November few people still clamored for revaluation. Under increased pressure from creditors, the mortgage banks, for example, now favored a mortgage-repayment moratorium. But while the Bavarian banks thought some individual revaluation would be necessary to get people to save again, the north German banks thought some nominal revaluation to show good faith would be sufficient.[73] The number of letters from creditors to the government dropped sharply in October and November, suggesting despair or loss of hope for assistance from the government.[74]

Politically, the revaluation conflict was stalemated—and stalemate generally favored the debtor. The creditors had for 18 months applied increasing, albeit diffuse, pressure for relief. In the chaos of hyperinflation, though, fiscal and economic concerns had easily prevailed over their pleas for fairness. Even with the chancellor's support, they had been unable to alter the status quo. Moreover, the Labor and Finance ministries were planning to tax away debtor inflation profits. If these taxes took effect, they would eliminate the financial base for any revaluation. Thereafter, a Reichstag that had already refused to protect creditor assets would almost certainly have hesitated to reverse itself and introduce the fiscal and economic unknown of a revaluation, especially since debtors would no longer be enjoying large, unearned profits. Given the strength of any status quo, creditor prospects seemed minimal.[75]

Legal Victory for the Creditors

As long as the courts held to the mark equals mark principle, inflation would expropriate creditors to the benefit of debtors. Ministers and civil servants seemed to assume the courts would continue to do so and would thereby bear much of the onus for the creditors' catastrophic losses.[76]

Yet during the course of 1923 that comforting assumption seemed increasingly questionable. Various Germans began to argue that a repayment moratorium was necessary to allow the judiciary to complete an evolution in private contractual relations that they expected to lead at least to mortgage revaluation.[77] And the Finance and Labor ministries felt compelled to seek an explicit revaluation ban to ensure that debtors' inflation profits would remain available for taxation. Hence, despite the creditors' political defeat, the judiciary's expansion of contract revaluation led to hopes and fears it might eventually introduce PM-debt revaluation, especially as several lower courts had ruled that the Civil Code mandated debt revaluation.[78]

The most important proponent of this view was the Darmstadt Appeals Court, under the presidency of Dr. Georg Best. Best was born in 1855 in Darmstadt, the son of a savings-bank director. Although he practiced law briefly, he eventually concentrated on the career judiciary, becoming appeals court president in 1914. He resented his mandatory retirement in 1924 and ascribed it to government retribution for his prorevaluation stand. Thereafter he became the creditor movement's political leader and a Reichstag deputy. His whole life seems to have become wrapped up in the revaluation problem, and he would substantially influence its development. Best obviously despised the materialism and unbridled competitiveness of capitalism. An apparently unshakeable faith in his own rectitude and in the justice of his cause marked his approach to revaluation.[79]

In 1922 and 1923 Best published several articles deploring legislative inaction and insisting that the *courts* could and should revalue debts. He argued that shifting court attitudes toward Paragraph 242 and the mark equals mark principle in contract cases suggested the moral and legal limits of the currency legislation. He also thought Paragraph 607 showed that even debts implied an equivalence. The 4 August and 28 September 1914 decrees, he asserted, were merely temporary measures and had not repealed GM *value* payment of debts; meanwhile, the Civil Code represented "ancient rights of the *Kulturstaat*." Therefore, he concluded, the "right of the judge must exert itself," and the courts must use Paragraph

242 of the Civil Code to correct the mark equals mark principle and adjust each individual debt.[80] His reference to the *Kulturstaat* implied that any government that did not revalue on the basis of equity and good faith was betraying the eternal and indisputable values of German culture and embracing a base materialism. Best was particularly upset that many debtors were trying to pay off their debts in near worthless paper marks before the state acted to protect creditor interests. Morally indignant, he characterized such debtor actions as usury and gouging.[81]

On 29 March and 18 May 1923 the Darmstadt Court of Appeals, at Best's instigation, issued rulings requiring revaluation. The grounds were basically those Best had presented in his articles. In the May decision, however, the court added that creditor protests, articles by legal scholars, and recent Reichsgericht decisions in contract cases showed that the mark equals mark principle no longer corresponded to the "prevailing usage" mentioned in Paragraph 242.[82]

One prorevaluation jurist characterized these decisions as "of the greatest importance."[83] In the absence of political action, courts were beginning to act for the creditor. The decisions heartened creditors and confirmed their feeling that their demands were just. These rulings also publicized the justification for revaluation that the Reichsgericht would later adopt and elaborate on, a justification essential for legitimating the judiciary's intervention—in the minds of the populace and of the judges themselves.[84]

Rebuffed by the political system but encouraged by the Darmstadt decisions, more and more creditors were appealing over the government's head to the judiciary, the weak point in the state's defenses against debt revaluation. By autumn 1923 various lower courts had handed down conflicting pro and antirevaluation decisions, creating considerable legal uncertainty that would somehow have to be eliminated.[85] Relative government inaction on debts had tended to favor debtors—but it also left scope for the judiciary to settle the issue on its terms.

Available evidence suggests that by summer 1923 many, perhaps most, judges favored helping the creditors, but only a few as yet felt the courts should take the initiative. They hesitated to challenge a valid statute or to "create" law (as opposed to applying it), fearing especially that any judicial initiative would only compound legal uncertainty.[86] Also, many thought that hyperinflation created such confusion that only after stabilization could anyone deal effectively with the problem. Many judges seemed to want immediate legislation establishing a repayment moratorium and providing guidelines—and perhaps special arbitration courts—to revalue debts.[87] Nonetheless, according to two appeals court presidents, hyper-inflation and government inaction were bringing ever more judges to support ever more drastic action.[88] Furthermore, in August the Reichsgericht Judges Association (*Richterverband beim Reichsgericht*) proposed legislation on the debt problem that suggests that many Reichsgericht judges may already have been leaning toward judicial revaluation.[89]

The Reichsgericht considered a debt-revaluation case in October 1923 but postponed a decision. The government had already publicized its intention to stabilize the currency. It issued the first Rentenmarks on 16 November but did not immediately fix the PM/Rentenmark rate. The court then postponed decision again, until 28 November, eight days after the government finally stabilized the currency de facto.[90]

These delays were hardly coincidental. The mark's catastrophic collapse, with prices eventually changing hourly, had accelerated the judicial swing toward debt revaluation. Nonetheless, the situation apparently had to be both desperate and irreversible before the judiciary would completely jettison legal positivism and a century of legal tradition. By introducing a new currency and stabilizing at one trillion to one, the government destroyed any meaningful value for the paper mark and confirmed its intention to end the inflation at creditor expense. In Austria, where the Krone (stabilized at 14,400 to one) retained some minimal value, the courts had rejected debt revaluation. One Reichsgericht judge, deeply involved in the revaluation issue, thought that if Germany had achieved a similar stabilization, the Reichsgericht might also have rejected revaluation.[91] Further, stabilization heralded the return of reasonably normal economic conditions and provided a stable measure of value—both preconditions for effective debt revaluation.

Under these circumstances, the German judiciary shifted from applying the law to making it. On 28 November 1923 the Reichsgericht's Fifth Civil Senate ruled that mortgage revaluation was required. The mortgage involved was on a plot of land at Lüderitz in the former German colony of Southwest Africa. The court's jurisdiction was in doubt because German law no longer ran in Southwest Africa and because the mark, paper or otherwise, was no longer legal tender there. The court hence prepared two sections in its opinion, one if the place of payment was Lüderitz and one if payment was in Berlin, where both parties now resided and where German domestic law might apply. The court's willingness to use so questionable a case for so far-reaching a decision suggests that the judges were convinced the time was ripe for action on debt revaluation. Conscious of the gravity of its decision, the Senate circulated the ruling among all Reichsgericht members (an unusual procedure), and virtually all the judges apparently concurred in it.[92]

The judges justified their decision by asserting that the unforeseen hyperinflation had created a conflict between the legal tender laws and Paragraph 242. Paragraph 242 was said to "rule all of legal life" and therefore to predominate over the currency legislation. In enacting the legal tender legislation, the court argued, the Reichstag could never have expected hyperinflation; in concluding a contract under stable monetary conditions the parties could never have expected the mark to become valueless (an implicit acceptance of *Geschäftsgrundlage*). The court cited previous decisions on contract revision as evidence of changing legal conceptions of Paragraph 242 and argued that Paragraph 607 showed the same principles applied to mortgages. (The court soon dropped references to *Geschäftsgrundlage* and Paragraph 607 and came to rely solely on Paragraph 242 in debt-revaluation cases.)[93]

The court declared individual revaluation the only appropriate means to revise the debt. In basing their decision on equivalence, the judges declared that a "fair consideration of the interests of both sides is required." Hence, the judge had to take into account not only the original amount of the debt but the type of property (industrial, urban, or agricultural) and the economic situation of both creditor and debtor. "A general principle requiring the revaluation of every mortgage cannot be established. Nor will the extent of the revaluation . . . be the same in every case."[94]

But individual revaluation had dangerous implications. It would have opened the gates to a flood of cases, as every mortgage creditor in Germany sought the highest possible revaluation. Because the court set no guidelines, lower courts throughout Germany would have been individually responsible for revaluation cases in their jurisdictions, creating the potential for a vast range of revaluation rates and for massive economic uncertainty. Lenders would have had no assurance as to a potential debtor's credit status until the courts had settled all revaluation cases against him, a process that could have taken years. In addition, a high average revaluation rate would almost certainly have forced up prices and could have increased the money supply, quite possibly reigniting the inflation—with disastrous consequences for German society.

The essential legal flaw in the 28 November decision was its analysis of the legislature's intentions. Certainly no one in 1909 or 1914 expected the currency legislation someday to expropriate creditors completely. Nonetheless, the potential for expropriation was inherent in the legislation. And the legislature had explicitly reserved to itself the decision on when to repeal the 1914 decrees. More important, as the legislation's inflationary effects became obvious, the Reichstag had by subsequent legislation confirmed the principles of the 1914 decrees. And it had in 1923 refused to hinder or reverse inflation's effects on debts. Finally, the legislature had most certainly never intended Paragraph 242—a mere statute—to "rule all of legal life."[95]

This decision was also flawed in a larger, political sense. The inflation was the legislature's fundamental policy decision about how to apportion the burdens of war and defeat among the German people. The state had sacrificed some men's lives to fight the war; it could surely sacrifice some people's capital to finance the war.[96] The method chosen seems grossly unfair, but one could hardly shift the final decision in this matter to the courts, who had no constitutional mandate to make such fundamental decisions.

Finally, individual judges quite simply lacked the expertise or the inclination to weigh crucial issues of monetary, fiscal, and economic policy in making the millions of decisions they would face in individual cases. The courts had arrogated to themselves the power to establish indirectly the value of the national currency, a power that was simply too important to be left to economically unlettered judges.[97] Further, in the short term Germany needed the taxes on inflation profits Luther had planned and that any substantial revaluation would preclude. And determining what level of revaluation burden the economy could bear would be a complicated and risky process.

Significantly, the judges based their decision not on the Weimar Constitution but on the Civil Code promulgated by Emperor Wilhelm II. Many writers argued that Article 153 of the Weimar Constitution, which forbade uncompensated expropriation, was adequate grounds to invalidate the mark equals mark principle (certainly as adequate as Paragraph 242). That the judges preferred instead to do so with a simple statute passed under the Empire suggests where they thought political legitimacy could be found. And, amazingly, the Reichsgericht itself ordered its documents relating to this case destroyed. This *most unusual* procedure suggests that Reichsgericht judges felt that, for whatever reason, they had something to hide.[98]

Despite revaluation's economic complexities, and despite the government's efforts to publicize its potential dangers, the creditors had successfully appealed over the government's head to the judiciary, had reversed political defeat in the legal arena. They did so not from any sophisticated political or legal calculation but out of despair and in the hope that the judiciary would prove sympathetic. And the judges had responded, but by *creating* law in a way that directly challenged executive and legislative prerogatives and ignored wider social and economic concerns.

Yet the German legal system did not logically and inherently require revaluation. To the contrary, the currency legislation still made mark equals mark the ruling principle for money debts. As various scholars have pointed out, jurists had to comb legal texts searching for grounds to revalue debts. And as Ludwig Bendix noted at the time, "These passion-filled exertions . . . do not ring true, because the *actual relevant grounds for decision* are *extra-legal*, but are dressed up [*frisiert*] as legal." Debt revaluation was clearly an "extension of justice [*Recht*] beyond the law [*Gesetz*]."[99]

Judges were clearly deeply distressed at the sufferings of impoverished creditors. In January 1923, in a personal letter to an English friend, Reichsgericht President Dr. Walther Simons complained that he headed the Supreme Court of a state "that has lost all power to uphold the right and prevent the wrong. . . . For it is too weak to do the latter and too poor to avoid the forgery of inflation, cause of all sorts of inequity. It is a miserable thing to be Lord Chief Justice of such a country." His letter reveals an awareness of inflation's wider implications that few jurists showed in their writing. But it also reveals a sympathy for the creditors that confirms in private correspondence the public expressions of concern of many prore-valuation jurists. And jurists, such as Oertmann, could and often did openly change their attitude toward legal positivism as inflation and existing law combined to produce unexpected horrors.[100]

Evidence exists that judges were themselves predominantly creditors. Best, who handed down the first important decision favoring debt revalu-ation, was a substantial mortgage creditor (to the extent of 97,600 prewar marks) and a government-bond creditor.[101] No statistics are available on the creditor status of judges as a group. All available anecdotal evidence, however, suggests that judges were thrifty and had relatively large savings and a substantial stake in revaluation. Further, civil servants in general were apparently more likely to be PM creditors and small businessmen to be PM debtors.[102] F. Dessauer, a liberal journalist, wrote that "uncon-sciously the decisions of the judges, who were consumers and money creditors, were indeed influenced by the situation of their *Stand* [class or status group]." E. Fraenkel, a socialist sociologist, thought that virtually every judge had capital invested in fixed-interest assets; he argued their class interest played some, probably subconscious, role in the Reichsgericht's revaluation decision. Reichstag Deputy Rademacher, a conservative industrialist, thought that most judges were either creditors or related to creditors and that "it is humanly explicable that this influenced the judicial attitude."[103] The evidence is not definitive, but it is consistent.

Yet the judges' apparent creditor status did not necessarily imply corruption or determine their views. As Dessauer pointed out, conflicts of interest are inevitable in modern society.[104] Best seemed astonished and mortified when revaluation opponents suggested his creditor status might have influenced his attitudes. He was, he exclaimed, "one of the robbed, not the robber." Debtors were self-interested, he thought, while he merely wanted his rights.[105] And Dessauer and Fraenkel suggested a subconscious influence.

Rather, creditor status probably affected the terms in which one perceived the issue. One could view revaluation as a question of economic efficiency, or of private-law equity, or both. Because Germany lacked any consensus on how to reconcile the conflicting aspects of the issue, personal economic considerations not surprisingly seemed to predispose individuals (creditor and debtor) toward one approach rather than the other—all the more so because the issue was so novel and complex that its implications were difficult to foresee.

Most creditors, and probably judges, would not consciously, or materialistically, have chosen to emphasize solely the more personally advantageous private-law viewpoint. Rather, having every reason to feel betrayed and robbed by their debtors, they were responding to the perception of the issue most immediate to their own experience. Judges faced a painful moral dilemma in dealing with inflation. Their apparent creditor status can help to explain why they solved that dilemma by ignoring broader economic and social considerations, in the process challenging the government and a century of legal orthodoxy by voiding a valid statute.[106]

Judges also had a legal training that emphasized handling issues on a case-by-case, private-law basis. Judges normally had no occasion to consider national economic policy in their decisions, so that they tended to ignore the damage they could inadvertently do when they began to set "economic-legal principles."[107]

"The law is not made by judge alone," Jeremy Bentham commented, "but by judge and company." And the company, the legal community, was prorevaluation. Lawyers were even more likely to be substantial creditors than judges, since they had relatively high incomes and depended on their savings for protection against disability or old age. Lawyers also had a potential professional self-interest: any revaluation would involve renegotiating debts; if even a fraction had to be adjudicated, legal business would increase tremendously. And lawyers were later overrepresented in creditor interest groups.[108] The legal community helped define legal issues, and legal writers increasingly came to emphasize the private-law approach to revaluation and the argument that the courts could implement it under existing law. If judges ignored the legal community's growing commitment to revaluation, it could raise questions in the minds of the general public. Courts did not and would not merely mirror the opinions and interests of lawyers, but the judges would be sensitive to the legal community's attitudes.

Judges also had to cope with a growing loss of public confidence. The judges had already come under attack from the political left, which accused them of politically motivated decisions, and this pressure had made them extremely sensitive.[109] Now judges had to expropriate creditors by forcing the latter to issue a *Löschungsbewilligung* even if the debtor repaid in near-worthless paper marks. (In a *Löschungsbewilligung* the mortgage creditor officially acknowledges that the mortgage has been fully redeemed and that he no longer has a claim on the debtor or his property. German law requires it as a normal part of repaying a mortgage.) Creditors and others were coming to feel that the Civil Code offered the courts the means to end this grossly inequitable expropriation; Germans on the political center and right increasingly blamed judges for creditor problems and expressed a loss of faith in the judiciary.[110] Creditors seemed to expect more from the courts than from the Weimar Republic and its legislature, which had refused to provide revaluation by statute.[111] Prorevaluation writers and some politicians in 1923 predicted danger for the legal system if the obvious inequity of the mark equals mark principle was not brought to an end.[112] Even Chancellor Stresemann criticized the judges for their inaction.[113]

In the summer of 1923 the Prussian justice minister asked the presidents of the various Prussian appeals courts about the judiciary's attitude toward revaluation. The presidents' replies showed that judges were very sensitive to the loss of confidence in the courts among creditors and suggest many judges actively feared losing all support among the populace. Of the thirteen respondents, four explicitly voiced serious concern that the reputability of the law and the courts was in danger;[114] all the answers showed some implicit or explicit concern about general faith in the law.[115] The continued implementation of the mark equals mark principle by the courts and the attendant expropriation of creditor savings had, one respondent wrote, "provoked among wide circles animosity [*Misstimmung*] not only against the judiciary, which had not thought itself able to prevent such a process, but also against the state as such."[116] Another warned, "A lasting failure by the legislature in this area would occur at the expense of the judiciary; the interests of the authority of justice necessitate the prevention of this."[117] In addition, in calling for aid for the creditors, the Reichsgericht Judges Association warned that if the judiciary did not want to become a "mockery of justice and equity," it would have to come to terms with the inflation.[118]

Some judges may have acted not merely to protect the courts' prestige, but to increase their own power. Many judges deeply mistrusted parliament. One appeals court president denigrated objections to a repayment moratorium bill because they "do not take into consideration to what degree the judiciary is already inclined to use the silence of the legislature for an expansion of their own power sphere, [an expansion] that in my opinion will be fateful [*verhängnisvoll*] for themselves." The 28 November decision certainly expanded judicial discretion, and in 1925 the Reichsgericht used revaluation to assert for the first time the power of judicial review. Even in the midst of hyperinflation, some judges may have pursued wider political goals.[119]

Different jurists presumably had differing constellations of reasons, but the judges' extraordinary decision to require debt revaluation can perhaps best be understood in terms of a confluence of motivations, all pushing judges toward rejecting legal orthodoxy and radically challenging government policy. Mandating debt revaluation was a qualitatively much more radical step than requiring contract revaluation because it meant invalidating a standing statute, the currency legislation, that was central to government policy. Sympathy with impoverished creditors, the gradual evolution in judicial perceptions of Paragraph 242, the judges' probable creditor status, professional self-interest, and mistrust of the Weimar Republic most probably combined, in differing degrees, to convince judges that equity demanded debt revaluation and that in this instance they were justified in invalidating a statute to preserve equity.

The way the judges manipulated legal concepts to reach decisions at nearly direct variance with the legislature's intentions suggests the extent to which the law was a social artifact, a reflection of the interests of different social groups. Under conditions of monetary stability the old idea of the *Rechtsstaat* protected creditors, whereas in the midst of hyperinflation it expropriated them. Faced with this situation, the courts redefined the *Rechtsstaat* to allow them to legislate on the creditors' behalf.

This decision could be seen as a kind of "class" justice—but not in the usual sense. Businessmen were predominantly debtors. Whether the judges were creditors or not, their rulings on revaluation favored creditors at the expense of those usually considered "the capitalists."[120] Revaluation initially confused debtor forces, but in the long run industry, commerce, and agriculture would not sit still for such an attack on their interests.

The Initial Impact
of Stabilization

Determining Who Would Pay for Stabilization

Germany was in crisis in late 1923. Without a new currency German society had faced collapse. But even with it, much remained to be done to prevent a descent into chaos. Government officials based their short-term attitude toward revaluation on the crucial need to preserve the stabilization.

The reparations issue haunted the government. Germany had to negotiate with the Allies a mutually acceptable compromise that would overburden neither Germany's budget nor its balance of payments. The government was thus deeply involved in the Allies' ongoing investigation of Germany's ability to finance reparations.[1] And to pay reparations and meet its social needs, Germany needed to restructure its economy fundamentally. Revaluation would influence any restructuring.

The government had to balance its budget. It devoted its major efforts in late 1923 and early 1924 to drastically curtailing expenditures and fundamentally reorganizing the taxation system to increase revenues. Its new "inflation taxes" on inflation profits were essential to these efforts. Because a high revaluation rate would eliminate the inflation profits of mortgage and possibly other debtors, revaluation threatened the core of the government's fiscal policy.[2]

War, defeat, and inflation had devastated the German economy. Germany had had to cede land, industrial plants, foreign assets, and population to its neighbors and enemies. Agriculture had "mined the soil" of nutrients and worn out equipment; industry had used up fixed capital; building owners had neglected maintenance, and virtually no housing had been built for a decade. Germany now had to pay reparations and help disabled veterans, widows, and orphans. The inflation had offered German business the opportunity to recover lost markets and rebuild ailing operations cheaply, but it had also created chaotic conditions that made it difficult to invest wisely.[3] Most contemporaries believed Germany's net national wealth had declined since 1914 by over 50 percent, and recent estimates largely confirm this impression.[4] Influential segments of public opinion believed, justifiably, that this loss of wealth limited the economy's ability to bear the burdens of reparations and stabilization—including revaluation.[5]

Industrial and agricultural interests strongly influenced the new cabinet that would deal with stabilization. Political conflict had prompted the SPD to withdraw from the government and had forced the new chancellor, Wilhelm Marx (Z), to form a minority government. Marx, a former jurist, was diligent and conciliatory but rather uncharismatic. He did not really dominate a cabinet that included such strong personalities as Luther and Stresemann. Although the new justice minister, Erich Emminger (BVP), sympathized with creditors, the new economics minister, Eduard Hamm (DDP [*Deutsche Demokratische Partei*, left liberals]), was an industrialist with close ties to industrial interest groups. The interior and finance ministers, Karl Jarres and Luther, both served as mayors of Ruhr industrial cities, while Foreign Minister Stresemann had worked for business interest groups and led the probusiness DVP. All three had a deep sympathy for industry's problems and a predisposition to accept businessmen's prescriptions for the economy. The agriculture minister, Gerhard Graf von Kanitz, saw himself as a representative of agriculture's interests.[6]

Because the measures needed to preserve the currency were bound to be unpopular and seemed to demand immediate action, the government sought the power to rule by decree. The Reichstag agreed and approved a new Enabling Act valid until 15 February 1924. For all decrees the government would have to consult, but not obtain the approval of, a "Committee of Fifteen" Reichstag members.[7]

The SPD had acquiesced in a grant of almost dictatorial powers to a coalition in which it was not represented and which clearly sympathized with employer and conservative attitudes. In October it had refused to concede more limited decree-granting powers to a cabinet in which it participated. After the chaos of November, however, it was afraid to demand a dissolution of parliament in the midst of social unrest. Basically, C. Maier has argued, by December 1923 the government had to "choose to contain social tension on conservative terms or not contain it at all."[8]

Stabilization required wide-ranging and severe measures that angered

most segments of German society—especially as the government generally spared big business. The government had offered to implement some
direct charge on German industry as a guarantee for reparations. Industry
was able to justify limiting its share of the stabilization burden so that it
might provide such a guarantee.[9] The economic orthodoxy of the 1920s
held that investment was the only key to economic growth and that to
obtain necessary credit business had to be spared any excessive burdens.
Further, the government and many others believed (with some reason) that
the effects of war and defeat had made German goods uncompetitive, so
that Germany had to reduce production costs to compete again in world
markets. Because high labor costs, taxes, and revaluation could all "burden" the economy, the government tried to deal with these issues in ways
least burdensome to industry and commerce.[10]

Workers had to work longer hours for less pay. The eight-hour day had
been the workers' major gain from the November Revolution. Employers
vehemently opposed it for economic reasons and as a symbol of worker
political influence and worker control over some aspects of production.
High postinflation unemployment weakened labor's bargaining power.
Many government officials and even many SPD politicians, union leaders,
and workers believed longer working hours and lower wages were now
necessary for economic recovery (albeit longer working hours do not
necessarily increase net production or profits). Employers hence succeeded in getting the eight-hour day suspended and in reducing real wages,
often drastically.[11]

These developments embittered many workers. Many Germans were
convinced industry's success in eroding its workers' gains guaranteed it
sure profits. The government had seemingly supported all of industry's
labor policies and condemned workers to bear the costs of stabilization and
economic recovery. Important segments of industry plainly wanted to shift
the burden of German economic recovery to the workers through longer
hours and lower wages, "often," as a liberal union official wrote, "in the
most brutal way [and] under the disapprobation of their own central [trade]
associations." These policies poisoned labor relations in many branches
of industry and seriously eroded workers' will to support the Weimar
Republic.[12]

Stabilization and the accompanying severe recession battered the *Mittelstand* as well. Business slashed its swollen white-collar work force,
many white-collar workers lost the eight-hour day, and white-collar unemployment remained high and wages low throughout 1924. These difficulties inspired considerable anger at the business community and the govern-

ment. Attempting desperately to balance the budget, the government laid off one-quarter of government employees, including some tenured civil servants. It drastically lowered wages and raised working hours for its remaining employees. Justifiably or not, civil servants felt that the government was demanding disproportionate sacrifices of them and was treating them unjustly. Meanwhile, many small and medium businessmen went bankrupt or suffered losses so severe they feared they might go out of business.[13]

These economic difficulties limited creditor options as well. With unemployment so high and credit so tight, impoverished creditors would find it difficult to find work or set up in business as an alternative source of income. And they could not easily turn for assistance to relatives who might themselves face unemployment, lower wages, or lagging incomes.

Despite massive unemployment after stabilization, the government set a fixed amount it would disburse in unemployment benefits. Often no additional aid was available to the unemployed, and many were pushed to subsistence. In addition, the government reformed the unemployment system so that employees and employers would provide four-fifths and the municipalities one-fifth of the funds. Only in extreme emergencies would the state provide additional monies.[14]

Balancing the budget required a fundamental tax reform. Committed to freeing business of all burdens, the government worked systematically to limit and then lower the tax burden on the propertied as much as politically possible.

The government set personal taxes (income, inheritance, and capital taxes) relatively low. Luther actually *lowered* the inheritance tax in December 1923 for the two highest classes, leading even scholars sympathetic to him to admit that he was ignoring taxable resources. The income tax was relatively regressive. The Dawes experts complained sharply that their fellow businessmen in Germany were so lightly taxed compared with upper income groups in Britain and the U.S.—while the poorer wage earners paid higher direct taxes in Germany than in the Anglo-Saxon countries. Taxes on industry and agriculture in general were also low, unjustifiably so in the eyes of many government officials.[15]

The government generally ignored the popular demand for inflation taxes to capture the windfall profits big business had often enjoyed. The center and left proposed various capital or capital-gains levies to finance the stabilization. Finance Minister Luther rejected any such levies, arguing they would be impossible to assess, would be an inducement to tax evasion, and would complicate the collection of other taxes. And if they were successful, he argued, they would disastrously erode the "substance" of the economy, seriously retarding economic recovery. He rejected as technically not feasible any profits tax on dealings in short-term credit or in so-called emergency money.[16] Many industrialists had at least tacitly supported inflation as a policy, but they were not to pay the price for its effects. Whatever the merits of Luther's arguments, many of his contemporaries considered such taxes feasible and were outraged when the government refused to introduce them and when it levied a meager 15 percent tax on industrial obligations redeemed in worthless PM.[17]

The only substantial inflation taxes were on agriculture and building owners. Farmers apparently often avoided or evaded their taxes, but the grossly regressive rent tax brought in 2.5 billion RM per year and was a major source of revenue. Although landlords remitted the rent tax, the government included it when calculating allowable rent increases under rent control. Hence tenants in fact paid the tax, as rents rose by 1925 to 110 percent of prewar in GM, even though wages lagged.[18]

Aside from the rent tax, by far the greater part of the government's income came from taxes on consumption. The turnover tax, set at 2.5 percent, was in 1924 the single most remunerative tax. Other consumption taxes were also high. In 1925, responding to agriculture's pleas for protection, the government imposed tariffs on imported food and fodder. These tariffs increased government revenues and helped agriculture but depressed the living standards of most Germans.[19]

The government exacerbated the impression that it unfairly favored industrialists by giving them massive subsidies. In 1923, the French had forced heavy industry in the Ruhr to make deliveries of goods for reparations. The German government had privately promised to compensate industry when the Reich could afford it.[20] Under the circumstances, the government probably should have compensated industry at least partially. But Finance Minister Luther did so secretly, creating a fait accompli, and he accepted all the companies' claims without question, quite probably giving them a profit.[21] Many Germans were outraged to discover that the government had made such a promise, that industry had used it to escape any sacrifice, and that Luther had disbursed public funds in such a manner—quite possibly illegally.[22] The government continued after 1924 to subsidize private businesses—often the most unprofitable and wildly speculative inflation-era conglomerates—as well as large agriculturalists.[23] Concern for the credit of the German economy, which large bankruptcies might have damaged, played a major role in these actions.

Although each measure the government took had some merit according to prevailing economic views, many Germans came to resent bitterly the ability of German businessmen to grow fat while other Germans suffered. The government was demanding cruel, if necessary, sacrifices from many citizens, including creditors, in the name of economic necessity. Revaluation was part of a pattern of policies that burdened disproportionately a truly amazing share of the population, while sparing or even benefiting businessmen who had often botched the inflation-sent opportunity for recovery. Many Germans perceived these policies as fundamentally unfair, with disastrous consequences for the legitimacy of the Weimar economic and political order.

The Yearning for Order

The six months preceding the stabilization had been a nightmare for the German people. Inflation's magnitude, with prices changing daily and eventually hourly, had destroyed all sense of certainty or security.

People accepted the Rentenmark as a stable currency in part because of a desperate desire for the reestablishment of some sense of order. Indeed, one German writing 23 years later remembered the first Rentenmark he saw as "that little wisp of paper from which now blessings were to flow, and which after all the froth and slippery deceit of the inflation mark . . . was once more something solid, to which one could hold and in which one could have confidence." He went on, "Through it we had the sense of becoming honorable people once again, for whom a word is a word that is worth something tomorrow too, even though it was given yesterday."[24] This psychological desire for a return to old verities—material *and* moral—influenced many people's initial reaction to revaluation.

Some civil servants and debtor and banking groups supported revaluation (*Aufwertung*) in December 1923 because they believed that Germany had to restore old moral as well as economic values (*Werte*) in order to reestablish faith in the state. Bavarian officials pointed out that small savers considered the November 28 decision merely the "necessary and self-evident recognition of their rights." If the government blocked revaluation, these savers would see the state as "unscrupulously" evading its obligations. Anger over this could lead to "new revolutionary movements." Ministerialrat Schlüter (Reich Finance Ministry) considered the government's planned revaluation ban so arbitrary and dangerous that he publicly expressed his opposition. No state, he wrote, could attack "justly acquired rights [*wohlerworbene Rechte*]" by banning revaluation without destroying all legal security.[25] Some debtor and banking representatives also used this argument, although their interests in this issue were complex.[26]

Many Germans worried particularly in these months about reestablishing the German economy's credit. They feared that a revaluation ban would be perceived as a declaration of national bankruptcy. Such an evasion of the moral obligation to repay debts might dissuade the German people from ever saving and foreign investors from ever trusting their money to German governments and entrepreneurs.[27] And some credit institutions, fearing that a savers' strike might threaten their existence, were briefly prorevaluation.[28]

Although savings patterns did change significantly as compared with those before the war, people did begin investing in Germany again, and this fear soon evaporated. By March 1924 many who had initially shared such fears would be arguing against revaluation.

Nonetheless, the German economy could suffer if the state countenanced the legal expropriation of creditors. Inflation had made Germans and foreigners leery of German assets, especially government bonds. Unless their confidence were somehow restored, their savings and investment rates might fail to meet the economy's needs. Economic efficiency—securing sufficient credit—did require that the government treat creditors "equitably" in the creditors' own eyes, so that they would willingly invest again. This requirement, however, clashed with Germany's need to limit revaluation for immediate fiscal and economic reasons.

Concerns about the revaluation issue's long-term effects were closely related to fears about the attitudes, indeed even the continued existence, of the *Mittelstand*. For decades government officials, politicians, and others had professed to consider the *Mittelstand* vital to the viability of the German state, an indispensable counterweight to the "Marxist" working classes. The creditors assiduously cultivated the idea that all members of the *Mittelstand* had a major economic interest as creditor and that a revaluation was crucial to preserving them as a bulwark of the state. Although the creditors were exaggerating the *Mittelstand*'s dependence on savings, many businessmen and, more significantly, politicians and civil servants believed them.[29]

Bavarian officials held this attitude most strongly. In June 1923 the Bavarian Justice and Commerce ministries justified a repayment moratorium as necessary to prevent the destruction of the *Mittelstand*, "whose maintenance is of great domestic political, social, and cultural significance."[30] In December 1923 the *Generalstaatskommissar* (a kind of temporary dictator) and the justice minister argued forcefully for revaluation because of the *Mittelstand*'s importance, particularly in Bavaria. "I share completely," the latter wrote, "the fears that the *Generalstaatskommissar* has expressed of new, severe damage to the *Mittelstand* and of the devastating effects on the patriotic feelings [*Staatsgesinnung*] of these segments of society, segments that are to a special degree supportive of the state."[31] Bavarian officials even opposed limiting revaluation: "The Bavarian government considers a limitation of the revaluation to 10 percent politically ill-advised; the government fears major unrest among the masses of the *Mittelstand*, whose effects would be highly dangerous to the state."[32] Such fears, however, soon diminished. Subsequently, the Bavarian government basically ignored this aspect of the revaluation issue.

In fact, bourgeois parties paid only lip service to the *Mittelstand*. Aside from undercutting support for specific parties, limiting revaluation could aggravate inflation's negative impact on the legitimacy of the Weimar system. Luther wrote that he, Interior Minister Jarres, and Stresemann discussed the political effect on the *Mittelstand* of limiting revaluation—but concluded that economic difficulties required limiting it. And Economics Minister Hamm argued similarly in February 1924.[33] Before World War I political rhetoric had been pro-*Mittelstand*, but political action had often been anti-*Mittelstand*.[34] The same attitude prevailed under Weimar. The "crucial role of the *Mittelstand*" made a fine topic for campaign speeches. In policy-making, however, the government and the bourgeois parties ignored any long-term necessity for satisfying *Mittelstand* sensibilities in favor of the productive sector's immediate needs, including the "need" to limit revaluation.

Initial Confusion over Revaluation's Implications

Revaluation was so complex that Germans had great difficulty understanding its implications, with considerable long-term consequences. It was an issue without a past: no industrial nation had ever had to deal with it before. Creditors, convinced their cause was just, failed to realize the degree of opposition they would face because of revaluation's economic effects. Many debtors at first misconstrued their real economic interest in the issue and subsequently underestimated the vehemence of the creditors' desire for redress. The government was among the first to recognize the dangers of individual revaluation, leaving it virtually isolated in its initial efforts to limit revaluation and planting seeds of suspicion about its motives.

Government success in stabilizing the currency suggested political and economic elites had more control over the situation, including revaluation, than creditors had previously imagined. Nonetheless, in this period creditors emphasized restitution, not the issue of responsibility for inflation. They expressed only a diffuse, "populistic" anticapitalism.[35]

The 28 November ruling decisively influenced the revaluation issue's development. Most Germans looked to the courts for guidance on what justice meant, and the courts had said that justice required private-law revaluation of each debt. This ruling vindicated the creditors' belief that they had a *justly acquired right* to nearly full revaluation. It remained a vivid symbol for creditors, proof that they were in the right and that all who opposed them were in the wrong. And even after the political parties became convinced of revaluation's potentially deleterious economic effects, they nonetheless felt compelled to provide some significant revaluation to meet what the judges had made the moral expectations of the German people.[36] Further, after the 28 November decision the creditors insisted that only the court-sanctioned individual revaluation was acceptable, even though they might have gotten more revaluation by trying to increase the rate under the unavoidable schematic revaluation.[37]

Creditors rushed to organize and lobby in this period. They now had a concrete policy to defend in the political arena, where organization counts. Local creditor-group chapters proliferated. They inundated Reich and Land ministries with petitions denouncing proposed revaluation bans or limits as monstrously unjust attacks on their justly acquired right to revaluation. Most simply spoke of "right" as a quality inhering in the natural moral order that no government, apparently for whatever reason, could in any way impair. Others decried a revaluation ban or limitation as unconstitutional because it conflicted with the provision against uncompensated expropriation.[38]

The creditors initially ignored revaluation's fiscal and economic implications. The government's revenue problems seemed to them irrelevant to the private-law issue of revaluation. And, convinced of the justice of their cause, they had little interest in addressing economic objections to their demands, especially as debtor groups were not supporting the government when it did refer to such objections.

Some debtors did feel some moral obligation to revalue their debts. In February 1923 one debtor had written that repaying his mortgage in PM would be an "unbelievable confounding [*Verwechselung*] of the concepts of mine and thine."[39] Some debtors would voluntarily revalue their debts at varying rates, depending on their own economic situation and on the date, but these were definitely exceptions.[40]

Building owners had suffered during the inflation and felt no one could expect them to revalue their mortgages. Because of rent control, most had operated at a loss for years. Continued rent control, the rent tax, and the desperate need to catch up on repairs limited their returns and the value of their property. Their creditors deserved assistance, but substantial revaluation could create a new inequity for many of these debtors in place of the old one for creditors.[41]

Some commercial and industrial debtors in this period also opposed revaluation. They argued it would only unfairly burden many honest debtors to the benefit of often undeserving creditors, while creating unacceptable uncertainty and an insupportable burden for the economy. They denied having made any inflation profits.[42]

Revaluation had complex implications for debtor tax burdens, given Finance Ministry plans to tax inflation profits. The more astute debtors recognized the intimate connection between the revaluation and the tax rate the government could impose: the greater the revaluation, the lower the debtor's net profits and the lower, presumably, the tax burden.[43]

All other things being equal, debtors would be indifferent whether they paid the government or their creditors; but all other things were not equal. Businessmen tended to see all funds diverted to the public sector as wasted. They preferred that the funds remain available in the private sector for investment. And although the proposed inflation taxes were supposedly temporary, taxes have a way of becoming permanent, unlike any one-time revaluation levy. For example, the rent tax was to have expired in 1926 but lasted until 1942. Finally, if the assessment base were sufficiently low because of a moderate revaluation or the appearance of revaluation, the tax yield might be so low that the government would abandon its planned inflation taxes. Debtors would then escape taxation altogether and could hope to retain more of their inflation profits.

Apparently motivated by a desire to decrease their net liabilities (revalued debt plus taxes), the national and several local Chambers of Commerce (*Handelskammern*) attacked government proposals to ban revaluation. They proposed instead some type of individual revaluation, usually through special arbitration courts to be staffed with economic "experts" from the Chambers of Commerce, artisans' guilds, and Agricultural Councils. They seemed to believe that individual revaluation would preclude any inflation taxes. They apparently assumed they could then obtain relatively low revaluation rates from the arbitration courts, which would be staffed by representatives of debtor groups.[44] They clearly believed the cost of individual revaluation would be lower than the tax burden a bourgeois government would impose.

Not all debtors made so subtle, or oversubtle, an analysis—or any analysis at all. The National Association of German Industry (*Reichsverband der deutschen Industrie*) failed to reach any consensus before the government issued its initial revaluation decree.[45] And in this period, traditional problems such as taxation, reparations, credit, and the eight-hour day, not revaluation, were the major concerns at meetings in agricultural, commercial, and industrial circles.[46]

As both creditor and debtor, credit institutions were ambivalent. Stabilization had destroyed almost all liquid capital, and saving temporarily collapsed in the ensuing liquidity crisis. The mortgage banks in particular feared a long-term collapse of saving resulting from an inflation-induced mistrust of paper assets. They therefore initially demanded some limited mortgage and mortgage-bond revaluation to restore lost confidence.[47] The savings banks and their association (*Deutscher Sparkassenverband*) favored mortgage revaluation as a solution to their own financial difficulties, but rejected savings-account revaluation as technically not feasible. They also emphasized that most of their remaining assets were government bonds and that only a government-bond revaluation would allow any significant savings-account revaluation.[48]

Government as debtor had a continuing interest in limiting any type of debt revaluation as much as possible. The biggest debtors were the various levels of government (Reich, Länder, and municipalities), who held about five-eighths of the revaluable debt as government bonds (*Anleihen*). At this time even creditors assumed that the inflation- and reparations-induced poverty of the governments precluded government-bond revaluation. Yet the governments' fiscal situations would certainly improve. Any private-debt revaluation would undoubtedly then be extended to the legally very similar public debts—and the private-debt-revaluation rate would set a precedent for the government-bond rate.[49]

Germany's fiscal and economic crises persisted, as revenues failed to keep up with expenditures. By 13 December 1923 the Finance Ministry seriously feared the Reich would imminently have to suspend all payments, leading to "immediate dissolution of the entire organization of the state, with incalculable political, economic, and social consequences."[50] Many ministers shared these anxieties, especially as the budget was not really in balance until July 1924.[51]

Hence, Luther, who bore responsibility for the budget, reacted to the revaluation decision with near panic. A high revaluation would eliminate the inflation profits he needed to tax away to balance the budget. Replacing the lost revenue would be virtually impossible. Only massive increases in other taxes could do so, and that was politically and economically inconceivable.[52]

Individual revaluation threatened to reduce the revenue from other taxes as well. Years would pass before the courts could revalue each debt and establish each asset's real value. Meanwhile, each debtor would post his debt as though it were going to be fully revalued, and each creditor his asset as though it were not going to be revalued at all, reducing the revenue from inheritance, capital, transaction, and property taxes.[53] Estimating the probable revenue loss is impossible, but in early 1924, when revenues and expenditures were in such precarious balance, any loss could have proved disastrous.

Many Germans also realized that individual revaluation could create economically harmful uncertainty. Even debtor groups and policymakers who favored some individual revaluation wanted a simplified arbitration procedure. Otherwise the economy might grind to a halt for years while the courts struggled to establish the economic situations of millions of debtors and creditors.[54]

Unfortunately though, no one was yet grappling publicly with the central issue, reconciling equity for creditors with the economically and politically possible for German society as a whole. Luther and some officials certainly recognized and raised revaluation's inflationary implications and the long-term dangers it might pose for the overburdened economy.[55] Yet the fiscal crisis and the risks of individual revaluation were so obvious that the government concentrated on them instead. Other debtors generally ignored revaluation's broader effects in their concern over the government's planned inflation taxes and over other issues, leaving the government isolated and creditors uninformed. Perhaps most important, by emphasizing primarily short-term fiscal difficulties in justifying its initial revaluation policies, the government left itself dangerously vulnerable to creditor counterattacks when those difficulties eased.

Regulating Revaluation by Fiat

Forestalling a Ban on Revaluation

Despite the 28 November Reichsgericht decision, Luther had not wavered in his determination to ban debt revaluation. Obsessed with taxation, convinced equity must give way to economic necessity, Luther saw the decision as irresponsible. When Bavaria pressed at a 30 November Reichsrat meeting for a mortgage-repayment moratorium, because of the 28 November ruling, Luther brushed the proposal aside. He convinced the Länder to postpone consideration of the moratorium. And he intended, he announced, to ban revaluation by decree immediately, "except as expressly allowed by law."[1]

When ministers first discussed revaluation in mid-December, Hamm, Jarres, Luther, and Brauns—the first three with ties to business and the fourth responsible for housing—demanded a revaluation ban on fiscal and economic grounds. They wanted the ban included in the crucial Third Emergency Tax Decree (*Dritte Steuernotverordnung*, hereafter Tax Decree). Emminger replied that the 28 November decision had created "a definite legal status for the creditors," so that a ban would be a "massive attack" on the courts. Stresemann supported Emminger, arguing that the state in its necessity "could ruthlessly have its way" in refusing to revalue government bonds but that private citizens could not do so with their debts. He thought it unjust "to completely proletarianize the strata of society that had previously been state-supporting." He also feared a ban would damage the German economy's credit, especially abroad. But even Emminger proposed limiting revaluation to 10 percent. In closing, Chancellor Marx waffled, saying he agreed with the financial basis of Luther's proposed ban but believed he must associate himself with Emminger's suggestions.[2]

Most ministers except Emminger apparently did not consider the 28 November decision really binding on the government. They were still living psychologically in the prewar era, when a single court ruling could not conceivably have committed the state to a particular policy course. They blithely assumed that the government could simply reverse the bothersome court ruling by banning revaluation.

The creditors were being run through an emotional roller coaster. Their hopes had dwindled over the years, and the stabilization on 20 November seemed to extinguish any possibility they might regain the security and social position their savings had once ensured. The 28 November decision, however, seemed to promise nearly full revaluation. But then reports of the government's planned revaluation ban appeared, crushing unmercifully their newly revived hopes. And Emminger's proposal for 10 percent revaluation must have seemed a cruel mockery to people who but a couple of weeks earlier had expected to recoup up to 100 percent of their losses.

Meanwhile, the Länder were becoming more receptive to measures favoring the creditors. On 21 December the Reichsrat met to discuss the projected Tax Decree. All Länder insisted on discussing revaluation first, and virtually all rejected a revaluation ban. Although they recognized that full revaluation was impossible, their concern that a ban would now offend the sense of justice and the patriotism of many Germans—especially in the *Mittelstand*—produced a consensus for partial revaluation.[3]

After the Christmas holidays the chancellor asked each minister to report formally on revaluation's implications. The eight responding split evenly. Opponents of revaluation stressed the fiscal crisis, and the Agriculture Ministry argued that revaluation would overburden the economy. Proponents stressed the demands of equity but also asserted that banning revaluation would impair Germany's credit, particularly abroad. Nonetheless, all eight saw a need to regulate the revaluation to eliminate the dangerous uncertainty that individual revaluation was creating. Emminger insisted, at length, that the government could not simply ignore the judiciary's ruling. But because he recognized the state's fiscal needs, he thought it permissible to limit revaluation to 10 percent, to regulate the rate of impoverishment the Reichsgericht had said had to be considered. The ministers did not split along party lines.[4]

Luther's plan to ban revaluation was under increasing attack. The ministers' replies suggest they were swinging toward revaluation, apparently as they came to understand the depth of popular feeling on the issue. Both Jarres and Hamm, for example, now supported limited revaluation predominantly because they thought it unavoidable for political reasons. And in early January the Reichsgericht Judges Association and the Catholic church gave revaluation additional impetus.

On 8 January 1924, in an unprecedented step, the Reichsgericht Judges Association sent the chancellor a letter threatening to invalidate any law or decree that banned or even limited the revaluation. The association's directing committee had moderated a draft letter prepared by Reichsgericht Judge Alois Zeiler and then, according to Zeiler, voted unanimously for it.[5]

The committee argued that the court had made the revaluation decision carefully and responsibly and that the ruling was necessary to avoid a gross injustice. The decision was based on the principle of equity and good faith, "which rules all our legal life." A revaluation ban would be incompatible with equity and good faith.

> It would be a severe blow, not only to the reputability of the government but also to the sense of justice of the people and to faith in the law, if the highest court were forced to declare against a revaluation ban that, despite all, had been promulgated, that this ban was not binding, was void [either] as an offense against [equity and] good faith, or as immoral or on account of its immoral effects, or as an expropriation without legal justification, or as a tax that makes a mockery of the constitutional principle of equal taxation. The serious danger of such a judicial ruling or a similar one against the planned measure exists, and it also exists if the government, perhaps under pressure of the recent popular opposition, decides not to impose the ban with the originally intended harshness.

The committee avoided explicitly defying the government. The judges couched their letter in the subjunctive and asserted only that "the serious danger . . . exists," not that they would definitely take action if the government banned revaluation.[6]

Despite the letter's circumspect tone, it represented a serious challenge to the constitutional order. The Reichsgericht would eventually assert the power to review statutes for constitutionality, but that was only a minor aspect of the letter. At this point the judges were asserting rather more—the power to invalidate a law based not on its incompatibility with an amendable constitution, but on whether it conflicted with the abstract concept of equity and good faith. The court had taken this concept from a regular statute passed under an earlier regime and raised it to the status of an immutable principle superior to any positive law. They tacitly assumed that whatever they might proclaim to be equity and good faith would in fact be so.[7] On that basis they were claiming for themselves a veto that apparently could not be overridden over all legislation.[8] Whatever role judicial review might play in guaranteeing the bases of a democratic polity, the scope of these judicial claims would seem to represent an antidemocratic development.

Like the 28 November decision, this letter departed radically from German legal tradition. Judges were refusing to acknowledge the government's desperate efforts to deal with fiscal and economic chaos and were challenging even more directly the constitutional order. Sympathy with the creditors, however sincere, seems insufficient to explain the judges' unwillingness to recognize revaluation's economic implications or their willingness to challenge the government over this issue. Some reference to the judges' probable creditor status and their apparent desire to expand their own powers would seem necessary to explain why they perceived the issue as they did and why they took a step so singular, so nearly revolutionary.

Sending such a letter challenged the government seriously enough, but the association also published it in two legal journals on 15 January. When newspapers quoted it extensively, it became a factor in the political conflict over revaluation. Although socialist papers ignored the letter, other papers tended to support it or treat it neutrally. For the creditors it was a tremendous boost. The judges (or at least the Reichsgericht Judges Association, which came to the same thing in popular opinion) had condemned as unjust not merely the government's efforts to ban revaluation, but even those to limit it.[9]

The government reacted cautiously, perhaps too cautiously. Marx and Emminger agreed that the judges' claims were unjustified. The Chancellery state secretary therefore drafted a reply to the association that excoriated the judges for overstepping their constitutional bounds; he sharply rejected any use of equity and good faith for judging the validity of properly promulgated laws. Emminger, however, considerably toned down this reply, though he did deny judges could use either judicial review or equity and good faith. The government published the reply, presumably to strengthen its position.[10] One legal historian has suggested that Emminger avoided vigorously contesting the judges' pretensions because he wanted to avoid a conflict that might split the conservative camp. In addition, Emminger's ministry had to work with the courts. In any event, "No one seemed to realize that thereby the as yet unsolved problem of the role of the judge [*Richterrecht*] was created and that in fact the '*dissolution*' of the traditional legal order and of the liberal conception of the judge had been announced by the Reichsgericht and not been prevented by the Reich minister."[11]

The Catholic hierarchy also denounced a revaluation ban. On 6 January Michael Cardinal Faulhaber of Munich preached a well-publicized sermon on the seventh commandment (Thou shalt not steal) denouncing any revaluation ban. On 14 January the Archbishop of Freiburg wrote Marx (a Catholic) attacking the proposed ban as "in contradiction to the constitution and the laws of natural morality." Besides, he said, the state had forced the church to invest in *mündelsicher* assets that the inflation had destroyed. In mid-January Adolf Cardinal Bertram, chairman of the Catholic Bishops Conference, sent Marx a letter denouncing the revaluation as a "new expropriation" of the church. The press reprinted Bertram's letter.[12]

Church opposition strengthened the creditors' position considerably, particularly within the Center Party. By rejecting the government's revaluation plans on moral grounds, the church seemed to many Germans to confirm the moral righteousness of creditor demands. Insofar as people recognized the church's economic interest as creditor, they generally saw it as a pastoral concern for the charitable activities that the church had financed from part of its income.[13] And according to a Reichsbank official, clerical lobbying was responsible for the Center's opposition to a revaluation ban.[14]

A wave of speculation in revaluable assets also helped the creditors. Germans in the 1920s despised speculators and profiteers with a particular virulence. War and inflation had provided myriad opportunities for economic and financial manipulation, and many Germans blamed speculators for much of what they had suffered. Renewed speculation after the 28 November ruling seemed a repulsive contrast to the creditors' own thrifty, measured investments from hard-earned income. It fueled the creditors' moral indignation, confirmed their sense of moral superiority, and created sympathy for them among noncreditors.[15] And it contributed to subsequent proposals to exclude "speculatively" acquired paper assets from any revaluation.

Facing strong opposition from creditors, the courts, and the Catholic church, and with virtually no support from debtors or anyone else in society, government officials realized they must find an alternative revaluation policy. Given the growing opposition to a revaluation ban, Marx told the Center Reichstag delegation the cabinet was abandoning the ban. The next day, 9 January 1924, the government withdrew the Tax Decree draft containing a revaluation ban.[16]

The Government Concedes as Little as Possible

Emminger dropped a bombshell in mid-January. On 17 January he asked the cabinet to allow him to commit it to a schematic revaluation at the Reichsrat meeting the next day. Otherwise, he argued, the Reichsrat might act on its own. The cabinet rejected his proposal and *explicitly* instructed him not to make any such commitment to the Reichsrat.[17] The chancellor might have abandoned a revaluation ban, but the cabinet was not yet prepared to commit itself to an alternative. Emminger, however, ignored the cabinet's instructions and told the Reichsrat that some schematic revaluation with an "average rate" was necessary to clarify the situation. He did exclude government bonds but added that he personally felt the government could someday fulfill a certain "moral duty to revalue" bonds purchased because of *Mündelsicherheit* requirements. The evening press reported his statement.[18]

Emminger's motives in breaching faith with his coalition colleagues are difficult to evaluate. As a jurist, he sympathized with the judges' moral dilemma over debt revaluation and was sensitive to the political and legal implications of bluntly reversing a judicial ruling. He also sympathized deeply with the creditors, and he fought for years for the highest revaluation he thought compatible with the national interest. Yet he refused to stoop to demagoguery and warned creditors frankly that economic considerations precluded full revaluation.[19] Perhaps he was convinced the Reichsrat would on 18 January vote an unfavorable and politically damaging resolution on the revaluation. Perhaps he considered the moral stakes in revaluation sufficiently high to justify breaking faith with his colleagues. That this apparently honorable man felt compelled to take an arguably dishonorable action suggests the moral ambiguity of the issue.

Although Emminger had been very indiscreet, his unilateral action probably did not by itself force the government to grant a partial revaluation. Given the political developments of early January, some restitution was almost inevitable, as Chancellor Marx clearly believed even before the Reichsgericht Judges Association and the Catholic church intervened publicly. None of Emminger's coalition partners seems to have complained that he had committed them against their wills. The other cabinet members probably believed that Emminger's declaration only committed them to something they would eventually have had to embrace anyway.[20]

At a 22 January cabinet meeting, Luther proposed simply granting the government the power to determine "when and to what extent" a revaluation would be allowed, a proposal that Emminger promptly rejected.[21]

This policy would have given the appearance of revaluation while allowing the government to implement any kind of revaluation it thought fit—including a revaluation ban if it could get away with one. The proposal reflected Luther's preference for an administrative state run by "impartial experts."

By the 25 January cabinet meeting time was running out. With the Enabling Act expiring on 15 February, Marx told the cabinet that they would have to reach a decision in principle on the Tax Decree that day.[22]

Labor Minister Brauns suddenly reversed his position. He had earlier been in the forefront of efforts to ban revaluation, and as recently as 8 January he had denounced individual revaluation as impossible. Yet he now embraced individual revaluation. In justifying his new position he merely stated that some revaluation was necessary for political reasons. Yet no other minister thought political reasons demanded individual revaluation. Further, Brauns subsequently reverted to his economically based opposition to revaluation.[23] Brauns was a Catholic priest, and subsequent to 8 January his religious superiors had declared revaluation necessary on moral grounds. His temporary and otherwise inexplicable change of heart presumably reflected the pressure he must have felt to follow his superiors in their argument that revaluation was a moral duty. Like Emminger, Brauns seemed to face a difficult moral dilemma.

Conscious of the political pressure in favor of revaluation, the cabinet rejected Agriculture Minister von Kanitz's proposal for a ban. Yet when they voted on the alternative of a "fixed limit" on revaluation, the finance, agriculture, interior, and economics ministers favored a mere 5 percent and the rest of those present (except Brauns) wanted 10 percent.

The ministers did not divide on party lines, and the key factor influencing their attitudes seems to have been the interests of the ministry or its clientele. Those ministers who represented economic groups or interests (e.g., Agriculture Ministry) voted for 5 percent while the other ministers voted for 10 percent. The exceptions are Jarres—who had ties to industry and voted for the lower figure—and Brauns—who temporarily shifted his views for apparently personal reasons.[24]

Revaluation proponents had not convinced the government that revaluation was economically wise, or even economically supportable, only that some revaluation was politically unavoidable.[25] What the government was willing to concede under duress was insignificant, but it was a start.

The Finance and Justice ministries quickly hammered out a new draft for the revaluation portions of the Tax Decree (which also included important sections on inflation taxes and on allocating tax revenues among the different levels of government). This revaluation involved only *Vermö-gensanlagen* (long-term capital investments for savings), whose paper value most probably exceeded Germany's 1924 real national wealth. The judiciary had generally refused to revalue short-term obligations (e.g., commercial credit and demand deposits) because of their ephemeral character, so the government could safely leave them to the courts and Paragraph 242.[26]

The key question at the 29 January cabinet meeting was still the nature and amount of revaluation. Reflecting Justice Ministry views, the draft decree provided that in "exceptional cases . . . to prevent an obviously gross inequity" revaluation could exceed 10 percent. The cabinet eliminated this de facto revaluation norm with no recorded discussion. Instead it decided with eight votes, one abstention (Brauns) to set a 10 percent maximum and allow *debtors* to sue for less if their situation required it. Creditors had gotten a schematic revaluation, while debtors had won a revaluation norm. Interest payments were to begin on 1 January 1925 at 1 percent per year and rise in yearly increments of 1 percent to the contractual rate.[27]

In some respects the Tax Decree revaluation was a gift to the banks, reducing immeasurably their problems and costs. The mortgage banks were to accumulate the proceeds from revaluing their assets in a special fund (later named the distribution fund). After reimbursing themselves for administration costs, they were to distribute the remainder of the fund proportionally among eligible mortgage-bond holders. This simplified scheme reflected bankers' access to government officials and their crucial role in a capitalist economy.[28] The cabinet excused the impoverished life-insurance companies and savings banks from revaluing their debits.

Significantly, the decree postponed any interest or redemption payments for pre-1924 Reich, Land, and municipal bonds until reparations had been settled. This relieved Germany of any foreseeable burden from PM government bonds while meeting the moral responsibility to recognize creditor claims to possible recompense, a recognition that many saw as vital to reestablish Germany's credit. And because the state had not "expropriated" its creditors but had merely delayed repayment indefinitely, the moratorium forestalled any constitutional objections to a ban on government-bond revaluation.

The Parties Force a Larger Revaluation

The cabinet could not settle the revaluation issue simply by promulgating its draft decree. De facto or de jure the government had to consult the Reichsrat, the Reich Economic Council, and the Committee of Fifteen. Further, it would need as much support as it could muster in these bodies to prevent the Reichstag from reversing its revaluation policies. Instead, it generated a muddled discussion that failed to convince the public that the decree as written was essential to Germany's economic recovery.

The Reichsrat seems generally to have accepted the government's fiscal and economic arguments. Despite some sentiment for higher revaluation, the government insisted on 10 percent, and only Bavaria, Württemberg, Silesia, and the Rhine Province voted for more. Hamburg's proposal for a general savings-bank-account revaluation failed to win support; other Länder apparently realized that only government-bond revaluation would enable the savings banks to offer any reasonable revaluation of their accounts. The Länder objected to the ban on all government-bond revaluation because they thought it unjust to prevent governments who could pay from doing so. The Reich argued that leaving government-bond revaluation to the discretion of the different governments would simply enable creditors to play governments off against one another. But it finally agreed to allow some municipal-bond revaluation if the Reich justice minister determined that it was appropriate—but only for bonds that cities had issued to acquire profit-making enterprises (e.g., streetcar lines, gas works) from which they could finance a revaluation.[29]

Nonetheless, the Länder did not help the government in winning over public opinion. Most Länder clearly felt revaluation was not a problem for them because they had little or no debt of their own. They could therefore quibble about details rather than vocally endorsing the Tax Decree revaluation.

The Reich Economic Council also rather hindered than helped the government. Its 7 February discussion of the Tax Decree seemed diffuse and produced little agreement on revaluation's implications. Although the members rejected individual revaluation 25 to 14, many felt 10 percent was so nearly confiscation that the government should forgo a fixed rate. Some argued that the debtor's right to sue for reduced revaluation would create nearly as many cases as individual revaluation. The council did agree that savings-bank deposits should be revalued, despite the government's doubts. Unable to agree quickly enough on any alternative to the Tax Decree revaluation, the members finally adopted Hilferding's proposal that revaluation be settled by law (not decree). Members believed that the Reichsgericht might invalidate the Tax Decree, but that it would hesitate to invalidate a law. Yet the council also wanted businesses to establish GM balances immediately. These two proposals were mutually exclusive. Until one knew what one's net revaluation position was, one could not establish a GM balance.[30] These confused deliberations failed to spark any general debate on revaluation's economic implications.

Political pressure had now become such that the parties could no longer avoid taking a stand on revaluation. Much more than most issues, revaluation cut across party lines, and each party (except possibly the KPD [*Kommunistische Partei Deutschlands*, Communist party]) had both supporters and opponents of revaluation within its ranks. Individual politicians had long supported or opposed procreditor measures but had done so as individuals. Unfortunately for the government, the parties now took up the issues in ways that exacerbated the difficulty of winning popular support for limited revaluation.

After dismissing revaluation through most of 1923 as a private, capitalist issue, the SPD now insisted on a revaluation ban. Its leaders believed with the Free Trade Unions that higher rents would shift mortgage revaluation's costs to the tenants. It also feared a revaluation would preclude any inflation taxes except the rent tax, which it *vehemently* opposed as an unconscionable burden on the poorest classes. The party wanted to siphon off inflation profits for the common good anyway, not disperse them among creditors.[31]

The other main nongovernmental party, the DNVP, was deeply divided. Important segments of the party (agriculture and industry) were debtors and would soon be antirevaluation. Other segments, however, were *mittelständische* creditors. The party had long supported rentier demands for relief—especially since, as a nongovernment party, it bore no responsibility for securing the necessary funds. Although the agricultural interests in the party rejected revaluation, party chairman Oskar Hergt proposed allowing individual revaluation within a fixed minimum and maximum. The party initially opposed revaluation of industrial obligations or personal loans, a position beneficial to industry and small business. This hodgepodge of proposals reflected the party's attempt to paper over its differences while still taking political advantage of the issue.[32]

The "government" parties were in an anomalous position. The Marx cabinet was a minority government ruling by decree. Hence the parties to which the various ministers belonged could distance themselves somewhat from government policies because they did not have to vote on the decrees in the Reichstag. Nonetheless, they could not completely divorce themselves from the cabinet's actions and had to preserve maneuvering room for the inevitable Reichstag debates on the cabinet's decrees.

The Center party stood fairly firmly behind its chancellor, Marx, and his government. Certainly the party was under considerable popular and church pressure to reject Luther's ban. And some members of the Center Reichstag delegation vehemently favored substantial revaluation. Nonetheless, party policy was that Germany could only maintain the stabilization by substantially limiting revaluation.[33]

The DVP apparently recognized that, politically, it would have to acknowledge the 28 November ruling, but it was still unwilling to accept individual revaluation. The party represented both industrialists, usually debtors, and many in the *Mittelstand* who were creditors. Some Reichstag delegation members, including Stresemann, had supported Düringer's repayment moratorium, although Heinze and others had prevented the party as such from supporting Düringer. Immediately after the 28 November decision, the *Deutsche Allgemeine Zeitung*, a DVP paper with ties to industry, favored individual revaluation under a simplified arbitration procedure. Yet the paper soon accepted, vaguely, the need somehow to limit revaluation. In January 1924 the DVP delegation voted unanimously for a revaluation based on the 28 November decision. Stresemann, writing to a creditor, implied that the DVP was thereby committing itself to a large, perhaps individual, revaluation. Nonetheless, "basing" a revaluation on the 28 November decision could mean almost anything. And in February and March the DVP supported the limited Tax Decree revaluation.[34]

The DDP delegation basically supported the Tax Decree revaluation, especially on the key issue—banning individual revaluation to create the necessary certainty in the economy. But even representatives of debtor interests in the party supported a modest revaluation, around 10 percent for mortgages.[35]

The government, then, got little support from nonpartisan bodies, from parties out of power, or from parties represented in the cabinet. Indeed, its complex revaluation proposal invited detailed objections and—increasingly—efforts to turn revaluation into a partisan issue.

To complicate matters, the DVP and DDP insisted that the government try to settle revaluation by law rather than decree. The DVP feared the Reichsgericht might actually declare any revaluation decree invalid; it argued that only a law, preferably with the two-thirds majority necessary for constitutional amendments, could preclude a court challenge and provide the necessary certainty. The DDP agreed, arguing that the Reichstag could achieve a compromise at 15 percent. The two parties presumably also wanted to get the larger parties to vote to limit revaluation, rather than have the government they supported bear all the onus.[36]

The government was certainly willing to accept a law if the parties could guarantee speedy passage, but such a guarantee proved impossible to secure. Despite initial signs of a general willingness to negotiate, compromise proved elusive. The government parties accepted the government's draft proposals, but the SPD ultimately held out for a ban, and the DNVP insisted on some individual revaluation within a minimum and maximum rate.[37]

The situation was still so confused that the parties were no more able than most Germans to weigh the full economic and moral complexities of revaluation. They generally recognized that neither individual nor large-scale revaluation was feasible, but the creditors' strong moral and legal position made any revaluation ban seem unjust and politically unwise. The parties did show themselves somewhat responsive to popular opinion, forcing the government to increase the revaluation amount slightly. But they did not address directly the conflict between equity and economic constraints, and so their initial intervention did not and could not advance the effort to cope with the fundamental dilemma the issue presented.

The government stuck closely to its draft decree, making only those changes that it thought would suffice to make the decree politically defensible.[38] Under extreme pressure from the SPD to extend revaluation's benefits to the working classes, the cabinet granted limited savings-account and life-insurance revaluation. However, it rejected the SPD's proposal to increase savings-bank assets by retroactively revaluing all debts paid off after 1 July 1922.[39] Instead, it explicitly banned retroactive revaluation unless the creditor had "reserved his rights" when accepting repayment. The courts had been forcing creditors to issue *un*reserved *Löschungsbewilligungen* until well into 1923, and officials expected this wording to prevent any retroactive revaluation. To avoid burdening debtors with sudden and often massive repayments, the government set 1 January 1932 as the earliest date on which creditors could demand repayment of revalued obligations. To allow higher revaluation *only* in certain special cases (e.g., debts among relatives or heirs), the cabinet added a new provision, Paragraph 3, allowing individual revaluation of mortgage-secured demands. This paragraph would later cause problems.[40]

The government added to the decree a vaguely worded provision intended to preclude any commercial-bank-account revaluation. Bank-account revaluation seemed impossible to many because commercial-bank assets consisted virtually entirely of short-term loans and treasury bills that were not revaluable. But the 29 January draft had implicitly allowed revaluation of term accounts (six months plus) at commercial banks. Using their influence with and ease of access to Reich officials, the banks apparently convinced the government such a revaluation was economically impossible (which it quite possibly was).[41]

In response to severe pressure from the parties, the cabinet accepted Emminger's 13 February suggestion that they increase the revaluation rate from 10 to 15 percent. Although an Agriculture Ministry representative and the economics minister denounced this rate as too burdensome, the cabinet voted five to three to set the maximum and usual revaluation rate at 15 percent.[42]

Luther asserted in his memoirs that after discussions with several representatives of agriculture, he chose 15 percent as the highest rate agriculture could support, given its credit and price problems and high tax burden.[43] This explanation says more about Luther's preference for nonpolitical policy-making than it does about the way the cabinet actually set the rate. Luther felt no qualms about presenting his one-sided discussion with a self-interested producer group as adequate grounds to make a decision in which an opposing, nonproducer group and the larger society and economy had a vital interest. And he could maintain that the decision resulted solely from expert analysis of the objective situation.

Documents on the revaluation show plainly, however, that the government set the revaluation rate not through objective economic analysis but in response to political pressure. Luther and some other ministers fought against revaluation every step of the way, giving ground only a little at a time, first 5 percent, then 10 percent, and only under extreme pressure 15 percent. Luther may have concluded that 15 percent was the maximum possible for agriculture, but he accepted that rate only under political duress.

Apparent Victory

The government had a revaluation policy, but that policy faced threatening judicial hurdles. The Reichsgericht Judges Association had threatened to invalidate any limited revaluation. If the court did so, the nation would face a dangerous and unprecedented situation.

The initial developments were not encouraging. On 23 February the Berlin Landesgericht (appeals court) found the Tax Decree's revaluation

provisions "judicially null and void (*rechtsunwirksam*)" because they conflicted with Article 153 of the constitution, which protected against uncompensated expropriation. For the first time, a German court had used
judicial review to invalidate an important measure. This decision was not
quite the major step it might appear. The measure was a decree under an
Enabling Act that specifically forbade changing the constitution by decree,
and judges had often ruled on the validity of decrees under the monarchy.

Nonetheless, for the government the decision was potentially catastrophic. It implied some expansion of judicial power. More important,
though, if the Reichsgericht upheld it on appeal, Germany would be
thrown into that chaos of individual revaluation cases the government
feared and the state would lose irreplaceable revenue from inflation taxes.
A number of nonsocialist newspapers explicitly rejected this decision,
arguing the court had overstepped its bounds in a way that threatened the
stabilization.[44]

Meanwhile, debtors and credit institutions finally began to rally to the
government's support. On 4 February the Central Federation of Associations of Building and Property Owners (*Zentralverband Haus- und Grundbesitzer Vereine*) had announced its acceptance of the Tax Decree revaluation, but only if the maximum was 10 percent. Apparently, the landlords
had decided that some revaluation was unavoidable but that a schematic 10
percent was better than individual revaluation. On 26 February the major
German banking, commercial, and industrial organizations issued a joint
statement rejecting unequivocally any further "upheaval" in the revaluation situation, either by law or judicial decision. Because Germany's
economy required certainty above all, they wanted the Tax Decree pre-
served as it was.[45] The lines of the conflict were now more clearly drawn as
creditor versus debtor, and creditors would no longer benefit from confusion in the enemy camp.

Two developments probably prompted this crucial shift. First, German
businessmen did want certainty. They would have to base economic decisions on assumptions about future costs. Once the government had established its Tax Decree revaluation policy, they could make these assumptions with some degree of confidence. Yet if either the courts or the
legislature amended the decree, a businessman might find a decision to
have become unprofitable.[46] Probably more important, Luther's inflation
taxes were relatively modest, while lower courts were requiring 75 percent
revaluation. Businessmen must have realized that they stood to lose far
more from high individual revaluations than they could ever save in lower
taxes.

On 1 March 1924 the Reichsgericht's Fifth Civil Senate, which had handed down the 28 November revaluation decision, ruled that the Tax Decree's revaluation provisions were "judicially valid (*rechtswirksam*)" and did not contravene Article 153 of the constitution or the principle of equity and good faith. The court acknowledged that the Tax Decree revaluation was a legitimate attempt to regulate the relations between creditor and debtor and that it was necessary to solve a complex legal, social, and economic problem that the judicial system could not solve alone.[47]

The judges had retreated from the assertiveness of their 8 January letter. Already on 25 January the Third Civil Senate had refused to invalidate a decree on the basis of Paragraph 242. In a 31 January reply to the justice minister, the Judges Association directing committee had renounced any debate over the scope of the court's powers and had merely claimed credit for preventing the "harsh measure" of a revaluation ban.[48] And the court's 1 March opinion characterized as "disputed" the use of a conflict between a decree and Paragraph 242 to invalidate the decree. Presumably, the judges recognized how revolutionary a step it would have been for them to invalidate not the 10-year-old currency legislation, but contemporary government policy on a vital and urgent issue.

Yet the courts did not retreat completely. By examining the decree's constitutionality, the Reichsgericht implicitly expanded its powers over policy-making, even if it had surrendered some of the power it had asserted on 28 November 1923 and 8 January 1924.

The court had finally acknowledged that the government must regulate revaluation to prevent a potentially disastrous scramble for the highest possible rates. The Judges Association letter had indirectly embraced the view that the 28 November decision had created a property right in GM for the creditor. The judges hence could have made a case that the decree introduced an unconstitutional expropriation of property. Yet they rejected creditor arguments to that effect. The decision's wording suggests that the judges were influenced by the government's fears for the stabilization, by recent pleas from the business community for economic certainty, and also by a recognition of the potential muddle—and disrepute—the courts might find themselves in if they actually tried to mediate every debt in Germany.[49] Whatever the mix of reasons, these judges had come to see beyond the private-law aspect of the issue.

The Tax Decree's basic principles would underlie all subsequent debt-revaluation jurisprudence and legislation. Most important, it replaced the court-ordered individual revaluation with a less equitable but economically necessary schematic revaluation for most mortgages, industrial obligations, and other long-term debts. It set up the distribution-fund system for revaluing mortgage bonds, savings-bank accounts, and life-insurance policies, while excluding deposits at commercial banks. The decree postponed repayment until 1932, but it ordered interest payments at least to begin in 1925. The government had, however, reasserted control over the value of the currency and thereby gained some influence over Germany's economic future.

Although the government had gotten its Tax Decree revaluation past the Reichsgericht, it had given much away. The government had acknowledged that it must redistribute some of inflation's costs from creditors to others in society. And, significantly, the various governments had not repudiated their bonds but had acknowledged the possibility of a future government-bond revaluation.

Germany had suffered major losses of national wealth in which the creditors ought to have shared, but the government disproportionately sacrificed creditor interests to short-term economic expediency. Reestablishing the state's sovereign powers basically reconfirmed the expropriation of holders of paper assets—even though the Tax Decree mandated the transfer of approximately 4.5 billion marks from debtors to creditors.[50] A 15 percent revaluation payable in 1932, with relatively low interest, had to be discounted and in fact meant the loss of over 90 percent of the creditors' assets, often to the benefit of wealthy and quite solvent debtors. And the government had ignored the long-term, and serious, problem of reestablishing Germany's credit.

The combination of judicial intervention and public opinion had constrained government actions. Without the mediating influence of existing institutions—the courts and the Catholic church—disorganized public opinion on creditor rights might very well have dissipated in ineffectual protest, as it had in 1923. But without such political pressure as the still weakly organized creditors brought to bear through the parties, the government could certainly have overcome the Reichsgericht's resistance.

Even though the government had drafted the Tax Decree revaluation without consulting creditors or debtors, debtor interests were represented in the process. Agriculture and industry stood in client relationships with the Agriculture and Economics ministries, respectively. Ministers von Kanitz and Hamm fought tenaciously—and without any apparent support from agricultural or business groups—against creditor demands. And when some schematic revaluation became inevitable, they sought to limit as sharply as possible the revaluation burden on the economy. And it was Hamm, von Kanitz, Jarres, and Luther, all with ties to industry or agriculture, who blocked any individual revaluation and held the line on the revaluation rate. They defended industry's and agriculture's interests when industrial and agricultural groups did not or would not.

Significantly, the government seemed isolated. The cabinet contended that revaluation would hurt the economy, yet the only debtor group to fight vigorously against revaluation was the central government. Even a concerted push against revaluation by debtor groups might not have provided the government with sufficient support to ban revaluation. But such support could have lent legitimacy to the government's economic arguments, helping both to forestall the parties' rush to play on creditors' discontent and to convince creditors of the Republic's sincerity in attempting to deal with the issue.

And the government itself failed to make a sufficiently compelling case for schematic revaluation to discourage creditors from organizing or to keep the issue nonpartisan. The government had justified its Tax Decree revaluation provisions primarily on the basis of immediate fiscal needs. But the economy and the fiscal situation would improve. The government could not permanently settle the revaluation issue by imposing a solution predicated on what would soon clearly be temporary factors. And it could not ignore indefinitely the creditors' demand for some measure of equity.

The Government's Revaluation Erodes

The Parties Attack the Tax Decree

The government's stabilization policies antagonized virtually everyone. With the Enabling Act no longer in force and the Reichstag scheduled to review government policies on 20 February, conflict was unavoidable.

Whatever their long-term advantages, government economic policies provided little but pain in the short run. The Reichsbank's restrictive credit policies raised costs and increased bankruptcies among farmers, business-men, artisans, and shopkeepers. The government continued reducing its work force until April. The relatively modest salary increases it granted thereafter only reminded civil servants of how much they had lost. White-collar unemployment remained high and salaries low. Although blue-collar unemployment was falling, wages stayed low and the conflict over the eight-hour day continued to strain labor relations.[1]

Many Germans found the government's fiscal policies unacceptable. The Tax Decree was particularly disliked. Its revaluation provisions en-raged creditors, whereas the inflation taxes on agriculture, industry, and building owners antagonized debtors. Incensed at the way rent increases would shift the rent tax to tenants, the SPD and the unions rejected the decree vehemently.

Reacting to the meager inflation taxes and limited revaluation of typical worker assets, the SPD in mid-February suddenly switched policy. It now demanded 20 percent revaluation, with retroactive revaluation of debts repaid after 1 July 1922. The party had wanted to ban revaluation and tax away inflation profits to the common weal. In the decree, however, the government repudiated such a policy. The regressive rent tax was the only significant inflation tax. Although the government had probably not excluded the working classes from revaluation deliberately, the Tax Decree revaluation would primarily benefit *Mittelständler* who had been able to afford mortgages, mortgage bonds, and industrial obligations. Workers' typical assets, savings deposits and life-insurance policies, were to receive only meager revaluation. The party may also have realized it could lose votes by opposing revaluation. Under these circumstances, a prorevaluation faction apparently secured a majority for a shift from Hilferding's economically based opposition to revaluation toward Reichstag Deputy Wilhelm Keil's politically based support for it.[2]

When the Reichstag discussed revaluation in late February, most parties favored repealing or amending the Tax Decree revaluation. The KPD rejected any revaluation as merely a bonus for speculators. Objecting to the government's revaluation as too schematic, the DNVP demanded a more flexible system, no matter how many cases it created. The Reichsgericht decision upholding the Tax Decree's validity led both the DDP and DVP to announce that they accepted the decree's basic outlines, but they reserved the right to propose amendments. The SPD considered the Tax Decree unconscionable and was determined to amend it. Although the party wanted the revaluation provisions changed, it apparently found the rent tax, not the revaluation, most objectionable.[3]

The pressure to amend the stabilization measures forced ministers to choose between governmental responsibility and political expediency. The government believed that the Tax Decree's various parts were so interdependent that if a process of amendment once began, the carefully crafted stabilization would rapidly and completely unravel.[4] As Marx later explained, "[i]t would have been very easy for an opposition party to introduce a motion on a domestic policy question that could not be rejected by the government parties but that would have been unacceptable for the government." To forestall any amendment of the decree, the government convinced President Friedrich Ebert to dissolve the Reichstag on 13 March 1924 and to set new elections for 4 May.[5] The ministers apparently hoped that postponing Reichstag action long enough would allow the stabilization to take hold, giving government and parties maneuvering room.

Courting the Creditor Vote

Germans had much to be unhappy about as the parties campaigned for the Reichstag. Germany's economic situation was still tenuous. The taxes necessary to maintain the stabilization were a heavy burden on all Germans. The French still occupied the Ruhr. And the foreign Dawes Committee of experts, who were to determine Germany's ability to pay reparations, issued their report on 9 April.

Reparations came to overshadow revaluation rhetorically, but the latter remained a significant issue. Bernhard Dernburg (DDP, prewar colonial minister and postwar finance minister) commented that "indeed until the publication of the Dawes Report it seemed as if [revaluation] would dominate all other questions."[6] After 9 April the government was partially successful in using the reparations debate to divert attention from its unpopular stabilization policies—but only partially. Popular anger at government policies had scarcely abated, and conflict over the stabilization, including revaluation, continued.[7]

After the debtor and banking groups' 26 February statement opposing any "upheaval" in the revaluation, they tended to ignore the issue. The Tax Decree seemed to provide a final settlement for the revaluation, and numerous other issues (e.g., taxes, credit, reparations) must have seemed much more immediate and vital.

The May election was the creditors' first political campaign, and they campaigned hard. Despite a degree of fragmentation, the movement was sufficiently united on basic policies that politicians did not face drastically differing proposals. The HGSSV and other organizations could now claim to speak for the creditors as a group. And because individual creditors writing to government officials almost universally demanded the same policies as creditor groups and their leaders, the creditor group claim seemed, and seems, generally convincing.

The creditor groups wanted the Tax Decree revaluation repealed, allowing individual revaluation of private debts based on Paragraph 242. Some of them recognized the need for a simplified arbitration procedure. Not having received any real income from their investments for years, many creditors had become dependent on relatives, charity, or public assistance. They resented this bitterly and desperately wanted to regain their independence. Although they recognized a need for a moratorium on the principal, they demanded that interest payments begin quickly, generally immediately, at the full contractual rate (usually 4 to 4.5 percent). Such a speedy resumption of interest payments would be necessary to ameliorate rentiers' poverty. And the lack of interest payments reduced the value of the investments substantially.

Creditors also consistently demanded general retroactive revaluation (i.e., for all mortgages, and occasionally other investments, repaid after a given date). Numerous creditors had had their investments repaid in worthless paper. In its 28 November ruling, the Reichsgericht had implicitly admitted that the judiciary had been wrong to force creditors to accept such repayments. Those who had suffered from that error considered revaluation of their assets only just.[8]

The creditors achieved less unity on government-bond revaluation. Although some local creditor groups ignored government bonds in this period, creditors increasingly demanded that the government revalue the bonds in GM *at face value*, either with a full moratorium on payment, or with a timely resumption of at least some interest payments.[9]

Although creditors developed a basic consensus on policies, they failed to reach agreement on tactics. Some groups merely urged the justice of their demands, apparently considering their case so unimpeachable that moral suasion would suffice.[10] Other groups, including the HGSSV, the largest creditor organization, threatened to instruct their members to vote only for those parties that promised to repeal or revise drastically the Tax Decree.[11] A few local creditor groups ran their own candidates in various election districts, promising little more than improved revaluation. These candidates got only a few thousand votes, but their presence undoubtedly reminded the major parties of the issue's potential impact.[12]

In justifying their policy proposals, creditors concentrated on their strongest argument and the one they themselves felt most deeply: the obvious inequity of inflation's effects on the relative wealth of creditor and debtor. They disregarded broader economic implications of their demands because revaluation's earlier development had made it seem a predominantly legal-cum-moral question to most Germans, despite the government's efforts in early 1924 to emphasize its fiscal and economic aspects. And debtors were not discussing revaluation's economic impact.

Some parties at this time seemed to consider revaluation a relatively minor issue. The Völkisch (proto-Nazis) supported substantial revaluation but concentrated on other issues. The Economics party (WP [*Wirtschaftspartei*, small businessmen]), KPD, and even SPD more or less ignored it as well.[13]

The parties of the center suffered for their implicit support of the Marx cabinet's policies. Popular (especially *Mittelstand*) anger at the impact of stabilization, coupled with attacks from right and left, threw these parties on the defensive. Revaluation was just one policy among many where the DVP, DDP, and even the Center were struggling desperately to retain their electoral bases.[14]

The DVP chose to campaign against the Tax Decree revaluation provisions, despite its ministers' support of them. Düringer gave the speech on revaluation at the DVP convention in late March. He attacked the decree revaluation as unacceptable and proposed, in the name of the DVP, a revaluation norm of 40 percent. Düringer said he knew that "many members of the Reichsgericht share fully my opinion" that the decree was unconstitutional, so that the Reichstag's first task must be to regulate the revaluation "according to the principles of justice."[15] Elsa Matz (a candidate in Pomerania, where creditor groups had their own slate) strongly seconded Düringer, emphasizing that the creditors deserved restitution, not welfare.[16] And in campaigning the party "promised the moon on the revaluation" and disowned Luther, who was close to it politically.[17]

Nonetheless, the party was by no means as prorevaluation as these developments might suggest. Düringer had in late February convinced 14 of his colleagues to cosponsor a bill to amend the revaluation, but none of the DVP leaders, not even Stresemann, would do so.[18] And when he rose to speak on his bill in the Reichstag on 10 March, the rest of his delegation ostentatiously left the hall, to indicate that he spoke only for himself and not for the party. And he commented that whenever he spoke in delegation meetings, his colleagues ridiculed him by shouting "Mortgage! Mortgage!"[19] The *Hannoversche Kurier* and the *Deutsche Allgemeine Zeitung*, both close to the DVP, downplayed the revaluation throughout the campaign, merely acknowledging the need somehow to assist the rentiers. And one DVP pamphlet and some party leaders defended the Tax Decree as unfortunate but necessary, saying the capital for a large revaluation simply did not exist.[20]

The DVP campaign platform on revaluation probably represented a combination of party infighting, differing political priorities, and political expediency. Düringer and Matz were sincerely and energetically prorevaluation. But most members, including debtor representatives, were apparently too concerned with other political problems to expend effort on what they considered a secondary issue. The creditors' desperate pleas for equity presumably swayed many uncommitted delegates, especially as no broad discussion of revaluation's economic implications was occurring. Also, the Reichstag delegation and the party as a whole quite probably had differing attitudes on the revaluation, as spokesmen for business were overrepresented among delegation members.[21]

The DDP felt compelled to respond to the DVP's revaluation rhetoric by acknowledging the inadequacy of the Tax Decree revaluation, but it was more cautious in its promises. DDP Reichstag Deputy Hermann Dietrich, a revaluation supporter, wrote in a pamphlet on revaluation, "It can of course not be a question of fully recreating the savings again." To "promise those involved, that is, the savers, specific measures . . . would be criminal" and "demagogic."[22] The DDP carefully emphasized that in the revaluation a "just solution is impossible" and that unfortunately Germans had to decide which should predominate, "individual interests" or the "public interest." The party did promise that as soon as the reparations situation had stabilized, it would work for a "more just solution."[23]

Unfortunately for the DDP, the politics of revaluation put a premium on irresponsible campaign promises, not probity. Creditors did not want to hear sweet reason; they wanted redress. They were convinced that full revaluation was feasible, but because revaluation had no history, they had no way to predict how much revaluation each party would actually offer if it got into power. The parties themselves could not even know exactly how they would or could act.

The Center party's ambivalence about how to handle revaluation reflected its difficult position. It could ignore neither its political responsibility, through Marx, for the Tax Decree nor the Catholic church's support for extensive revaluation. One party publication could hence defend the Tax Decree revaluation as unfortunate but necessary, whereas the Reich General Secretariat of the Center could promise that once the economic situation had improved, the party would work to amend the decree. In general, however, the party reacted to its revaluation dilemma by downplaying the issue, ignoring it in most election articles.[24]

The DNVP was particularly immoderate in seeking creditor votes. The party had a strong contingent of revaluation supporters, including the party chairman, Hergt. And because the party had never participated in a government and had never had to bear responsibility for its political rhetoric, its campaign promises were extravagant.

DNVP statements convinced creditors it was committed to substantial revaluation. Hergt probably never promised 100 percent revaluation, as some creditors believed; he did call for a *minimum* revaluation and an arbitration court to set the exact rate, although he soon amended this to a revaluation norm.[25] Most important, although the DNVP said that full revaluation was out of the question, it also proclaimed that "an equitable settlement of the interests involved according to the principle of equity and good faith can and must take place." Creditors were convinced that all debtors were inflation profiteers on a grand scale and that equity and good faith required individual revaluation; they hence construed this as a promise of very high or even 100 percent revaluation. And the DNVP made no real effort to clarify its position.[26]

Many in the DNVP, from debtor groups and otherwise, were antirevaluation, but neither these groups nor their representatives in the party appear to have objected to DNVP attacks on the Tax Decree. This inaction reflected the temporary apathy, not the weakness, of debtor groups in the DNVP. It presumably also reflected a desire not to weaken the party's electoral chances by antagonizing creditor voters.

Significantly, debtor apathy and partisan expediency had set the creditors up for high expectations and subsequent disillusionment and bitterness. Because debtors believed the Tax Decree had settled the revaluation in their favor, they let creditors turn the revaluation into a political issue, instead of emphasizing its deleterious economic implications.[27] Debtor silence encouraged prorevaluation politicians and left the uncommitted susceptible to the creditors' pleas for equity. The promises the parties then made confirmed the creditors in their exaggerated idea of what was feasible and left the parties committed to some revaluation reform.

The collapse of the political center in Germany began in the aftermath of stabilization in 1924, not with the rise of Nazism after 1928. The inflation had to some extent papered over conflicts of interest within German society and, particularly, the *Mittelstand*. Stabilization only exacerbated these conflicts, and its massive burdens meant real pain for most Germans. Voters' desperate attempts to avoid or redistribute these burdens created additional conflicts more fundamental than the traditional liberal parties proved able to reconcile.

The May 1924 election hence had a devastating and permanent impact on the liberal parties (the DDP and DVP). Artisans and creditors fled the parties, as did many civil servants. Between 1920 and May 1924 the DDP vote dropped from 8.3 percent to 5.6 percent, the DVP vote from 14 percent to 9 percent. In particular, the clear correlation between rentier status and liberal voting that had existed in 1920 disappeared in 1924, never to reappear. Many Germans were seeking political alternatives, with crucial implications for the Weimar Republic's stability.[28]

Several parties benefited from this liberal debacle. Individually insignificant, the splinter parties together collected 8.3 percent of the vote in May, up from 3.7 percent in 1920. The political extremes also gained. The KPD vote jumped six times (mostly at the expense of the pro-Weimar SPD) as workers protested wage cuts and longer working hours. The Völkisch scored their first big success, going from nil in 1920 to 6.3 percent in May 1924. They benefited from small business, rentier, and civil servant anger at the stabilization and the existing system.[29] Probably the biggest winner was the DNVP, whose vote jumped from 14.9 percent in 1920 to 19.5

percent in May 1924. The party played with considerable success on *Mittelstand* and agricultural discontent with the stabilization and the Dawes Plan, emerging as the largest party in the Reichstag (after allying with smaller parties).[30] The revaluation issue proved particularly fruitful, providing the DNVP with "countless votes," according to a Center politician.[31] A DNVP supporter agreed, identifying the "socialist policies" of the Marx-Stresemann government in taxes and revaluation as the major grounds for DNVP gains. Nonetheless, he characterized the party's new voters as "crazies," as an "oscillating mass" with old National Liberal, not conservative, ideas; he doubted whether they would provide a reliable political base.[32]

The revaluation issue had become too important to ignore. Economic and fiscal recovery were making the severe limits the Tax Decree set on revaluation seem less justified. And the need of all parties to pay at least lip service to their campaign oratory meant that the new Reichstag would debate major changes in the revaluation.

The Tax Decree Revaluation Undermined

To deal more equitably with revaluation's complexities, the government had added the ill-fated Paragraph 3 to the Tax Decree. The cabinet had intended to provide individual revaluation for selected *Vermögensanlagen*, including obligations that one relative owed another, support payments (e.g., alimony) secured by a mortgage, and seller-financed mortgages. In each instance a special "personal demand" existed between creditor and debtor that the government believed entitled the creditor to a higher revaluation.[33]

The drafters of Paragraph 3, however, so worded it that it legally mandated an individual revaluation of *all* mortgages, a result diametrically opposed to the cabinet's express intent. Courts began using the paragraph to offer individual mortgage revaluation on a broad scale.[34] When a worried finance ministry official telephoned the justice ministry about this, his interlocutor (unnamed) blithely replied that the justice ministry had intended the result all along. Indeed, Emminger later boasted, "I was successful in Paragraphs 3 and 12 of the Emergency Tax Decree in helping to bring to a breakthrough the so-called *individual principle*, and in considerable magnitude beyond the 15 percent set by the decree."[35]

The wording of Paragraph 3, then, reflected Emminger's and the justice ministry bureaucracy's conscious intent to reverse government policy secretly. Civil servants and a government minister apparently saw as honorable what others might see as irresponsible.

The government tried to eliminate individual mortgage revaluation through the extensive—indeed, constitutionally questionable—decree-writing power it had granted itself in the Tax Decree. On 1 May 1924 it promulgated an implementation decree that effectively repealed Paragraph 3 and legislated a new provision explicitly limiting individual revaluation to the special cases the cabinet had originally had in mind. The cabinet decided to publish the decree only after the 4 May election, and it failed to show the Reichsrat the provision amending Paragraph 3 (as it was supposed to), ostensibly because speed was crucial.[36]

The government had opened itself even further to creditor wrath. It seemed to be almost tormenting creditors by repudiating those aspects of its own Tax Decree that favored creditors. And the constitutionally questionable implementation decree would face a court challenge in November that would confirm creditor suspicions of the government's good faith.

Savings banks wanted a revaluation system that they could implement cheaply while still providing their creditors with revaluation rates comparable to those that other debtors offered. During the war, however, they had patriotically shifted their assets from mortgages to government bonds, whose revaluation the Tax Decree postponed indefinitely. Debtors had repaid most of the remaining mortgages in 1922 and 1923. Hence, the average savings-bank revaluation would be a mere 2 to 3 percent. This insignificant rate, especially compared to the 15 percent for mortgages, would seem contemptible to potential new savers. Indeed, creditor groups were attacking the banks for negligence in managing their assets. The banks considered a higher savings-account revaluation essential for reviving the propensity to save in general and the propensity to save at savings banks in particular.[37]

The savings banks hence called with increasing frequency for measures that would increase the funds available for savings-account revaluation. They demanded an increased mortgage-revaluation rate and general retroactive mortgage revaluation. The savings bank association eventually favored some government-bond revaluation. In addition, some banks suggested that the municipalities and counties that guaranteed savings-bank deposits should contribute to the savings revaluation. In the past, these guarantors had shared in savings-bank profits. Equity seemed to demand that they now share in the banks' losses by contributing to restoring the real value of deposits.[38]

The savings banks were breaking ranks with the rest of the production-oriented groups in the producer/creditor conflict. Unlike the commercial and mortgage banks, they demanded substantive changes in the Tax Decree revaluation because it directly threatened their competitiveness and viability. The Reich eventually met most of their demands, and their support for increased revaluation presumably weakened the government's position.

The churches openly supported substantial revaluation. Although tacitly accepting the need for some schematic revaluation, the Catholic church denounced the Tax Decree. Cardinal Bertram wrote again in September 1924 to Marx, urging revision of the decree because it did not conform to the "principles of Christian morality and equal justice" and because of the losses the church's charitable operations had suffered. He released this letter to the press. Protestant churches also denounced the decree publicly as an offense against Christian morality and justice; they too added that the low revaluation was preventing them from fulfilling their charitable functions. Furthermore, Catholic and Protestant clergymen published prorevaluation articles and were active in creditor groups.[39]

The impact of church attitudes is difficult to measure. Reichstag Deputy Rudolf Schetter wrote that his Center party was conscious of the Catholic church's position—but not what actual effect this had. Except for demanding retroactive revaluation, church leaders usually confined themselves to general requests for increased revaluation. Their statements did, however, confirm creditors in the belief that morality and justice required increased, presumably individual, revaluation.[40]

Judges continued to influence the revaluation issue. The judiciary sent no more quasi-official letters to the government or the press, but several well-known judges (such as Best and Zeiler) continued to support revaluation on legal and moral grounds. The courts characterized the Tax Decree as establishing "exceptional prescriptions"; they then generally interpreted the revaluation as much as possible in the creditors' favor. Some lower courts issued rulings that ignored the Reichsgericht's 1 March 1924 decision approving the Tax Decree revaluation. The resulting legal confusion convinced many the government would have to confirm its revaluation policy through regular legislation. Further, judicial interpretations of the revaluation provisions for seller-financed mortgages, bank accounts, and trustees' liability forced the government to clarify these issues in drafting the 1925 Revaluation Law.[41]

Perhaps most important, the courts' obvious tilt in the creditors' favor must have strengthened the latter in their demand for individual revaluation. Implicit in that demand was the expectation that judges would order more revaluation than the 15 percent established in the Tax Decree or the 25 percent or even 40 percent Reichstag deputies were proposing.

Finally, the courts substantively changed the retroactive revaluation of mortgages. By allowing retroactive revaluation only where an individual had "reserved his rights," the government had expected to preclude it in all but a tiny minority of cases. Over the course of 1924 and early 1925, however, the courts gradually redefined the phrase "with rights reserved." First the courts declared that the reservation could be oral, then that it need not have occurred at the time the creditor handed over the *Löschungsbewilligung*, and finally that the reservation did not have to be explicit, but only that it be clear "that the creditor wanted to explain that he was not completely satisfied with the paper mark sum."[42] After rumors of a moratorium or a revaluation in 1922 and 1923, many creditors must have expressed dissatisfaction with the PM repayment. These decisions made most mortgages repaid in late 1922 or in 1923 potentially revaluable.

Nonetheless, neither government nor Reichstag expressed any objection to this judicial legislation. Indeed, when the Reich proposed a more explicit limit on retroactive revaluation, the south German Länder rejected it as futile—because the courts would just widen further the concept of reserving one's rights.[43] Numerous creditors had accepted repayment without explicitly reserving their rights—but only because the government and the courts had forced them to do so. A firm national consensus in fact existed, including within the Reichstag, that equity demanded some general retroactive revaluation, despite the uncertainty it would bring. The courts seem once again to have succeeded in making policy against government wishes because they more accurately reflected popular conceptions of what was legitimate.

Debating the Viability of Revaluation

The Government Temporizes

Efforts to form a government with a parliamentary majority failed after the May election. Marx then reconstituted his centrist, minority government, and it maintained a precarious existence.[1]

The Völkisch, DVP, BVP, and DNVP immediately introduced differing bills to revise the revaluation to the creditors' benefit.[2] When the Reichstag debated the issue on 28 June, all parties at least nominally supported amending the Tax Decree revaluation—but disagreed about how to do so. Hence, at Düringer's suggestion, the Reichstag created a Revaluation Committee to prepare alternative legislation.[3]

The cabinet sought to postpone any committee session until after the reparations situation had been settled. Government officials were desperately short of time as they prepared for the London conference on reparations, to be held in early August. Also, a government-sponsored revaluation proposal on the eve of the conference might have created a bad impression abroad. Nonetheless, even the government parties agreed the revaluation must not be postponed, and most parties wanted an early appearance by Finance Minister Luther.[4]

The creditors reacted with seemingly disproportionate anger when Luther refused to take any time to work on the revaluation question before the implementation of the Dawes Report.[5] His attitude was an affront to their moral indignation over revaluation, and he was insensitive in the brusqueness with which he refused to testify. Yet the creditors' vituperativeness might seem a bit surprising, given the London conference's crucial implications for Germany's future.

The Allies, however, had already implicitly recognized the relationship between reparations and revaluation. By eliminating Germany's public and private domestic debt, the inflation had decreased the obligations on its economy as compared with the victors. Both General Jan Smuts and David Lloyd George had expressed the fear that without a compensating reparations burden, the German economy would be too competitive internationally.[6] The Dawes Report both justified and based its reparations proposals explicitly on Germany's debt-free status, and it burdened two major debtor sections of the economy, government and industry, with obligations that limited their ability to finance revaluation.[7]

Creditors hence concluded that an increased debt burden, such as higher revaluation would create, would force the Allies to lower their reparations demands: "Yet how much greater would this progress have been if our government had not, in an incomprehensibly shortsighted step, smoothed the way with the Third Emergency Tax Decree for this [Dawes] report. . . . The total sum could have been considerably smaller if the Third Emergency Tax Decree had not introduced a complete elimination of the debt of the Reich, Länder, and municipalities and a nearly complete [elimination] of private debt." Many creditors accused the government of impoverishing its own people in order to pay the enemy.[8]

However, no domestic German policy consideration was at all likely to dissuade the Allies from imposing a high reparations burden. Creditors refused to take seriously France's determination to obtain high reparations. Nor did they seem to recognize how Allied occupation of the Rhineland and Germany's need for foreign markets and, especially, foreign credit made the country vulnerable to Allied pressure on reparations. The *New York Times* reported during Germany's December 1924 election campaign that the Dawes Plan supervisors would reject any increase in revaluation that threatened reparations. And on 2 February 1925 Parker Gilbert (the reparations agent) made it clear to Chancellor Luther that the reparations committee would not accept any effects of a large revaluation as grounds for reduced reparations payments.[9]

Revaluation Opponents Make Their Case

Despite the cabinet's refusal to talk about revaluation, Reichstag deputies were determined to act. All that government officials were doing about revaluation was to work behind the scenes to convince all the major economic interest groups to condemn the parties' new revaluation proposals. The government hoped thereby to shift responsibility for the Tax Decree's preservation to "the economy." Meanwhile, however, the Revaluation Committee had decided (at the SPD's suggestion) to hear testimony from "economic experts," mostly representatives of those very same interest groups.[10]

The creditors hence got a hearing for their position. Their representatives promoted retired Appeals Court President Best's draft bill, which mandated individual revaluation of private debts. They also demanded government-bond revaluation. Although they emphasized considerations of equity in justifying their demands, they also blamed Germany's liquidity shortage on inadequate revaluation and suggested government-bond revaluation might limit the Allies' demands for reparations.[11] The creditors had nominal allies in the savings banks, who privately suggested amending the Tax Decree to increase savings-account revaluation.[12]

Yet as the hearings continued, creditors found themselves otherwise alone. Before the Revaluation Committee or in subsequent petitions to it, the National Association of German Industry, the wholesalers association (*Centralverband des deutschen Grosshandels*), the National Committee of German Agriculture (*Reichsausschuss der deutschen Landwirtschaft*), the Federation of Renters Associations (*Bund deutscher Mietervereine*), the liberal and Christian trade unions (*Hirsch-Dunckel* and *Christlichen Gewerkschaften*), and representatives from insurance companies and mortgage banks all denounced any increase in revaluation, indeed any amendment of the Tax Decree revaluation, as economically deleterious and potentially inequitable.[13]

The creditors were learning the hard way that erstwhile allies could suddenly become enemies. Mortgage-bank officials had demanded a repayment moratorium in early 1923 and had later supported revaluation to encourage savings. Now, mortgage-bank representatives rejected an increase in revaluation as unnecessary because small investors had already begun buying the new GM mortgage bonds.[14] Reassured by the gradual revival of saving, these banks now worried about the economic uncertainty and the administration costs revaluation would bring.

These hearings were a mixed blessing for the creditors. They did get some support from the savings banks. More important, the Reichstag had invited them to testify, thereby officially recognizing their right to a hearing. Yet these hearings also revealed the breadth of opposition the creditors faced. Worse, various noncreditors used the hearings to begin articulating the antirevaluation arguments they would develop and emphasize.

Although the interwar years were a time of ferment in economic theory,

Keynes's demand-oriented theories were still a decade away. Indeed, in Germany the improvised and inefficiently administered wartime economic controls and the inflation had discredited government intervention in the economy. And Germany's economic weakness strengthened calls for reducing burdens on the economy.

What still held sway in Germany was the prewar, producer-oriented economic orthodoxy. The crux of this orthodoxy was a rejection of any significant role for consumers, consumption, or demand in economic growth. Germans from virtually all walks of life, including socialists, believed that in a capitalist economy economic well-being required the careful cultivation of the producer side of the economy. They thought that only by freeing the producers of all constraints and burdens—and subsidizing them if necessary—could the economy continue to operate efficiently and to grow optimally.[15]

Because revaluation seemed to favor consumers over producers, debtors tarred it as heretical and dangerous. They argued that the war and defeat had reduced the nation's real wealth, so that increasing revaluation would increase the burdens on an already weakened economy. They specifically asserted that revaluation could refuel inflation; decrease Germany's international competitiveness; make it difficult to obtain new credit; and increase "wasteful" consumption at the expense of "necessary" saving and investment.[16]

Revaluation could refuel inflation because it would re-create extinguished claims to goods and services without increasing commensurately the total goods and services available in the economy. Just as deficit spending or easy money policies could increase demand and force prices up, so could revaluation, as creditors spent their revaluation payments. To cover their new obligations, debtors would have to raise prices, rents, and (in the government's case) taxes, setting off an inflationary spiral. And the revalued debts would provide creditors with collateral to obtain new credit and the financial system with the assets and reserves to provide it, potentially leading to an increase in the money supply and a new inflation. For a people who had just experienced an unprecedented hyperinflation, this scenario seemed terrifying indeed.[17]

Even a moderate increase in German prices, as debtors sought to finance their revaluation payments, would weaken Germany's competitiveness in world markets. Yet Germany had to improve its competitiveness, so that it could increase its exports to pay reparations and offset its balance-of-payments deficit. It also had to restrain domestic prices to forestall a flood of relatively cheap imports. And if cheap imports forced German producers to restrain prices despite their new revaluation burdens, business-men might well fail to accumulate earnings that could finance needed investment.[18]

Debtors pointed out that the ability to obtain new credit depended on the potential lender's perception of the borrower's ability to repay the loan. The German economy already looked a shaky proposition because of its loss of national wealth, higher postwar taxes, and continuing reparations burden. Debtors maintained that by further increasing the burden on them, revaluation would make them and the economy appear even less able, quite possibly unable, to repay any new loans. Hence, any substantial revaluation could frighten off new lenders, especially foreign lenders.[19]

Debtors insisted that further revaluation would harm Germany because it would transfer funds from the "productive" sector (i.e., debtors) to "wasteful" consumption. The remaining PM creditors were apparently predominantly elderly and smaller investors who hoped to live on their savings. Many would spend all or most of any revalued wealth, rather than reinvest it.[20] One revaluation opponent also complained that the Tax Decree revaluation would increase food imports and thereby exacerbate the balance-of-payments problem.[21] What mattered most to debtors was creating an economic environment that they considered conducive to invest-ment and economic growth, not dabbling with possibly inflationary or economically debilitating social policies.

Revaluation opponents also emphasized the danger that economic un-certainty could lead to a potentially disastrous credit freeze. These Ger-mans now insisted (as had creditors before the inflation) that a capitalist economy required a set of fixed, almost immutable, written laws applied neutrally and objectively. They argued that without such certainty invest-ment either would not occur, or would occur only at damagingly high interest rates (to provide an adequate premium to the investor for the risk of legal uncertainty).[22]

An individual revaluation, debtors argued, would completely undercut this certainty. Many individuals and enterprises were both creditor and debtor or had more than one debt or asset, and the revaluation rate for any particular debt might depend on the rate for any number of other debts. The courts would hence need years to untangle and settle all the cases, mean-while leaving the credit position of every PM debtor unclear.[23]

Revaluation opponents went farther and asserted that *any* amendment of the Tax Decree, or even debate in the Reichstag, would create uncertainty about Germany's future policy stability and would lead to a credit freeze. The gold balances that had provided the basis for postinflation loans to the

German economy had been based on the Tax Decree revaluation. Increased revaluation would make the balances inaccurate, and lenders might feel they had been deceived about debtors' ability to pay. Revaluation opponents asserted that lenders would then suddenly withdraw short-term funds from the German economy, resulting in serious dislocation, and that no one, especially foreigners, would thereafter be willing to invest in the German economy.[24]

The trade unions and the renters association rejected revaluation on somewhat different grounds. Their members were more likely to be small creditors than debtors because the only debt most Germans could incur was nonrevaluable short-term debt. Both groups argued that debtors would not bear the new burden revaluation would create but would transfer it to consumers and taxpayers. In general, only those who had more than average savings stood to gain from revaluation. Small savers could expect to pay more in higher prices, rents, and taxes than they would get from revaluation of their modest savings.[25]

Like the creditors, revaluation opponents tended to see the aspect of the revaluation closest to their own interests and experience and to ignore other aspects. Confusion, uncertainty, chaotic and harmful pricing conditions, and the direct effects of inflation had dominated the lives of revaluation opponents for years, and in 1924–25 they experienced a severe recession and credit squeeze. They believed (often sincerely and often justifiably) that they could not afford any greater burden, despite the creditors' moral claim. Consumers and small savers hence opposed revaluation to the extent it would be passed on to them in higher prices, rents, and taxes. Producer/debtors opposed it to the extent it would *not* be passed on, affecting their incomes. Both consumers and producers opposed revaluation to the extent it would burden or appear to burden the economy, making German goods less competitive, credit more difficult to obtain, and economic growth slower. And the debtor/producers' ability to appeal to a productionist economic orthodoxy in support of their position predisposed many nondebtors to accept their arguments.

The Creditors Counterattack

Despite the debtors' attempt to shift the debate from the moral to the economic, many creditors continued to believe moral considerations should predominate—at any cost as far as some were concerned. One retired Prussian officer wrote, "Nonetheless, it is just as true according to centuries old German law [*Recht*] that debts, even state debts, are to be paid, and that as long as one of the two parties has to go bankrupt this has to be the debtor and not, as is now the vogue to construe things in the new German law, the creditor." Prussian officers were in theory devoted defenders of the state, yet this man was implicitly demanding that the German state bankrupt itself in an attempt to pay the debt owed a portion of its citizens. Although no other creditor seems to have rejected so baldly any consideration of larger, national-economic aspects, numerous creditors and creditor leaders so vehemently emphasized moral considerations as to implicitly reject national economic considerations.[26]

Nonetheless, the powerful economic arguments revaluation opponents had begun to raise prevented the creditor movement from simply retreating into a moral fortress. For political reasons they had to argue that revaluation would not produce negative economic effects. But most creditors would want to believe that debtor economic objections were groundless— or indeed that revaluation might help the economy. And given revaluation's complexity, one could justifiably doubt that the debtors' prodebtor evaluation of the situation was adequate.

Creditors simply denied that debtors could transfer the revaluation burden to the mass of the population. And as potentially important as this objection to revaluation was, it apparently had in 1924 and 1925 no significant impact outside the Catholic workers' press.[27]

Most creditors did not believe increased revaluation would be an insupportable burden for a weakened economy because they did not believe Germany had suffered any net loss of wealth. Because debtors' buildings, farms, and factories usually still existed, they argued that the capital stock must not have diminished, at least not *their* debtors' capital.[28] Houses and agricultural land were supposedly selling for more than their pre-1914 prices. Creditors denied that agriculture's burdens were greater than before 1914, and they cited several profitable companies as evidence of industry's ability to pay.[29]

By late 1924 creditors refused to believe that the governments were too impoverished to revalue their debts. Creditors were outraged that foreign governments were to get staggering sums in reparations, while German creditors got nothing. Meanwhile, the central government and various municipalities began to show small budget surpluses, making them seem more capable of paying. Creditors argued that cities could finance revaluation from profit-making enterprises they owned.[30] In November 1924 Luther took advantage of a Reich budget surplus to cut taxes by presidential decree, to reduce the burden on the economy. Government-bond creditors protested that the government had a moral obligation to devote at least part of any surplus to redeeming its debts. Their anger grew into outrage when the press revealed in February 1925 that Luther had secretly compensated Ruhr industrialists for costs incurred during the French occupation. The secretiveness of the decision convinced creditors that a double standard was at work and that if the government could afford to compensate industry it could well afford to compensate its creditors.[31]

Not every creditor maintained that Germany had suffered *no* losses since 1914. Some creditor leaders acknowledged that the events of the preceding ten years had reduced Germany's wealth, as did some individual creditors. Creditors could, however, still well believe that Germany could afford a revaluation far above the 15 percent for private debts and the 0 percent for government bonds that the Tax Decree offered.[32]

Creditors acknowledged that massively expanding revaluation would create some uncertainty; they denied, however, that it would create unacceptable uncertainty. Investors might not like policy changes, but they ought to have seen that some revaluation reform was a distinct possibility. Any uncertainty that individual revaluation or a norm might create would, they argued, last only a very short time. A few representative court rulings would show creditors and debtors what the usual revaluation should be in various cases. Both would then have an incentive to come quickly to some agreement to avoid legal costs.[33] Some creditors also argued that the hardship clause for debtors had created individual revaluation for debtors and would lead to uncertainty anyway.[34]

The creditors were not content merely to counter debtor charges. They were convinced that increased revaluation would have positive economic benefits.

Creditors had argued all along that the inflation had made Germany seem a horrible credit risk and that only substantial revaluation could once again make investment in Germany seem secure and profitable. Investors are concerned with debtors' willingness to repay debts as well as with their ability to do so. Without meaningful revaluation, creditors argued, no potential lender could have confidence in the willingness of German debtors to repay or of the German state and legal system to protect creditor interests in the event of future difficulties. Germany desperately needed saving and investment, but the creditors claimed that without substantial revaluation they themselves, and other Germans, would decline to save. And they cited dozens of foreign newspaper articles, foreign visitors, and Germans returning from abroad who asserted that Germany could expect no foreign loans until creditors had received an equitable revaluation.

Indeed, foreign PM creditors were often vehemently prorevaluation because they were so incensed at how inflation had consumed their assets.[35]

Creditors further argued that increased revaluation would stimulate the economy by boosting liquidity. Because they believed Germany's real wealth had not declined, creditors argued that only a credit shortage and high interest rates prevented economic recovery. An influx of liquidity would itself be sufficient to put the "frozen fixed capital [*Sachwerte*]" to work and revive the economy. The increase in the money supply that this implied would not, they thought, ignite a new inflation because the existing money supply was inadequate (indeed, substantially below its real 1913 level in 1925) and, especially, because debtors would repay their loans over several years.[36]

Creditors embraced as a positive development the partial shift of funds from producers to consumers that revaluation would bring. Rejecting claims that only expenditures by producers could result in economic growth, creditors asserted that increased revaluation was imperative just because it would increase the purchasing power of consumers, thereby stimulating economic activity. One creditor group said revaluation would mean more purchasing power for one-third of the population, leading to an economic boom. Another identified consumers as the most important part of the economy because overall economic health depended on the health of the internal market.[37]

Some Germans, convinced by the debtors' arguments, proposed a social revaluation to meet the creditors' complaints about the impoverishment of honest savers. Instead of revaluing each debt individually (private-law revaluation), they proposed to revalue public, and perhaps private, debts as highly as economically feasible, pool the resulting funds, and apportion them among creditors based on individual *need*, not on any general legal right to revaluation.

Yet social revaluation could only threaten the creditors' sense of personal identity and worth by making them permanently dependent. Influenced by the *Mittelstand*'s mores, creditors had worked hard and saved diligently to be able to support themselves independently in the event of disability or old age.[38] Basing their self-respect on the visible, economic aspects of their status as *Mittelständler*, they differentiated themselves in no small part from the proletariat they disdained by their claim to independence.

Hence, the creditors' sense of self-respect prevented most of them from supporting social revaluation, even though it would probably have provided a considerably higher revaluation for individual creditors, especially those in most need, than could a private-law revaluation. As early as May 1924, in a symptomatic letter, a creditor had bitterly rejected the meager Tax Decree revaluation because, he said, "We [savers] also consider ourselves citizens with equal rights, just as much as the owners of real property; we too want to be able to pay taxes again and not to be fed from the soup kitchen." When Luther proposed a social revaluation of government bonds, the creditors rejected it vociferously. They insisted that they did not want charity but justice. As a DDP pamphlet later noted, the creditors did not want to "remain in the, for them, unbearable and shameful role of welfare recipients." This refusal to be turned into welfare recipients did not merely express the interests of those who would not be eligible for social revaluation; it clearly reflected the deeply felt conviction of most creditors.[39]

In an important sense, status considerations were more important to creditors than merely economic self-interest or the considerable evidence that the economy could not meet their demands. If the creditors had accepted the current economic orthodoxy, they would have had to accept minimal private-debt revaluation and the humiliating social revaluation of government bonds that was the best orthodoxy could offer. The creditor economic theory had some plausibility, and the orthodoxy obviously catered to producer (debtor) interests. Under the circumstances, creditors not surprisingly rejected orthodoxy and social revaluation in favor of their own ideology and individual revaluation.

But even though the creditors' theory grew out of their policy needs, rather than some disinterested analysis of the workings of a capitalist economy, their emphasis on maintaining liquidity and demand cannot merely be dismissed as self-serving rationalization. Among economists, monetarists argue that the money supply must keep pace with (although not excessively outpace) economic growth, in order to provide the means of exchange for economic activity, and Keynesians emphasize the importance of effective demand in maintaining prosperity. The creditors developed their alternative theory inchoately, but it did in fact express naively a number of themes that academic economists would subsequently elaborate.

Evaluating Creditor and Debtor Claims

The creditor movement had developed a coherent and plausible theory, but one that misled its members as to the economically and politically feasible.

Debtors did overstate their case, and increased revaluation might have improved Germany's abysmal postinflation credit situation. But creditors failed to appreciate the depth of Germany's immediate economic problems and the mischief revaluation could play in a weak economy. Even if they could have maintained the political momentum of 1924, they still could not have secured their goals.

Although creditors insisted individual revaluation, including a norm, would not create unacceptable uncertainty, it probably would have been far more confusing than they assumed. Many Germans were simultaneously creditor and debtor, often to numerous others, and many creditors believed that *their* debtor could afford nearly full revaluation. Where the government allowed individual revaluation, the procedure led to such long delays that even Emminger complained about the consequent confusion. Such uncertainty, and the relatively high revaluation rates judges would undoubtedly have imposed, would probably have drastically reduced the amount of credit available to the German economy. And one New York bank did explicitly threaten to withdraw its offer of credit if Germany imposed an individual revaluation—because of the consequent uncertainty.[40]

Equally dubious, though, was the debtors' assertion that *any* increase in revaluation would create disastrous uncertainty. Much as they may dislike uncertainty, investors cannot hope to avoid it entirely. Debate on reforming the Tax Decree revaluation began before its promulgation, and investors had to know change was possible, indeed probable. And investors did invest in Germany after the 1925 increase in the revaluation rate to 25 percent.[41] Clearly, a modest revaluation increase would not of itself preclude further investment.

What mattered most for revaluation was that Germany had suffered real losses of wealth between 1914 and 1923. The creditors personalized the issue by pointing to the continued existence of specific buildings, farms, and factories. But rent control, the need for repairs and new investment, and the loss of foreign and domestic markets had decreased the return on and therefore the value of such property. Various observers, for example, valued apartment houses in 1924 at 10 to 40 percent of prewar prices. And the net capital imports Germany enjoyed from 1925 to 1930 merely covered the massive payment deficits the country suffered without fully compensating for pre-1924 losses of wealth.[42]

This decline in real national wealth precluded creditors ever realizing their fondest hopes: recognition of government bonds in GM and individual and nearly full revaluation of private assets. By 1924 the real value of Germany's national wealth most probably was less than, but certainly not much more than, the paper value of the revaluable debt. And of course many other domestic and foreign claims on the wealth existed. Although some revaluation was certainly possible, anywhere near full debt revaluation would only have reignited the inflation, destroying anew the value of the revalued assets.

Although creditors were right to argue that the destruction of their assets had reduced the availability of credit and raised its cost, simply recreating the liquid capital would not have solved the problem. The real money supply was lower in 1925 than in 1913, so some scope for monetary expansion did exist. But Germany faced more than a liquidity shortage. When the Reichsbank pursued an easy money policy in early 1924 (in response to massive private demand for credit to replace the reserves destroyed by inflation and stabilization), considerable new inflationary pressure developed. Only a severely restrictive credit policy stabilized the mark. And subsequent Reichsbank efforts to ease credit resulted in rapid declines in its reserves.[43] Some modest revaluation might have stimulated the economy, but too much would apparently have put inflationary pressure on the mark.

Central to the creditors' argument that increased purchasing power would stimulate economic growth was the implicit assumption that Germany's problem in the interwar years was a lack of effective demand. Although debate exists over this issue, Germany's interwar problems were such that simply increasing demand would probably not have solved them.[44]

World War I had stimulated the creation of massive industrial and agricultural overcapacity worldwide, and the ensuing structural changes in world economic relationships weakened Germany's economic position. Despite the short-term advantages inflation brought, Germany had not successfully adapted. Industry and agriculture had responded primarily with defensive measures, using cartelization, tariffs, and government subsidies to avoid fundamental restructuring. Banks proved more willing to loan to stagnant industries than dynamic ones. The German economy had therefore not regained its prewar competitiveness on world markets.

Hence, increased demand simply sucked in more imports, while sluggish world trade and Germany's own lack of competitiveness prevented the country from financing imports with increased exports. The balance-of-payments problems that developed were not solved but were masked by massive inflows of capital after 1923. Without changes in the world and the German economies, increasing demand even further with large-scale revaluation could only have worsened Germany's trade and payments deficits and hence would most probably have been untenable over the long run.[45]

Furthermore, Germany ran budget deficits in the late 1920s and was in fact pursuing expansionary economic policies (albeit unintentionally and not in the way creditors wanted). They were not a success.[46]

With rapid economic expansion unlikely, revaluation would have put upward pressure on taxes, rents, and business costs, creating problems for governments, building owners, and businessmen. Debtors would have had to cover the cost of revaluation either by improving the efficiency of operations, reducing pretax income, or increasing taxes, turnover, or prices.

Basically, the Reich, Länder, and municipalities—who held two-thirds of the revaluable debt—could only revalue their debts by raising taxes. Increased taxes on consumers would have burdened many Germans who were no better able to bear the cost than impoverished creditors. And if the government had increased taxes on producers, it would have further burdened essential elements of the economy who were often barely competitive even without added taxes to finance revaluation.[47] Moreover, financing substantial revaluation with budget deficits was scarcely an option because virtually no one in the late 1920s was willing to loan the Reich money long-term.[48] Room certainly remained, however, to shift some government spending toward meeting creditor rights, even if not enough actually to meet their demands.[49]

Substantially revaluing urban mortgages would also have been problematic. Most were on buildings subject to rent control. Any increased revaluation would have required either raising rents (as after the 1925 revaluation increase) or cutting the crucial rent tax. The former would have burdened often impoverished renters, and the latter would have aggravated the government's severe fiscal problems.[50]

Improving the efficiency of government and business operations was probably not a viable alternative for financing additional revaluation. The various levels of government had cut their expenditures severely in 1923–24 and already faced pressure to restore spending. Building owners had to make up for years of neglected maintenance. Agriculture already suffered from an increasingly severe depression brought on by low world prices. Improving efficiency to meet existing burdens was difficult enough. Industry was trying to rationalize its operations to make good the losses of the war period and the misinvestment that had occurred during the inflation. In general, however, it was more inclined to seek defensive solutions. Business felt mortally threatened by the potential for workers to defend their interests through collective bargaining or the Republic's democratic institutions. In the uncertain climate of the late 1920s, business seemed to focus its efforts more on fighting with its workers and on attacking the Republic than on fundamentally restructuring itself.[51]

Financing revaluation by forgoing some profits was no option for the government and presented problems for other debtors. To obtain any credit, businesses had to maintain profits to reassure investors of their viability. Some firms paid dividends in 1924 and 1925, but most did not. With credit expensive, much of investment was probably self-financed. Reducing net income would have left less funds for this desperately needed self-financing.[52] Revaluation would shift funds from producers (and investors) to consumers at a time when increased investment was most probably more important than increased consumption. Morally, revaluation was an issue between creditors and debtors, but economically its broad ramifications created complex interactions among creditors, debtors, producers, taxpayers, tenants, and consumers.

Germany's economic situation made increasing turnover difficult. World trade was stagnant in the interwar years, and by the late 1920s the mark was probably overvalued, severely weakening Germany's competitiveness at home and abroad.[53] Domestically, demand was rather weak, and Germany's balance of payments and competitiveness problems limited the ability of German business to increase domestic sales.[54]

In fact industry and agriculture would have to increase prices to cover most of whatever public- and private-debt revaluation occurred. Businesses' ability to increase prices would depend on the elasticity of demand for various products, on relative competitiveness, and on profit margins. Establishing the exact weight of these factors is impossible at this late date, but the profit margins of German business were sufficiently thin, and their control of domestic markets through cartels, tariffs, and other factors sufficiently great, that many businesses would have been able to or would have felt compelled to raise prices. Aside from allowing debtors to transfer much of the cost of any revaluation to consumers, as some Germans feared, increased prices would have further hurt the competitiveness of many sectors on world and domestic markets.[55]

Not surprisingly but unfortunately, creditors were not thinking too hard about how any revaluation would actually have to be financed. When Luther argued that the government needed to settle its revenue and expenditures before it could settle revaluation, creditors responded with vague assertions about revenues that might be secured from inflation taxes or extra funds that might be available from reducing the welfare rolls or, somehow, reparations.[56] And their analysis of the financing capacity of private debtors seemed to reflect predominantly wishful thinking. If the creditors had realized that full or even substantial revaluation could probably only have been financed with a new inflation, they might have had a different attitude toward their situation and the Republic.

Curiously, creditors ignored how other European countries dealt with revaluation, although considering foreign experiences might have been instructive. Britain, Italy, and France each experienced war and postwar inflations, albeit not on the scale of Germany's. Each dealt with its monetary difficulties differently, although each sooner or later revalued its currency. Revaluing a currency was not the same as revaluing debts, but its effects on costs, prices, and investment were arguably similar. These countries stabilized too late to provide comparative experience before the Reichstag enacted the revaluation laws, but creditors might eventually have become more reconciled to those laws if they had considered other national monetary experiences in the 1920s.

Britain decided to revalue its currency at prewar par. With lower deficits during and after the war than the other European belligerents and with substantial holdings of foreign assets, Britain remained a net foreign creditor. Generally, British business, political, and public opinion was ideologically committed to the gold standard as the basis for prosperity. And the economically important financial community and many other Britons considered restoring the pound's prewar par indispensable for maintaining London's central and quite profitable international financial predominance. Britain also had many rentiers who favored returning the pound to its prewar value.

Hence, when the postwar boom ran down in 1920, the British government was determined to return to fiscal orthodoxy. It even ran budget surpluses to reduce its debt. Knowledge of the Central and Eastern European inflations had meanwhile further discredited managed money. Many experts even feared that *not* returning to gold when the pound was so stable and so close to prewar par would create difficulties. The government also hoped to increase the value of British assets abroad. The return to gold at the prewar rate, in April 1925, met no real opposition.

The return to par did, however, bring severe problems. When American prices failed to rise as expected, only a severe deflation in Britain could

forestall a devaluation that would harm its financial position. This deflation in turn caused high unemployment in Britain and lost investment
opportunities. Thus, British financial institutions, creditors, and consumers profited at the expense of industry and industrial workers.[57]

Italy's situation was more precarious. Much poorer than Britain or
France, it had depended predominantly on foreign and domestic loans to
finance its war effort and postwar reconstruction—on top of substantial
prewar debt. By 1922 the debt had more than quintupled above its 1914
level, and the value of the lira had fallen proportionately. After 1922 the
new Fascist dictatorship continued the debt consolidation the liberals had
begun. It also more or less balanced the budget. Nonetheless, by the mid-
1920s capital flight and speculation were fueling inflation and undermin-
ing the currency.

By 1926 drastic measures to stabilize the lira seemed necessary to
Mussolini and most Italians. Britain and the U.S. held over half the debt,
and Italy's success in negotiating very favorable reschedulings with them
strengthened the lira. Yet the chaotic debt structure, with short-term debt
constantly coming due, remained a major problem. The Fascists had to
combine its forced conversion into long-term debt with restrictive foreign
trade regulations to stabilize the situation in early 1927.

Mussolini was determined for prestige reasons to set as high a value for
the lira as possible. Despite opposition from some sectors of industry,
other sectors and the middle classes pushed for a high rate. His government hence chose, more or less arbitrarily, to stabilize at 19 lira to the
dollar (90 to the pound), about 28 percent of the prewar rate. This rate was
too high, and Italy suffered serious deflation as Mussolini fought to defend
it.

Although Italian creditors got more than an economically optimal rate
might have provided, they still lost nearly 75 percent of their assets. Yet the
country's difficulties in maintaining the chosen rate suggest that any higher
currency revaluation was impossible.[58]

France also experienced considerable problems with monetary and fiscal
policy. The Third Republic had always had difficulty taxing its citizens,
and in 1914 the government decided to assume it would win the war and
could force Germany to pay France's war costs. France hence relied on
foreign and domestic borrowing for 94 percent of its war expenditure.
After victory, the government borrowed more to cover the massive costs
for demobilization and reconstruction, assuming reparations from Germany would cover all war-related costs. France had already experienced

sufficient inflation that long-term borrowing was difficult, so the state relied on short-term bonds and discounting at the Bank of France to tide it over until reparations began in earnest.

During the early 1920s the government recognized the problems inflation entailed, but it could not bring itself to stabilize. France had too many rentiers and others who hoped for a return to par, and the massive, unfunded short-term debt complicated the situation. Hence the legislature was unwilling to take drastic action to balance the budget, especially given continued hopes for reparations and the splits within coalition governments on how to balance—at what cost and whose expense. When parliament discussed a forced conversion of the short-term debt in October 1925, creditors panicked. A vote rejecting forced conversion scarcely affected the ensuing capital flight and inflation.

By 1926 a consensus existed that some measure of stabilization was imperative to forestall chaos. As Eleanor Dulles argued, stabilization came because those desiring stable money had come to far outnumber those desiring compensation for the decline in the value of government and other securities. The government balanced the budget in the spring. The July appointment of the conservative Raymond Poincaré as prime minister, with a strong mandate, finally allowed a series of confidence-building measures that stabilized the franc, de facto, by late 1926.

Although Poincaré was temperamentally inclined to revalue the franc at or near its prewar value, he eventually decided that doing so was economically impossible. Much of the debt had changed hands at inflated prices since 1918, so speculators, not the original purchasers, would often benefit. Any attempt to return to par would necessitate massive deflation. The business groups who opposed raising the franc's value could point to the problems Britain had experienced from its revaluation. On one estimate, French wages and salaries would have had to have been cut 60 percent, leading to massive social unrest. Hence on 25 June 1928 the legislature stabilized the franc at about 20 percent of its prewar value.[59]

All these countries faced monetary difficulties similar to Germany's, and they were the victors, not the losers. Britain alone risked full revaluation. With relatively little debt, with extensive foreign holdings, with a crucial international financial sector dependent at least partially on financial and monetary stability, British leaders felt that they had to return to par. Yet such a return proved more than even the relatively wealthy British could afford. France and Italy agreed with Germany in seeing revaluation as economically disadvantageous, agreed implicitly that they had to sacrifice creditors to protect producers. And although debt and currency revaluation are not the same, the economic difficulties faced by the two who did overvalue their currencies slightly, Britain and Italy, suggest the dangers inherent in substantial revaluation.

Despite creditors' blindness to some economic problems, they did correctly appreciate the need to restore faith in Germany's *willingness* as well as her *ability* to repay her debts. By pursuing inflationary policies and then refusing to provide substantial revaluation, the German state and German debtors were arguably showing an unwillingness to repay honest debts that called into question the security of any future investments in Germany.

And many investors apparently did not fully trust debtors or the German state to prevent a new inflation or to pay up in real terms if one did occur. Theodore Balderston's calculations suggest Germany's savings rate dropped from 15.5 percent in 1899–1913 to 8.5 percent in 1925–29 (compared with a drop from 13.5 percent to 10.5 percent for the U.K.). The relatively high interest rates in Germany in the late 1920s also suggest a shortage of savings. Investment seems to have fallen as well.[60] German business and German governments had great difficulty in obtaining long-term loans in this period, as investors shifted to short-term assets in apparent fear of a future inflation. The stock of bonds in 1929 was only half that of 1913. Indeed, by 1930, the Reich found itself simply *unable* to borrow long-term because no one would lend it money. And German industry was often forced to look abroad for funds. Substantial capital flight by Germans unsure of the mark's stability also characterized this period.[61]

This lack of trust caused real economic, fiscal, and political problems. The overwhelmingly short-term nature of savings and investment made it difficult for German business to plan and invest rationally. It also left German financial institutions dangerously weak in the face of economic fluctuations. German capital flight and the banks' dependence on volatile foreign deposits were predominantly responsible for the disastrous banking crisis of 1931. And the Reich's near inability to borrow money decisively narrowed its options in the great crisis of 1930–33.[62]

Yet the creditors did exaggerate when they predicted that no one would save if the government refused to increase revaluation. Germans had to continue saving. Pensions, disability and unemployment insurance, and medical plans were only imperfectly developed. If a German wanted to protect himself and his family against age, disability, unemployment, illness, or accident, if he wished to accumulate funds for a child's education, a vacation, a new suit, or any other purpose, he had to save. And given the complexities of investing abroad, most (although not all) Germans had to save *within* Germany.

Thus, despite the lack of revaluation, the German people did regain sufficient confidence in the willingness of credit institutions to repay that they entrusted their funds to those institutions, at least short-term. They deposited at savings banks slightly more in real terms 1924–30 than they had 1907–13. They invested with public and private mortgage banks approximately twice as much in real terms 1924–30 as they had 1907–13. They apparently deposited with credit cooperatives approximately as much 1924–30 as 1907–13.[63]

More important, creditors were wrong about the attitudes of foreign investors, who proved more concerned with ability to pay than with willingness to do so. Foreign PM creditors might vehemently demand revaluation, but the big foreign banks and brokers (through whom new loans to finance German economic recovery would have to flow) vigorously opposed any increase in revaluation. According to the *Journal of Commerce of New York*, "The worst blow that could be dealt to German credit in foreign markets would be delivered if Germany were to try to meet her old public obligations in substantial amounts."[64] American bankers warned they would cut off all credit to German agriculture if the government introduced individual revaluation. In discussing the Dawes loan, all foreign exchanges except the Dutch favored a ban on government-bond revaluation.[65] And Ben Strong, Governor of the New York Federal Reserve Board, wrote in November 1924 that American lenders hesitated to make further loans to Germany because they feared a high revaluation would make German debtors unable to pay.[66]

Only by defaulting on its PM loans could Germany seem attractive to potential new lenders. In the short term Germany apparently could not afford to revalue.

Even had large-scale revaluation been economically feasible, it probably would not have solved Germany's post-1923 credit shortage. Investors want liquidity as well as ultimate repayment. Many foreign and domestic investors presumably cared less about revaluation than about controlling inflation in the first place.[67] They might well have feared that the German state, having once pursued inflationary policies, could do so again, especially given the possibly inflationary consequences of attempting to finance a large revaluation. Also, given the mid-1920s political conflict over revaluation, investors could scarcely count on a revaluation in the event of a future inflation.

Even though limited revaluation hurt the German economy, substantially increased revaluation does not seem to have been feasible. Its short-term consequences were just too damaging and its long-term advantages too long-term, limited, and uncertain. On grounds of equity creditors deserved as much revaluation as society could afford—but Germany apparently could afford far less than creditors thought. Had creditors admitted the very real short-term economic difficulties revaluation implied and accepted that the political system was trying sincerely to make the best of a difficult situation, they would have had far less reason to withhold their savings or question the Republic's legitimacy.

Creditors, however, remained unconvinced that any economic difficulties constrained policymakers. The debtor counterattack on economic grounds called on an economic orthodoxy but came from an obviously self-interested group. Indeed, the producers proved willing to abandon important elements of that orthodoxy once Adolf Hitler had destroyed the democratic Weimar Republic they mistrusted.[68] And the government was obviously biased toward producers/debtors, not least by its own debtor status.

Buoyed by support from judges, churches, and many politicians, the creditors had responded to this situation by inventing their own countervailing and very compelling ideology. Like other ideologies, the creditors' rationale for revaluation was a morally charged and logically coherent set of beliefs; it structured economic, social, and political reality to the point of misrepresentation, but it made the world seem comprehensible. Also like other ideologies, the creditor perspective was both comprehensive, attempting to explain all aspects of social reality, and exclusive, denying the validity of other ideologies. It constituted a revolt by creditors against orthodoxy and elites. And because the creditor ideology appealed to creditor interests in moral terms, it was extremely effective in mobilizing creditors both behind specific policies and for fundamental change.[69]

For many creditors, then, the net effect of debtor counterattacks had been to strengthen their resolve by arming them with a powerful and coherent, if somewhat skewed, view of their situation. As one-sided as debtors often were, many creditors responded with an equally one-sided rejection of any suggestion that the society might have to limit revaluation. And creditors based their rejection of significant limits on revaluation not merely on vague hopes or economic self-interest, but on a systematic theory that seemed to prove both the justice and the feasibility of their demands. Their faith in their ideology made them a determined, potentially powerful, and potentially revolutionary political force.

Miseducating the Creditors

The Revaluation Committee Makes Some Progress

Government officials missed a chance to use the Revaluation Committee to educate politicians and public about revaluation's complexities. Indeed, because ministers saw it only as a threat to stabilization, they sought to postpone committee action as much and as long as possible. They apparently hoped the Tax Decree revaluation would become so completely a part of economic expectations that amending it would be impossible.

This attitude only awakened suspicions among committee members, so that even the Finance Ministry agreed that the government could not put them off completely. Therefore, on 8 August the cabinet decided to work with the committee, but very carefully, and especially to avoid "any hint of a positive attitude."[1] But only on 24 September, nearly two months after the Revaluation Committee's hearings, did a subcommittee of one representative from each of the eight major parties finally begin a series of meetings on revaluation reform.

The subcommittee deputies unanimously agreed that some reform was necessary. All except the DDP and KPD seemed to favor increasing private-debt revaluation substantially. Some deputies supported individual revaluation of mortgages (Karl Steiniger [DNVP] and Gottfried Feder [Völkisch]) or a revaluation norm (Hergt [DNVP]), but most deputies were less explicit. Government representatives unanimously rejected general retroactive revaluation because they feared it would cause tremendous legal and economic problems. The committee, however, generally favored it, especially as it was a prerequisite for any significant savings-deposit revaluation.[2]

The deputies did moderate their parties' earlier demands. Even Hergt was apparently having second thoughts about individual revaluation. Hans Wunderlich (DVP) subsequently commented that 25 percent was the highest mortgage rate to which anyone would commit himself.[3] On industrial obligations, Dernburg, Wunderlich, and Paul Fleischer (Z) all suggested that the Dawes Plan charges against industry were too burdensome to allow any increase.[4]

Committee members generally believed the time had come to allow some government-bond revaluation. Hergt favored such a revaluation for original purchasers up to some as yet undetermined amount. Fleischer proposed a detailed but totally impractical plan for confiscating speculatively acquired bonds and using them to finance revaluation of other bonds. His proposal would have used worthless paper to pay off worthless paper; it was literally laughed out of the committee. Nonetheless, newspaper reports on the Fleischer and Hergt plans seemed to corroborate the creditors' conviction that government-bond revaluation was now feasible.[5]

According to the KPD, Fleischer introduced his improbable plan in hopes of driving up bond prices. A bank of which he was a director might then recoup some of its losses from speculation. The Communists said Fleischer expected the newspapers to concentrate on the attractive revaluation rate he proposed, not the ludicrous financing procedures. Such rosy reports did appear, and the SPD newspaper *Vorwärts* hinted that Fleischer did have ties to the ailing bank. The Center newspaper *Germania* and Fleischer himself denied the accusations.[6] Fleischer may have been naive or misled, but the accusations did have a certain plausibility.

In any event, committee members and many creditors agreed that any revaluation must somehow exclude government bonds acquired for speculative purposes. Speculators had often obtained bonds during and after the inflation for a tiny fraction of their original worth. The self-sacrificing patriots who had bought government bonds at their GM value before or during World War I, so-called old holders, would get a greater share of the funds available for bond revaluation if the government excluded postwar purchasers, so-called new holders. For practical reasons, the government defined old holders as those who could prove they had acquired a PM asset before an arbitrary cut-off date, 1 July 1920, and had held it continuously. Obsessed with limiting the government's liability, Luther naturally supported such proposals.[7]

These attacks on "speculation" glossed over certain very real difficulties. Any investment in a capitalist economy is of course a speculation. And new holders had often made their purchases simply because government bonds were a *mündelsicher* asset or, indeed, out of patriotic enthusiasm, rather than in an attempt to profit from others' poverty and uncertainty. And punishing "speculation" was likely to reduce the value of future government bond offerings by limiting their liquidity (the ability of a bond holder to sell the bond for cash), if investors feared a future inflation might lead to another annulment of bonds not held by the original purchaser.[8]

This willingness, indeed eagerness, to seize speculatively acquired assets to the benefit of "honest" creditors reflects the creditor movement's antipathy toward capitalism. Nominally, the moral case for revaluation rested on the sanctity of contracts and private property. Yet when the property in question was speculatively acquired (whatever that might mean), the creditors denied it any right to protection, indeed wanted it "expropriated." Clearly, the creditors did not believe in competitive capitalism or in private property per se. They wanted rather a social guarantee of those assets acquired by hard work and thrift in reputable occupations—that is, their assets.

The committee discussed at length a social revaluation of government bonds. In an apparent attempt to forestall general government-bond revaluation, Luther suggested limiting such revaluation to needy old holders of war bonds (not all Reich bonds). He insisted the government could afford at most 50 million marks per year for interest on government bonds. Spreading it over all PM government bonds would provide a mere 0.1 percent interest. Limiting payment to needy old holders would at least provide some creditors with significant revaluation while excluding those regarded as speculators.[9] Only Dernburg was willing to support this proposal. Feder tentatively supported Luther, but his party had its own plan for a social revaluation of private and public debts, in addition to its recent proposals for individual revaluation. The KPD did prefer social revaluation, but not Luther's version.[10]

Social revaluation was not well-received. The creditors consistently and vehemently opposed it, as did, initially, most of the parties.[11] Believing that the government had a moral obligation to all (except speculators) who had bought its bonds, the parties and the creditors also usually wanted to revalue not merely war bonds, but all bonds.

The committee barely discussed the important problem of finding revenue to finance government-bond revaluation. Characteristically, none of the supporters of substantial revaluation was willing to deal concretely with this problem. Hergt, for example, simply assumed increased revaluation would bring large savings on the welfare rolls, although he did suggest taxing municipal enterprises.[12] Being out of power, creditors and their strongest supporters could ignore the extent to which revaluation involved taking from some to give to others. Yet the bourgeois parties' choice of expedient silence on this problem would return to haunt them in 1925, when they actually had to finance government-bond revaluation.

The revaluation subcommittee made no concrete decisions, but it did contribute to a consensus on some issues. Despite vehement government opposition, deputies had accepted retroactive revaluation. Speculatively acquired government bonds seemed almost certain not to be revalued. The committee had generally rejected social revaluation as a solution, but Luther had raised the possibility of some social revaluation of government bonds. Significantly, however, the committee did not endorse individual revaluation, and it apparently could not agree on increasing the revaluation rate above a relatively modest 25 percent, although perhaps as a norm. Even though the parties had sent prorevaluation representatives to the subcommittee, it had implicitly rejected the creditors' chosen policy.

Even though committee discussions had educated some politicians, they had the opposite effect on the parties and the public. Each party except the KPD and DDP had sent a revaluation supporter to the subcommittee. Discussions were hence predicated on the assumption that the government must and could expand private-debt revaluation substantially and that it should and could revalue government bonds. Newspaper reports thus tended to give the impression to politicians and public that creditor demands had gotten a legislative stamp of approval. And before events could erode that impression, the pressures of an election campaign intervened.

The Creditors Get Another Electoral Opportunity

When efforts to form a majority government failed in October 1924, Marx decided a new election was unavoidable. Although some ministers (including Luther) feared the results of such an election, Marx thought that it would increase the number of seats held by moderate parties and make working with the new Reichstag easier. And so, on 20 October, the president dissolved the Reichstag and set new elections for 7 December 1924.[13]

The prospects of the middle-of-the-road (government) parties were mixed. By the fall of 1924 the economy and the political situation had improved markedly. Unemployment was generally down and wages up. Most businessmen were enjoying some prosperity. Reichstag acceptance of the Dawes Plan, and the DNVP split over it, seemed to have weakened that party somewhat.[14] Yet serious problems remained to lessen the government parties' appeal. White-collar unemployment remained high and wages relatively low. Civil-service salaries lagged. Bankruptcy rates were still considerably higher than prewar. Many Germans remained unreconciled to the Dawes Plan. Above all, the government's fiscal and revaluation policies antagonized many. Even its November tax cuts would predominantly aid business, confirming the unequal distribution of burdens.[15]

Well aware that revaluation could prove politically dangerous, the government sought to defuse the issue. Luther urged his fellow ministers to influence government-party candidates not to take firm positions on revaluation, or at least not to repudiate the government's policy.[16] Although Luther wanted to limit revaluation reform to the little he had already proposed, Brauns argued that the government would have to offer more. And in a 6 November statement, the cabinet promised that it could now "go past the previously foreseen limitation to the needy, within the framework of the economically possible" and that after the election it would amend the Tax Decree revaluation.[17] Although this statement undoubtedly represented a defeat for Luther, it was too vague to impress most voters.

The revaluation was the issue that generated the most discussion and controversy in the December election. Some newspapers, for example, the *Westdeutsche Arbeiter Zeitung* (a Catholic workers' paper) and the *Deutsche Allgemeine Zeitung* (a paper with ties to industry) did ignore revaluation completely, and papers sometimes reported speeches selectively, editing out references to revaluation. Nonetheless, it came up at almost every election meeting, often through bitter heckling from the audience. And according to the political parties, it was the most popular issue.[18]

A combination of interest and indignation underlay the creditors' single-minded determination to speak out again and again until someone satisfied their just demands. For many elderly or disabled creditors, with time on their hands to attend campaign meetings, revaluation seemed almost literally a matter of life or death. Unless they turned to charity or welfare (options most found abhorrent), their livelihoods depended on a revaluation of their savings. Creditors also felt basely betrayed by the government and self-righteous about their inalienable right to redress through (individual) revaluation.

Their single-mindedness and volatility made creditors an irresistible target to the political parties. Other issues (e.g., taxes, tariffs) appealed to more voters, but such voters knew from past battles roughly what they could expect from each political party. New flights of rhetoric might move some of them to vote for a different party, but not any great number. The creditors were different. They had no concrete experience with how each political party would actually vote on revaluation in the Reichstag, as opposed to talk in political or committee meetings. Thus, as one local party official wrote, there were "infinitely many small savers who still set their hopes on this [revaluation], and who instinctively allow themselves to be captured by the party that offers the most hope."[19] Such creditors (perhaps 3 percent of the electorate) undoubtedly constituted the largest pool of voters whom campaign promises alone might sway, a pool no party could ignore.[20]

The election campaign hence put a premium on rhetoric at the expense of analysis. The complex debate that had developed over revaluation's economic implications disappeared in a flood of campaign slogans.

Creditors believed they had the "moral factor (*Moment*)" on their side and that no party could reject them. They continued to emphasize the investor's right to protection from expropriation. Only by implementing the principle of equity and good faith, they argued, could Germany ensure its political and economic reconstruction.[21]

Creditors continued to emphasize that revaluation was necessary to preserve the *Mittelstand*. The creditors viewed the Tax Decree as a disaster in this respect: "Through this disinheritance [by the decree] the culturally indispensable *Mittelstand* is delivered into despair, because it loses in large part its possibility for existence. . . . If the culturally most valuable sector of the German people . . . is destroyed and annihilated, then all the ostensible, illusory 'economic blossomings' of the nation will not save the nation from ruin."[22]

In fact the inflation had not destroyed the *Mittelstand*, even if it had impoverished individual *Mittelständler*, such as the prorevaluation creditors. The education, social attitudes, and contacts that characterized the *Mittelstand* were responsible for their access to better and better-paying jobs and enabled them to perpetuate their social position. The *Mittelstand* and other middle-class groups in Germany accumulated considerable savings between 1924 and 1930, and their children continued to have access to higher education in much the same proportion in the late 1920s as before the war.[23] *Mittelstand* assets reflected higher earning power more than they caused it.

Nonetheless, the inflation had increased the *Mittelstand*'s sense of social insecurity and their mistrust of unrestrained capitalism and of the new

Republic. Creditors were inextricably intertwined with the *Mittelstand* as a whole. The loss of creditor assets had constrained the availability of credit and purchasing power. The destruction of paper assets had forced many rentiers to enter the labor market, presumably raising the unemployment rate somewhat. Many in the *Mittelstand* had friends and relatives whom inflation had reduced to poverty.[24] And no one in this period seriously challenged the creditor assertion that inflation had obliterated the *Mittelstand*.

Hence, when prorevaluation forces identified themselves with the "indispensable" *Mittelstand*, they were fairly successful in convincing those parties that claimed to represent the *Mittelstand*, or that saw it as indispensable, to support some revaluation reform. Such an identification widened revaluation's appeal to all *Mittelständler* who had any savings, however small. And it strengthened the creditor movement among the many Germans who shared the belief that the *Mittelstand* alone could mediate between capitalists and workers and provide a secure basis for the state.

If creditor rhetoric was predictable, their tactics were not. They could: confine themselves to principled exposition of their position; use their votes as a bargaining tool; or found their own political party. The Reichstag's failure to revise the Tax Decree had discredited the first option, but the creditors divided over the other two.

In the autumn election no less than five revaluation parties ran candidates. They assumed that the major parties were not to be trusted—an assumption that proved correct. They had little impact, however, obtaining no seats and only 275,000 votes (less than 1 percent), part of which was undoubtedly noncreditor protest votes.[25] This splintering of a splinter group was symptomatic of the *Mittelstand*'s political problems.

The largest creditor group, the HGSSV, decided not to form a revaluation party and instead used its members' votes to extract promises from the parties. It prepared a list of questions (three in one version, five in another) and demanded from the various parties an affirmative answer to each one. The basic questions were: (1) Will you support immediately revoking the Tax Decree, implementing Dr. Best's draft revaluation bill, and considering resumption of interest on government bonds? (2) Will you support taxing inflation profits and using assets bought by speculators to the benefit of government-bond holders? (3) Will you support replacing Luther as finance minister?[26]

Best's draft called for revaluing private debts according to the principle of equity and good faith, that is, for individual revaluation. The government was to implement general retroactive revaluation for all debts. Interest payments were to resume immediately and were to be based on the relative economic situations of creditor and debtor. The creditor was also to share in future increases in the value of any property against which he had loaned money.[27] Allowing the creditor to share in future increases in property values was particularly problematic, for it would have drastically increased the uncertainty and decreased the value of new investment.

The attack on Luther was no surprise. As *Vorwärts* later commented, "In the eyes of the victims of the inflation, Herr Luther was a monster without feeling or compassion for the situation in which the rentiers and savers who had been robbed of their capital found themselves."[28] His responsibility for the Tax Decree, his refusal in July to take time out to testify on revaluation, and his probusiness tax cuts had angered the creditors. They thought he was "indifferent" to the "death of the rentiers" because their "consumption capital" could never be made productive. They characterized him, rightly, as "under the influence of the economy [*die Wirtschaft*], i.e., the debtors."[29] Creditors believed, with good reason, that so long as Luther had responsibility for revaluation, they could not achieve their goals.

The HGSSV had probably been wise not to form its own party. Single-issue parties in the Weimar Republic (including the creditors themselves in the late 1920s) were relatively ineffective. They could never attract enough voters to have an impact on the Reichstag, and once they had tied up the votes in a weak special interest party, the larger parties had less incentive to make concessions on the issues. But if the creditor groups could convince the larger parties that they could deliver the votes, they would have leverage to extract campaign promises and some action from the parties.

The Parties Commit Themselves

The DNVP's electoral success in May must have been convincing, because creditor groups in fact obtained substantial, but infeasible, promises from major political parties. The HGSSV thereupon endorsed the DNVP, Center, and Völkisch parties, whereas the German Rentiers Association (Deutscher Rentnerbund, which represented landlords and pensioners, as well as some creditors) supported the DNVP, DVP, BVP, and Center.[30] Other parties failed to satisfy creditor groups.

Although the SPD officially favored a limited and partially social revaluation, its revaluation spokesman, Keil, campaigned in his own district for a considerably increased private-law revaluation. If party leaders did not explicitly reject Keil's misleading version of party policy, they would be encouraging creditor misapprehension about what was feasible. But disavowing one of their own candidates would be politically embarrassing. Presumably aware that the party could lose votes by openly opposing revaluation, the SPD leadership—like the revaluation opponents in other parties—chose silence.[31]

The WP's fuzzy revaluation policy reflected the *Mittelstand*'s divergent interests. The party supported a "just, general revaluation of all debt obligations in the framework of what our impoverished German people can support"—whatever that might mean.[32] Although the party claimed to speak for the entire *Mittelstand*, including creditors, its major constituency was still the landlords (*Hausbesitzer*), who were debtors. To appeal to creditors, the WP and the landlords argued that they and the creditors were really allies. They argued that landlords could only afford the mortgage revaluation that creditors wanted if the government abolished rent control. And the landlords offered a political alliance if the creditors would help eliminate rent control.[33]

Although the two groups might have had some community of interest if rent-control reform had been possible, no evidence is available that the creditors responded to this proposal or indeed sought any political allies. This attitude, typical of the creditors, undoubtedly contributed to their relative failure. They found the *Kuhhandel* (logrolling) of the political process base and despicable. They considered morality, not interest, the proper basis of public policy. And of course they assumed morality lay solely on their side. They apparently did not even consider breaking out of their self-imposed isolation, did not consider acting politically while attempting to realize their aims in the political arena.

The DDP probably lost the most because of revaluation. It resolutely rejected demagoguery, despite the loss of votes it knew that would entail. It answered all the HGSSV questions affirmatively, but it declared forthrightly, "The DDP will go as far with its proposals as is possible without danger of a new inflation or of further economically damaging tax and rent burdens."[34] At a time when other parties were promising at least a revaluation norm, such honesty could not satisfy the creditors; it merely seemed a surrender to debtor claims and debtor interests. The DDP got no creditor endorsements.[35]

The BVP managed to satisfy the Rentiers Association, but not the HGSSV. Emminger, the BVP revaluation spokesman, touted his earlier efforts on revaluation; he proposed a probably infeasible 25 to 30 percent private-debt revaluation norm, general retroactive revaluation, 20 percent government-bond revaluation with 2.5 percent interest, and extra government-bond revaluation for savings banks. Yet he also emphasized the limits to the economically feasible, warning that the Tax Decree was part of the "great work of reconstruction and stabilization" and could only be amended cautiously.[36]

Emminger's refusal to pander to creditor illusions suggests that he supported revaluation from conviction, not expediency. His politically responsible stand probably prompted the HGSSV's refusal to recommend the BVP to the creditors. The major creditor group had turned its back on the politician who had actually done the most to help creditors in favor of politicians who only promised the most.

The DVP emphasized its ties to the creditors' great friend, the late Dr. Düringer, and to his policies. The party spokespersons on revaluation, Wunderlich and Matz, proposed a revaluation norm, perhaps of 25 percent, a general retroactive revaluation, and interest payments on government bonds, with speculators excluded. Wunderlich admitted that the party was split on revaluation but asserted that the majority favored it and that "even those who were earlier very skeptical toward revaluation have now entirely accepted the point of view of the majority," including Heinze. Although Stresemann insisted the Tax Decree had been necessary when promulgated, he now supported a revaluation norm.[37]

The procreditor forces had again won the intraparty battle over revaluation rhetoric, but not necessarily over revaluation policy. Debate over economic consequences had apparently moderated party policy slightly compared with the spring. And despite Wunderlich's claim that debtor representatives had "entirely accepted" the creditor view, opposition within the party to these promises did continue.[38]

Pulled one way by debtor interests and economic arguments and another by creditor demands for equity and creditor votes, the DVP chose a revaluation platform that proved counterproductive. Even though it obtained Rentiers Association support, it could not win over the HGSSV. Memories of Heinze's actions in 1923 and the DVP's close identification with the hated Luther and with big business left most creditors unconvinced that their friends within the party had really succeeded in changing its policies. And the party set itself up for charges of demagoguery when it had to back away from its campaign promises in 1925. Meanwhile, unrealistic DVP promises and assertions further strengthened creditor faith in the feasibility of large-scale revaluation.[39]

The Völkisch obtained approval from the HGSSV but not the Rentiers

Association. The Nazi ideologue Gottfried Feder, the party's revaluation spokesman, had initially proposed a social revaluation of public and private debts.[40] Yet as soon as the HGSSV made its demands, the Völkisch embraced the Best draft and promised 100 percent revaluation.[41] It also placed an HGSSV leader, Paul Seiffert, in a safe Reichstag seat. The Nazis were nothing if not flexible in making extravagant promises to any and all groups. The revaluation was no exception.

The HGSSV also endorsed the Center party (as had the Rentiers Association), despite the party's lukewarm attitude toward revaluation. The party and Marx did concede the need to revise the Tax Decree. Yet Marx bluntly rejected "demagogically phrased claims" that a large revaluation was possible. The official party position was hardly more encouraging; it proposed revising the decree on the basis of justice *unless* the economic existence of private debtors or the state was threatened. Specifically, it called for "recognition" of government bonds (but no immediate revaluation), social revaluation for needy government-bond holders, a 25 to 37.5 percent private-debt revaluation, including some retroactive revaluation, and more revaluation for municipal bonds than for other government bonds. The Center responded to the HGSSV questions by referring the group's leaders to its official revaluation policy.[42]

The Center's relative moderation on revaluation presumably derived from its role as the quintessential government party in the Weimar system. Because it participated so often in governments, its leaders realized they would be responsible for whatever promises they made. And its ideology and broad constituency made it aware of the need to reconcile conflicting interests.

The HGSSV apparently endorsed the Center because the party agreed to place a creditor representative on the Center party Reichstag list.[43] The Center had promised less than the DVP, and its leader emphasized the limits on revaluation. Yet creditor leaders seemed to imagine they had won the Center over to large-scale revaluation—or that their representative could do so by moral suasion once he was in the Reichstag.

All three parties that received a HGSSV endorsement placed a creditor leader in the Reichstag. The symbolic value of this gesture is understandable. But if creditors based their endorsements on it, they showed no little naiveté about one deputy's influence in a delegation. This attitude reflects creditors' idealistic, and unrealistic, view of the political process. And it set the creditors up to feel betrayed when their representatives could not convert the party Reichstag delegations to the creditor position and were not allowed to dictate party revaluation policies.

DNVP support for individual revaluation eroded after the May election. In the summer and fall, a number of DNVP members with ties to debtor groups rejected any increase in revaluation.[44] More significant, the prorevaluation party chairman, Hergt, had come to believe that the Best draft was economically infeasible. Best and creditor leaders apparently knew of this development.[45]

Yet despite Hergt's change of heart, in early November the party and Hergt answered the HGSSV questions affirmatively, adding, "The German National People's Party will also continue to exert itself, under full consideration of the extremely valuable Best draft, to reestablish and reactivate, insofar as economic conditions permit, those rights that the Third Emergency Tax Decree eliminated." The party also affirmed its commitment to interest payments on government bonds according to the ability of the debtor (Reich, Land, or municipality) to pay, and it offered a safe Reichstag seat to Dr. Best, leader of the creditor forces and author of the draft bill it had promised to support.[46]

Although the DNVP had subtly qualified its support of the Best draft, the sum of its pronouncements grossly misled creditors. Creditors continued to talk as though Hergt had promised 100 percent revaluation, and he made no effort to correct their misapprehension.[47] Most important, however, the party characterized the Best draft as "extremely valuable"[48] and accepted Best as one of its candidates, an action it touted as "indeed a sure proof that we are prepared, in common effort with him, to reestablish justice and equity."[49] A large percentage of DNVP candidates came out "expressly for the Best draft" and all for a "just revaluation."[50] As one HGSSV local later wrote, "In similar fashion, Graf Westarp and other representatives of your party . . . have *promised revaluation according to equity and good faith*, thus according to the essential characteristics, well-known to all creditors, of the Best draft." As newspaper articles and creditor letters and petitions show, DNVP statements convinced the overwhelming majority of Germans that the party had committed itself to substituting the Best draft for the Tax Decree revaluation provisions. In mid-November, therefore, the HGSSV endorsed the DNVP as a party that had given "binding assurances" in answer to the group's demands.[51]

The DNVP cannot escape the creditor accusation that it deliberately, demagogically, misled voters, especially since it made no effort to correct the obvious misapprehension among creditors as to its real intentions. The way the party made revaluation policy subsequently led some of its own members to characterize its promises as "fraud" and to say the party had handled the issue "not objectively but demagogically." Even Hergt later admitted the party had created the impression that more would result for the creditors than it could actually offer.[52] The DNVP was not alone in making elastic promises, but its were the most elastic.

Yet the responsibility for whatever demagoguery occurred did not lie with revaluation supporters. To all appearances, revaluation supporters in the DNVP (except Hergt) and other parties were generally sincere, believing into 1925 or later that some individual revaluation was possible. They may have been economically naive, but not hypocritical.

Rather, responsibility lay predominantly with the debtor and other anti-revaluation forces. Fully believing that the Best draft was infeasible, the antirevaluation forces in the DVP and the DNVP, and Hergt, allowed their parties to make unfulfillable commitments.[53] The prodebtor DNVP Reichstag Deputy Praetorius von Richthofen did speak out forcefully against revaluation in 1924, but he complained that delegation members attacked and then ignored him.[54] Most antirevaluation DNVPers and DVPers ignored an issue they could hope the Tax Decree had settled definitively; they were unwilling to spark intraparty battles by challenging party revaluation supporters too strongly on an issue that meant so much to the latter; and they hesitated to speak out against revaluation when speaking out could cost the party votes. They acted demagogically, tacitly or explicitly supporting extravagant campaign promises that they would fight to keep from being implemented.

Evaluating the actions of those who switched from supporting revaluation in 1924 to opposing it in 1925 is more difficult. Many in each party who were neither particularly creditors nor debtors supported revaluation in 1924 because it seemed equitable and because no one was raising forcefully enough its economic disadvantages. Revaluation was so complex people could differ sincerely on its viability, making it tempting to accept the procreditor economic theory that justified doing the apparently equitable—and politically advantageous—thing. Yet if a political system is to survive, its leaders must learn not to make promises they will inevitably have to break. The DNVP, and to a lesser extent the DVP, made irresponsible promises, and to some extent those who let themselves be lulled into supporting revaluation in 1924 share responsibility for that demagoguery.

The DNVP's actions reflected its political legacy. Political parties in the Empire had found extravagant campaign promises relatively easy to make because they would never hold governmental power and the responsibility for implementing their promises.[55] And the DNVP, created in 1918, had not yet held office in the Weimar Republic, sparing it the burdens of responsibility. Yet it was already the biggest party and had every hope of obtaining office in the near future. It had not, however, learned how to act in the shadow of that responsibility.

Although the DNVP's demagoguery would come to haunt it, the election seemed to confirm its tactics. The radical parties of right and left (Völkisch and KPD) lost the most, 35 seats between them. The big winners were the SPD and the DNVP. The SPD increased its vote from 20.5 percent in May to 26 percent in December. Despite the bitter conflict within the DNVP over the Dawes vote in August, the DNVP not only held its own but added seven seats, bringing it to 103 and making it the largest bourgeois party. The DNVP's revaluation strategy played a major role in this success, as the party increased its share of the creditor vote over May. The Center, DVP, and DDP made only slight gains. The splinter parties dropped from 8.3 to 7.8 percent, but they remained a political force.[56]

The DNVP's successes and the DVP's unwillingness to form a coalition with the SPD meant that the next government would be right-of-center. The new government would have to revise the policies established during the stabilization and make them permanent in new legislation. The right-of-center Reichstag majority and government would maintain the stabilization predominantly according to the desires of industry and agriculture and at the expense of public and private employees, consumers, and creditors.

The improvement in the economy had not reversed the dissolution of the traditional party system that had begun under the impact of stabilization. Many voters obviously remained unreconciled to the Republic and its policies. The KPD retained 9 percent of the vote and would continue to attack the SPD from the left. The middle-of-the-road, democratic parties were in serious trouble. They had increased their vote only slightly, while the DNVP had attracted more voters and the Völkisch and the splinter parties had survived.[57]

A year after the Reichsgericht decision, politicians had still not confronted the creditors with the realities of the situation, with the necessity of reconciling the creditors' claim to equity with the pressing need for economic recovery. Perhaps politicians could never have convinced the majority of creditors of those realities. But the election campaigns of 1924 had seduced politicians into doing the opposite, into strengthening the creditor belief that full revaluation was feasible. The parties had committed themselves to the impossible. They could only settle the revaluation by betraying their promises.

The Debtor Viewpoint Predominates

The State Apparatus Closes Ranks

In late November judicial assertiveness threatened to hamstring the German economy again. The government had in May amended the Tax Decree's Paragraph 3 to prevent judges from using a technicality to introduce individual revaluation of mortgages. Unfortunately it used a mere implementation decree to do so. The Kammergericht (the second highest court in Germany) quite properly invalidated the amending provision because it was actually new legislation. The Kammergericht ruling effectively reintroduced individual mortgage revaluation.[1]

To guarantee its stabilization program against judicial interference, the cabinet repromulgated *all* its stabilization and implementation decrees as an emergency presidential decree (under Article 48 of the Constitution). The new decree was explicitly temporary, until the Reichstag could pass regular legislation. President Ebert signed it on 4 December, but at his insistence the government did not publish it until two days after the 7 December election.[2] The Bavarian Supreme Court soon declared the decree valid because it was necessary to avoid economic chaos.[3]

Ebert's good political senśe in delaying the decree's publication could not obviate its significance. The courts revealed once again their potential power to influence policy, even though the Bavarian court had given the government a breathing space. The government's willingness to resort to decree reflected the administrative tradition of the German state and many ministers' qualified commitment to democracy. It was one of the sorry precedents for presidential dictatorship after 1929. Most important in the short term, creditors believed the government was once again arbitrarily and unfairly denying them their judicially sanctioned rights.

Although negotiations on forming a new cabinet became stymied, the caretaker government asked the Länder governments in January about their attitudes toward revaluation reform. Länder officials suggested mortgage-revaluation rates ranging from the existing 15 percent to individual revaluation. Virtually all Länder officials, however, favored a relatively modest 20 to 25 percent mortgage revaluation. The Länder generally agreed the banks lacked sufficient assets to revalue demand deposits. Nonetheless, some Länder did argue that term accounts at banks were just like savings-bank accounts and hence deserved a similar revaluation. Only the government and the Prussian Finance Ministry objected when the Prussian justice minister proposed a general retroactive revaluation. The government also opposed some Länder officials' desire for increased industrial-obligation revaluation.[4]

Because Länder finance ministries were directly responsible for the state's fiscal needs, they were most sensitive to revaluation's potential difficulties and most opposed to it. The Prussian Finance Ministry was most vocal, with ministry officials in January 1925 denouncing proposals to increase revaluation because of "the credit and monetary interests of the Prussian state and of the Reich" and "state-political, national economic, state-fiscal reasons."[5] Alfred Dehlinger (Württemberg, nonparty) did want to allow increased government-bond revaluation once Germany's economic situation had improved. But, he commented, his proposal to delay setting a GM value on government bonds "had been rejected out of hand by everyone" at a conference of Länder finance ministers.[6]

Other Länder ministers, however, also recognized the issue's economic and fiscal implications for the Länder. The Württemberg interior minister, for example, conceded that the municipalities' need for new credit made low revaluation a necessity so they would seem able to repay new loans. Some Länder were debtors, and all Länder revenue came out of a pool shared with the Reich and the municipalities. The Länder hence had a community of interest with the Reich and the municipalities in a low, uncomplicated revaluation that would least burden the common revenue pool. And the Länder had already recognized this in August 1924.[7] Members of the governmental apparatus had their own interest in revaluation, an interest in simplifying administration and revenue assessment, guaranteeing collection of all taxes, and limiting avoidable budget items.

Hence the Länder favored relatively moderate changes in revaluation.

Debtor and banking groups had not yet launched their concerted attack on revaluation reform, but Länder governments—from conservatives to socialists—were leaning strongly toward the debtor view. The Länder felt compelled to make some concessions to equity, and they did pressure the government to increase revaluation in several ways. Yet on the whole, interest as debtor and as state in limiting revaluation prevailed over the political pressure and moral suasion creditors could bring to bear.

The municipalities—most of whom owed considerable PM debt—vehemently opposed revaluation. They feared not only that the Reichstag might revalue their bonds, but that it might require them, as guarantors of the savings banks, to contribute toward savings-account revaluation. They bent every effort toward limiting as much as possible all types of revaluation, but especially those directly affecting them.

The cities and the German Association of Cities (*Deutscher Städtetag*) strove to decrease the cities' obligations at creditor expense. The association pressured cities that wanted to revalue not to do so, to avoid setting any precedents.[8] From early 1923 cities also began quietly buying up their bonds at a low real rate, to reduce their potential revaluation burden. The association struggled to hold the cities to a common GM purchase rate (*not* to be acknowledged as a revaluation) of 5 to 6 percent of face value, to keep one city from "overbidding" the others. And despite pressure from numerous city assemblies for higher purchase rates or increased revaluation, the association was sufficiently well-organized to hold its members in line.[9]

The cities also worked diligently to limit the statutory revaluation. In December 1923 cities demanded a ban on municipal-bond revaluation, citing their fiscal weakness. When the Tax Decree provided for the possible revaluation of municipal bonds issued to finance "income-earning" enterprises, the cities and their association successfully dissuaded the Reich justice minister from implementing the provision. They constantly emphasized their own weak financial position and their involvement (through the revenue allocation) in the general, reparations-induced poverty of the German state. Subsequently, the cities association opposed increased revaluation in general, arguing it must represent the "standpoint of general fiscal and tax economics" against the creditors' demands.[10]

The municipalities also recognized clearly their interest *as municipalities* and as debtors in limiting revaluation as much as possible, an interest separate from that of the taxpayers who would ultimately foot the bill. Like the Länder finance ministers, municipal authorities wanted to avoid the effort and potential trouble of dealing with a fiscal conundrum such as revaluation. The cities association privately rejected revaluation as "not in the general interest of the cities."[11] And the Executive Committee of the Westphalian Association of Cities asserted that "A high revaluation . . . is in general not in the interests of the cities. . . . It is very ill-advised [*bedenklich*] that the Land governments should obtain such extraordinarily far-reaching competence, in whose exercise they will most probably allow themselves to be led to a much greater extent by the well-being and favor [*Wohlwollen*] of the savings-bank creditors than by the fiscal interests of the municipalities."[12]

The impact of the interests of the various governments as governments on the revaluation's development is difficult to measure. Absent the 28 November decision, the central government almost undoubtedly would have banned private-debt revaluation, if only de facto; it and the other governments would presumably also have refused to revalue their bonds, claiming the war and the Versailles Treaty had impoverished them. Once the Reichsgericht introduced debt revaluation, the governments were unable to prevent its implementation. Nonetheless, they maintained the initiative on the issue, set the terms for parliamentary debate, and were responsible for implementing the revaluation laws. They could and did use their powers to limit revaluation's scope.

When partisan conflict stalemated negotiations on forming a cabinet, Ebert asked Luther, as a "nonpartisan neutral expert," to form a government. Luther devised a system whereby the parties "standing behind" the government (DNVP, DVP, BVP, Z, and later WP) sent "trustees [*Vertrauensmänner*]" to fill some cabinet posts, while he filled the rest with nonpartisan specialists. The Reichstag accepted this system, and Luther became chancellor on 15 January 1925.

This arrangement accorded well with Luther's faith in administration and his mistrust of politics. It reflected the imperial tradition of government as administration—of the possibility of nonpartisan rule. And it seemed an attempt to recreate the nonparliamentary—nondemocratic—ministerial governments of Germany's prewar monarchy. While Luther was emboldened to install the antirevaluation civil servant Otto von Schlieben as finance minister, the parties cultivated the illusion they could disavow any unpopular cabinet action by saying that the government was responsible, not themselves—just as they had before 1918.[13]

Luther and other government officials moved to seize the initiative on revaluation. Realizing they could not prevent revaluation reform, they still sought to "find an expedient bearable for government finances and the economy."[14] And by preparing its own draft legislation, the government set the terms of the debate and put the creditor movement on the defensive.

The government's relative monopoly on expertise increased its ability to maintain the initiative. Best drafted his own bill, and some deputies threatened a Reichstag vote on it in place of government proposals. Yet even Emminger, who favored substantially more revaluation, said one had to work from the government drafts because only the government had the information to legislate competently.[15]

Revaluation Opponents Speak Up

Despite having flirted with revaluation in the confusion of early 1924, businessmen subsequently found it difficult to recognize the issue's potential seriousness. As a one-time problem, it was not part of their mental agenda of vital questions.[16] Further, PM investments seemed to them merely an unwise speculation. As one industrialist later wrote, "These people [PM creditors] speculated on the preservation of the body politic as a guarantee of the mark. . . . Their state succumbed in the revolution. It may sound harsh and severe, but it remains true that they suffered a not entirely undeserved fate when the loss arose."[17] Given this attitude and the impossibility of reversing ten years of economic change at the stroke of a pen, businessmen saw promises of substantial revaluation as utopian nonsense.

Nonetheless, the "extravagantly prorevaluation attitude [*Aufwertungs-freudigkeit*]" of the courts terrified debtors (and government officials), leaving them panic-stricken at the prospect of court decisions on important revaluation issues.[18] To all appearances, most judges (if not the Reichsgericht) remained committed to individual or large-scale revaluation.[19] Yet they had neither the training nor the inclination to consider the economic implications of their decisions. As one industrialist wrote, "Surrendering this question [revaluation] to the courts means, therefore, the unlimited victory of the law and the exclusion of economic counterarguments." He predicted that the result would be a 70 to 80 percent average (and often 100 percent) mortgage revaluation.[20] The bankers association complained that debtors faced a "tendentious jurisprudence . . . that, wherever scope for interpretation exists, would come to an interpretation in the sense of revaluation."[21]

Given these fears and the events of December 1924, debtors suddenly began vigorously to defend their interests. The DNVP had committed itself to the Best draft. It had quickly introduced a bill to revoke the 4 December presidential decree, which would have reintroduced individual revaluation of mortgages. And, under pressure from the parties, the government was clearly going to have to amend the Tax Decree revaluation. The National Association of German Industry hence asked the government to show any amendments to the relatively proproducer Reich Economic Council before showing them to the Reichsrat and Reichstag. More important, it asked Economics Minister Albert Neuhaus (DNVP) to meet with the central associations of the various (producer/debtor) economic interest groups to discuss revaluation because of its "special significance" for the economy. The Central Association of German Banks and Bankers and the Central Association of German Wholesalers seconded this request.[22]

Neuhaus accepted these proposals, as well he might, given the government's need for support for its antirevaluation policy. He met on 28 January with spokesmen for the industrialists, wholesalers, bankers, retailers, artisans, agriculture, the Berlin Chamber of Commerce, the Justice, Finance, Agriculture, and Labor ministries, and the Reichsbank.[23] The groups that sent spokesmen represented the producer side of the economy—and they all had potentially revaluable debts. Neuhaus did not invite the creditors. The meeting produced a resolution that, at the groups' request, Neuhaus sent to the Reichstag Revaluation Committee.[24]

In the resolution the associations ignored the moral issues and instead "set forth the demand that this subject be handled exclusively from the standpoint of the interests of the economy as a whole and of the populace as a whole." They insisted that any increase in revaluation would endanger the currency and the GM balances (the bases of Germany's credit). The associations especially opposed any general retroactive revaluation as creating confusion and disorder. A final regulation was absolutely necessary to provide certainty: "It is the conviction of the associations represented that in such a regulation one must under all circumstances hold firmly to the fundamental principles of the Third Emergency Tax Decree."[25]

Debtors were equating the nation's economic well-being with their own (short-term) prosperity, and government officials clearly accepted this view. It was the economic orthodoxy of the day. Debtor interest groups hence had no need to manipulate the government on their behalf. Government officials themselves tried to recruit the interest groups as allies in the campaign against revaluation.[26]

Industry lobbied vigorously, and virtually unanimously, against revaluation. Its central trade associations publicly denounced as dangerous all plans to increase revaluation; they successfully urged their member groups and members to lobby the politicians and officials close to them.[27] The groups also used their members who were in political parties or the Reichstag to influence the parties and delegations to resist increased revaluation.[28] Local Chambers of Commerce and regional industrial groups pressured Länder governments.[29]

Industry had a special champion in the Economics Ministry. Ministry civil servants accepted unquestioningly the industrialists' version of the producer orthodoxy. They believed their task was to represent the economic viewpoint as over against that of equity. They hence opposed any greater increase in revaluation—especially of industrial obligations—than was absolutely necessary from a political standpoint.[30] At the behest of ex-Economics Minister Hamm, a Bavarian industrialist, they solicited and presented to the Reichstag data from selected, unprofitable companies to counter the creditors' argument that industry could afford industrial-obligation revaluation (because, as Hamm told them, it would look better if the government, not industry, made this argument).[31]

Agriculture was divided over revaluation because some farmers were net PM debtors, some creditors. Agriculturists generally opposed increased mortgage revaluation and retroactive revaluation, arguing they were too impoverished to finance additional burdens. But many of them owned government bonds and mortgage bonds, and some had even mortgaged their farms to buy war bonds.[32] These agrarian creditors had an interest in having their assets revalued *in the same degree* (whether 15 percent, 25 percent, or 0 percent) as the mortgages for which they were debtors. Only after three months of apparently heated debate could the Reichslandbund, the largest agricultural group, establish a common policy, demanding that the Reichstag limit mortgage revaluation to 15 percent, offer government-bond revaluation at the mortgage-revaluation rate, and provide tax and tariff breaks for agriculture.[33]

On balance, though, agricultural lobbying worked against revaluation. Agriculture used its ties with Reich and Prussian Agriculture Ministry officials to promote its revaluation policies.[34] Its spokesmen influenced deputies close to them to oppose individual or increased mortgage revaluation. This contributed to the swing of the parties, especially the DNVP, away from their earlier procreditor positions.[35] Agriculturists were, however, extremely upset with industry for not supporting their demand for some government-bond revaluation and angry that industrial-obligation revaluation was less complete than mortgage revaluation (because they felt industry was better able to pay).[36]

The Reichsbank proved a firm and powerful opponent of increased revaluation. Its president, Hjalmar Schacht, and other representatives expounded in several forums the standard bankers' arguments against monetary experimentation. As the putative expert on money, Schacht emphasized continually the danger revaluation posed to the economy and the currency, especially the danger that it would spark a new inflation.[37]

The bankers association lobbied diligently against increased revaluation. Its representatives attended the 28 January meeting, and it petitioned central government officials.[38] Its regional associations wrote to Länder officials, and all the south German states said they were under great pressure from the banks.[39] The banking committee of the German Chamber of Industry and Commerce emphasized to its members that "everyone must, insofar as it is at all possible for him, work on the influential [*massgeblichen*] individuals and convince them of the impossibility of any such revaluation." The association especially opposed judicial and political efforts to introduce bank-account revaluation.[40]

The commercial banks' lobbying was particularly effective because they were nearly indispensable for channelling new credit—foreign and domestic—to industry and the state. This role and the banks' relative wealth assured them of access to and influence on politicians and officials.[41] All the Länder except Bavaria would oppose bank-account revaluation. The Reich Finance Ministry rejected bank-account revaluation because it "would need the good will of the banks for future financial transactions."[42] The bankers did not have veto power (e.g., the government maintained the distinction between old and new holders of government bonds over their vehement objections), but their demands carried tremendous weight.

The mortgage banks petitioned the Reich Economics Ministry and Reich Economic Council, but the Länder felt the brunt of their pressure, with the mortgage bank association and individual banks sending memos and petitions pleading their case for limited and easily administrable revaluation. Generally successful in defending their interests, they emphasized their (nearly) indispensable role in providing credit for agriculture, small business, and municipalities: "[T]he public has an interest in the preservation of the mortgage banks . . . and those claims of the [PM] mortgage-bond holders must find in this interest their limit."[43]

The savings banks continued to lobby for changes that would substantially increase the funds available for savings-deposit revaluation. Yet they also apparently came to an arrangement with the Association of German Cities not to press for too great an increase in municipal-bond revaluation.[44] Savings banks often held municipal bonds, but city officials usually dominated their boards of directors. Some officials even recognized the conflict between their creditor interest as savings-bank officials and their debtor interest as city officials concerned to limit bond revaluation. The banks, though, opted to moderate their demands for municipal-bond revaluation, at the expense of their depositors.[45]

The building owners opposed retroactive revaluation bitterly; beyond that they split. Their central association accepted as unavoidable the relatively modest revaluation increases the government proposed. Some local associations, however, would only accept any increases in revaluation as part of a package involving an end to rent control.[46]

Because many small businessmen were net debtors, the national level associations of both retailers and artisans joined industry in opposing revaluation. As one artisan newspaper asserted in rejecting increased revaluation, "The artisans are well aware that the interests of the whole must stand above those of the individual and that these interests of the whole demand ultimately a final stabilization of the whole economy and in addition no endangering of our currency."[47] Some individual artisans and local groups favored substantial revaluation—but always based on the needs of elderly artisans.[48] Artisans and retailers active in economic organizations seemed generally aware that revaluation could be detrimental to their immediate economic interests.

The various unions feared revaluation would harm their members. The Christian trade unions continued to oppose revaluation, fearing that its cost would fall on the masses in the form of higher prices, rents, and taxes. They promoted this position in petitions to government officials and in articles in the Catholic labor-movement press and presumably brought pressure to bear on the Center party through union officials in its Reichstag delegation. The liberal unions opposed increased revaluation for the same reason, although they advocated a social revaluation if the Reichstag introduced any changes.[49] The free unions, which were close to the SPD, generally ignored revaluation but later condemned the revaluation laws as a special benefit to capitalists whose costs would be shifted to the masses. The possibility of a large revaluation apparently never worried the free unions sufficiently to divert their attention from other issues.[50]

Although the newspapers of the organized white-collar workers and civil servants often printed prorevaluation material, none ever officially took a prorevaluation position. The German Civil Servants Federation (*Deutscher Beamtenbund*), for example, said it would take a position after studying the draft revaluation laws—but never did. After the Revaluation Law's enactment it merely commented that the law was "inadequate."

Indeed, white-collar groups with ties to the Christian unions eventually opposed revaluation, as did the *Deutsche Handlungsgehilfe Verband* (shop clerks).[51]

These employee groups probably had mixed motives. They presumably hesitated to antagonize any debtors in their ranks by promoting revaluation, even though most members were likely to have been at least small PM creditors. They also concentrated on issues such as taxation that concerned all their members. Perhaps most important, the leaders of these groups probably shared the orthodox view that revaluation was not in the best interest of the German economy or German consumers.

After over a year of having the best of the argument, creditors suddenly faced a solid phalanx of public opposition. Significantly, the employee groups that represented millions of nominal PM creditors were showing themselves indifferent or even opposed to increased revaluation just when debtor-group protests were beginning to impress politicians and other noncreditors. And the DNVP's and DVP's close ties to many debtor groups prompted speculation about the future of revaluation reform.

The Creditors Lose Faith

Creditors had felt a cautious but real optimism in December 1924 and early January 1925. They had obtained significant concessions from the bourgeois parties, and their leader, Best, had entered parliament. Luther's days as finance minister appeared numbered. And the major bourgeois parties had introduced resolutions demanding that the government amend the Tax Decree revaluation.[52]

The first blow to this optimism, in mid-January, was the selection of Luther as chancellor, a step one creditor newspaper characterized as "a slap in the face of the German saver."[53] The mere willingness of the DNVP and other parties to negotiate with Luther produced anger and acrimony. Despite DNVP efforts to reassure creditors that they had nothing to worry about, creditors were outraged. They railed bitterly about Luther's promotion.[54]

This choice demonstrated vividly the limits to the bourgeois parties' willingness to cater to creditor demands. Revaluation was a one-time issue, of overriding importance to only a minority of the population. If Luther alone could form a government to handle appropriately more "important" issues such as taxes, tariffs, and foreign affairs, then they would make Luther chancellor. Their decision implied insensitivity to creditor feelings and a degree of contempt for creditor political influence. No one could doubt where Luther stood: he would never accept any individual revaluation or any major increase in the rate. Whatever the parties might tell creditors—or themselves—Luther's appointment was the death knell for the creditors' more optimistic hopes.

Shortly thereafter came striking evidence of ambivalence toward revaluation within the DNVP and other government parties. In mid-December the DNVP had introduced a bill that would revoke the 4 December decree, thereby reestablishing individual revaluation of mortgages. Once a bourgeois government took office, Keil suddenly demanded immediate passage of the DNVP bill, something the government could not allow and the government parties, including the DNVP, did not want. The Revaluation Committee therefore tabled the original DNVP proposal, with even the DNVP's assent. Instead, on 28 January, the committee voted to revoke the 4 December decree but to postpone all revaluation cases until the Reichstag passed a new revaluation law. The creditors were already upset because neither the DNVP nor any other party had actually introduced a new revaluation draft. This development only aggravated their suspicions.[55]

In early January a scandal involving government officials and politicians with the speculator Julius Barmat became public knowledge. Barmat had arranged food shipments from neutral countries to Germany during the chaotic days after the Armistice. He later exploited the contacts he had gained among government officials to obtain the use of government funds for various speculations. When his finances collapsed after the inflation, much of those government funds were lost, and he was eventually indicted.

This whole sorry spectacle called into question the integrity of the political system, especially in the eyes of creditors. They complained that the Weimar Republic could find money for venal speculators, but none for honest creditors.[56]

Their bitterness was heightened in late January when the public and the Reichstag learned that Luther had secretly disbursed 715 million RM to compensate industry, especially heavy industry, for losses from the French occupation. He had accepted without question industry's own estimates of its losses, giving neither the people nor the Reichstag an opportunity to weigh industry's claims against those of other groups. A popular uproar developed as people became aware of the magnitude of this so-called Ruhr compensation and of the underhanded way in which rich industrialists had obtained massive payments for themselves while the government abandoned the less affluent to poverty and misery. Over the next several months the daily press, politicians, and common citizens attacked the government's favoritism toward the propertied. Creditors felt particularly ill-used because Luther had been telling the Revaluation Committee that no money was available for government-bond revaluation just when he was preparing to give 700 million to industry.[57]

The final blow to creditor illusions was the apparent collusion between government officials and private debtors. In early January, Finance Ministry officials met with bank officials to discuss bank-account revaluation and the proposal to distinguish between old and new holders of government bonds.[58] More important was DNVP Economics Minister Neuhaus's 28 January meeting with economic interest groups, which made front-page news. The creditors panicked. They rightly saw the groups' unanimous rejection of any larger revaluation as a dangerous and powerful threat to their hopes for recovering their lost savings.

As significant as these developments might have been individually, the timing of their appearance on the public scene made them devastating. Each of these major attacks on creditor sensibilities—the Barmat scandal, the Ruhr compensation, DNVP waffling on the 4 December decree, and Neuhaus's meeting with debtor representatives—was a major news story on 28 and 29 January 1925. The last two became public knowledge on 28 January. If Luther's appointment had been a slap in the face, this aggregation of shocks was a hammer blow. Debtors, the government, and the parties seemed suddenly to be conspiring against the creditors and to the benefit of speculators and big capital.

The creditors counterattacked, calling into question the objectivity and motives of the economic organizations. They identified the organizations as "self-chosen groups of debtors, inflation profiteers, and grafters," as "representatives of international capital" who were destroying Germany. They accused the groups of using specious economic arguments as a screen behind which to hide their personal interests.[59] Their tendency to personalize issues led them to accuse Schacht and Luther of being in league with these pernicious speculators.[60]

Despite the traditional anti-Semitism of many Germans and their association of Jews with financial manipulation, creditors expressed little explicit anti-Semitism. A few anti-Semitic slurs did appear in letters to the chairman of the right-wing DNVP. And creditor references to Barmat (who was Jewish) and attacks on "international big capital" as the cause of the inflation and of the limits on revaluation probably often reflected anti-Semitic attitudes.[61] Nonetheless, whatever anti-Semitism existed among creditors had not yet become overtly political.[62]

This creditor counterattack involved not so much a change in arguments as a dramatic increase in the level of mistrust and a marked radicalization of many creditors. The events of November 1923 had suggested that the government could have stopped the inflation earlier if those in control had had the will. And many creditors were certainly suspicious of big capital. Nonetheless, debtor reticence and party promises of revaluation reform apparently allowed most creditors to believe in 1924 that their enemies were Luther and a few inflation profiteers.[63] The events of January 1925—especially Luther's appointment as chancellor, DNVP waffling on revaluation reform, and Neuhaus's meeting with the trade associations—destroyed such illusions.

The enemy now seemed to be all the big capitalists and the whole political system. The creditors came to see the Weimar Republic as a nefarious conspiracy by big (international) capital to expropriate the creditors and destroy the German economy. The government, they asserted, was merely a tool of the rich. The HGSSV saw the Finance Ministry consultation with bank officials as an attempt by the government to use the specious arguments of so-called experts—really self-interested debtors—to support it against the public interest.[64] At the beginning of February an HGSSV local attacked the major economic interest groups: "They know exactly that their goals are the economic, physical, and spiritual annihilation of the greatest part of the people, now and forever."[65] Another local argued that big business had caused the inflation: "These inflation profiteers believe they can introduce a new, a communist/big capitalist economic method."[66] Yet another local wrote in April to Marx: "The view is pervasive among the people that our current government is only a willing tool of big capital, of big industry."[67] The creditor movement's leader and mentor, Best, accepted this view wholeheartedly, seeing in the government's supposedly objective paper on revaluation "a total capitulation to the demands of big capital." He adopted a virulently anticapitalist stand.[68]

This onslaught against the capitalist system came from more than just the creditor-movement leadership. Starting immediately after the 28 January meeting, before that leadership could have had a determining influence on creditor attitudes, individual creditors and local groups began to write bitterly anticapitalist letters that expressed a corrosive disillusionment with the Weimar Republic.[69]

The anticapitalism of these small capitalists was not surprising. Most Germans had never fully accepted laissez-faire. *Mittelständler* certainly supported the idea of private property as a guarantee of economic security and social status. Yet they did not really believe in free markets and the risk of failure such freedom entailed, especially as those markets became dominated by big businesses that used cartels, protectionist legislation, and other measures to shield themselves from competition. *Mittelständler* hence clung to a sense of limits on competition, of a government responsibility to protect the weak and to support the economic and social position of the "indispensable" *Mittelstand*.[70] In this respect the Weimar Republic—a regime already tainted by its association with revolution, the Versailles Treaty, and reparations—struck the creditors as a dismal failure.

Surprisingly, revaluation supporters claimed creditor disillusionment was inducing many of them to swing to communism. Already in 1924 a few creditors had warned that unless the government dealt fairly with them many would turn to the KPD.[71] Nonetheless, only in 1925 did numerous creditors make extravagant claims about "millions" being "driven into the communist camp."[72]

Yet these claims, like the threats of German peasants before 1918 to "vote red" if their demands were ignored, were basically only an expression of anger and an effort to intimidate the bourgeois parties. Creditors in fact never wrote, "*I* will join the KPD or SPD," but always, "Many creditors will join." The SPD complained of the creditor leaders' "strong antipathy toward the left." One DNVP member expressed his own bitterness at length and claimed to have seen hundreds of fellow creditors join the SPD. But he said only that he was quitting the DNVP, not that he would join one of the left-wing parties. And he had earlier said that he would never vote left.[73]

A substantial creditor vote for the left was indeed scarcely likely and rarely taken seriously. Creditors were overwhelmingly *Mittelstand* in origin and rightist in political ideology. One group even declared proudly, "Racketeers, speculators, and war and postwar profiteers are not accepted into our association. Also no one who is not well-disposed toward the *Mittelstand* and therewith conscientiously patriotic [*vaterländisch*]."[74] Marxist parties could hardly be a home for such people, no matter how disillusioned they became. And an ecological study of voting patterns throughout the Weimar Republic shows consistently negative or insignificant correlations of rentier status with SPD and KPD voting.[75]

And despite their radicalization, creditors were as yet no more ready to embrace the radical right than the radical left. Their anticapitalist, anti-Marxist rhetoric, with its emphasis on German nationalism and the Weimar Republic's "betrayal" of the German people, was very similar to right-wing Völkisch rhetoric. Yet in 1925 creditors seem not to have considered the Völkisch a realistic alternative.[76] After resigning from the DNVP, Best entered the Völkisch Reichstag delegation. But it was reported, "This transfer has solely the goal that he might retain voice and vote in the Revaluation Committee; he [Best] explained that politically he was completely uncommitted [*indifferent*] and thought only of working for the revaluation."[77] One DNVP local leader did mention the Völkisch party as a possibility for disillusioned creditors, but only if it overcame its divisions.[78]

Apparently, then, the Völkisch were not yet a credible force. They were still too divided, too crude, too obstreperous, too exotic for the generally conservative creditors. The latter were quite willing to use the more familiarly anticapitalist left as a club with which to beat the bourgeois parties. Yet the inflation and its aftermath had not driven them directly into the arms of the Nazis. Although some had voted Völkisch in 1924, most were not yet prepared to support the radical right.[79]

Although the extent of creditor radicalization is impossible to prove, the weight of the evidence strongly suggests that already in February 1925 most organized and quite possibly many unorganized creditors had lost faith in the Weimar Republic and the existing capitalist order. They were waiting for someone, anyone, to offer them a credible (non-Marxist) alternative. The parties hence faced a volatile and complicated situation as they sought to come to terms with debtor protests, government intransigence, creditor outrage, and economic realities.

The Parties Reverse Themselves

In the winter of 1925 all but two of the major political parties did an about-face on revaluation. Participation or nonparticipation in government, responsibility for or freedom from responsibility for policy, seemed to determine the position a party would take. The government parties, all of whom but the WP had received some creditor-group endorsement, ended by arguing for relatively limited increases in revaluation. The nongovernment parties, of whom only the Völkisch had received a creditor endorsement, began to support substantial increases in revaluation.

The two parties that maintained essentially consistent positions on revaluation were the Völkisch and the KPD. Neither had any immediate prospect of bearing the responsibilities of office. The Völkisch continued to support Best's proposal for large-scale individual revaluation. Having given the HGSSV's Seiffert a safe seat, they made him their initial revaluation spokesman.[80] When Best quit the DNVP in disgust, the Völkisch welcomed him and made him their spokesman. The party portrayed itself as the creditors' best friend, a portrayal it exploited in the future.[81] The KPD continued to propose a social rent for all needy individuals, including creditors. It also took the offensive against the bourgeois parties, particularly the DNVP. It accused them of demagoguery in their earlier promises and denounced their revaluation compromise as proof of duplicity.[82]

The WP remained in the difficult position of being the avowed representative of small businessmen, mostly debtors, and the *Mittelstand* as a whole, often creditors. The party quickly committed itself to its core constituency, though, and resisted increased revaluation, especially retroactive revaluation. When it acquiesced in the government compromise, which did increase revaluation somewhat, some of its supporters repudiated its policy. It tried to recoup by threatening to withhold its Reichstag votes unless the government granted concessions on other issues. Yet it had to support the government's revaluation proposals to avoid even worse if the Reichstag were left to its own devices. Ultimately, it voted with the government and left all its constituents dissatisfied.[83]

The BVP played a relatively restrained role in the revaluation conflict of 1925. Emminger favored some individual revaluation or norm, but he recognized the need to reconcile equity and economic efficiency. He hence acquiesced grudgingly when his party accepted Luther's adamant rejection of any individual revaluation or norm. The party supported the government's modest compromise revaluation proposals. As late as 27 June, however, Emminger proposed a 40 percent revaluation in individual cases if special circumstances justified it. And in later years he continued to seek ways to improve the revaluation. Clearly, Emminger did not accept the government's proposals as the maximum consistent with reconciling equity and efficiency. He had simply submitted to a party majority.[84]

Center party deputies generally accepted the draft revaluation laws as the optimal solution, given Germany's unfortunate situation. Reichstag Deputy Josef Andre (Z) favored individual revaluation but wrote that an "overwhelming majority" of Center Reichstag deputies felt compelled to reject it as economically unsupportable and as likely to create unacceptable legal uncertainty.[85] They believed, as Franz Ehrhardt (Z) wrote, that "only secure legal conditions make possible growth (*Aufstieg*), which is in the interests of the whole populace"; they did not consider the compromise completely satisfactory but felt that "[i]n spite of everything," the government revaluation drafts meant "an essential step forward." Because of its relatively responsible campaign promises, the party had to make only minor concessions when it supported the revaluation laws. General retroactive mortgage revaluation was, however, an absolute prerequisite for Center support for limiting the revaluation rate.[86]

Not every Center member accepted party policy—and creditors knew it. Some Center politicians and the Catholic church were pressing for individual or at least substantial revaluation. Schetter (Z) commented to the Revaluation Committee that some Center deputies considered 25 percent mortgage revaluation too little, while some thought it too much.[87] Andre wrote two articles in a Christian trade union paper proclaiming his support for individual revaluation, and he broke party discipline to vote against the Revaluation Law.[88] Even more troublesome was Deputy Emil Ross, a creditor leader with a Center seat on the Revaluation Committee; he abstained several times and once embarrassed the government by voting against it in committee. He too voted against the Revaluation Law.[89]

Despite the apparent sincerity of its revaluation spokespersons, the DVP's far-reaching revaluation promises proved more than many of its supporters and Reichstag members could accept. By 1925 (according to the bankers association) many debtors in the DVP felt the party had betrayed them on revaluation and were inclined to withdraw their support, even though they had apparently not challenged party policy in 1924. Party leaders were also having second thoughts. In 1923 Stresemann had supported creditor demands and in 1924 had accepted the party's call for a revaluation norm, even while pointing out that unlimited revaluation was impossible. Yet in 1925 he told three bankers that he agreed with their analysis of revaluation's deleterious economic implications; he was, however, unsure how far he could go with them, recognizing that some increase in mortgage revaluation was politically unavoidable. As he wrote to a DVP member, the party had to strike a "diagonal" on the revaluation "between the just demands of the individual and the need to maintain the financial strength of the state and its economy."[90]

Yet the DVP only slowly brought itself to shift its policy publicly. After a "very exhaustive discussion" of revaluation on 9 March, the party decided to wait until the issue had been settled within the DNVP. The DVP went into the decisive 18 March meeting of government-party and government leaders still proposing a revaluation norm. But when Luther threatened to resign if the parties insisted on a norm, Wunderlich answered, apparently immediately, that if the other parties opposed individual revaluation, the DVP would reconsider.[91]

The DVP's general political complexion and the alacrity with which Wunderlich gave in suggest that by March 1925 there was no firm majority for individual revaluation in the DVP delegation. None of the government parties wanted to expose itself to attack by being the only party, or even the first, to publicly reject a revaluation norm. Each party apparently now had a majority against substantial revaluation but was waiting for the other parties to act before committing itself. Hence Wunderlich's majority for a norm had probably already eroded. Once it came to a conflict with the chancellor, Wunderlich knew he had to yield if the DNVP too abandoned a norm, as it in fact did.

The DVP now struggled to develop a coherent policy. Trapped by past campaign promises and by fear of attack from other parties, the DVP could not repudiate Wunderlich or the creditors' demand for their rights; it worked in the Revaluation Committee for general retroactive mortgage revaluation and some other increases in revaluation. Nonetheless, it generally took its cue from the government and from debtor/producer economic arguments and sought to limit, not expand, revaluation.[92]

In early 1925 the DNVP was still loath to acknowledge its ambivalence about revaluation—perhaps even to itself. Hergt later admitted that he and other party leaders had long known the Best draft was infeasible, claiming they had only supported it and given Best a seat so that the draft could be discussed.[93] Yet in January and February 1925 the new party chairman, Kuno Graf von Westarp, replied to creditor complaints with assurances the party would keep its promises, something he would hardly have done if he had expected to have to break those promises completely.[94] A struggle soon developed within the DNVP between a group around Best and Hergt, who still believed in at least a revaluation norm, and the "agriculturists and other businessmen," who opposed any increase in revaluation.[95] This struggle became increasingly public, and by late February Westarp had to acknowledge to creditors that while the DNVP kept its promises, there were problems.[96]

Nonetheless, change in party policy did not come easily. On 11 and 12 February the DNVP Reichstag delegation held meetings on the revaluation. The economics, agriculture, and finance ministers (each with ties to the DNVP) gave speeches sharply attacking individual revaluation and emphasizing the fiscal and economic objections to large-scale revaluation. The speeches impressed the deputies strongly, but many still favored some increase in private- and public-debt revaluation. After inconclusive discussions the party still could not settle its position on major aspects of revaluation. By early March the prorevaluation Steiniger and a cautiously antirevaluation Westarp were publicly debating party policy over revaluation. And by mid-March Westarp was blaming the party's failure to help creditors on the government, "whose majority is not German-National."[97]

Meanwhile, Best was becoming more and more upset by the delays. He began pushing hard to introduce his draft legislation in the Reichstag, but he lacked the necessary 16 signatures. Indeed, the DNVP initially forced some DNVP deputies who had signed it to withdraw their signatures. Only by threatening to obtain them from the Völkisch could Best on 7 March extort the necessary signatures from the DNVP.[98] The latter informed its coalition partners that it was only allowing the draft's introduction on "party-tactical grounds."[99] And Joel of the Justice Ministry, in close communication with the various parties, informed the cabinet on the very day Best introduced his draft that as a serious option it was "objectively finished . . . and indeed also in the German National People's Party."[100]

The prospect of a presidential election campaign in March forced the DNVP to make up its mind. Fearing a new contest in demagoguery over revaluation, the government and the government parties decided to commit themselves to compromise revaluation legislation before the campaign got underway. The DNVP Reichstag delegation met early on 18 March to set policy for the upcoming government/coalition parties meeting on revaluation. The deputies voted against individual revaluation and, apparently, for Hergt's proposals for a norm. Then, instead of Best, the leadership sent to the meeting Schultz, the delegation chairman, and Oberfohren, a representative of debtor interests. After perfunctory efforts to secure a norm, the two surrendered to the government's insistence on limited, schematic revaluation.[101]

The DNVP suffered a flood of obloquy for this complete reversal of the party's earlier position. It had opened itself to charges of demagoguery, and with electioneering in full swing, the charges flew. The KPD, SPD, and DDP certainly could not resist baiting the party each saw as a dangerous enemy, but even the DNVP's coalition partner, the Center, pointed out the gap between DNVP promise and DNVP practice. And when the compromise revaluation became public, Westarp had to shift ground, eventually asserting the DNVP had never "promised" individual revaluation, but only revaluation "as economically possible." The creditors were not convinced.[102]

Sentiment for substantial revaluation remained strong within the DNVP. Best resigned from the delegation (although not from the Reichstag), but leading party members such as Hergt and Reichstag Deputy Wilhelm Bazille (party chairman and minister-president in Württemberg) remained vocal revaluation supporters.[103] Only three DNVP deputies voted against the Revaluation Law, and Bazille was absent. Nonetheless, both Best and Bazille claimed a number of DNVP deputies preferred individual revaluation, only voting for the Revaluation Law because of party discipline. And local DNVP leaders were "rather upset" about the change in party policy.[104]

The DNVP acted as it did in substantial part because of the economic interests of many of its Reichstag deputation and members. Thirty percent of the party's deputies and most of its money came from industry, and the generally antirevaluation agriculturists were also very important in the party. The party presumably feared weakening this support if it left the government over revaluation. Several party members emphasized the importance of staying in the government, even at creditor expense, to protect the economic interests of the producer groups that supported the party. Westarp also cited foreign policy issues as a reason not to bring the government down over revaluation.[105]

But broader considerations of economic recovery and equity also forced the delegation to reconsider its support for the Best draft. The DNVP was now for the first time in the government and responsible for the hard economic and social consequences of the policies it supported. And Best's draft could have had very deleterious consequences. As a Center party member later wrote, "The revaluation issue brought for the DNVP a further education in objectivity." He quoted Hergt's confession that representatives of the economy had proved statistically that the Best draft meant disaster for the economy and hence for most Germans. As Joel had said in early March, the Best draft was finished within the DNVP on "objective grounds."[106]

If participating in the government provided an incentive to objectivity for the DNVP, exclusion from the government seems to have had the opposite effect on the SPD and DDP. They saw the revaluation as a club with which to beat the government parties, especially the DNVP. Both parties abandoned their earlier preference for modest increases in revaluation and began in 1925 to demand substantial increases.

The SPD's Damascene conversion to support of the Best draft, a 40 percent revaluation norm, and 20 percent government-bond revaluation was not completely convincing.[107] Keil, the party's revaluation spokesman, insisted that he was always objective and sincere on revaluation and that he spoke for the party. Yet he acknowledged that most SPD deputies were indifferent toward the issue. And he ultimately voted against the Best draft, admitting the SPD had never "stood on the basis of the Best draft" but had only wanted it discussed (the same argument the DNVP's Hergt was using to justify his 1924 campaign rhetoric). Further, when the Revaluation Committee voted on Keil's proposal for a substantial government-bond revaluation, his fellow SPD committee members abstained. None-theless, Keil most probably did want a substantially higher revaluation, probably even the 40 percent private-debt revaluation he subsequently promoted.[108]

In fact, SPD efforts to embarrass the DNVP for its betrayal of the creditors led the Social Democrats into policy positions very nearly as demagogic as those the DNVP had once promoted. SPD newspapers attacked DNVP revaluation demagoguery continuously, in articles on re-valuation and in other articles as well. When Keil spoke in the Reichstag on the draft Revaluation Law, he spoke more about DNVP demagoguery than about the validity of creditor demands. And Keil tacitly admitted the SPD's goal when he said that the SPD partly supported the Best draft because it "of course also wanted to establish to what extent equity and good faith still count in the DNVP revaluation policy."[109] The DNVP's revaluation antics had made it a perfect target. Mistrusting the DNVP, believing it an implacable enemy of democracy and the working class, the SPD simply could not ignore the opportunity to attack it, perhaps even to win over some creditor votes.

After being excluded from the governing coalition in 1925, the DDP adopted a somewhat opportunistic revaluation policy. In January and Feb-ruary it pressured the government to introduce a revaluation draft, while avoiding precipitous actions that might damage the economy. Nonetheless, as the presidential campaign picked up, it increased its attacks on the DNVP's revaluation maneuvers and began to imply that it supported large-scale revaluation.[110] In April, May, and June it temporarily supported the Best draft, and a DDP representative on the Revaluation Committee pushed for substantial government-bond revaluation. And the party voted against the revaluation laws.[111]

Like most parties, the DDP was split between supporters and opponents of revaluation. Local DDP party meetings in May 1925 urged the party to work for increased revaluation. In the Reichstag delegation, Hartmann von Richthofen (Hannover) led the revaluation supporters. Theodor Heuss believed von Richthofen was promoting individual revaluation "for tactical reasons," although the latter told Heuss he had "neared" this position for objective reasons. Nonetheless, von Richthofen seemed sincere in pro-posing substantial government-bond revaluation.[112] Dernburg, a former banker, led the opponents and reflected the conviction of the party's Trade and Industry Committee that increasing revaluation would be economi-cally disastrous.[113]

Von Richthofen's efforts to increase revaluation led to a sharp conflict.

Fearing revaluation's economic effects, Dernburg was determined to reverse party policy and occasionally voted with the government in the Revaluation Committee. This fostered considerable ill-feeling. The prorevaluation Dietrich complained, "In the revaluation Herr Dernburg noises all about, ruining again all that Richthofen and I have made good. . . . We run the risk of neglecting the interests of numerous modest and small creditors just to shine up to some industrialists who give their money to right-wing parties anyway."[114]

Anton Erkelenz too reacted angrily to Dernburg's actions, but for quite different reasons. He wrote to party chairman Erich Koch, "Dernburg carries on against [our revaluation proposals] and indeed completely unnecessarily; for the present revaluation compromise of the government parties will be accepted in any case. . . . Yet by the nature of his actions Dernburg destroys all the tactical advantage that we obtained through our attitude in the period January to April."[115] And when Dernburg and Georg Gothein complained about the economic implications of the Best and von Richthofen revaluation proposals, Koch responded only that "[w]e must create a rallying point for those streaming from the right who perceive the absurdity of the policy of the right from the DNVP's broken promises in the revaluation."[116]

Although Dietrich and von Richthofen sincerely favored increasing revaluation, Erkelenz and Koch seemed to see in it predominantly a means to increase the DDP's electoral base. Safe in the knowledge that the government parties would pass only a modest revaluation increase, the DDP could allow some of its members to promote a substantial increase. In the end, the DDP too apparently could not resist the temptation to make political hay from the DNVP's embarrassment—even at the expense of itself seeming to adopt the demagoguery for which it was attacking the right-wing party.

By April 1925 a crucial shift had occurred in the balance of forces on revaluation. The debtor appeal to orthodox economics and the influence of debtor interest groups had had a powerful impact. Despite the parties' continued desire to meet creditor demands as fully as possible, considerations of immediate economic efficiency had clearly won the upper hand, especially with Luther and von Schlieben in charge of government revaluation policy.

David Blackbourn has recently emphasized the importance of the "politics of demagogy" in Imperial and Weimar Germany.[117] Conservative elites had since the 1880s faced a political self-mobilization by *Mittelstand* and working-class Germans no longer content with notable politics. These elites were unwilling to make real concessions but needed mass support. In attempting to harness newly politicized groups, Blackbourn argues, conservatives adopted a demagogic style of politics in which they combined appeals to popular prejudices with extravagant promises of assistance to various voting groups. They could do so under the Empire safe in the knowledge the political system allowed them rhetoric without real political responsibility. DNVP and DVP politicians resumed this practice in Weimar Germany, but they now had the political responsibility for their promises.

The revaluation conflict provides strong support for Blackbourn's argument about the politics of demagogy in the Weimar period. Creditors had mobilized themselves and had rejected elite efforts to convince them of the limits of the economically possible. The conservative parties had sought political advantage by adopting creditors' demands more or less wholesale, despite the very real constraints on Germany's ability to meet those demands. Unfortunately for the conservatives, they now had political responsibility and had to expose their own demagoguery by breaking their promises when they actually made policy. They were, in effect, sorcerer's apprentices.

The shortsightedness or demagoguery of all the parties from the Völkisch to the SPD had created a situation in which the creditors had reason to believe that almost all parties were more or less untrustworthy and that the economic system was stacked against the *Mittelstand* by big-business control of the Weimar Republic. Most Germans perceived the government, and especially Luther, as prodebtor. The government parties' dramatic reversal from more or less procreditor campaign rhetoric to more or less anticreditor draft bills had obviously taken place under considerable debtor pressure. And just when the DVP and DNVP were recognizing the needs of the economy, the DDP and SPD were repudiating their earlier emphasis on economic necessity and touting the virtues of creditor ideology and the demands of equity. Under the circumstances, the Republic faced a herculean task in convincing its citizens that its chosen revaluation policies were actually reconciling equity and economic necessity to a reasonable degree.

Compromise or Betrayal?

A Presidential Election Forces the Pace

Luther was obsessed with economic considerations. For him, Germany's future depended on re-creating economic prosperity through hard work and sacrifice. Production had to take precedence over all else. His public and private comments on revaluation always emphasized its economic aspects. When he did comment on the need for equity, he did so in passing and to all appearances grudgingly. He may well have believed that Germany had to sacrifice the creditors to secure long-term equity for most Germans. But he did not succeed in clearly articulating such a vision. Creditors and many other Germans hence perceived him as at best completely insensitive and at worst a tool of greedy debtors, especially the industrialists with whom he had such close ties and whom his policies favored.[1]

The ministers Luther had chosen generally reflected his antirevaluation attitude. Except for Justice Minister Josef Frenken (Z, a retired judge and civil servant), Luther's colleagues seemed to share his concern with economic efficiency and his indifference to the creditors. The agriculture and interior ministers (von Kanitz and Martin Schiele [DNVP]) had close ties to agriculturists, many of whom were debtors. Economics Minister Neuhaus (DNVP) was clearly sympathetic to industry. And Finance Minister von Schlieben was notoriously antirevaluation. Indeed the latter would publicly express serious misgivings about even the limited concessions the government finally made.[2]

Von Schlieben's Finance Ministry further tarnished the government's image when it prepared an obviously biased white paper on revaluation. The paper dealt solely with revaluation's economic disadvantages. It was so transparent that it merely outraged creditors while impressing no one else. It even annoyed some antirevaluation ministers.[3]

Although other issues dominated the press in February 1925, the parties behind the government found their revaluation policies in increasing disarray. The DNVP was deeply embarrassed when on 6 February it had to vote in the Reichstag against its own bill revoking the 4 December decree. The Reichstag then suspended all revaluation cases pending new legislation. The ensuing uncertainty meant the government would have to introduce some new revaluation legislation fairly expeditiously.[4] Meanwhile, the creditors were loudly demanding relief; procreditor forces within the government parties, especially Best, were vigorously resisting debtor counterattacks; and the left-of-center parties and their newspapers were sniping at the DNVP and other government parties.[5]

The government's initial attempt to prepare revaluation legislation had an air of unreality. Even the politically inexperienced Frenken warned the cabinet that the Reichstag would insist on substantially more revaluation than the government was preparing to offer. Buoyed by support from the Länder and other debtors, however, the cabinet ignored his diffident warnings. By late February it had finally accepted drafts that provided a minor increase in private-debt revaluation, forced the conversion (but not repayment) of all PM government bonds at 5 percent of face value, and offered a modest social revaluation for needy old holders of war bonds. Yet despite its promises of and the need for speedy action, the government did not dare publish its own proposals.[6]

President Ebert died suddenly on 28 February 1925, and the consequent need for an election helped force the government's hand. Hoping to placate creditor voters, the DNVP felt compelled to allow Best to introduce his draft. Seeking to embarrass the DNVP and the government and to attract voters, both the SPD and DDP introduced Reichstag motions to force action on the revaluation. Aided by Völkisch and some Center party votes, they outvoted a right-of-center effort to postpone debate. The Reichstag then passed a DDP motion to demand a revaluation bill immediately and sent to committee a SPD motion revoking the Tax Decree revaluation as of 31 March 1925. The Reichstag enacted the SPD bill on 21 March, with revocation set for 30 June 1925. If the legislature and new president had not approved new revaluation legislation by then, the courts would be free to reintroduce individual revaluation of private debts. The government now had only three months to prepare a revaluation law and to have the Reichstag and Reichsrat debate and enact it.[7]

To forestall a renewed contest in demagoguery, Schiele convinced the cabinet to tie all the government parties to specific draft revaluation legislation. The cabinet and the parties had already been promising a bill for months and had missed several self-imposed deadlines. Their inability to present promised new legislation had cast doubt on their sincerity. The SPD and DDP bills were clearly only the first steps in a campaign to embarrass the right-of-center parties for their past demagoguery and their present temporizing. And despite pressure from debtor forces and ministerial responsibilities to keep revaluation in check, the parties felt compelled to mollify creditors and their own local party groups. Unless the government acted, the dynamics of a political campaign could well induce a new round of extravagant promises.[8]

On 16 March the cabinet finally admitted that some meaningful increase in revaluation was inevitable. It decided to leave the revaluation rate at 15 percent but to offer a supplemental revaluation of 10 percent for *mündelsicher* mortgages only. It also offered a limited and much smaller retroactive revaluation of *mündelsicher* mortgages, and some taxes on industry in lieu of increased industrial-obligation revaluation. Apparently against von Schlieben's bitter resistance, it also decided to provide 80 million RM toward amortization and interest for old holders of war bonds.[9]

At an 18 March meeting, the cabinet seemed to succeed in tying the government parties to its drafts. The parties' initial proposals were unacceptable to the government. Luther particularly, and vehemently, attacked the DVP's call for a revaluation norm as "the suicide of the German people"; he declared he would resign if the parties implemented such a policy. Faced with this threat, the parties agreed to abandon a norm. Georg Schultz (DNVP) insisted, however, that the government declare individual revaluation or a norm to be unsupportable, and Luther did so. The DNVP leadership could now say that it had supported Best's draft "insofar as it is economically possible," but that the government had said that it was economically impossible. Although the parties firmly resisted committing themselves to a final decision on government-bond amortization, Luther convinced them to accept a statement acknowledging the need for "a substantial differentiation" between public- and private-debt revaluation rates.[10] The cabinet breathed a figurative sigh of relief.

Yet even before the government could publish its drafts, victory seemed to slip from its grasp. Several DNVP leaders clearly believed they retained the right to introduce substantive amendments. Luther, however, was determined to resign if the parties introduced such amendments without cabinet approval. Although the DNVP insisted on its right to propose amendments, the party did agree on 22 March to consult with the government before introducing any new proposals—to prevent a "competition" among the government parties over revaluation promises. And government-party leaders agreed on 2 April to refrain from discussing or proposing amendments to the government drafts until after the Reichsrat had passed them. At that time they would consult with the government on a common basis for finally settling the revaluation.[11]

The government parties just wanted to publish *some* draft legislation before the election, to show good faith, while excluding revaluation from the presidential campaign as much as possible by mutually muzzling each other. Their 18 March agreement with the cabinet had been a tactical maneuver, a truce for the duration of the election campaign. It was not a viable compromise.

Creditor mistrust of the right's first-round presidential candidate, Jarres, may have contributed to the decision to switch to Field Marshal Paul von Hindenburg as the right's second-round candidate. Creditor groups urged their members to abstain in the first round, a suggestion that Jarres believed cost him votes. At least one HGSSV local specifically urged its members to vote against Jarres because of his antirevaluation bias. Immediately after the first round, at least one creditor group announced that neither Marx (the center-left candidate) nor Jarres deserved creditor support.[12]

Especially in southern Germany, creditor groups often told their members to vote for Hindenburg over Marx. They blamed Marx for the Tax Decree and repeated the rumor, probably unfounded, that he had derided "stupid saver types." However, the revaluation issue probably just reinforced for most creditors their inclination to vote for Hindenburg, who was after all the choice of most elderly, middle-class, conservative voters.[13]

Although the presidency was largely ceremonial, the electoral victory of the highly respected Hindenburg brought creditors new hope. They assumed he would refuse to sign an inequitable revaluation law. He never mentioned revaluation in the campaign and was apparently virtually totally ignorant of the issue. But he did say, "The Reich President is especially called upon to uphold the sanctity of justice (*Recht*)"—a delphic pronouncement that creditors seized upon as ironclad proof of the new president's unshakable commitment to full revaluation. The right had touted Hindenburg as "the savior"—and many creditors now clearly believed he would prove their savior.[14]

The Government Prepares a Compromise

Desperate for support, Luther promptly submitted the draft revaluation laws to the Reich Economic Council. Although council members insisted on minor changes that increased revaluation somewhat, they rejected individual revaluation and generally accepted as necessary the government's limits on revaluation.[15] The council's resolution drew no dissenting votes, although 14 members abstained. Interestingly, 12 of the abstainers represented employee organizations; they declared that "in the revaluation the employees are involved in the smallest degree, so these gentlemen [capitalists] can settle this thing among themselves."[16]

The council's action strengthened the government's position with the political parties and noncreditors, but it only left many creditors more convinced than ever that the system was conspiring against them. The council's revaluation subcommittee reported that it had decided to discuss the drafts "only with respect to the overall economic situation of Germany. It therein must place especially in the foreground the effects on production, credit, and price relationships." Revaluation, it added, was clearly in part a compensation for an unjust capital shift; "nonetheless, one must warn against viewing this aspect as decisive."[17] And published reports of council discussions showed that it had followed its constitutional mandate and its subcommittee's advice and more or less ignored considerations of equity. Yet for the creditors equity was paramount, and they rejected the producer orthodoxy that the council appealed to in supporting the government's position. The fact that most council members represented debtor interest groups only deepened creditor suspicions.[18]

The government's expectation of full support from the Reichsrat proved overly optimistic. Länder ministers believed full revaluation was impossible, but many considered the government drafts inadequate. And even though the government forestalled the most far-reaching Länder proposals, it failed to stop the Reichsrat from voting some amendments it found unacceptable. Hence, the Reichsrat sent to the Reichstag a so-called double version of the revaluation bills (where some paragraphs were in two conflicting versions, one supported by the government, the other by the Reichsrat).[19]

These developments did not bode well for revaluation opponents. Although the Reichsrat was constitutionally subordinate to the Reichstag, these discussions reinforced the pressure on the government and the government parties to make additional concessions. Also, conflicting proposals by DNVP representatives from different Länder occasioned newspaper stories about DNVP ambivalence and demagoguery.[20]

The Reichsrat's behind-the-scenes conflict over bank-account revaluation reflected the difficulty of reconciling equity and efficiency. Bavarian officials attacked a Reich proposal to explicitly ban term-account revaluation in the Revaluation Law. Although conscious of account revaluation's economic implications, the officials feared allowing the Revaluation Law to become a "bank protection law."[21] Most commercial banks probably could not have afforded any significant revaluation. Yet it hardly seemed fair that the government should completely protect them while limiting creditor rights severely. But because the banks played a vital role in Germany's capitalist economy, bankers and their shareholders could not be allowed to suffer, even if creditors must be reduced to misery. The Reichsrat rejected term-account revaluation.[22]

In April debtor/producers were very vocal in opposing revaluation, both behind the scenes and publicly. The German Chamber of Commerce and Industry, for example, held its annual meeting in late April. In well-publicized addresses, several speakers—including Chancellor Luther—denounced any proposals to increase revaluation above the amount the government drafts offered. They all emphasized economic necessity and neglected considerations of equity.[23]

Although German securities brokers generally approved of the revaluation drafts, their representatives met in April to condemn vehemently the distinction between old and new holders of government bonds and the unfavorable treatment accorded the latter. They argued that "old holder/new holder" did not equal "noble sacrificer for the Reich/greedy speculator" and that the distinction was unworkable. They also insisted that investors would fear they could *never* sell any future government bonds to other investors because of the danger a future government would introduce another old/new distinction, making any transferred bonds worthless. Hence, the brokers argued, old/new would ruin the German government's credit.[24]

This issue illuminates strikingly the government's dilemma. Germany could only afford any significant government-bond revaluation rate by introducing the old/new distinction and limiting the number of bonds eligible for revaluation. And keeping the revaluation rate high was essential to proving its willingness to repay its debts to some meaningful degree. Yet denying revaluation payment to new holders called into question its willingness to repay all its debts. Any policy would damage its credit.

The creditors were active in April too. They held mass meetings and prepared pamphlets and petitions to anathematize the government drafts. To many creditors, the drafts eroded the few advantages the Tax Decree had offered while providing only risible improvements. In particular, the forced conversion of PM government bonds at 5 percent of face value worsened the creditors' position by eliminating any possibility of full recognition in GM. Also, many creditors expected the state to restore the original Paragraph 3 of the Tax Decree, which had allowed de facto individual revaluation of mortgages. For the HGSSV the drafts showed that "[t]he government is and remains openly disposed *one-sidedly in favor of the debtors*." The creditors also demanded that the government consult them on revaluation legislation, asking how it could ignore them while soliciting private debtors as advisors and "neutral" experts.[25]

The government obviously had no credibility with the creditor movement—and scarcely deserved any. Not only were its officials disinclined even to mention equity, not only were its drafts a mockery of earlier promises, not only had the Reichsrat and many politicians dismissed the drafts as patently inadequate, but the government had excluded creditor representatives from its discussions while openly consulting representatives of debtor interests. No wonder the creditor movement was convinced that the government was, at the least, "disposed one-sidedly in favor of the debtors."

Luther's first compromise was doomed, and unless the government acted quickly, it might completely lose control of the situation. On 7 May the Revaluation Committee defeated a government-party motion because Best (DNVP) and Ross (Z)—creditor leaders whom their parties had given Reichstag seats—voted with the left. Emminger threatened that if the parties could not agree on a common program, he would go his own way, presumably to promote a revaluation norm. Best was supposedly using delaying tactics to prevent the enactment of any revaluation law before 30 June. He believed the Reichstag would never extend the Tax Decree revaluation and that judges would then use the civil law to provide individual revaluation. And with the presidential election campaign at an end, the parties behind the government were determined to rewrite the drafts.[26]

The generally procreditor Emminger (BVP), Wunderlich (DVP), Hergt (DNVP), and Schetter (Z) met on 7 May to establish revaluation guidelines for the government parties. Under considerable political pressure to prove their good faith, the government parties agreed to support the policy these men formulated: 30 percent revaluation of *mündelsicher* mortgages (but only 15 percent for other mortgages), retroactive revaluation of all mortgages repaid since 15 December 1921, 25 percent industrial-obligation revaluation, and 10 percent Reich-bond and 30 percent municipal-bond revaluation for old holders.[27]

The government found these policies unsupportable, and after sharp negotiations the parties and the government agreed on a compromise and a means to maintain it. A complicated system would raise industrial-obligation revaluation to 25 percent for old holders, but most big companies would owe only 15 percent revaluation. Mortgages, owed mostly by small businesses and individuals, would be revalued at 25 percent, including any repaid in PM after 15 June 1922. The government would convert all PM bonds to redemption bonds at 5 percent, but only old holders would receive any immediate repayment, nominally equivalent to 10 percent revaluation for Reich and Land bonds and 12.5 percent for municipal bonds. One-thirtieth of the old-holder bonds, selected by lottery, would be repaid each year. A "preferential annuity" proportionate to their bond holdings would provide a modest social revaluation for the needy among the Reich- and Land-bond old holders.[28] To ensure that this compromise would survive, on 15 May each of the government parties signed identically worded statements promising to support the compromise and to deviate from it only after consulting the other parties.[29]

Fueling Creditor Anger

The government parties struggled to put the best possible face on their compromise. At Revaluation Committee meetings on 15 and 16 May, they defended the drafts and their support for the compromise. Hergt said that he had hoped for a partially individual solution, but that as he went deeper into the issue he had learned better. The society required certainty in everyone's bookkeeping, and if the Reichstag did not settle the issue the struggle would be perpetual. Schetter also emphasized the insupportable uncertainty individual revaluation would create and the need for compromise. Emminger pointed out that the compromise brought the creditors 4 billion RM over what the government had offered.[30]

The *Kreuzzeitung*, a major DNVP newspaper with ties to debtors, had trouble placating creditors. Its obvious sympathy for the debtor position had angered creditors in January and February. And in May and June, despite occasional acknowledgements of creditor disappointment, it basically emphasized the economic constraints on revaluation. It insisted that the compromise actually benefited creditors because it brought certainty, a feeling that creditors certainly did not share. It also dismissed the creditors as simply one more interest in society that had to give way before broader national interests. Creditors repudiated such a perception of the issue, especially from a mouthpiece for the debtor interests they despised. The paper and the DNVP also tried to blame the economic limits on revaluation on the revolution and the Republic, but creditors were already convinced the inflation had been a plot by the debtor groups the *Kreuzzeitung* represented.[31]

By May 1925 creditors were sufficiently outraged by political developments that it is difficult to imagine how the DNVP could have salvaged its honor. Yet the *Kreuzzeitung*'s emphasis on economic considerations, dismissal of the creditors as just another economic interest, and lack of sympathy for the creditors' desperation and sense of betrayal could only aggravate creditor anger at the DNVP.

The May compromise drove Best out of the DNVP. He had become increasingly disillusioned but had held on in hopes he could somehow influence DNVP policy. The party's decision to remove him from the Revaluation Committee—to prevent him from voting against the government drafts—precipitated his resignation. Best remained in the Reichstag as a guest of the Völkisch delegation, which had no seat on the Revaluation Committee because it had had too few deputies when the committee was formed. Surprisingly, the SPD gave Best one of its seats on the committee because of his expertise on the issue—undoubtedly to embarrass the DNVP.[32]

The DNVP had required all its candidates to sign an affidavit promising to resign their Reichstag seats at the party's request. Best, however, refused to leave the Reichstag, arguing that he had a higher responsibility to the creditors to promote their interests. He submitted himself to a "Court of Honor" that was to determine whether he was acting as a "German man of honor." The court was composed of a Prince Löwenstein, three members of the Völkisch party, and the prorevaluation DNVP Deputy Steiniger (who participated without his party's knowledge). Not surprisingly, these men found unanimously that Best had acted honorably in refusing to resign.[33]

The DNVP would probably have been well-advised to accept the verdict of the "court" silently. The affidavits were almost certainly unconstitutional (although Best never appealed to the Weimar Constitution in support of his refusal to resign). The party had in 1924 dealt in bad faith with Best. Arguably, it had thereby forfeited its right to hold him to any promises. Instead, the party proclaimed that if Best did not give up his seat he would be breaking his solemn word of honor. Best countered that if the DNVP did not retract, he would sue for libel, and the public could decide from the court testimony whether he or the DNVP had broken its word. The DNVP did not respond.[34]

Shortly thereafter Best published an extensively quoted article on his relations with the DNVP that confirmed creditors' worst suspicions about the democratic political process. He claimed that a DNVP leader (unnamed) had dismissed his complaints about broken campaign promises, saying such promises were "meaningless" and had always to give way before "the higher interests of the state." Best also suggested that personal economic interests of some members were determining DNVP policy.[35] The DNVP vehemently rejected Best's charges, asserting that DNVP party practice was to allow only "objective grounds and state necessities," and certainly not "the selfish economic interests of individual members," to determine policy. But Best stood by his claims, threatening to "name names" if the DNVP further disputed his word. DNVP leaders were sufficiently alarmed to seek an "authentic report" on whether Best were a creditor or debtor in the revaluation, so they could decide whether to answer his attacks.[36]

This squabble soon degenerated into a slanging match. Keil charged in the Reichstag on 26 June that the influence of interests was delaying the revaluation proceedings.[37] When the DNVP challenged him next day in the Revaluation Committee, he cited Best's assertions, demanding their confirmation or denial. Best then named names, making charges that he admitted were based predominantly on anonymous letters, hearsay, and innuendo. All those he named were "fortuitously" present. They all denied his charges, often recounting sad stories of their own and their families' economic sufferings from inflation. They also asked Best if he were not himself a creditor; apparently mortified, he answered that he was, but protested he was "one of the swindled, not the swindler."[38] The Reichstag refused on constitutional grounds to permit libel suits among the deputies.[39]

The DNVP's public feud with Best may have given some noncreditors second thoughts about the creditor position, but it seems only to have solidified creditor opposition to the compromise. The derogatory implications of the DNVP attack on Best's creditor situation only increased creditor defensiveness; the same accusation could apply against all creditors. Creditors especially resented the implication that they and Best were on a level with debtors whom the creditors considered thieves. Best and the vast majority of creditors sincerely believed that debtors were self-interested while they, having been swindled, were merely exercising their rights. Even before the Court of Honor had approved Best's refusal to resign his

Reichstag seat, the HGSSV backed his actions to the hilt. And in the aftermath of the chaotic 27 June committee meeting, the HGSSV Executive Committee publicly reiterated its full support for him.[40]

After Best's attacks on the DNVP, the *Kreuzzeitung* apparently gave up hope of winning over the creditor movement. In mid-July it took to calling Best the revaluation fanatic and chided him for cooperating with Marxists in opposing the revaluation bills. It also blamed Best and the creditor movement for creditor disappointment, asserting they were thoughtlessly building up false creditor hopes anew.[41]

Hergt's efforts to justify himself and his party only created new controversy. In a widely quoted article, he blamed the creditors for their own disappointment. He admitted that he had abandoned individual revaluation as infeasible in the summer of 1924. The DNVP, he said, had only given Best a seat to ensure a hearing for the latter's popular draft. Hergt asserted that when Best's draft lost its majority in the DNVP, Best and the creditors ought to have revised their views. Instead they had clung to an infeasible position and left their friends in the lurch.[42]

Hergt's tone and his revelation that he had already in mid-1924 opposed the Best draft touched off a furor. The center and left-of-center press scornfully dismissed his attempt to blame the creditors. The creditors were apoplectic. Hergt had in effect admitted to the demagoguery and betrayal they had suspected and now blamed them for having believed his promises. Creditors sent him stinging letters and published vituperative articles attacking him and the DNVP for treachery.[43]

Although creditors should have recognized the economic limits on revaluation, the DNVP and Hergt did seem to have a very cavalier attitude toward the electorate, one that presumably reflected their authoritarian conservatism and the politics they had learned under Bismarck's authoritarian system. Even if DNVP leaders never said that campaign promises were meaningless, Hergt and DNVP leaders acted as though they were. Hergt's comments implied a certain contempt for the electorate. Voters apparently were not to develop and promote their own opinions or to hold their representatives accountable for fulfilling promises. Rather, they were to revise their views whenever their leaders changed policy. As ambivalent as many creditors may have been about democracy, they certainly believed *their* opinions had value and deserved respect.

According to *Vorwärts*, Hergt suffered further embarrassment in mid-June when he tried to defend DNVP revaluation policy at a DNVP meeting. Although he sought to explain the issue's economic complexities and the need for compromise, the paper reported that his audience was unsympathetic. When he pointed out that Germany had just lost a war and had to bear massive costs, a heckler asked derisively if Hergt had only just figured that out. Hergt complained bitterly, "Because of the delegation's policy, I receive almost daily about forty letters with threats, complaints, insults, such as traitor, blackguard, swine, and so on. That cuts me to the quick, and my wife is near desperation." Far from eliciting his hearers' sympathies, his lament was reportedly followed by a veritable inquisition from the floor. Finally, Hergt burst out in exasperation that he had said all he could and wished the SPD were in the government. The *Frankfurter Zeitung* found it hard to feel sorry for Hergt because he was only reaping the bitter fruits of his and the DNVP's demagoguery. The DNVP later claimed that Hergt had in fact won over the crowd—but the *Vorwärts* version was widely reprinted.[44]

The DDP and SPD, meanwhile, were having a field day. Despite their earlier opposition to substantial revaluation increases, they now promoted numerous prorevaluation amendments, at least partially to embarrass the government and the government parties. Their politicians and newspapers, and those of the KPD, excoriated the government parties for their demagoguery and neglect of the creditors. These strenuous efforts embarrassed the government parties, often forcing the latter to vote against proposals they had once touted.[45]

Yet this change of heart does not seem to have won the SPD or DDP significant creditor support. The SPD attracted some creditors to "revaluation meetings" it held, but it complained bitterly about the opposition it faced from creditor leaders. And neither the SPD nor the DDP seems to have gotten any great access of rentier votes at the next election.[46] These parties had apparently done nothing to restore creditor faith in themselves or in the system.

The Reichstag Enacts Legislation

Against this background of economic constraints, political conflict, and policy reversal, the government parties could only devise a compromise revaluation that was sure to offend many on both sides, especially among creditors. Moreover, the mechanics of compromise, particularly on so technical and complex an issue, were such that the whole process took on an unsavory aura of political dealing.

To the undoubted relief of the government parties, Dernburg (DDP) moved on 16 May that the Revaluation Committee base its discussion on the government compromise and not on the Best draft (although he did say his party reserved its position). All but the SPD agreed to Dernburg's motion, the latter objecting that it excluded Best's draft.[47]

The committee took several initiatives on behalf of creditors. Most important, it raised the revaluation for old-holders of Reich and Land bonds from 10 to 12.5 percent. It increased the maximum income old holders could have and still be eligible for some social revaluation from 600 to 800 RM per year and provided 10 million RM per year for 15 years for charitable and religious organizations that were bond creditors. It also provided some funds for early repayment of government bonds held by savings banks and social insurance and pension funds.[48] The committee made various arrangements for creditors to mobilize some revalued assets quickly for cash (albeit at a substantial discount). The committee also accepted SPD proposals guaranteeing more or less individual revaluation of employees' savings and pension plans and other deposits with their employers.[49]

The committee also aided debtors. It stipulated that mortgage banks could deduct a maximum of 10 percent of the distribution fund for administration costs, arguing that more would be a bonus to the banks. (The government had proposed 12 percent and Emminger had demanded 5 percent.) And at the WP's insistence, it strengthened the hardship clause to protect anyone who had in good faith made investment decisions on the assumption of no retroactive revaluation.[50]

The committee offended many debtors and probably hurt the propensity to save when it sought to further punish speculators. Although the government had already created two unequal classes of government-bond revaluation, for old and new holders, Keil proposed annulling new holders' government bonds completely. The committee rejected this popular but drastic measure. Instead it reduced the originally proposed conversion rate for PM government bonds from 5 to 2.5 percent, while raising old holders' repayment from 2.5 to 5 times the redemption bonds' face value—preserving government-bond revaluation of 12.5 percent for old holders. New holders would still get no repayment until reparations had been settled, but their bonds now had even less nominal value.[51] This sudden erosion of bond holders' rights so outraged securities brokers that they went on a (self-described) one-day strike. And in the future the government would have trouble selling its bonds.[52]

Of course, creditors were bound to be dissatisfied with anything less than individual revaluation of private debts. Any schematic revaluation rate would inevitably be to some extent arbitrary. As one creditor wrote, there is no such thing as "25 percent justice," and establishing statistically the effects of any given rate was impossible. Schetter admitted as much in the Revaluation Committee.[53] The committee nonetheless rejected a revaluation norm, although some members of the government parties continued to urge some sort of norm up until between the second and third readings of the Revaluation Law.[54]

Perhaps the most unsavory aspect of the legislation from the creditors' point of view was that it *was* a compromise with a life of its own, independent of the merits of individual provisions or of the honest opinions of individual deputies. On a substantive issue involving seller-financed mortgages, Wunderlich actually broke the government-party silence (apologizing to his colleagues for doing so) to say that although he personally opposed the government position on the issue, the need to maintain the compromise required that he support it. According to *Vorwärts*, Hergt chimed in that one must stick it out and not let sentimental feelings interfere.[55] Newspaper reports of conflict between antirevaluation leaderships and many prorevaluation deputies, especially in the DNVP, added to the aura of political expediency and backstairs dealing surrounding the revaluation and strengthened creditor suspicions.[56]

The Reichstag and Reichsrat passed the revaluation bills fairly quickly after the Revaluation Committee finished its work. Best, Keil, and Karl Korsch (KPD) did virtually all the talking in the Reichstag, excoriating the government parties and Luther and introducing amendments to force roll-call votes on substantive issues. Government-party members usually appeared in the chamber only to vote. Despite evidence of considerable dissatisfaction with the bills among government-party deputies (and government fears of a collapse of party discipline), the government majority held on all the votes, although some government-party deputies absented themselves from the voting. And on the final vote, only three DNVP deputies and three Center deputies broke ranks on 15 July 1925 to vote against the (private-debt) Revaluation Law, while one Center deputy abstained. On 16 July 1925 the same three DNVP deputies and two of the Center deputies voted against the (public-debt) Bond-Redemption Law, while one Center and one DNVP deputy abstained.[57] (The Appendix to this volume summarizes the more important provisions of the revaluation laws.)

Creditor forces successfully challenged the Revaluation Law under a constitutional provision allowing one-third of the Reichstag members to call for a referendum on a statute. Even if the revaluation referendum ultimately failed, the courts could meanwhile provide individual revaluation in many cases. If, however, a majority of the Reichstag and Reichsrat declared a law urgent, the decision on holding a referendum rested with the president.[58]

When majorities in both chambers agreed the Revaluation Law was urgent, creditor hopes came to rest on "the savior," Hindenburg. Germany's most popular military hero, Hindenburg still commanded a great fund of good will. Creditors had taken to heart his vague campaign promise to maintain justice and had convinced themselves he would permit a referendum by refusing to sign any unjust bill. He raised these hopes even more when he received six creditor representatives in late June. He assured them he was very sympathetic because he had lost all his savings too and had been very fortunate to have a large pension. He asked for the creditors' demands in writing and closed with, "The last word on this question has not yet been spoken." Creditors were ecstatic at this evidence of presidential sympathy.[59]

Hindenburg in fact confounded creditor expectations. After his sympathetic talk with creditor representatives, he continued to be flooded with written and oral requests not to sign the revaluation bill. He answered all with the promise he would read the final bill and then decide. So that he could be seen to do so, his state secretary proposed that the justice minister and the chancellor meet with Hindenburg, explain the bill, and "then the president decides for the execution and promulgation of the bill"—in sum, a nice charade for the creditors' benefit. The scenario was played out, and Hindenburg signed the Revaluation Law.[60]

Tragically, different institutions and individuals had for over 18 months kept encouraging the creditors to believe that their fondest hopes could be realized—only to reject creditor demands in the end under pressure of economic and political realities and debtor influence. Creditor demands may have been excessive, but because creditors kept getting new, if usually temporary, support for those demands, they had difficulty recognizing the limits on revaluation.

Although the government had fought vigorously, it had had to make major concessions. It had originally planned a government-bond revaluation costing 50 million RM per year, and its first draft offered 80 million per year. The Reichstag bill apparently offered about 187 million.[61] In making these calculations, however, the government had assumed that old holders held only 20 billion of the 70 billion PM in outstanding government bonds. In fact they held 40 billion, and government redemption expenditures averaged 250 million RM per year, 1926/27 to 1932/33. The Reich also disbursed about 70 million per year for the preferential annuity, although this reduced municipal welfare payments by an indeterminable amount.[62] Further, even though a 12.5 percent repayment rate would not provide much to the individual creditor, it would shift more than 5 billion RM of principal, plus interest, from taxpayers to creditors. The annuity was an additional burden because annuity payments were higher than welfare payments.

The revaluation laws mandated the transfer of a substantial amount of capital from debtors to creditors. The data are scattered, incomplete, and to some degree contradictory, but the total to be transferred was approximately 16 billion RM (ca. 5 billion for government bonds and ca. 11 billion for private-law debts). The government drafts probably would have transferred 8.7 billion RM, and the May compromise and the Reichstag apparently added over 7 billion. This was a substantial increase over the Tax Decree's 4.5 billion. And the revaluation principal equalled about 30 percent of Germany's annual GNP in the mid-1920s.[63] (A comparable burden would be about $1.25 trillion for the 1986 United States of America [GNP] and about DM 580 billion for the 1986 Federal Republic of Germany [GDP].)

Although some specific provisions of the Bond-Redemption and Revaluation Laws (e.g., the relatively low revaluation of industrial obligations) were undoubtedly inadequate, the legislation probably did provide about as much revaluation as the society could afford. Reich payments to PM government-bond creditors were about 3.6 percent of all its expenditures, 1924/25 to 1932/33 (ca. 2.2 billion RM of 61 billion). The Reich's deficit in these years averaged 12.5 percent of expenditures, on top of a tax burden substantially greater than prewar.[64] Hence, scope for further expenditures was arguably quite limited, especially since reparations were a major drain and the government soon ran into difficulty borrowing money. On the other hand, the Reich made various expenditures (e.g., often massive subsidies to industry and agriculture, occasionally questionable military expenditures) that scarcely seemed to deserve priority over the creditors' moral claim.[65] Evaluating private-debt revaluation is even more problematic because of the varying situations of individual debtors, but Germany's economic weakness did make substantial or individual revaluation impossible.

Imperfect as the revaluation laws were, the political system had at least partially fulfilled its basic function. The parties' efforts to overbid one another in campaign promises in 1924 had been a sorry spectacle. Yet they had been responding to a difficult and unprecedented situation. Political expediency had motivated some politicians. But many others—such as

Emminger and Steiniger—clearly sought to reconcile equity and economic necessity as much to the benefit of the expropriated creditors as feasible. They and the parties had challenged the government's apparent indifference to creditor rights and had forced the government to make significant concessions to the creditors' just demands. Even if they had not succeeded in educating much of the public as to the nature of the revaluation problem, they had helped to mobilize popular opinion and to give it representation in the policy-making process.

Nonetheless, the creditors and the parties failed to achieve their ends completely. Organized producer/debtors and the executive were a powerful combination; they could appeal to an economic orthodoxy; and the economic constraints Germany faced made it impossible to reverse a decade of economic developments. Debtors, including the state, had left creditors to pay a substantial portion of the burdens of war and defeat with inflation. They were not powerful enough to make so obviously unjust a policy permanent, but they were economically important and powerful enough to limit sharply the costs creditors could shift back to them.

The Creditors Feel Betrayed

Nothing that the debtors, the government, or the government parties had said had shaken the creditors' fundamental faith in the economic feasibility of substantial revaluation. Underlying their rejection of economic counter-arguments was a continued emphasis on debtors' moral obligation to repay in full. But even where creditor groups, for tactical reasons, indicated a willingness to accept less than full revaluation, they insisted that debtors could afford substantially more than the revaluation laws offered. Creditors could and did argue that no one had brought forward any concrete evidence that 25 or 12.5 percent were the appropriate rates—the government had pulled them more or less out of thin air.[66]

The creditor movement had long mistrusted Luther and his government. The debate on the revaluation drafts only reinforced their conviction that the government was a tool of big capital and that it had produced legislation that "stood fully on the side of the debtor."[67]

To the creditor movement the revaluation laws represented not a politically and economically necessary compromise, but base betrayal, and they blamed the government parties. The creditor group in Bavaria was particularly vitriolic, accusing the government parties and their members of betrayal, economic self-interest, and shameless horse trading. They threatened to struggle against any deputy who voted for the compromise, denouncing such individuals "as enemies of moral and economic recovery, as despoilers of folk and Fatherland." The HGSSV too threatened to urge all savers to struggle against these parties' deputies if they enacted the compromise drafts.[68] The demagoguery of some of the government parties—their cavalier attitude toward campaign promises—had returned to haunt them.

The creditor movement further suggested that its defeat resulted from political finagling or from an abuse of party discipline by unscrupulous debtors seeking to prevent an open vote on the issue's merits. As Best commented bitterly, creditors did not believe that "justice, equity, and objective arguments could play any role for [our] opponents in the problem's solution."[69] Creditors emphasized how the Reichstag debated the revaluation legislation before empty benches. They believed that not only a majority of the German people, but a majority of government-party deputies supported substantial revaluation. Only party discipline and backroom deals, they believed, had allowed deceitful government and government-party leaders to railroad through the unjust revaluation legislation. And Wunderlich had even admitted publicly the role of compromise and party discipline in holding the parties together behind the revaluation drafts.[70]

For creditors, the legislative process had itself been fundamentally dishonest, a sham, reflecting the illegitimacy of a parliamentary system that represented only rich interests and neither justice nor the popular will. Weimar democracy had not adequately defended their rights and seemed to them incapable of doing so.

The creditors were not alone in doubting whether the revaluation laws provided a just solution to the problem. For all his readiness to use the revaluation issue to embarrass the DNVP, Keil was sincere in denouncing the legislation as inadequate. Steiniger and Bazille remained in the DNVP but publicly opposed its revaluation policy. And Emminger continued to seek ways to improve the creditors' situation.[71] Such support could only strengthen the creditors' conviction that they had been betrayed.

Significantly, the relatively independent *Frankfurter Zeitung* became increasingly concerned with what it perceived as the government and government-parties' failure to provide a just and politically acceptable solution. Close to the DDP, the *Frankfurter Zeitung* distanced itself from that party's 1925 prorevaluation stance because of the newspaper's fundamental, economically based, fear of substantial revaluation. Yet by June the paper was warning that the legislation was seriously flawed, especially in the extremely favorable terms industry had obtained. Even while attacking the creditors' emotionalism and unwillingness to believe in their opponents' integrity, it called for improvements in the legislation. Although still convinced the Best draft and substantial revaluation would be highly deleterious to the German economy, the paper explicitly agreed with Best that the final legislation was socially unjust. It clearly feared by July that the government parties' inability or unwillingness to deal justly with the creditors was undercutting the legitimacy of the republican order. It warned in an article on the bills that careful work in political education would be necessary if democracy were to prosper.[72]

The determination of Germans after World War II to treat seriously creditor and other demands for equity provides strong evidence for the revaluation question's corrosive effect on faith in democracy and in capitalism. Most Germans who wrote on currency reform and related matters in the later 1940s had lived through the political and economic problems of Weimar. They frequently emphasized the imperative need visibly to tax holders of real capital to provide a socially just distribution of war and postwar burdens (*Lastenausgleich*). As one newspaper columnist wrote, "This social equalization is, however, also indirectly of economic and political significance. For neither the economy nor democracy can flourish in a society burdened with social tensions and riven by envy." Others referred explicitly or implicitly to the unfortunate effects of the revaluation conflict on support for democracy. Even men who shared Luther's belief in the primacy of economic considerations often acknowledged explicitly the need to provide some equitable compensation to those the war had damaged; they could even support substantial levies on real capital to finance that compensation. All these writers appeared convinced that another unjust or unequal solution to the problem of war losses would both undermine the legitimacy of any political order that implemented it and deleteriously affect faith in saving and in capitalism.[73]

As sincere as many government-party members may have been, the parties had not succeeded in fully reconciling equity and economic necessity in the revaluation controversy—certainly not in the creditors' eyes, but not even in the eyes of reasonably objective contemporary or subsequent observers. The parties might never have convinced all or even most creditors that substantial revaluation was infeasible, but they had not even succeeded in creating the appearance of a good-faith effort. The often sorry record of demagoguery, the long delays, and the political maneuvering that had preceded the revaluation legislation had instead called into question for the creditor movement, for many creditors, and perhaps for other Germans, the very legitimacy of a democratic order. To the creditors' disgust and dismay, not even the great Hindenburg had prevented the Weimar parliament from denying them what they still saw as their fundamental rights.

The creditors had given the Weimar Republic every chance. They had tried the legitimate avenues of protest that the system offered. Yet it had in their eyes failed them. The question now was where they would turn.

Revaluation's Bitter Denouement

The Revaluation and Judicial Review

Although the government had succeeded in promulgating a Revaluation Law, its problems were not yet at an end. Among other things, the creditors had discovered judicial review.

Germany had had no tradition of judicial review. Under the prewar legal philosophy, the judge was simply to apply the law as written, not to question its source or legitimacy. Indeed, under that system, any law the emperor signed was ipso facto constitutional. And German courts under the empire had, as late as 1917, explicitly rejected any right to review the content of laws for constitutionality.[1]

After the 1918 revolution, judicial attitudes changed. Because most judges continued to believe in monarchical sovereignty, they rejected the legitimacy of the new Republic (which was based on popular sovereignty) and of its parliament. The judges decided that they now had a special responsibility for maintaining legality.[2]

Judges also began to assert their right to, indeed their responsibility for, judicial review of the Republic's legislation. Between 1921 and 1924 the Reichsgericht issued three *obiter dicta* asserting the right of judicial review of Reich statutes.[3] In October 1924 the Reichsversorgungsgericht declared a 1922 law unconstitutional, and in February 1925 the Reichsfinanzhof declared some aspects of the 4 December 1924 presidential revaluation decree unconstitutional.[4] The latter two courts were the highest appeals courts only for cases involving social security and taxation respectively, so their rulings did have limited authority.

Other developments in 1924 and 1925 suggested judges were preparing to act. Reichsgericht President Simons spoke favorably of the court's February 1924 *obiter dictum* asserting the right of judicial review. Senate President Adolf Lobe publicly proclaimed the judges' right to review the constitutionality of laws.[5] Most significantly, Simons wrote to the chancellor in May 1925 asserting for the Reichsgericht the same power to determine the constitutionality of laws that the U.S. Supreme Court and the Swiss Bundesgericht had. This power was, he wrote, necessary as a "counterweight to popular sovereignty."

> In a constitutional monarchy the crown offers at least theoretically, if not always actually, the necessary guarantee for the preservation of tradition in constitution and administration, so that the political counterweight of a high court to guarantee the constitution can be dispensed with; in a parliamentary republic, on the other hand, the danger exists that without such a counterweight a transitory majority could, under the influence of fleeting opinions and political passions, introduce disorder and uncertainty into the constitution's organic development. For Germany, it is hence more important under the Weimar Republic than under Bismarck's constitution that there be a high court above the daily political struggle, one that protects parliamentarianism from itself and from the serious dangers existing in its own excesses.

Simons especially feared conflicting rulings from the multiple high courts (e.g., Reichsversorgungsgericht), and he did not want every lower court to be able to rule on constitutionality. He therefore suggested legislation to regulate the scope of the courts' powers of judicial review.[6]

Politicians initially resisted judicial review. The Weimar constitutional convention had discussed it. The delegates reached no explicit decision, although Ernst Huber believes most of them opposed it as a limitation on democracy.[7] After the 1921 Reichsgericht *obiter dictum*, a Reichstag committee debated inconclusively a proposal to vest judicial review in the Staatsgerichtshof (a special quasi-political court).[8] In December 1923, in discussing the draft Enabling Act, the Justice Minister stated that "the general legal opinion was, the courts possessed no right to review the constitutionality of laws." And in answering the judges' 8 January 1924 revaluation letter, the justice minister rejected judicial review, especially on the basis of Paragraph 242, an opinion in which the chancellor and Chancellery state secretary concurred and in which all were merely echoing German legal tradition.[9]

Yet the politicians came around quickly. At a 31 January 1925 meeting on legal certainty, Reich Justice Ministry and Land officials agreed, tacitly but apparently unanimously, that judicial review was an established fact and that the government would have to regulate it.[10] The government then drafted legislation reserving the power of judicial review to the Staatsgerichtshof, and then only if the Reich government or one-third of the Reichstag or Reichsrat members requested a review. The Reichsrat passed the bill, but the Reichstag never acted on it. The statute would drastically have narrowed the scope of judicial review—but it represented a startling departure from the government's earlier attitude.[11]

Judicial pressure contributed to this change. Judges continued to assert that the courts had the power to review statutes. The Reichsversorgungsgericht undoubtedly played a crucial role by actually invalidating a law. The judges' letter on revaluation asserted judicial review. Equally important, the Reichsgericht reviewed the constitutionality of the Tax Decree revaluation (a decree with virtually the character of a law) and found it valid. Happy to have the court approve schematic revaluation, the government raised no objection to the constitutional principle the judges had asserted.[12]

The creditors' insistence on the courts' right of judicial review probably also influenced these developments. Creditors were obsessed with the issue. To them, schematic revaluation was uncompensated expropriation and hence patently unconstitutional. They began to assert this unconstitutionality in December 1923, and they continued to do so despite the Reichsgericht decision confirming the Tax Decree's validity. Indeed, Zeiler and Düringer asserted that many Reichsgericht judges disagreed with the decision and suggested that the court might reverse it.[13]

When a creditor sued for individual revaluation on the grounds the Revaluation Law was unconstitutional, the Reichsgericht got its chance. In its 4 November 1925 ruling, it first laid out in some detail the legal and constitutional basis of its right to review the constitutionality of Reich statutes. It then reviewed the Revaluation Law and found that it was in fact constitutional because it was a regulation of creditor/debtor relations and not an expropriation.[14]

In this landmark decision, the Reichsgericht successfully asserted its right to judicial review, substantially increasing its power at the expense of parliament and the executive.[15] Similarly to the U.S. Supreme Court in *Marbury vs. Madison*, the court had established a precedent for judicial review while giving the government what it wanted in the substantive decision. And the German government, apparently relieved that the court had upheld its much-disputed revaluation provisions, did not challenge the constitutional principle involved.

The decision had limited immediate significance. Although the Reichsgericht declared a minor law unconstitutional in 1929, judicial review suffered a hiatus under the Nazi regime. Its explicit inclusion in the Federal Republic of Germany's Basic Law probably resulted primarily from the experience of Nazi violence and arbitrariness, rather than from the 1920s precedents.[16]

The courts seemed to be using inflation's effects, and particularly the revaluation, to expand their power. Many Germans were sure to view a judicial revaluation decision with favor, the more so the more convoluted the issue became. The judges initially chose the payee and creditor side, and in the process arrogated to themselves major new powers to intervene in the economy using Paragraph 242. On 1 March 1924 and 4 November 1925 they acknowledged the government's and debtors' arguments against individual debt revaluation, but this time they arrogated still more power, the power of judicial review. Popular approval forestalled a challenge to the legal principle behind their first ruling. Subsequently, the government's need for judicial sanction of its revaluation policy prevented it from attacking the judges' constitutional claims.

One can never know with certainty how politically calculating various judges were in deciding the revaluation cases, but judges were far from ignorant of the broader political and constitutional implications of their rulings. The revaluation was a difficult and crucial issue, and the judges' three major decisions presumably did reflect primarily their perception of its legal, economic, and social implications. Yet at least three contemporaries, a journalist, a legal writer, and an appeals court judge, suggested that an awareness of revaluation's usefulness for expanding judicial powers influenced some judges.[17] Many, perhaps most, judges clearly wanted the powers they were arrogating, and some at least were conscious that revaluation was a favorable issue for obtaining those powers.

The Creditors Seek Salvation

Dissatisfied with the July 1925 legislation, the creditor movement fought on. Although many elderly PM creditors must have died in the years after 1925, new supporters were available from disappointed heirs and PM creditors approaching retirement.

The most important creditor political party, the Reich Party for Popular Justice and Revaluation (*Reichspartei für Volksrecht und Aufwertung*), insisted that reestablishing equity and good faith was crucial to creditor and noncreditor alike. To prosper again, Germany would have to recreate the *Rechtsstaat* by reintroducing individual revaluation and by acknowledging that in the long term economic efficiency presupposed equitable policies. Like other creditor, and *Mittelstand*, parties, the Popular Justice party was vehemently anti-Marxist and anticapitalist, claiming that the nation must replace the egoism and materialism of capitalism and Marxism with a more just social order based on community, not self-interest or conflict. Convinced the capitalists and the Weimar governments were conspiring against the German people, the party identified itself as a political movement opposed to the existing party system of government.[18]

The main creditor groups were still seeking redress within the existing order—but in vain. They began collecting signatures for initiatives to supersede the revaluation laws. The main creditor initiative proposed a 50 percent revaluation norm, a 50 percent bank-note revaluation, and a 50 percent government-bond revaluation. On one estimate it would have increased the revaluation amount from 15.4 billion to 74.4 billion RM. Other creditor groups promoted an initiative mandating 100 percent revaluation.[19] Reacting in panic, the government arbitrarily banned the initiatives on a constitutional technicality.[20] To the creditors this was yet another example of the duplicity of the "democratic" system.

In 1926 creditor frustration led them to the self-contradictory posture of supporting the expropriation of princely fortunes. Creditor moral and legal demands rested on the sanctity of contracts and of private property. Yet when the left-wing parties supported an initiative to expropriate the ruling princes of the pre-1918 German states (arguing that the princely fortunes actually represented state assets), all the major creditor groups instructed their members to vote for the initiative. Believing they had been expropriated, creditors decided that if the government refused to protect their assets, it had no business protecting those of the princes.[21]

The creditors' reaction to this issue illuminates just how disillusioned, angry, and desperate they had become. In part they simply wanted to dramatize their cause and expose their opponents' hypocrisy. But by supporting this expropriation, they showed the extent to which they considered private property not a good in itself but rather a means to guarantee their economic security and independence and their social status. They thereby undercut their own moral claims.

Any substantial increase in the revaluation amount was unlikely after

1925, but conflict, petty jealousies, and fraud within the creditor movement certainly weakened its political influence. Some policy differences did exist, reflecting a split between those who recognized the need for some concessions and those who would brook no compromise. Personality differences also created divisions.[22] Worst of all, petty swindlers preyed on the movement. The HGSSV's leaders were almost undoubtedly completely sincere and honest. But many involved on the fringes sought only to line their own pockets through scams aimed at the desperate, bewildered, and all too often gullible creditors.[23]

Despite creditor efforts, the government was able to preserve the 1925 limits on revaluation. The survival of determined creditor groups and pressure from some government-party members did worry Weimar governments, but the governments and the revaluation opponents succeeded in holding the parties in line. Although the Reichstag twice amended the Revaluation Law, it merely corrected minor flaws in the statute's original drafting—and not always to the creditors' advantage.[24]

Even worse, in the face of the depression of the 1930s the government promulgated decrees (discussed below) enabling debtors to postpone the repayment of debts, including revalued debts. This new attack on creditor rights undoubtedly helped cut the last ties many creditors had to political moderation. The Republic seemed to be taking back even the paltry concessions it had made to private-debt creditors. For many creditors this meant more years of poverty and misery. And because the Weimar Republic had once again shown its preference for debtors over creditors, creditors could only fear future arbitrary limitations on their rights.[25]

Initially, many creditors had expected the Popular Justice party to attract enough votes to secure revaluation reform and to fundamentally restructure the political order. Yet although the party got 1.6 percent of the vote and two Reichstag seats in 1928, it was too small to achieve anything, and from 1930 to 1933 its vote dwindled to almost nothing.

Having given up in turn on the liberal parties, the DNVP, and the creditor parties, many creditors ultimately turned to Hitler. Available statistical and anecdotal evidence indicates that creditors voted overwhelmingly for the Nazis after 1929.[26]

Although the Nazi party attracted Germans from all classes, just as it repelled Germans from all classes, members of the *Mittelstand* were overrepresented in the party and among its voters and almost certainly constituted over half its electoral support. *Mittelstand* votes alone certainly did not bring the Nazis to power, but they contributed significantly to Hitler's rise. And creditors considered themselves *Mittelständler*.[27]

Creditors turned to the Nazis in part for seemingly practical reasons. The inflation and stabilization had revealed how diverse and conflicting the interests of different segments of German society and even of the *Mittelstand* were. Yet support for creditor and other splinter parties had not ended these conflicts or produced the public policies *Mittelständler* demanded. And the depression further exacerbated social conflicts. Meanwhile, the Nazis claimed to offer a new kind of society that would somehow reconcile these conflicts and achieve the demanded reforms. The party supported individual revaluation, even promising 50 or 100 percent revaluation, as part of its policy of promising everything to everybody. And Hitler vociferously denounced the "inflation criminals" and the "robbery of the savers"—albeit without mentioning revaluation.[28]

Beyond economic self-interest, most creditors saw revaluation as a moral issue in which the Republic had failed dismally. Like many other Germans, they rejected the materialism of capitalism and Marxism and believed in a social order where virtue would prevail. They looked back nostalgically to the prewar period when they believed that order had been maintained, conflict overcome, and the unjust punished. The war and inflation created a chaotic situation where virtue (hard work, thrift, and patriotism) was often punished and vice (speculation) often rewarded. Convinced by events and their ideology that "equity" could be restored, they repudiated as fundamentally unjust the Republic that had failed to secure that equity.

Thomas Childers has emphasized how each of the professedly *Mittelstand* splinter parties in the late 1920s was more than a mere party of economic interest, how each shared an ideological dimension. They were all both anti-Marxist and anticapitalist, often bitterly so, and each criticized the existing system "in highly moralistic terms," especially in comparison with their assumptions about "traditional German justice." Their electoral successes had represented a fundamental rejection of Weimar's legitimacy. An examination of creditor experience and attitudes confirms this very important insight.[29]

The Nazis were in a position to exploit the situation, once the creditors and other Germans had found other alternatives wanting. Beyond promises of specific policy concessions to different segments of the society, Nazism's major appeal was its claim to offer a new, communal social order, anti-Marxist and anticapitalist, that would reward hard work, thrift, and patriotism and guarantee social status according to social contribution. The party claimed to offer a new state based on a moral legitimacy to replace the discredited Weimar Republic and its capitalist system.[30]

The Weimar Republic bore heavy burdens from the start. Founded in a revolution many Germans repudiated, blamed by many for defeat in World War I, forced to sign a punitive peace treaty, saddled with unpayable and much-resented reparations, shackled by economic constraints, it was never able to secure itself in the hearts of its citizens. Its stabilization policies alienated virtually every social group. It never really had any economic golden years in the 1920s, and the disastrous severity of the depression had a devastating impact on many Germans. Germany's continuing problems after 1918 called into serious question the effectiveness and viability of the democratic and capitalist orders—and this in a country where antidemocratic and anticapitalist attitudes were already widespread. Arguably, the Republic was ripe for collapse by early 1930.

Nonetheless, the Third Reich was not predestined to take the Republic's place. National Socialist electoral successes stemmed from the collapse of the political center and right that had begun in 1923–24. Yet they also depended on the kinds of ideologies that many Germans, especially in the *Mittelstand*, subsequently adopted. Although economic losses made many Germans critical of the status quo, so did their cultural, social, and political traditions and assumptions. And the ideologies they developed created perceptions of the morally necessary and politically possible that predisposed many to accept the often similar rhetoric of National Socialism, when other alternatives proved ineffectual.

Many creditors clearly shared this receptiveness to Nazism. The Nazi promise to reestablish equity and good faith seemed to creditors to offer a new political order and a moral legitimacy in terms of their own ideology. Hence the party not only catered to creditor policy preferences, it also acknowledged their moral indignation and spoke to their perceptions about Germany's situation and about the nature of the just society. Many, if not most, revaluation supporters apparently became convinced that Adolf Hitler (perhaps "tamed" by the responsibilities of office) offered not merely economic benefits but also a social, political, and moral order superior to that of the Weimar Republic—incredible as that may seem in retrospect.

Not surprisingly, then, when Hitler became chancellor, creditors naively expected him to increase the revaluation, despite the existence of a severe economic crisis. They flooded the government in the spring of 1933 with letters and petitions.[31]

What creditors got instead was a gradual suppression of their movement. Creditor groups were *gleichgeschaltet* (placed under Nazi supervision) in June 1933. On 14 July 1933, Hitler and the cabinet rejected any revaluation amendment. Instead of publicly announcing this decision, they instructed the newspapers to avoid discussing revaluation. When this proved insufficient, the government ordered newspapers to ignore the issue completely and called in revaluation leaders to advise them their efforts were futile. In March 1934 the government banned nine revaluation groups. Although individual creditors continued to petition for improved revaluation, the remaining creditor organizations limped along by generally ignoring revaluation and lobbying on behalf of savers and saving in general. Finally, in 1938, S.S. Chief Heinrich Himmler banned the HGSSV and confiscated its assets.[32]

The creditors had been betrayed once again, more basely than before. They had ceased to be a political force in 1933. Within five years the Nazi state obliterated their independent organizations and forceably incorporated them into its "people's community." They had gotten a new social, political, and moral order—but not quite the one they had expected.

The Creditors Get Some of Their Money

The municipalities, with Länder support, cooperated to limit revaluation at their creditors' expense. (See Table 2 for an overview of actual revaluation of the various types of debt.) The Reichstag had empowered the *Treuhänder* (trustee-supervisors) for municipal bonds to increase the revaluation rate if a municipality's fiscal situation permitted, but "in practice all the cities—with the approval of the Länder—have jointly determined not to exceed 12.5 percent." The *Treuhänder* (almost invariably Land officials) only required more than the statutory 12.5 percent in 2 percent of the cases.[33] The municipalities owed about 1.1 billion marks plus interest for revaluing their bonds and other debts, but many of them probably could have afforded higher payments.[34]

The government had assumed that old holders owned only 20 billion of the 70 billion marks in outstanding PM Reich and Land bonds, but creditors registered 40 billion as old holdings. Relatively few had responded to inflation by unloading their government paper. Some of the 40 billion was really new holdings, but the government had to accept it as old holdings because certain perfectly legal, and usually legitimate, banking practices made it impossible to distinguish. Many redemption-bond creditors were individuals, but the larger creditors, usually financial or nonprofit institutions, held 75 percent of the debt. The social composition of the old holders in fact reflected fairly accurately the composition of the original signers of the bonds.[35]

Table 2. *Actual Revaluation*

		Type of Asset	Revaluation Rate	Interest Rate	Payment Made[a]
Primary Revaluation	Private	Mortgage	25%	3% 1926–27 5% 1928–31 6–11% 1932	1932–48
		Industrial obligation	15%	3% 1926–27 5% 1928–31 6–11% 1932	1932–48
		Genusschein	10%	0%	1926–48
	Government	Old-holder Reich bond	12.5%	4.5%	2/3 paid, 1926–44
		Old-holder Land bond	12.5%	4.5%	2/3 paid, 1926–44
		Old-holder municipal bond	12.5%[b]	5%	2/3 paid, 1926–44
		New-holder Reich bond	2.5%	0	never
		New-holder Land bond	2.5%	0	never
		New-holder municipal bond	2.5%	0	never
Secondary Revaluation	Private	Mortgage bond	17–46% (most around 20%)	4.5%	1935–38
		Sparkasse (savings-bank) account	15–46% (most 20–25%)	ca. 4.5%	1928–36
		Employee savings and pension plans	50–100% (most ca. 65%)	varied	1927–30

Table 2. *continued*

		Type of Asset	Revaluation Rate	Interest Rate	Payment Made[a]
⌐Secondary⌐	Revaluation	Commercial bank account	0	0	never
	⌐Private⌐	Life insurance	8–25% (most around 15%)		1932 or death of policy holder

[a] For all private assets, some debt remained unpaid in 1948, when currency reform substantially devalued the assets.

[b] In 2% of the cases, municipal bond revaluation exceeded 12.5%.

Frightened by the increase in the Reich's liabilities (to an eventual 3.8 billion RM owed old holders plus a nominal 750 million owed new holders), the Finance Ministry began urging its officials to demand rigorous proof of old holder status. This action may or may not have reduced the state's liabilities, but it certainly antagonized many Germans and called into question once again the government's good faith.[36]

Despite the flood of 3.85 million redemption claims, plus over 726,000 requests for a preferential annuity, and despite its fiscal difficulties after 1928, the government faithfully paid its obligations to old holders. Beginning in 1926, it drew one-thirtieth of the redemption bonds each year until the Reich collapsed in 1945. The government did provide special payments (over 15 years) to charitable and religious organizations that held its bonds. It repaid in all about two-thirds of the bonds (with accumulated 4.5 percent interest on the redemption amount). Some bonds whose numbers the government called were never submitted for payment.[37] Preferential annuity payments also continued until 1945, with annuitants receiving on average less than 100 marks per year. Originally, any old holders of Reich or Land bonds who became needy could apply for the preferential annuity. In 1935, however, the government decreed that creditors must apply by 31 March 1937 or lose the privilege.[38] Bond payments in West Germany resumed under complicated new legislation, and at yet lower rates, after the 1948 currency reform.

The government did not begin redeeming new holders' bonds when it stopped making reparations payments in 1932, as the Bond Redemption

Law seemed to mandate. In fact the end of reparations was only de facto, and the law provided that the Reichstag must fix the end of reparations by statute. The government did not introduce such legislation in 1932, and there is no evidence it ever made any payment to new holders. This policy provoked considerable ill-feeling.[39]

Foreign bond holders were entitled to revaluation if they could prove they were old holders. Most foreigners were new holders because they had only bought German war bonds after the war. Yet at least among Americans, even many old holders failed to redeem their bonds. Perhaps they were unaware their bond had been drawn for payment, perhaps the revaluation amount proved so small they did not consider redemption worth the trouble. But the greatest disincentive was presumably the rigid controls on capital export that Germany imposed in the 1930s.[40]

By providing that all revalued private debts were due on 1 January 1932, the Revaluation Law had created a dangerous situation. The German economy was still too weak to provide on one day the 7 to 8 billion RM in capital that would be due. Credit institutions would probably not have been too insistent, given governmental pressure for moderation. But most private creditors would probably have demanded their money, especially because market interest rates exceeded those on revalued debt. And private creditors held over half the outstanding revalued mortgage debt.[41]

The Reichstag hence promulgated in July 1930 a law regulating the repayment of revalued mortgages. After 1 January 1932 the interest on revalued mortgages would be 7.5 percent, sufficiently high that many creditors presumably would not have given notice. If creditors did give notice, they would still have to wait one year for repayment. If the debtor was unable to pay, he could sue for a postponement to as late as 31 December 1934, albeit only if he paid 11.5 percent interest in 1933 and 14.5 percent in 1934. The law was not a general moratorium and was weighted toward the creditors.[42]

Under pressure of economic depression, the government reduced creditor rights substantially by imposing more draconian moratoria on revalued and all other private debts. The government included revalued industrial obligations in its general decree of 10 November 1931, allowing debtors to postpone repayment. A 17 November 1931 decree allowed agriculture to reduce its interest payments. A decree of 8 December 1931 effectively reduced interest rates for all private debt to 6 percent or 75 percent of the existing rate, whichever was greater. Subsequent decrees extended the repayment moratoria in time (eventually into the late 1930s) and brought all revalued private debts under the new moratoria. These decrees did not, however, impose general debt moratoria: each debtor had to sue individually and show an inability to pay each time. The government did repeal the moratorium for revalued debts first, in December 1936, except for extreme hardship cases. By October 1938 outstanding revalued mortgages had generally been converted to fully amortized mortgages (*Tilgungshypotheken*).[43] To what extent creditors had converted their mortgages voluntarily and to what extent under pressure of the moratoria is unclear.

Because courts handled the moratoria on a case-by-case basis, any comprehensive statement about their effect on revaluation is impossible. The government did report in late 1932 that 126 companies had requested postponement of payment on revalued industrial obligations. Twenty-four companies had been denied, two cases were pending, and 100 companies (with some 20 percent of all the revalued industrial-obligation amount) had secured delays of from a few months to three years. Other sources spoke merely in vague generalities. This reticence presumably reflected the difficulty of gathering data about millions of individual mortgages and other debts, especially as new suits would be filed constantly. But the Nazi regime also sought to eliminate pressure for revaluation reform by forbidding discussion of revaluation.[44]

Nonetheless, the moratoria clearly reduced the value of creditor assets. If a debtor successfully sued for postponement, the creditor's loss would be obvious. But any threatened suit might force a creditor to negotiate an unfavorable compromise rather than face the costs of contesting the suit and the risk of losing it. And the market value of revalued assets fell generally because of the risk a debtor might suddenly sue for postponement.[45]

This new decision by the state to sacrifice creditor interests to economic expediency outraged creditors. When prices were rising they wanted their assets revalued, but they were loath to see them devalued when prices fell, as they did after 1929. Nonetheless, creditors did have reason for thinking the state simply found them the most easily expendable sector of the economy.[46]

The savings banks had few revaluable assets and should have been able to offer only minimal revaluation rates (e.g., 6 percent in Bavaria). The banks did not want to offer revaluation rates significantly lower than those of other credit institutions, so they introduced the so-called Wilhelmshaven System. Under this system, the banks recalculated inflation-era deposits into GM, while subtracting at PM face value prewar GM deposits withdrawn after 1918. (The Revaluation Law's ban on retroactive revaluation of savings-account withdrawals made this procedure legal.) Because a 1,000 PM deposit in 1922 might be worth only 1 GM, this system could substantially reduce the nominal value of the accounts. A bank's revaluation liabilities remained the same: if it had 10 million RM in its distribution fund, it still had to disburse all 10 million RM to its creditors. But its administration costs were lower because it did not have to recalculate all the withdrawals into GM. More important, by reducing the nominal value of its creditors' accounts (e.g., from 100 million to 50 million marks), the system increased the revaluation *percentage* it could offer (in this case, from 10 to 20 percent). The higher percentage might improve the savings banks' attractiveness to new depositors after 1925.[47]

Savings-bank procedures were legal but unfair. Some simplified recalculation system was probably necessary, given the tremendous number of inflation-era withdrawals and deposits. But the Wilhelmshaven System concealed the banks' ineffectualness in dealing with inflation. And it was so complex that most creditors could not make the calculations themselves, leaving them dependent on the accuracy of an overworked bank employee's calculations. Most important, it benefited depositors who had made few inflation-era withdrawals while often grossly and unjustly penalizing those who had made substantial PM withdrawals after 1918. One creditor, for example, complained that the system reduced from 1,120 to 233 marks one account his family held, with lesser reductions in other accounts. Also, the banks did not revalue accounts with very small GM values (less than 8 to 30 GM, depending on the Land). Berlin thereby excluded over one-third of its accounts.[48]

With such procedures the banks could offer revaluation rates ranging from 15 percent to 46 percent, with most between 20 and 25 percent. Prussia's savings banks offered 17 to 25 percent revaluation, yet the banks had distribution funds totaling only about 8.5 percent of 1918 GM deposits. The savings banks did, however, absorb the administration costs, unlike the mortgage banks. The banks began payments for small accounts in the late 1920s and, after some delays because of the depression, completed them in the mid-1930s.[49]

Mecklenburg, Saxony, and Württemberg did act to protect depositors' interests. Each either banned the Wilhelmshaven System or required savings banks and their guarantors to contribute to the distribution fund to raise the revaluation amount instead of just the revaluation rate.[50]

On paper the savings-bank creditors had done far better than government-bond creditors and as well as many other private-debt creditors; but in fact most had probably done rather poorly. Despite vehement creditor protests at these misleading, if not deceitful, maneuvers, the Reich did nothing—except expressly to allow the banks not to publish their revaluation balances, enabling them to conceal the real relationships among their prewar and postwar assets and liabilities.[51] Protecting the credit of the savings banks apparently justified more or less defrauding many depositors.

These developments reflect a fundamental weakness of the creditor position. The debtors, including financial institutions, were crucial parts of the society's productive forces. Whenever producers' vital interests were threatened, governments felt compelled to protect them, whatever the merits of the individual cases. This happened under the Second Reich; it happened under the Weimar Republic; it happened under the Third Reich. Under three different regimes, the German state decided economic necessity required sacrificing creditor interests.

Employees who had saved with their employer in company savings or pension plans often did significantly better than other private creditors. Sometimes a public or private insurance fund administered the employee's assets or the employer administered the assets separately from company funds. In those cases the employee received a proportion of the revalued assets of the fund or separately administered holdings, in theory no more than 25 percent. The Bond Redemption Law did provide some funds for speedy redemption of government bonds held by social-insurance funds. But if the employer, as he often did, used employee pension or savings contributions in the firm's operations, the Revaluation Law entitled the employees to a kind of individual revaluation through a special bureau. The revaluation rates varied from 15 percent (in the case of one bankrupt company) to 100 percent, but they apparently ultimately averaged around 55 percent. This was substantially more than virtually any other creditors received, including industrial-obligation creditors. No estimate was available of the total funds involved. Companies had established pension and savings plans to secure employee loyalty, so they were presumably well-advised to revalue them liberally. Some had even done so voluntarily.[52]

The government revalued civil-service pensions separately. The state based its pensions on the salary at retirement. From 1920 it provided cost-of-living increases for pensions. When the inflation ended, it tied pensions to December 1923 salary rates for the grade at retirement. The "revaluation" rate varied slightly, and inversely, with grade. Civil servant salaries were low after the inflation, but the government increased pensions somewhat in 1927. So even though government pensions did not regain real prewar levels, most civil servants had by 1927 come fairly close to full pension revaluation.[53]

Industrial-obligation revaluation created relatively few problems. Apparently only one company initially sought to reduce its revaluation with the hardship clause. Only about 30 percent of the industrial obligations were entitled to the special additional payment for old holders (the *Genusschein*). Although industry estimated its revaluation burden would be 750 million RM, revalued industrial obligations apparently totaled about 364 million marks. Some companies began repaying their obligations in the late 1920s, but in 1931 others obtained delays in repayment because of the depression. By 1934, 141 million RM remained outstanding. In the mid-1930s the government promulgated decrees improving *Genusschein* amortization, since many companies had made few if any payments on them. By 1940 only 70 million in obligations remained unpaid.[54] Most obligation creditors got their money eventually—insofar as the Revaluation Law had allowed.

Mortgage revaluation was a nightmare. Creditors registered about 4.5 million revalued mortgages. With debt moratoria, legal conflict dragged on into the 1930s. Prussia alone had to hire 1,000 extra judges and 2,000 other civil servants to handle revaluation. Court costs, legal fees, and delay hurt many creditors. Retroactive mortgage revaluation required action by both the special revaluation bureaus and the Land Register bureaus. The latter faced severe problems when the property had changed hands or property owners had registered new debt. (In Bavaria well over half of the mortgage cases involved retroactive revaluation.) But even though special legislation was necessary in 1930 to clear up the land registers, retroactive revaluation per se apparently went remarkably smoothly.[55]

In 1925 revalued mortgages totaled about 10 billion RM. Some mortgages were quickly transformed into fully amortized mortgages, and some debtors repaid early. Nonetheless, over 7 billion RM was due on 1 January 1932 (even though some creditors never applied for revaluation). With the debt moratoria of the early 1930s, over half the debt remained in 1936 and a substantial amount still in 1941. Most remaining debt was by then fully amortized mortgages. The interest rate on revalued mortgages exceeded that on new mortgages in the late 1930s. Creditors who did not need cash immediately, especially credit institutions, thus had every incentive not to accept repayment unless they had to. But creditors had had to wait an unconscionably long time for repayment, and presumably some creditors were expropriated again in Germany's second great inflation after 1944.[56]

The terms of insurance-policy revaluation excited relatively little concern among creditors, perhaps because of the element of gambling in insurance, perhaps because beneficiaries could feel uncomfortable about squabbling too vehemently over a right to money contingent on someone's death. The companies were able to offer rates ranging from 8 to 25 percent, with most around 15 percent. They had revalued assets of 815 million RM. Given administration costs of 1 percent, that means they repaid about 807 million marks.[57]

Mortgage-bond revaluation also proceeded fairly successfully. The government had settled on an 8 percent deduction from the distribution fund for administration costs. This provided the banks with a profit on revaluation despite the (meager) contributions to the distribution funds the Länder often required. Nonetheless, because some of their mortgages were retroactively revalued whereas mortgage bonds were not, the banks could offer relatively high revaluation rates, with most around 20 percent for mortgage bonds and 15 percent for *Kommunalobligationen* (which the mortgage banks issued to finance loans to municipalities). The mortgage banks allowed creditors to exchange their PM mortgage bonds for GM liquidation bonds that paid 4.5 percent interest. The creditors could sell the latter (albeit at a substantial discount) if they wanted cash. The banks redeemed the liquidation bonds only after 1935.[58]

Many disabled or elderly creditors received so little from revaluation that they had to turn to government welfare programs. The special welfare program the government had created during the inflation for impoverished small rentiers continued into the 1940s. For a lucky few it could provide substantial revaluation, although in the form of the welfare creditors despised. Reliable statistics are only available after 1925. They show a maximum of about 274,000 recipients receiving an average 440 RM per year, in 1929. Reich and municipalities expended about 700 million RM, 1926–1933, of which the Reich provided 244.3 million. Creditors who did not qualify for this special program or who needed additional help had to turn to public assistance. General welfare payments resumed in real terms after the stabilization, but never at substantial rates. Indeed, during the early 1930s they occasionally fell substantially below the subsistence minimum. Part of the income from revalued assets and from the special rentier welfare program could be excluded in calculating need for and levels of general welfare payments.[59]

Available evidence suggests that revaluation did affect where and how Germans saved. Credit and consumer cooperatives had voluntarily revalued their savings accounts, usually at about 25 percent. By 1930 credit co-op deposits had regained 1913 levels, and consumer co-op deposits were at six times those levels, whereas savings banks, which often still had not finally settled their revaluation rates, had only 55 percent of their 1913 deposits. Many attributed this discrepancy primarily to the good will the co-ops had obtained by their voluntary action. Similarly, mortgage banks attributed their relative success in regaining 1913 asset levels to the relatively high revaluation rates they offered. The mortgage bond's recovery came despite a general trend away from long-term assets. Conversely, the private-mortgage market, a major factor before World War I, never fully recovered.[60]

More important, the uncertain investment climate that inflation and minimal revaluation had created hurt both savings and investment, with deleterious economic consequences. Overall, savings were low, probably too low. Much of the money loaned out in Germany after 1923 was in the form of short-term credit and at relatively high interest rates. And Germany experienced substantial capital flight in the 1920s and 1930s, in no small part because of memories of inflation and meager revaluation. This situation made investment difficult and contributed to economic instability.[61]

Further, Germans reacted negatively to the Reich's collusion in the expropriation of creditors by basically refusing to loan the central government money after 1923. This unwillingness proved disastrous after 1929, when the Reich's near inability to obtain long-term loans drastically restricted its fiscal and economic options. The Reich was burdened with massive reparations obligations that made it seem a bad credit risk. The inflationary implications of Reich budget deficits and the fact that Weimar governments had once allowed an inflation must also have made investors wary of Reich borrowing, revaluation or no revaluation. But the nature of the revaluation the Reich had so grudgingly allowed undoubtedly contributed to its problems. The old/new distinction and the reduced revaluation rate for very large individual government-bond creditors clearly antagonized the financial community. And many other creditors, and perhaps their relatives and friends, were outraged at what they viewed as official fraud and deceit.[62] These factors can perhaps explain why private individuals and the municipalities could borrow more easily than the Reich.

These economic and fiscal difficulties reflected in part a self-fulfilling prophecy, but the creditors had also been right in insisting that long-run economic efficiency required that the government treat them equitably. Far from reassuring investors, the government's revaluation policy seems merely to have aggravated an already pernicious situation.

Because of the relatively low interest, the long delay until repayment, and real doubts among Germans about the stability of the revaluation settlement, revalued assets were worth substantially less than their face value to creditors, as Table 3 suggests. The apparent present value of revalued assets in 1925 was around 74 percent of face value for private debts and only 47 percent for old-holder Reich redemption rights. The lack of firm payment dates for interest or principal makes it difficult to calculate even apparent present values for mortgage bonds, new-holder conversion bonds, savings accounts, life-insurance policies, or the *Genusschein*. Even by 1930 (with lower interest rates on new investment) the apparent present value of private debt was only around 97 percent, of Reich debt about 76 percent (despite the considerable accumulated interest each redemption bond would offer). Significantly, market values show that investors generally discounted revalued assets below apparent present value, presumably in fear of further government intervention in the repayment of revalued debt. Market values for the *Genusschein* and new-holder bonds gyrated wildly, from a high of 65 percent in 1926 to a low of 15 in 1932 for the former, and from a high of 34.5 percent in 1927 to a low of 2.5 in 1932 for the latter.[63]

The drop in market values between 1931 and 1932 reflects the impact of various debt moratoria the government did in fact impose. Debtors had secured delays in the repayment of many remaining revalued private debts, reducing their value. And the possibility that debtors could postpone repayment yet again and that the government might further limit creditor rights reduced the value of all assets (e.g., old-holder bonds, revalued mortgages that had been transformed into fully amortized mortgages). Ironically, though, the government suspended the debt moratoria for revalued assets first, so they proved to be more secure than nonrevalued assets.

Discounting these assets further to reflect the inflation in gold seems unwarranted. Postinflation prices in gold were 50 percent higher than 1914 prices, but this was in line with the inflationary expectations implicit in prewar interest rates of 3.5 to 5 percent.

Hence the real value of the revaluation in 1925 was *at best* about 18.6 percent for mortgages, 11.2 percent for most industrial obligations, and less than three-quarters of the nominal revaluation rate for mortgage bonds. But the debt moratoria of the 1930s made these calculations meaningless for many private debtors who suddenly found they could not obtain repayment until 1934 or 1938 or later, although often with higher interest. A portfolio of old-holder redemption bonds apparently had a real value of 5.8 percent in 1925. But those bonds not paid by 1944 were either annulled or subject to new and complex payment and "revaluation" provisions after

Table 3. *Market and Approximate Present Value of Revaluation (as Percentage of Face Value of Revalued Asset)*

	Private Debts						Government Bonds	
	Mortgages		Mortgage Bonds[d]		Industrial Obligations		Old-Holder Conversion Bonds	
	25% Revaluation Payable 1932		Variable Revaluation Payable 1932		15% Revaluation Payable 1932		12.5% Redemption 1/30 Payable Each Year	
Year Interest Rate[a]	Present[b] Value	Market Value	Present[b] Value	Market Value	Present[b] Value	Market Value	Present[b] Value	Market Value
1925 9.5	74.0	—	?	—	74	—	46.7	—
1926 8.3	82.9	66 70	?	—	82.9	—	55.7	—
1927 7.9	90.2	—	?	—	90.2	—	61.1	—
1928 7.0	93.9	—	?	—	93.9	70	70.6	43–45 50 52
1929 7.4	94.6	—	?	76.6[c] 67–80	94.6	67.6[c]	70.9	52.13[c]
1930 7.2	96.9	80–86	?	85.2[c]	96.9	70.7[c]	75.8	55.87[c]

1931	7.0	99.0	—	?	89.7^c	?	99	72.47^c	73	80.8	54.45^c	44
1932	8.4	?	—	?	78.5^c	?	?	59.08^c		74.4	47.29^c	41
1933	7.2	?	—	?	86^c	?	?	74^c		86.8	68^c	

a. Interest rates are the *annual averages* of yields on GM mortgage bonds (Deutsche Bundesbank, *Bankwesen*, p. 278).

b. Present value was calculated as of 1 July of each year, using the annual average yields to smooth out the often substantial monthly or even weekly fluctuations in interest rates, 1925–1933. The debt moratoria of the 1930s allowed debtors to sue for substantial changes in repayment dates and interest payments for private debts. Because the courts settled such suits on a case-by-case basis, no general calculation of their effects on present value is possible. The present values for private debts given in the table assume interest payments according to the Revaluation Law and principal repayment on 1 January 1932.

For old-holder redemption bonds, payment stopped after 1944, so that about one-third of the bonds suddenly had no value. Because payment resumed under varying conditions for varying redemption bonds and varying creditors (and never resumed in many cases), no general calculation of the "real" revaluation for old holders is possible. Individual creditors would usually have held only one or a few bonds. For them, present value would depend on when or if the government redeemed their bonds. For the few individuals with extremely large holdings, it also would depend partially on the size of the holdings. The present values given here assume a portfolio of bonds would have been redeemed, on average, at the rate of one-thirtieth of the bonds per year. Financial institutions and many substantial investors would have viewed such calculations as the best approximation of present value in the 1920s and 1930s.

These figures are hence *very* inexact. They do suggest what many creditors and would-be investors would have assumed after 1925 that revalued debts were worth. Such assumptions often influenced political and economic decisions in the period under study.

c. These market values are yearly averages and are from *Statistisches Jahrbuch für das deutsche Reich* 52:364. The remaining market values are scattered and *not necessarily representative* quotations from various periodicals and from various times of year.

d. Creditors received interest on mortgage bonds (at 4.5 percent p.a.) only as the various banks issued "GM Liquidation Bonds" in 1927 or later, and the banks periodically added small cash settlements above the face value of the liquidation bond. Hence, no general calculation of present value is possible. Market values would take account of the cash settlements and of delays in repayment after 1931.

1945 that substantially reduced their actual value below the apparent post-1924 values. Those clever or cautious enough to dump their revalued assets at the low market rates of the late 1920s might in fact have come out ahead, but only if they secured much higher interest or avoided those investments subsequently subject to repayment moratoria.

On paper, the German creditor had not done all that badly compared with French and Italian creditors. Those victors had stabilized their currencies at around 20 and 28 percent of prewar values, respectively.[64] Nominally, German mortgage creditors had obtained around 25 percent, and mortgage-bond creditors and savings-bank depositors had generally regained around 20 percent of their prewar investments. Government-bond creditors had nominally received 12.5 percent plus the possibility of a preferential annuity.

Psychologically, however, German creditors were not comparing their situation in 1925 to that of the French or Italians. Creditors believed the revaluation laws robbed them of justly acquired and vested rights. They hence compared their 1925 situation to their December 1923 situation, when the courts had granted them an individual revaluation that they believed would provide them with nearly full recompense.

Even in real terms the German creditor was in a far worse position than his French or Italian counterpart. The data cited in Table 3 suggest how low the real revaluation rates of German revalued assets were. Moreover, the figures do not take into account changes and delays in repayment after 1930. The values given also cannot account for the losses in interest German creditors suffered from about 1920 to 1925. In addition, many older creditors must have died between 1920 and the 1930s and thus have received only meager interest payments.

Subsequent events and government actions had conspired to deprive German creditors of the full fruits of even the modest success they had secured in the revaluation laws. The loss of interest in the 1920s, the repayment moratoria of the 1930s, the new inflation after 1944, all chipped away at the revaluation's real value, so that creditors still paid much of the cost of the German inflation. Having served before the inflation their economic function of accumulating capital, the creditors were dispensable afterwards. The German state sacrificed, resacrificed, and sacrificed them again to the perceived demands of economic necessity.

Conclusion

Any revaluation policy Germany pursued would have harmed the economy. The government could not have reversed its unjust inflationary policies without seriously impeding production. German producers, usually debtors, lacked the resources both to finance substantial revaluation and to invest enough to rebuild operations and regain competitiveness. And without a productive, competitive business sector, Germany faced immediate, severe economic difficulties. Indeed, offering anywhere near the full revaluation creditors deserved would have reignited the inflation, with disastrous consequences. But by limiting revaluation the government only increased Germans' postinflation unwillingness to save and invest. Germany suffered a serious capital shortage in the later 1920s. Sacrificing creditors also meant deleterious economic consequences, albeit longer-term ones.

Because Germany always needed production to meet current needs, it tended to neglect long-term problems and nonproducers' interests. Hence, three German governments treated creditors as more or less dispensable, once the latter had performed their economic function of making savings available to producers. The Second Empire and the Weimar Republic chose to use inflationary policies, and the Republic and the Third Reich rejected substantial revaluation and imposed moratoria on debt repayment.

German creditors, though, were set up in the 1920s to believe that their demand for substantial revaluation was incontrovertible. Their own assumptions, the attitudes of judges, and the actions of political parties obscured their real situation.

The judiciary gave creditors an exaggerated sense of the indisputability of demands for revaluation. Considerations of economic and professional self-interest almost certainly influenced the judiciary, but judges also seemed convinced that the expropriation of creditor assets had been grossly unjust. Reichsgericht judges therefore both ruled that equity required (individual) revaluation and publicly condemned government efforts to limit revaluation. And although the Reichsgericht eventually acquiesced in legislation that did limit revaluation, numerous judges remained publicly committed to substantial revaluation. Many creditors and other Germans hence concluded that justice required that debtors revalue their debts no matter what the cost—to the debtor or, apparently, to the German economy. The revaluation jurisprudence hence became an independent force inducing the political system to respond to creditor demands.

Debtors, usually producers, rejected revaluation out of hand. The "productive" sectors (industry, agriculture, craft production, commerce, and finance) saw themselves as "the economy," as though no one else mattered, including the savers who provided them with necessary capital. Because revaluation could interfere with debtors' competitiveness and profits, they denounced it as economic suicide for Germany. They cited the prevailing economic orthodoxy to justify their indispensability and the impossibility of revaluation. They basically refused to acknowledge that equity could play any role in the issue.

Creditors considered the debtor attitude merely a ploy to evade the moral responsibility to repay honest debts. They denounced the producer/debtor economic orthodoxy as merely self-interested rationalization. This denunciation was not wholly unfounded. Producers did prove willing to abandon important elements of that orthodoxy once Hitler eliminated the democratic Republic they mistrusted.

The economic ideology creditors developed did identify the pitfalls of avoiding revaluation but was otherwise flawed. Creditors were right that rejecting revaluation could lead future savers to invest—or not invest—in ways that weakened the economy. But debtors were right that they and Germany lacked the resources to meet creditor demands, so that substantial revaluation would have weakened the economy even more and would have seriously eroded the positions of many economically marginal Germans. Equity for creditors did mean inequity for others.

More than mere self-interest, though, determined the conflicting and only partially accurate perspectives that creditors and debtors adopted. Revaluation was so new and complex that one could (and still can) honestly debate its exact effects and just how much Germany could afford. Each side could point to ways in which the other's assertions about revaluation were clearly wrong. Indeed, no grand synthesis was available that would solve the intractable economic and moral problems revaluation presented. Given the muddle, Germans tended to choose the perspective most congenial to their interests.

Unfortunately, Weimar politicians were poorly equipped to handle so controversial and complex an issue. Under the Empire, parties had had no incentive to temper their rhetoric because they had had no responsibility for running the government. This legacy shaped Weimar parties. They were more inclined to excessive campaign promises and legislative intransigence than parties with more experience of governmental responsibility might have been. Weimar politicians also lacked economic expertise to understand revaluation. And they faced a real moral dilemma in deciding to what extent they should sacrifice often impoverished creditors to economic expediency. The parties hence promised much more revaluation than they could really provide—in part through intemperate efforts to attract creditor votes, in part through real confusion. Revaluation opponents in the parties were especially negligent; they generally remained silent while their parties touted revaluation reforms the opponents believed were deleterious.

The DNVP was particularly irresponsible. It only secured governmental responsibility in 1925, after it had built up unfulfillable expectations among creditors. Authoritarian in perspective, it expected party supporters to acquiesce unquestioningly whenever party leaders chose to reverse policy. This gave it a cavalier attitude toward campaign promises. DNVP revaluation rhetoric was so misleading that even some of its own supporters accused it of demagoguery.

By late 1924 creditors had every reason to be absolutely convinced of the rectitude and feasibility of their position. The courts had pronounced revaluation the only equitable policy. Creditors had developed a convincing ideology to justify their demands on moral and economic grounds. And most politicians had implicitly or explicitly supported that ideology, simply reinforcing creditor illusions. Although politicians could never have convinced all creditors that substantial revaluation was impossible, policymakers had contrived to leave most creditors convinced of the opposite. To creditors, opponents of revaluation could only be self-interested, suborned, or duped.

The ruling parties' 1925 revaluation policy could then strike creditors only as a travesty of good government. The cabinet sought antirevaluation support by consulting debtor representatives as impartial experts, but it ignored creditor spokesmen. And debtors were obviously putting tremendous pressure on the parties to abandon the creditors to their impoverished fate. The DNVP and DVP then broke campaign promises to accept a government revaluation compromise that even its supporters admitted was flawed. Convinced that equity was the central issue, creditors rejected as immoral the government parties' efforts to justify that compromise on primarily economic grounds. And because creditors believed they were just defending their rights, they were particularly incensed at assertions that they, like debtors, were just another interest whose demands had to give way before economic necessity. Finally, revaluation supporters in the parties asserted, with some justice, that only party discipline kept Reichstag deputies from rejecting the government's modest revaluation laws. Unwilling to abandon their hopes, creditors concluded that Weimar democracy was a sham democracy, actually controlled by unscrupulous economic elites.

Moreover, because parliamentary democracy made compromise obvious, many creditors came to associate it with compromised justice, rather than with the reconciliation of competing but legitimate interests. The Reichstag did secure more revaluation than debtors or the cabinet wanted, but the creditors simply saw the legislature making deals. For creditors, there was right, and there was wrong. (Nearly) full revaluation was right; any other policy, any compromise, was evil. Creditors considered the very concept of partial revaluation immoral: there could be no "25 percent justice."

Although many scholars have emphasized the ability of organized economic interests and the executive to dominate policy-making in the twentieth century ("corporatism," "organized capitalism"), the struggle over revaluation suggests some of the limits to that power. Access to the courts enabled the unorganized creditors to obtain revaluation in 1923. The creditors were able to secure substantial campaign promises in the 1924 elections because of their votes and of sympathy for their sufferings. The government parties retreated from those promises in 1925, but primarily for their own political and economic reasons, not because the executive wanted them to. And the parties and the Reichstag did overrule the government and organized interests with the revaluation laws. Creditors did manage to obtain something approaching the maximum revaluation Germany could afford.

But even though organized producer/debtors could not control revaluation policy, they could prevent creditors and the parties from implementing the most equitable revaluation policy. These producers were so important economically that no government could sacrifice their viability to any group's demand for equity. They could appeal to an economic orthodoxy to justify their policy preferences. And their economic power gave them access to political power. Debtors, including the state, had shifted much of Germany's postwar burdens to creditors with inflation. They could not make so obviously unjust a policy permanent—but they were economically important enough that the maximum revaluation Germany could afford was limited, and they were powerful enough to secure somewhat more than economic necessity demanded.

The postinflation stabilization process may have been economically necessary, but it had extremely corrosive effects on Weimar democracy.

The effects of revolution and defeat burdened the Weimar Republic from the start. Inflation then so weakened Germany economically and so unjustly redistributed social burdens that no government could have stabilized equitably. But the government's decision to favor big business (to secure the stabilization and promote economic recovery) angered most Germans and discredited both capitalism and parliamentary democracy. For many Germans, this decision showed conclusively the inordinate and unjustified power of big business to corrupt the political system. Capitalism meant not equal opportunity for all but unequal advantage for the economically powerful. The weaknesses of the Weimar political order and the ineptitude or demagoguery of politicians only aggravated the situation by creating unfulfillable expectations.

The Weimar party and political systems then began dissolving. The liberal parties were in a particularly weak position. Their individualistic political philosophy failed to offer many Germans sufficient sense of community to mediate the conflicts over economic advantage that stabilization promoted. The liberal parties collapsed in the 1924 elections, never to recover. The DNVP and the splinter parties were the initial beneficiaries, but the DNVP discredited itself by its failure to fulfill campaign promises.

The bitter conflict over revaluation helped foster this dissolution. Creditors repudiated the liberal parties in 1924 as too weak or too unreliable—because corrupted by ties to debtors. In early 1925 they rejected the existing capitalist system as a cabal of unscrupulous profiteers who were determined to preserve their ill-gotten inflation profits. After mid-1925 creditors anathematized the DNVP for basely betraying them and the whole political system for failing to protect their rights. Creditors had economic grievances against the existing order—but they had moral grievances as well. Many creditors then supported creditor political parties, which were developing a creditor, and anti-Weimar, social ideology.

The creditors' ideology was a political, economic, and moral whole. It rejected both Marxism and liberal capitalism because of their materialistic premises. Creditors insisted that people should base their actions on morality, not interest; equity, not profit; community, not individualism. Only by doing right for all could a society and an economy hope to prosper. Yet a proper balance in society—a just recognition of status, hierarchy, and contribution—were also indispensable. In particular, only a solid *Mittelstand*, including creditors, could mediate between elites and workers and ensure political and economic stability. Such a *Mittelstand* could survive neither the cutthroat competition of capitalism nor the leveling of Marxism. This ideology reflected economic self-interest (especially a desire for security) and social self-interest (a desire to preserve their superior status). But it also reflected a moral vision of society as an organic, hierarchical community, dependent on mutual responsibility.

Creditors had no faith, after the revaluation laws of 1925, that parliamentary democracy could promote such an organic community. They hence sought a new kind of society that would actively seek justice instead of merely balancing conflicting interests. And they favored a movement that would unify all Germans, not the interest-based parties (*Interessenparteien*) that divided them.

The creditor ideology shared many important concepts with other *Mittelstand* ideologies—and with Nazi ideology. Other *Mittelstand* groups also perceived deficiencies in Weimar capitalism and Weimar democracy. The groups faced similar problems in defending their interests in a capitalist system beset by virtually intractable economic problems. And they developed out of a common *Mittelstand* culture that believed in community, morality, and status, not interests, as the bases of a legitimate, viable society. As vicious as many elements of Nazi ideology were, it too developed out of this milieu and shared many communitarian, antimaterialistic, and hierarchical values with *Mittelstand* and creditor ideologies.

Against this background of political instability, efforts to deal with the depression further alienated many Germans. Weimar Germany had never been able to meet its citizens' desires for consumption, its economy's need for investment, and the Allies' demands for reparations from its own resources. As the economy slid into depression after 1928, with the end of foreign lending, the German government increasingly had to squeeze its citizens to forestall economic disaster. To creditors, though, the government's introduction of debt moratoria after 1930, to avoid mass debtor bankruptcies, seemed incontrovertible proof that the Republic was both implacably hostile to creditors and morally untrustworthy. Meanwhile, creditor (and other) splinter parties declined, as they proved too weak to protect what their voters perceived as vital interests.

The Nazis were then positioned to sweep up many creditor (and other *Mittelstand*) votes. The Nazis promised to end the depression and to meet the creditors' specific economic demands. Just as important, they promised a new society that mirrored creditor hopes for justice, status, and community. And they increasingly seemed a viable mass party that could obtain sufficient political power to deliver on its promises. Despite Nazi brutality and excesses, many creditors—and other Germans—apparently became convinced that Adolf Hitler offered a moral and social order superior to that of the Weimar Republic. And by the time creditors could realize the Nazis were betraying their promises, it was too late to do anything about it.

The creditors mobilized themselves and made their own choices. Economic elites tried unanimously to convince creditors that substantial revaluation was impossible—and failed. The Nazis certainly preached the inadequacy of democracy and the advantages of hierarchy and authority, but they did not simply seduce the creditors. The latter had already rejected Weimar democracy and embraced a status-based alternative for their own reasons. Nazi ability to benefit from the Weimar Republic's decline reflected the way Nazi promises fit in with many Germans' perceived needs and values. The Nazis were clever, but they faced a receptive audience.

The *Mittelständler* were certainly not alone in abandoning Weimar and voting for Hitler, but they were nonetheless his fundamental base. Upper and upper-middle class Germans were probably more likely to support Hitler than *Mittelständler*, and many workers voted Nazi as well. But *Mittelstand* voters probably provided well over half of Nazi electoral support. They were the core of Hitler's movement, especially in the 1920s. Without their support he scarcely would have seemed a viable enough alternative to the existing system to attract substantial elite or working-class support.

Although analyzing the attitudes of social groups such as creditors contributes to an understanding of Weimar's decline and Hitler's rise, a crucial residuum of individual decision remains. The experiences of a specific group and the shared desires of its members can help explain why group members voted disproportionately for or against democracy, for or against Hitler. But no social group's members voted unanimously. Each German had to weigh various factors, and *individual* calculations of self-interest, values, and social responsibility ultimately determined what each creditor, debtor, employer, employee, farmer, industrialist, and so on would actually do in the voting booth.

Memories of the 1920s revaluation conflict strongly influenced West German politics after World War II. War and defeat had once again expropriated many Germans. Creditors lost their savings anew; Allied bombing and invasion left many Germans homeless; East European governments expelled millions more Germans with little more than the clothes on their backs. Remembering the revaluation conflict's disastrous impact on Weimar democracy, West German policymakers seemed determined not to make the same mistakes. The major parties refused to make extravagant promises to these war-damaged, but they were very careful, often painfully careful, to emphasize and reemphasize the society's moral obligation to provide as much compensation as possible to all those who had suffered. And they ensured that owners of real property would be seen to pay a share (even if not *too* onerous a one) of the burden of war and defeat. Bonn is not Weimar for many reasons. One was that politicians had had a chance to learn some important lessons about rational and responsible politics in a democracy.

Appendix

The Major Provisions of the Revaluation Laws

The key characteristic of the revaluation legislation (see Table 4) was a rejection of individual revaluation, even a revaluation norm, for long-term investments. Unfortunately, under a schematic system such as the government imposed, the revaluation rate had to be low enough that weaker debtors could afford it—leaving a clear profit for stronger debtors and substantial losses for often needy creditors.[1]

Any schematic revaluation rate would be more or less arbitrary. The 25 percent chosen was simply the minimum the parties thought would be politically acceptable. Also, the state could commit only limited funds to government-bond revaluation, and policymakers feared creating too great a gap between private- and public-debt revaluation. Further, the parties wanted to keep the mortgage and savings-account rates close together, and the latter depended primarily on the necessarily limited government-bond rate. Finally, the government did not want to raise rents any more than absolutely necessary, yet it still had to allow landlords enough after mortgage payments and overhead to pay the rent tax.[2]

The government left the industrial-obligation revaluation rate at 15 percent but, at the parties' insistence, offered a *Genusschein* for an additional 10 percent revaluation. Only old holders, who held less than 30 percent of the outstanding obligations, could claim the *Genusschein*. The *Genusschein* entitled its holder to a payment every time the company's dividend exceeded 6 percent. The payment would be proportional to the amount by which the dividend exceeded 6 percent. The *Genusschein* would be extinguished when the old holder had received dividend payments equivalent to 10 percent revaluation of the industrial obligation (with no interest). The government chose the *Genusschein* because it would not affect the company's GM balance or, presumably, its credit. The *Genusschein* would also be less burdensome than increasing the revaluation rate because the company could stretch out its repayment virtually indefinitely and without paying interest. Because it applied to less than 30 percent of the bonds, it would also burden the economy less.[3]

Significantly, only large companies obtained funds with industrial obligations. Whereas they owed in most cases only a 15 percent revaluation, smaller companies that obtained credit on mortgage had to pay the higher 25 percent rate. Indeed, the extensive short-term credits industry had obtained during the inflation were not revalued at all.[4]

The Revaluation Law offered some limited retroactive revaluation. Basically, PM assets only faced such revaluation when creditors had reserved their rights, an apparently infrequent occurrence. As a special exception, all mortgages repaid after 15 June 1922 were revalued retroactively at 25 percent unless this would create undue hardship for debtors or subsequent investors who had acted in good faith. The government parties chose mid-1922 in part as a political compromise but also because of the mark's collapse in the summer of 1922 and because of the

Table 4. *Provisions of the Revaluation Laws*

		Type of Asset	Revaluation Rate	Interest Rate	Payment Due
Primary Revaluation	Private	Mortgage	25%	5%[a]	1932
		Industrial obligation	15%	5%[a]	1932
		Genusschein	10%	0%	varies with company
	Government	Old-holder Reich bond	12.5%	4.5%	1/30 each year
		Old-holder Land bond	12.5%	4.5%	1/30 each year
		Old-holder municipal bond	12.5%	5%	1/30 each year
		New-holder Reich bond	2.5%	0%	?
		New-holder Land bond	2.5%	0%	?
		New-holder municipal bond	2.5%	0%	?
Secondary Revaluation	Private	Mortgage bond	varies with bank	4.5%	1932
		Sparkasse (savings-bank) account	varies with bank	ca. 4.5%	1932, but special provisions for needy
		Employee savings and pension plans	individual revaluation	individual revaluation	individual revaluation
		Commercial bank account	0%	0%	never

Table 4. *continued*

	Type of Asset	Revaluation Rate	Interest Rate	Payment Due
┌─ Secondary Revaluation ┌─ Private	Life insurance	varies with company	0%	1932 or death of policy holder

a. 1.2% from 1/1/25, 2.5% from 1/7/25, 3% in 1926 and 1927.

subsequent flood of repayment notices from debtors. Further, the courts had identified the summer of 1922 as the period when the mark equals mark principle had ceased to be valid and therefore as the general limit for retroactive revaluation.[5]

Retroactive revaluation was extremely important because credit institutions had apparently accepted repayment of most of their mortgages between 15 June 1922 and 28 November 1923. Hence savings-account, life-insurance, and mortgage-bond revaluation rates all depended on the degree of retroactive mortgage revaluation.[6] It may have as much as doubled the amount of mortgage revaluation, although, according to one estimate, only about 40 percent of retroactively revalued mortgages would actually be reestablished because of the hardship clause or conflict with subsequent mortgages established in good faith. Unfortunately, the available data are inadequate to establish its exact effects.[7]

The law subjected seller-financed mortgages to a partial individual revaluation. These debts were not long-term capital investments but expedients in concluding a contract; they seemed clearly entitled to individual revaluation. Nonetheless, debtors argued that if a creditor held one long enough it changed character and obviously became a long-term investment. Despite strong objections from agriculture and industry, the Reichstag mandated that only pre-1909 seller-financed mortgages would be subject to schematic revaluation. The revaluation rate for those seller-financed mortgages dated 1909–11 was not to exceed 75 percent; for those dated 1912–21 it was not to exceed 100 percent.[8] Industry was especially unhappy that revaluation could exceed 100 percent for post-1921 mortgages because courts were granting extremely large revaluations (800 percent in one case).[9] Industry and agriculture lost decisively on this issue, but in the absence of data on how many mortgages were at stake or what average rates the courts set, the implications of their defeat—or indeed the reasons for it—are unclear.

Although creditors and many others saw commercial banks as symbols of wealth, the government succeeded in banning all bank-account revaluation. Demand-deposit revaluation was almost certainly impossible because of its complexity and because the banks had no revaluable assets. Despite unrelenting popular pressure, the Reichstag agreed that term-account revaluation was also impossible.[10]

The assets of savings banks, public and private mortgage banks, and life-insurance companies were entitled to a secondary revaluation. The financial institution collected all its revalued assets in a distribution fund. Mortgage banks could then deduct 8 percent for administration costs. The other institutions covered these costs from their own resources. The Länder could require the mortgage bank or the city or county that guaranteed a savings bank's deposits to contribute to the distribution fund. The financial institution then divided the fund's assets among its PM creditors proportional to their investment. The revaluation rates hence depended on how effectively each financial institution had been able to deal with inflation, given the economic and legal environment in which it had had to operate. Because mortgages were retroactively revalued while savings deposits, mortgage bonds, and life-insurance policies generally were not, the institutions could often offer revaluation rates higher than the usual 15 to 20 percent. Credit cooperatives revalued voluntarily at 25 percent.[11] The Revaluation Law in effect granted individual revaluation to most employee savings and pension plans with employers. If a company administered employee funds separately from its own funds, though, revaluation generally followed the procedures for savings banks.[12]

The government set the interest rate for revalued private debt at 5 percent from 1 January 1928. The rate was 1.2 percent from 1 January 1925, 2.5 percent from 1 July 1925, and 3 percent in 1926 and 1927, low enough not to interfere with the rent tax.[13] The delay burdened many poor creditors who needed all the income they could get as soon as possible, but the state's fiscal interests predominated.

In general, revaluation creditors could not demand repayment until 1 January 1932. This provision only postponed repayment until the midst of the depression and concentrated the transfer of over 7 billion RM of capital on a single day. Although the Reichstag made some provisions for debtors to pay in installments and for creditors to cash in their assets at a discount, the long delay meant misery for many and problems in 1932.[14]

For calculating the GM value of assets purchased during the inflation, the Revaluation Law stipulated an index based on an arithmetic average between the dollar index and the wholesale price index on the day the loan transaction occurred. The law and the courts spilled much ink over determining exactly when judges should deem the transaction to have been consummated for different types of debt. The creditors demanded use of the cost-of-living index—reflecting their consumption orientation and the more favorable result that index would have provided them. The government rejected their argument because borrowers would presumably have used the loan for purchases at wholesale or in dollars, and because for the creditors to have saved by buying consumer goods would have been illegal or speculative hoarding. Some creditors went farther and demanded the use of Reichsgericht Judge Zeiler's index, which took account of the inflation in gold since 1914. Prices in gold were 50 percent higher in the mid-1920s than they had been in 1914, so that a 25 percent revaluation was actually equivalent to only 17 percent in terms of 1914 purchasing power.[15] This abstruse debate over indexes had very real economic implications—and the creditors lost.

To ensure a permanent solution and low expenditures, the Bond Redemption Law required creditors to exchange all outstanding PM government bonds for new redemption bonds at 2.5 percent of face value. *Only* the redemption bonds might henceforth receive any payments. The law further distinguished between old and new holders. The government chose 1 July 1920 as the dividing date because earlier legislation had required all Germans to officially register their assets, including PM long-term investments, from that day forward. Only old holders who could prove continuous possession of the bond since July 1920 would have any immediate claim to payment. New holders would have to wait until reparations had been repaid (about 40 years). This policy significantly reduced the state's debt burden. The cabinet grudgingly agreed to repay old holder Reich and Land bonds at five times face value (12.5 percent revaluation), although for constitutional reasons the Länder retained a nominal right to increase repayment on their (and municipal) bonds. At the SPD's instigation, the law established a graduated scale for payment. If a natural person had claim to more than 12,500 RM of redemption bonds (i.e., held more than 500,000 PM in government bonds), he could receive only 1,000 RM of redemption right for each 2,000 RM of redemption bonds up to 25,000 RM; 1,000 RM for each 3,000 RM up to 50,000 RM; and 1,000 RM for each 4,000 RM above 50,000 RM. As with the old/new distinction, the intent was to punish speculators—and the rich.[16]

Despite some opposition, the cabinet chose to redeem the redemption bonds by lottery, by selecting at random each year 3.33 percent of the outstanding bonds for repayment. Officials claimed this method would stimulate higher redemption-bond quotations on the exchanges, to the creditors' benefit. The government also thought it could more easily stop payment temporarily under a lottery system (by simply not drawing numbers for a few years) if the reparations burden became excessive. And finally, this method provided for a lump sum repayment, which the government thought would be better for capital formation than smaller payments spread over many years. For this reason the government paid the (uncompounded) 4.5 percent interest only when it redeemed the bond.[17]

The government tried to defuse pressure for higher revaluation by allowing a preferential annuity (social revaluation) to needy old holders of government bonds. The annuity was a yearly payment of 80 percent of the redemption bond's face value, that is, 2 percent interest per year in RM on the bond's PM face value, about half the pre-inflation return. The normal maximum payment was 800 RM per year, rising to as much as 1,200 RM per year for individuals over 60 who surrendered their right to redeem their bonds. Individuals could apply for the annuity as long as they held a bond. Their bonds would not participate in the lottery as long as they chose to receive the preferential annuity. Up to 270 RM per year of the annuity would not count as income for those seeking public assistance.[18] As much as the creditors seemed to dislike social revaluation, the preferential annuity did provide some substantial revaluation for eligible creditors.

The government also provided a fund of up to 10 million RM per year for 15 years, financed from tariffs on agricultural imports, for a special annuity to charitable and religious foundations that held redemption bonds. The agricultural tariff bill was at that time before the Reichstag. Left-wing parties attacked this provision, quite possibly correctly, as a cynical attempt to buy small rentier support for the tariffs.[19] It may also have been an attempt to buy off the churches, which had vehemently opposed government revaluation policy and which were substantial creditors.

Municipal PM bonds would receive redemption payments equivalent to a 12.5 percent revaluation, redeemed by lottery over 30 years. The redemption payment was to be repaid with 5 percent accumulated interest. The government parties considered the municipalities well able to pay because they usually had profit-making enterprises, often financed through bond sales. Hence, if the city's fiscal situation permitted, the *Treuhänder* (Land-appointed supervisor of municipal-bond revaluation) could increase the municipal-bond redemption to as much as 25 percent. He could also reduce the repayment period to as little as 20 years. Municipal-bond holders were not entitled to a preferential annuity.[20]

The actual revaluation payments creditors received often differed considerably from the legislation's provisions, as Chapter 10 above shows.

Notes

Abbreviations

In addition to the abbreviations used in the text, the following abbreviations are used in the notes.

Akten RK	*Akten der Reichskanzlei*
BAK	Bundesarchiv Koblenz
BayHStA	Bayerisches Hauptstaatsarchiv
CEH	*Central European History*
DAZ	*Deutsche Allgemeine Zeitung*
DIHT	Deutscher Industrie- und Handelstag (national chamber of commerce)
DJZ	*Deutsche Juristen Zeitung*
DSt	Deutscher Städtetag
FZ	*Frankfurter Zeitung*
G&G	*Geschichte und Gesellschaft*
G&S	*Gläubiger und Sparer*
GLA	Generallandesarchiv
GStADahlem	Geheimes Staatsarchiv Preussischer Kulturbesitz (Dahlem)
HStA	Hauptstaatsarchiv
JW	*Juristische Wochenschrift*
LA	Landesarchiv
MA	Ministerium des Aeussern
MJU	Ministerium der Justiz
ML	Ministerium der Landwirtschaft
MWi	Ministerium der Wirtschaft
NL	Nachlass (personal papers)
OLG	Oberlandesgericht (appeals court)
RAM	Reichsarbeitsminister(ium) (Labor Minister/Ministry)
RdI	Reichsverband der deutschen Industrie (Association of Industry)

REM	Reichsernährungsminister(ium) (Agriculture Minister/Ministry)
RFM	Reichsfinanzminister(ium) (Finance Minister/Ministry)
RGZ	*Entscheidungen des Reichsgerichts in Zivilsachen*
RIM	Reichsinnenministerium (Interior Minister/Ministry)
RJM	Reichsjustizminister(ium) (Justice Minister/Ministry)
RK	Reichskanzler (Chancellor)
RWM	Reichswirtschaftsminister(ium) (Economics Minister/Ministry)
RWR	Reichswirtschaftsrat (Reich Economic Council)
StA	Staatsarchiv
StM	Staatsministerium
Verh RT	*Verhandlungen des Reichstages*
VZ	*Vossische Zeitung*
ZSg	Zeitgeschichtliche Sammlung
ZStA	Zentrales Staatsarchiv

Introduction

1. See, e.g., Childers, *Nazi Voter*; the articles in Feldman, ed., *Nachwirkungen*.

2. A number of recent works have discussed revaluation: see Maier, *Recasting*, pp. 441, 483–84, 491–94, 508–11; Jones, "Inflation"; Southern, "Revaluation Question"; Southern, "Impact of Inflation"; Holtfrerich, *Inflation*, pp. 315–27, 331; also, Balderston, "Links," passim. Portions of this book appeared in a somewhat different form in Michael L. Hughes, "Economic Interest, Social Attitudes, Creditor Ideology: Popular Responses to Inflation," in Feldman et al., eds., *Deutsche Inflation*, pp. 385–408, and Michael L. Hughes, "Private Equity, Social Inequity: German Judges React to Inflation, 1914–1924," *CEH* 16:1 (Mar. 1983): 76–94.

Chapter I

1. See the graph in *Fontana Economic History of Europe*, 4, 1:96; Feldman, *Iron and Steel*, pp. 6–7; P.-C. Witt, "Einleitung," Feldman et al., eds., *Anpassung*, p. vi.

2. Holtfrerich, *Inflation*, pp. 111–12.

3. See the extensive discussion in Roesler, *Finanzpolitik*; also, Heck, "Urteil des Reichsgerichts," pp. 218–19.

4. *Verh RT*, Vol. 315, Anlage #26, p. 7.

5. Dr. Sontag, "Zur Polemik gegen die Ansprüche der Hypothekengläubiger," *JW* 52:21/22 (Nov. 1923): 908; Einspruch des HGSV, 27 Sept. 1923, ZStA, RWM, Nr. 15413, Bl. 140–42.

6. O. Mügel, "Die Frage der Aufwertung der Hypothekenforderungen vom Standpunkt des geltenden Rechtes aus," *JW* 52:21/22 (Nov. 1923): 875; Roesler, *Finanzpolitik*, pp. 47–48.

7. Peter-Christian Witt, "Finanzpolitik und sozialer Wandel in Krieg und Inflation," in Mommsen et al., eds., *Industrielles System*, p. 408; Holtfrerich, "Reichsbankpolitik," p. 194.

8. Holtfrerich, *Inflation*, Table 11; Henning, *Deutschland*, p. 66.

9. Henning, *Deutschland*, p. 60.

10. C.-D. Krohn, "Geldtheorien in Deutschland während der Inflation," in Feldman et al., eds., *Anpassung*, pp. 3–45; Ellis, *Monetary Theory*, passim.

11. Ibid., pp. 121, 161, 180, 247–50 and passim; also, the discussions of revaluation and payment moratorium proposals in *DJZ* and *JW*, 1923, and the numerous letters from creditors to government officials in ZStA, RJM, Nr. 781–85.

12. Henning, *Deutschland*, pp. 63–64, 61.

13. Holtfrerich, *Inflation*, Table 11.

14. Holtfrerich, "Reichsbankpolitik," pp. 199–201, 209; Holtfrerich, *Inflation*, pp. 130–32, 207, 296–98; Feldman, *Iron and Steel*, pp. 206, 280, 282; Witt, "Finanzpolitik," p. 416; Knut Borchardt, "Die Erfahrung mit Inflation in Deutschland," in Borchardt, *Wachstum*, p. 153; Feldman, "Political Economy," especially pp. 188–90, 202–3; Stephen Schuker, "Finance and Foreign Policy in the Era of the German Inflation," in Busch and Feldman, eds., *Prozesse*, pp. 351, 354–57; Kunz, *Civil Servants*, esp. pp. 186, 265. See also Charles Kindleberger, "A Structural View of the German Inflation," in Feldman et al., eds., *Erfahrung*.

15. Holtfrerich, "Reichsbankpolitik," p. 207; Holtfrerich, *Inflation*, p. 167; Schacht, *Stabilization*, p. 49.

16. Holtfrerich, *Inflation*, pp. 67–69, 77–78, 279–94; Holtfrerich, "Verteilungsfolgen," pp. 280–81.

17. See Holtfrerich, *Inflation*, Tables 2 and 4.

18. Halperin, *Germany*, pp. 248–53; Henning, *Deutschland*, p. 66.

19. Luther, *Politiker*, pp. 113–16; Beusch, *Währungszerfall*, pp. 49–51.

20. Luther, *Politiker*, p. 140; Schacht, *Stabilization*, pp. 87, 99–102, 114–15, 117, 119, and passim.

21. Luther, *Politiker*, pp. 140–46, 165, passim; Krohn, *Stabilisierung*, pp. 27–28; Beusch, *Währungszerfall*, p. 73; Kabinettssitzung, 7 Nov. 1923, *Akten RK, Stresemann*, 2:986, 989.

22. Winnewisser, *Aufwertung*, p. 30; Childers, *Nazi Voter*, pp. 160–63.

23. Childers, *Nazi Voter*, p. 277.

24. C. L. Holtfrerich argues this too: *Inflation*, pp. 265–66.

25. See also, Zeiler, *Mitarbeit*, p. 173; Betr.: Reichspartei für Volksrecht und Aufwertung, ZStA, Reichskommissar für die Ueberwachung der öffentlichen Ordnung, Nr. 299, Bl. 24–25; Bayerisches Statistisches Landesamt, *Verelendung*, pp. 49, 53; and for inflation's redistributive effects in West Germany in the 1950s, Mückl, *Wirkungen*, p. 152.

Chapter 2

1. Roth, *Aufwertung*, pp. 8–9, 15–17; for quotation, Dr. E. [Ludwig] Bendix, "Geldentwertung und Rechtsfindung," *JW* 52:21/22 (Nov. 1923): 916. See also Dr. H. Hattenhauer, "Vom Reichsjustizamt zum Bundesministerium der Justiz," in Hattenhauer, ed., *Reichsjustizamt*, pp. 47–48, 51; Dawson, *Oracles*, p. 458; Dr. Wunderlich, "Der kommende Hochkapitalismus," in Oelenheinz, ed., *Spiegel*, p. 70.

2. See, e.g., Sitzung des Reichsministeriums, 25 Jan. 1924, BAK R43 I/1391, Bl. 245.

3. Rüthers, *Auslegung*, pp. 92–93; also, G. Dilcher, "Das Gesellschaftsbild der Rechtswissenschaft und die soziale Frage," in *Das wilhelminische Bildungsbürgertum*, edited by Klaus Vondung (Göttingen, Vandenhoeck and Ruprecht, 1976), p. 58.

4. Dawson, *Oracles*, pp. 432–65.

5. Rüthers, *Auslegung*, pp. 50–51. Even some prorevaluation writers recognized this. See Simonson, "Aufwertungsfrage vom rechtlichen Gesichtspunkt aus," in Grossmann, *Kampf*, p. 71. For use of 242 before 1914 and since the 1920s, see Dawson, *Oracles*, pp. 464–65, 496; Wieacker, *Präzisierung*, pp. 12–13, 37.

6. Dawson, *Oracles*, pp. 438–40.

7. Ibid., pp. 478–81.

8. Ibid., p. 465.

9. *RGZ* 88, 172–78; also, *RGZ* 92, 322–25.

10. Dawson, "Effects of Inflation," p. 183.

11. Cf. Eyck, *Weimar*, 1:287–88; Hattenhauer, *Hierarchie*, pp. 223–25; the discussion in *NS-Recht in historischer Perspektive*, esp. pp. 114–23; and Hans Mommsen, "Beamtentum und Staat in der Spätphase der Weimarer Republik," in *Am Wendepunkt der Europäischen Geschichte* (Göttingen: Muster-Schmidt, 1981), pp. 136–38.

12. Dawson, "Effects of Inflation," pp. 184–86, and 186, n. 48; Rüthers, *Auslegung*, p. 13.

13. For prices, Laursen and Pedersen, *Inflation*, p. 134; Dawson, "Effects of Inflation," pp. 187–88.

14. *RGZ* 103, 328–34; Dawson, "Effects of Inflation," pp. 190, 192–94.

15. Dawson, "Effects of Inflation," p. 192; Paul Oertmann, "Geschäftsgrundlage," in *Handwörterbuch der Rechtswissenschaft*, edited by F. Stier-Somlo and A. Elster (Berlin: de Gruyter, 1926), pp. 803–4.

16. For the quotation, "Rechtsprechung. Reichsgericht," *JW* 51:12 (15 June 1922): 910; also Dawson, "Effects of Inflation," pp. 195–97.

17. Rüthers, *Auslegung*, pp. 42–43.

18. See Bauer, *Wertrelativismus*, which deals in detail with this issue; Rüthers, *Auslegung*, pp. 53–55, 87, and passim; and Huber, *Verfassung*, p. 127.

19. I am grateful to Gunther Teubner for pointing out the laissez-faire basis of the old idea of the *Rechtsstaat*.

20. *RGZ* 104, 402.

21. Rüthers, *Auslegung*, p. 34.

22. Cf. Dawson, *Oracles*, p. 480, n. 2.

23. Hattenhauer, *Hierarchie*, pp. 229–30.

24. *Akten der Reichskanzlei: Kabinett Fehrenbach* (Boppard am Rhein: Harald Boldt Verlag, 1975), p. 1384; Titze, *Richtermacht*; articles in *JW*, 50–52 (1921–23); Hattenhauer, *Hierarchie*, pp. 225–27, 230; Wieacker, *Privatrechtsgeschichte*, pp. 518–20.

25. Heck, "Urteil des Reichsgerichts," p. 205; *RGZ* 101, 141–48.

26. See, e.g., Roth, *Aufwertung*, pp. 8–9, 15–17; G. Best, "Zur Aufwertung von Hypotheken, Industrie-Obligationen und sonstigen langfristigen Geldforderungen," *JW* 52:23 (1 Dec. 1923): 980.

27. See Wieacker, *Industriegesellschaft*, pp. 14–21.

28. Holtfrerich, *Inflation*, p. 31; Lutz, *Kleinrentnerfürsorge*, p. 40; Bayerisches Statistisches Landesamt, *Verelendung*, p. 53.

29. Matthias Rösberg to Dietrich, 11 Mar. 1924, NL Dietrich, #294; H. Kuntze to Erkelenz, 20 Nov. 1924, NL Erkelenz, #33, Bl. 268–70; Verband der Interessenten zur Erlangung der Aufwertung von Reichs-, Staats-, und Kommunalanleihen to Reichspräsidenten et al., 24 Jan. 1925, ZStA, RWM, Nr. 15423, Bl. 326.

30. For quotation, Denkschrift über die Unterstützung notleidender Kleinrentner, 16 Dec. 1921, BAK, R43 I/1373, Bl. 115; Besprechung der Reichsressorts, 17 Oct. 1921, BAK, R38, #69, Bl. 173; *Verh RT*, vol. 352, 152. Sitz. (17 Dec. 1921), pp. 5351–52. Sitzung des Reichsministeriums, 22 Dec. 1922, BAK, R43 I/1381, Bl. 166; *Verh RT*, vol. 358, 294. Sitzung (31 Jan. 1923), p. 9576.

31. G. Best, "Goldmark und Papiermark," *JW* 51:23 (1 Dec. 1922): 1670; Deutscher Rentnerbund to RJM, 22 Jan. 1925, ZStA, RJM, Nr. 853, Bl. 218; and numerous other creditor letters; E. Hoos, "Die Vorzugsrente I," *FZ* 69:333 (6 May 1925); *Verh RT*, vol. 389, 167. Sitz. (1 Mar. 1926), pp. 5810–15.

32. O. Mügel, "Gesetzliche Massnahmen aus Anlass der Geldentwertung," *JW* 50:20 (15 Oct. 1921): 1270–77.

33. See Chapter 3 below, for creditor emphasis on this.

34. See, e.g., A. Zeiler, "Eine Berücksichtigung der Geldentwertung nach dem geltenden Recht," *JW* 51:10 (15 May 1922): 684–88; Best, "Goldmark," pp. 1670–71; [newspaper clips], ZStA, RJM, Nr. 773, Bl. 24, 35.

35. O. Mügel, "Kreditgewährung und wechselnder Geldwert," *DJZ* 27:3/4 (1 Feb. 1922): 73–81; Bund gegen Wucher und Teuerung to RK, 14 Dec. 1922, BAK, R43 I/1246, Bl. 357.

36. Jastrow, *Prinzipienfragen*, p. 20, n. 7.

37. See, e.g., *RGZ* 107, 91.

38. For jurists, see Mügel, "Kreditgewährung," p. 73; A. Düringer, "Schutz der Hypotheken," *JW* 52:10 (15 May 1923): 434. For creditors and Paragraph 607, see, e.g., G. Best, "Dritte Steuernotverordnung, Aufwertungsgesetz und Gesetzentwurf des Sparerbundes," in Bauser, *Wahrheit*, p. 12; Landesverband des HGSSV Mecklenburg, "Die Aufwertung vom wirtschaftlichen Standpunkt aus betrachtet," ZStA, RWM, Nr. 15423, Bl. 340–44.

39. Prussian Justice Ministry to RJM, 5 Dec. 1922, GStA Dahlem, Rep 84a, #5885, Bl. 23; also, Anlage, 5 Dec. 1922, ZStA, RWM, Nr. 15413, Bl. 29.

40. See Mitteilung des Bayerischen Städtebundes, [ca. 25 June 1923], LA

Berlin, Rep 142, #2795/I, and creditor letters; cf. Schwartz in Sitzung des RWR, 2 May 1925, ZStA, RWR, Nr. 397, Bl. 269–70.

41. Anlage, 5 Dec. 1922, ZStA, RWM, Nr. 15413, Bl. 29; Fritz Steyr (Direktor, Bayerische Handelsbank), "Zur Frage der Hypotheken-Kündigungen," 22 Jan. 1923, BAK, R43 I/836, Bl. 91; Georg Best, "Richter und Schuldnerwucher," JW 52:4 (15 Feb. 1923): 111. For debtor notice, Kammergerichtspräsident to Prussian Justice Minister, 8 June 1925, GStA Dahlem, Rep 84a, #5889, Bl. 927–28.

42. Cf. petitions in ZStA, RJM, Nr. 781–84.

43. RWM, 29 Dec. 1922, ZStA, RWM, Nr. 15413, Bl. 30; Abschrift, RJM to RK, 30 Dec. 1922, ibid., Bl. 32; Prussian Justice Minister to Minister President et al., 7 Nov. 1922, GStA Dahlem, Rep 84a, #5885, Bl. 13.

44. RAM to RFM, 5 Dec. 1922, ZStA, RJM, Nr. 845, Bl. 69.

45. See Generallandschaftsdirektion der Provinz Sachsen to Prussian Agriculture Minister, 27 Oct. 1922, ZStA, RJM, Nr. 845, Bl. 11; RdI to RJM, 25 Oct. 1922, ZStA, RJM, Nr. 781. Bl. 6.

46. RWM, 29 Dec. 1922, ZStA, RWM, Nr. 15413, Bl. 30; Abschrift, RJM to RK, 30 Dec. 1922, ibid., Bl. 32–36; [untitled memo], 28 Dec. 1922, GStA Dahlem, Rep 84a, #5885, Bl. 37.

47. For cabinet meeting see Sitzung des Reichsministeriums, 10 Jan. 1923, BAK, R43 I/1382, Bl. 31; for statement see "Keine gesetzgeberischen Eingriffe im Hypothekenwesen in Aussicht," FZ 67:31 (13 Jan. 1923).

48. See, e.g., Bayerische Hypothekenbanken to Bavarian Justice Ministry, 26 Feb. 1923, BayHStA, MJU 15503.

49. Ibid.; Preussischer Landtag. Hauptausschuss, 176. Sitzung, 22 Feb. 1923, ZStA, RJM, Nr. 845, Bl. 117.

50. See, e.g., Bayerische Hypothekenbanken to Bavarian Justice Ministry, 26 Feb. 1923, BayHStA, MJU 15503.

51. Anlage #5597, Verh RT, Vol. 378.

52. See Chapters 5 and 6 below, for Düringer's future activities; Gotthard Jasper, Der Schutz der Republik (Tübingen: J. C. B. Mohr, 1963), p. 85, n. 43, for Düringer's departure from the DNVP; Zur Frage eines Hypothekensperrgesetzes und der Aufwertung alter Hypotheken, 7 June 1923, BayHStA, MJU 15503.

53. "Die Rückzahlung der Hypotheken," FZ 67:188 (12 Mar. 1923); Bayerischer Stellvertreter zum Reichsrat to Justice Ministry, 10 Mar. 1923, BayHStA, MJU 15503.

54. A. Bauser, "Die Geschichte des Aufwertungskampfes," in Bauser, ed., Wahrheit, p. 6; "Reichstagabgeordneter Düringer," Der Sparerschutz 1:5/6 (Sept. 1924), in BayHStA, MA 103775.

55. [Draft, Düringer speech to DVP Parteitag, 29/30 Mar. 1924], BAK, R45 II/28, Bl. 42–43; see Vorstand des deutschen Anwaltsvereins to RJM, 7 Feb. 1923, ZStA, RJM, Nr. 781, Bl. 383; see JW and DJZ for 1923 for articles and reviews of pamphlets; see later in this chapter for court actions. Also, Dawson, "Effects of Inflation," p. 204, n. 6.

56. For examples: newspaper clippings in BayHStA, MJU 15503 and ZStA, RJM, Nr. 773; also articles in, e.g., VZ and Kreuzzeitung for 1923; Bayerischer Landtag, 175. Sitzung (1 Mar. 1923), BayHStA, MJU 15503; Preussischer Landtag, 160. Sitzung (31 Jan. 1923), GStA Dahlem, Rep 84a, #5885, Bl. 47 and

Stenogramm des Landtages, 261. Sitzung (22 June 1923), ibid., Bl. 187; Amtliches Gutachten, 15 Mar. 1923, GStA Dahlem, Rep 84a, #5885, Bl. 63; Mitteilung des Bayerischen Städtebundes, [25 June 1923], LA Berlin, Rep 142, #2795/I; Regierung von Schwaben und Neuburg, Kammer des Innerns to Interior Ministry, 31 Jan. 1923, BayHStA, MJU 15503.

57. Heck, "Urteil des Reichsgerichts," p. 206, argues this as well.

58. RJM to Reichsregierung, 5 Apr. 1923, ZStA, RWM, Nr. 15413, Bl. 73; Geheime Sitzung der wirtschaftspolitischen und finanzpolitischen Ausschüsse unter Hinzuziehung des Ausschusses für Siedlungs- und Wohnungswesen, 2 May 1923, ZStA, RWR, Nr. 397, Bl. 226–75.

59. "Aus dem Reichswirtschaftsrat," *FZ* 67:325 (5 May 1923); "Die Entwertung der Hypotheken," *Kreuzzeitung* 75:204 (4 May 1923).

60. *Verh RT*, vol. 360, 374. Sitzung (4 July 1923), pp. 11602–8; "Die Hypothekenrückzahlung," *FZ* 67:485 (4 July 1923); "Justiz Minister Dr. Heinze über die Hypothekengläubiger," *Kreuzzeitung* 75:306 (5 July 1923).

61. Emminger, *Aufwertungsfrage*, p. 5.

62. "Aufwertung von Pfandbriefforderungen," *Die Sparkasse*, #1126 (17 Oct. 1923); Reichschuldverwaltung, Schuldbuch, G621 im Juni 1923, BAK, R2/1978; Mitteilungen des DSt, 28 June 1923, LA Berlin, Rep 142, #2975/I.

63. Besprechung der Reichsressorts, 17 Oct. 1921, BAK R38/69, Bl. 169; Anlage, RAM, 22 Sept. 1923, ZStA, RWM, Nr. 15413, Bl. 104.

64. RJM, 26 Sept. 1923, ZStA, RWM, Nr. 15413, Bl. 294.

65. For Radbruch see Abschrift, RJM, 4 Aug. 1922, ZStA, RWM, Nr. 15413, Bl. 3–9; Radbruch, *Rechtsphilosophie*, p. 83; RJM to RAM, 17 Oct. 1923, BAK, R43 I/2343, Bl. 330. For SPD, see, e.g., *Rheinische Zeitung*, 32. Jhrg. (1923) and *Vorwärts* 40. Jhrg. (1923); Keil *Erlebnisse*, v. 2, pp. 305–6.

66. REM to RJM, 3 Oct. 1923, ZStA, RJM, Nr. 846, Bl. 7.

67. See "Luther, Hans" in *Biographisches Wörterbuch zur Deutschen Geschichte* 2:1740–41 (Munich: Franke Verlag, 1974); *Akten RK, Luther* 1:xxi–xxii; Luther, *Politiker*, passim; James, *Reichsbank*, p. 162.

68. For the meeting, Sitzung des Reichsministeriums, 12 Oct. 1923, BAK, R43 I/2343, Bl. 322; for the RJM see RJM to RAM, 17 Oct. 1923, ibid., Bl. 330; for RWM see RWM, 26 Oct. 1923, ZStA, RWM, Nr. 15413, Bl. 298 (which was, however, marked "Not sent!").

69. Düringer to Stresemann, 7 Oct. 1923, NL Stresemann, 3104/154195.

70. Stresemann to H. Luther, 10 Oct. 1923, NL Stresemann, 3104/154223; for quotation, Stresemann to Pfarrer P. Luther, 10 Oct. 1923, NL Stresemann, 3104/154221; Stresemann to Rose, 13 June 1924, NL Stresemann, 3117/155932.

71. RFM, VD4179, Oct. 1923, Vermerk; Oberfinanzrat Frommer to Staatssekretär Schroeder, 16 Oct. 1923; Brückner, 13 Oct., zu VD4179; and [memo], Schr., 1 Nov. 1923; all in BAK, R2/1858.

72. [Draft memoirs], NL Luther, #463, Bl. 333–34. But cf. Luther's published memoirs, where he praises the civil servants for always fulfilling their duties faithfully, even when they disagreed politically. Luther, *Politiker*, p. 133.

73. Entwurf, 31 Oct./1 Nov. 1923, ZStA, RJM, Nr. 846, Bl. 77–78 and Preussische Central Boden-Kredit AG to RJM, 13 Nov. 1923, ibid., Bl. 85–87. See also Direktor Dr. Hildebrandt, Rheinische Hypothekenbank, to Minister des In-

nern, 2 Nov. 1923, GLA Baden, Abt. 237, #29425, opposing the RFM's planned revaluation ban. See also Prussian Justice Minister to Minister President, 15 Nov. 1923, GStA Dahlem, Rep 84a, #5885, Bl. 519–28 and Prussian Minister for Science, Art, and Education to Minister President et al., 26 Nov. 1923, ibid., Bl. 571.

74. See ZStA, RJM, Nr. 784 and 785.

75. Zeiler thought so as well: *Mitarbeit*, pp. 129, 145, 152.

76. See, e.g., Schlegelberger's comments in Zur Hypothekenfrage [10 July 1923], ZStA, RJM, Nr. 845, Bl. 233. Also, RWM, 14 Nov. 1922, ZStA, RWM, Nr. 15413, Bl. 24.

77. See, e.g., Wermuth and Schwartz in Geheime Sitzung der wirtschaftspolitischen und finanzpolitischen Ausschüsse unter Hinzuziehung des Auschusses für Siedlungs- und Wohnungswesen, 2 May 1923, ZStA, RWR, Nr. 397, Bl. 228, 270.

78. See RAM, "Plan zur Umgestaltung des Wohnungswesens," BAK, R43 I/2343, Bl. 291–93; REM to RJM, 3 Oct. 1923, ibid., Bl. 307; [memo] to Herrn Minister [of Finance], 28 Nov. 1923, BAK, NL Pünder, #25, Bl. 89–90.

79. "Oberlandesgerichtspräsident Dr. Best," in *Wer ist?* (Berlin: Verlag Herrmann Degener, 1928), p. 114.

80. Best, "Goldmark," pp. 1670–71.

81. Best, "Richter," p. 111.

82. "Urteil des OLG Darmstadts, 29. Marz 1923," *JW* 52:10 (15 May 1923): 459 and "Urteil des OLG Darmstadts, 18. Mai 1923," *JW* 52:11 (1 June 1923): 522. For Best's role see Zeiler, *Mitarbeit*, p. 49.

83. Zeiler, *Mitarbeit*, p. 49.

84. See Becker, *Behavioralism*, pp. 41ff., for a general discussion of the constraints set by the judicial role.

85. See the letters from the various Prussian OLGpräsidenten in GStA Dahlem, Rep 84a, #5904; "Denkschrift zur Unterstützung des Antrages Düringers," *JW* 52:21/22 (1 Nov. 1923): 874; "Hypothekenrückzahlung in entwertetem Geld," *Die Sparkasse* #1106 (30 May 1923), p. 228.

86. OLGpräsident Frankfurt to Prussian Justice Minister, 23 Oct. 1923, GStA Dahlem, Rep 84a, #5904, Bl. 86; see also OLGpräsident Celle to Prussian Justice Minister, 20 July 1923, ibid., Bl. 36–37.

87. OLGpräsident Breslau to Prussian Justice Minister, 27 July 1923, ibid., Bl. 23–28 and OLGpräsident Celle to Prussian Justice Minister, 20 July 1923, ibid., Bl. 36–38.

88. OLGpräsident Köln to Prussian Justice Minister, 29 July 1923, ibid., Bl. 136 and OLGpräsident Düsseldorf to Prussian Justice Minister, 6 Aug. 1923, ibid., Bl. 46.

89. Richterverein beim Reichsgericht, "Gesetzentwurf neben Begründung," *DJZ* 28:15/16 (1 Aug. 1923): 442, 445.

90. "Hypothekenaufwertung," *VZ*, #517 (1 Nov. 1923); "Zur Hypothekenaufwertung," *VZ*, #551 (21 Nov. 1923).

91. Zeiler, *Mitarbeit*, p. 153; cf., Dawson, "Effects of Inflation," p. 203.

92. *RGZ* 107, 78–94; Nussbaum, *Money*, p. 206; also, "Zur Hypothekenaufwertung," *VZ*, #551 (21 Nov. 1923).

93. *RGZ* 107, 78–94; for future cases, Jastrow, *Prinzipienfragen*, p. 20.

94. *RGZ* 107, 78–94; for quotation, 87.

95. See, e.g., the prorevaluation Dr. Lehmann, "Artikel 151, Absatz 1," in Nipperdey, ed., *Grundrechte und Grundpflege* 3:147.

96. See Heck, "Urteil des Reichsgerichts," p. 210.

97. Rüthers, *Auslegung*, p. 77; also, Heck, "Urteil des Reichsgerichts," pp. 210–14, 219.

98. Cf. Lehmann, "Artikel 151, Absatz 1," p. 147; Eyck, *Weimar* 1:287–88; for Reichsgericht destruction of documents, oral communication from ZStA staff.

99. Bendix, "Geldentwertung," p. 916, his emphasis; see also, Dawson, "Effects of Inflation," p. 176, and Oertmann, *Aufwertungsfrage*, pp. 7–8.

100. Dr. W. Simons to Sir Graham Bower, NL Simons (Kleine Erwerbungen 378), #1, Bl. 8; see the articles on revaluation by jurists in *JW* and *DJZ*, 1923, and Oertmann, *Aufwertungsfrage*, pp. 7–9.

101. Dr. G. Best, "An dem Herrn Präsidenten des Reichstages," "Offener Brief," and "Niederträchtige Verleumdung," all in *G&S* 1:1 (8 July 1925).

102. Cf. Enquete-Ausschuss, *Wohnungsbau*, p. 271 and Bayerisches Statistisches Landesamt, *Verelendung*, p. 49; for judges, see David Southern, "Impact of Inflation," pp. 64–65; and cf. Reichsgerichtspräsident Simons to RK, 30 May 1925, BAK, R43 I/1211, Bl. 317.

103. Dessauer, *Recht*, p. 89; Fraenkel, *Klassenjustiz*, pp. 15, 26; Rademacher to Westarp, n.d., NL Westarp, 1925, Aufwertung (albeit, Rademacher was a representative of industry and therefore of debtor forces). Also, Eyck, *Weimar*, 1:288. Cf. Bauer, *Wertrelativismus*, pp. 237–38; J. Lehmann, "Die Aufwertungsliteratur II," *Steuer und Wirtschaft*, 3:12 (Dec. 1924): 1674; and Southern, "Impact," pp. 64–65.

104. Dessauer, *Recht*, p. 89.

105. Teilbericht über die 34. Sitzung, 18. Ausschuss, 27 June 1925, NL Marx, #412.

106. Cf. Dessauer, *Recht*, p. 65; Heck, "Urteil des Reichsgerichts," pp. 210–11; Roth, *Aufwertung*, pp. 41–42. For economic implications, see Chapter 6 below. For the creditor insistence that revaluation was not a problem of national economics but of (private) morality, see e.g., Mügel, *Aufwertungsrecht*, p. iv; Grossmann et al., *Kampf*, p. 9 and passim. See Chapters 6 and 8 below, for the corresponding debtor obsession with economic efficiency.

107. Wieacker, *Privatrechtsgeschichte*, pp. 438–39. My thanks to Prof. James Gordley for raising this issue.

108. See Chapter 1 above.

109. See Fraenkel, *Klassenjustiz*, passim, and articles in *Deutsche Richterzeitung*, 1922–23.

110. See, e.g., the letters reprinted in Oelenheinz, ed., *Spiegel*, pp. 62, 69; Schutzverband der Hypotheken-, Pfandbrief-, und Obligationengläubiger in Bayern, Ortsgruppe Steinach, 18 June 1924, BayHStA, MJU 15503; Neue Sparcasse to RJM, 31 Mar. 1925, ZStA, RJM, Nr. 884, Bl. 42–44; R. Wüst, *Aufwertungsproblem*, p. 2.

111. Schutzverband der Hypotheken-, Pfandbrief-, und Obligationengläubiger in Bayern, Ortsgruppe Steinach, 18 June 1924, and Erklärung, Sparerkommittee,

Rott a. d. Inn, 3 Feb. 1924, BayHStA, MJU 15503.

112. Best, "Richter," p. 111; Dr. H. Abraham, "Die Gefährdung der Zivil-rechtspflege," *DJZ* 28:9/10 (1 May 1923): 269–71; Prussian Justice Minister to Minister President et al., 15 Nov. 1923, GStA Dahlem, Rep 84a, #5885, Bl. 519–20.

113. [draft article], Für *Die Zeit*, 1923 [ca. Oct./Nov.], NL Stresemann, 3099/146083; Stresemann to Rose, 13 June 1924, NL Stresemann, 3117/155932, and Preussischer Richterverein, OLGbezirkverband Königsberg to Stresemann, 12 Dec. 1924, NL Stresemann, 3120/157768; and G. Stresemann, "Vom Rechte, das mit uns geboren" [newsp. clip, ca. Mar. 1923], ZStA, RJM, Nr. 782, Bl. 157.

114. OLGpräsident Düsseldorf to Prussian Justice Minister, 6 Aug. 1923, GStA Dahlem, Rep 84a, #5904, Bl. 47; OLGpräsident Hamm to Prussian Justice Minister, 15 Aug. 1923, ibid., Bl. 96; OLGpräsident Kiel to Prussian Justice Minister, 28 July 1923, ibid., Bl. 126; OLGpräsident Köln to Prussian Justice Minister, 29 July 1923, ibid., Bl. 145.

115. All the letters are in GStA Dahlem, Rep 84a, #5904.

116. OLGpräsident Hamm (see n. 114).

117. OLGpräsident Kiel (see n. 114).

118. Richterverein, "Gesetzentwurf," p. 442.

119. Dessauer, *Recht*, pp. 11, 23–24; Reichsgerichtspräsident Simons to RK, 30 May 1925, BAK, R43 I/1211, Bl. 315; for quotation, OLGpräsident Celle to Prussian Justice Minister, 20 July 1923, GStA Dahlem, Rep 84a, #5904, Bl. 37; *RGZ* 111, 322–23; Nussbaum, *Money*, p. 212.

120. Cf. Roberto Unger, *Law in Modern Society* (New York: Free Press, 1976), pp. 188–89.

Chapter 3

1. See BAK, R43 I/1390–92 (Kabinettsprotokollen).

2. Ibid. See also, Luther, *Politiker*, pp. 215–18, 230, and passim; Netzband and Widmaier, *Finanzpolitik*, p. 43 and passim.

3. Hardach, *Wirtschaftsgeschichte*, pp. 18–19, 23–26, 31–35; Henning, *Deutschland*, pp. 52–55, 59–61.

4. Luther, *Feste Mark*, pp. 17–18; Holtfrerich, *Inflation*, p. 275; Menders-hausen, *Recoveries*, p. 27.

5. Cf. BAK, R43 I/1389–91 (Kabinettsprotokollen) and below.

6. Maier, *Recasting*, pp. 384–86; *Akten RK, Marx*, p. vii; Krohn, *Stabilisie-rung*, pp. 23, 29–30; M. Vogt, "Rudolf Hilferding als Finanzminister im Ersten Kabinett Stresemann," in Feldman and Busch, eds., *Prozesse*, pp. 136–37.

7. Halperin, *Germany*, pp. 284–85; the cabinet protocols for early December in BAK, R43 I/1390, especially Bl. 10–11; and *Verh RT*, vol. 361, 397. Sitzung (8 Dec. 1923), pp. 12375, 12386.

8. Maier, *Recasting*, pp. 385–86.

9. F. Ramhorst, *Die Entstehung der deutschen Rentenbank* (Berlin: Selbstverlag des Reichsverbandes der deutschen Industrie, 1924), p. 4; "Kabinettssitzung vom 7. September 1923," *Akten RK, Stresemann*, p. 210; "Kabinettssitzung vom

10. September 1923," ibid., pp. 225–26; G. Feldman and I. Steinisch, "Die Weimarer Republik zwischen Sozial- und Wirtschaftsstaat," *Archiv für Sozialgeschichte* 18 (1978): 381.

10. Luther, *Feste Mark*, pp. 10–12, 24, 37–38, 43; Steinisch, "Auswirkungen," p. 422; see Chapter 6 below, for further discussion of these attitudes.

11. Feldman, *Iron and Steel*, pp. 387, 427–33; Feldman and Steinisch, "Weimarer Republik," esp. pp. 354, 368–69, 384, 388–98, 411; Maier, *Recasting*, pp. 403, 444–47; "Gemeinsame Sitzung des Reichskabinetts und des Preussischen Staatsministeriums, 5. Dezember 1923," *Akten RK, Marx*, 1:43; for working hours and productivity, Enquete Ausschuss, IV. Unterausschuss, *Verhandlungen*, esp. vol. 9.

12. For the quotation, see "Das Auswärtige Amt an Staatssekretär Bracht, 2. Februar 1924," *Akten RK, Marx*, pp. 315–16; also, Feldman and Steinisch, "Weimarer Republik," pp. 412, 414–19, 436–37; Krohn, *Stabilisierung*, pp. 54, 58.

13. Childers, "Inflation," p. 416; Childers, *Nazi Voter*, pp. 87–89, passim; Netzband and Widmaier, *Finanzpolitik*, pp. 224–25, 231; Krohn, *Stabilisierung*, pp. 37, 102; *Akten RK, Marx*, 1:72, n. 2; "Besprechung mit Vertretern der Beamtenorganisationen, 19. Februar 1924," ibid., pp. 381–83 and Kunz, *Civil Servants*, esp. pp. 378, 381.

14. Krohn, *Stabilisierung*, pp. 37–38; Netzband and Widmaier, *Finanzpolitik*, pp. 124, 169–74.

15. Netzband and Widmaier, *Finanzpolitik*, pp. 153–63; Krohn, *Stabilisierung*, pp. 41–43, 70, 113–15, 151–52, 156, 181.

16. "Sitzung des Reichskabinetts, der Ministerpräsidenten der an der Besatzung beteiligten Länder und des Fünfzehner Ausschusses, 17. November 1923," *Akten RK, Stresemann*, p. 1124; Beusch, *Währungszerfall*, pp. viii, ix; Luther, *Feste Mark*, pp. 30–32; Netzband and Widmaier, *Finanzpolitik*, pp. 185–86, 190–92, 194–96.

17. Krohn, *Stabilisierung*, pp. 51–52.

18. Krohn, *Stabilisierung*, pp. 43–44; Netzband and Widmaier, *Finanzpolitik*, pp. 198–202.

19. Krohn, *Stabilisierung*, pp. 43, 52, 134, 174–86.

20. "Kabinettssitzung vom 20. Oktober 1923," *Akten RK, Stresemann*, pp. 666, 668; "Kabinettssitzung vom 1. November 1923," ibid., p. 934.

21. "Kabinettssitzung vom 7. Februar 1925," *Akten RK, Luther*, 1:59–63; Krohn, *Stabilisierung*, pp. 106–9; Netzband and Widmaier, *Finanzpolitik*, pp. 259–65.

22. "Kabinettssitzung vom 7. Februar 1925," *Akten RK, Luther*, 1:59–63; Krohn, *Stabilisierung*, pp. 110–12; see also Chapter 9 below.

23. Krohn, *Stabilisierung*, pp. 212–22; Dietmar Petzina, "Staatliche Ausgaben und deren Umverteilungswirkungen—das Beispiel der Industrie- und Agrarsubventionen in der Weimarer Republik," in Fritz Blaich, ed., *Staatliche Umverteilungspolitik in historischer Perspektive* (Berlin: Duncker & Humboldt, 1980), pp. 59–106.

24. Hellmut Lange, "Die ersten Rentenmark," *Frankfurter Hefte* 1:9 (Dec. 1946): 885; Luther, *Politiker*, p. 143.

25. See, e.g., Ministerium des Aeussern, Betrifft: Entwurf einer 3. Steuernotverordnung, 5 Feb. 1924 (for quotation) and StM der Justiz to StM des Aeussern, 20 Dec. 1923, BayHStA, ML 1689; Ministerialrat Schlüter, "Grundsätzliches zum Entwurf der dritten Steuernotverordnung," *Germania* 54:37 (6 Feb. 1924); Prussian Justice Minister to Minister President, 15 Nov. 1923, GStA Dahlem, Rep 84a, #5885, Bl. 519–20.

26. President, Preussische Boden Kredit-Anstalt to RFM Luther, 3 Dec. 1923, ZStA, RJM, Nr. 786, esp. Bl. 30; DIHT, Handelskammer zu Berlin, "3. Steuernotverordnung," 7 Feb. 1924, ZStA, RWM, Nr. 15423, Bl. 8–9. See this chapter below for debtor group interests.

27. See, e.g., Deutscher Braunkohlen Industrie Verein to RWM, 16 Jan. 1924, ZStA, RWM, Nr. 15413, Bl. 234; Landeskulturrentenstelle to StM Landwirtschaft, 1 Feb. 1924, BayHStA, ML 1689; Stadtsparkasse Reichenbach o/ Laus. to Deutschen Sparkassenverband, 4 Feb. 1924, LA Württemberg, E130/II, Bushel 392, Bl. 55.

28. See Chapters 4 and 6 below.

29. See, e.g., Sitzung des Hauptausschusses [DIHT], 13 Feb. 1924, Stiftung Westfälisches Wirtschaftsarchiv, K-2, #346; Sitzung des Reichsministeriums, 17 Dec. 1923, BAK, R43 I/1390, Bl. 219; Hamburg Gesandtschaft, Bericht über die Beratungen der vereinigten Reichsratsausschüsse über den Entwurf einer 3. Steuernotverordnung, 21 Dec. 1923, StA Hamburg, Cl. I Lit. T, No. 15b, Vol. 70, Fasc. 1, Cour. II.

30. For quotation: Zur Frage eines Hypothekensperrgesetzes und der Aufwertung alter Hypotheken, 7 June 1923, BayHStA, MJU 15503; and also, StM für Handel, Industrie und Gewerbe to Ministerpräsidenten Knilling, 23 June 1923, ibid.

31. For quotation: [StM der Justiz] to StM des Aeussern, 29 Dec. 1923, ibid.; also, Abschrift, Generalstaatskommissar, 17 Dec. 1923, ibid.

32. For quotation: Vermerkung, 8 Feb. 1924, BayHStA, MA 103772; cf. Gordon, *Beer Hall Putsch*, pp. 413–15.

33. Luther, *Politiker*, p. 243; For Hamm, Sitzung des Hauptausschusses [DIHT], 13 Feb. 1924, Stiftung Westfälisches Wirtschaftsarchiv, K-2, #346.

34. For Wilhelmine rhetoric see, Volkov, *Popular Antimodernism*, esp. pp. 273–75, and Gellately, *Politics*.

35. Bund gegen Wucher und Teuerung to RK, 6 Feb. 1923, BAK, R43 I/1246, Bl. 348–51; Witwe Pastor Hermann Schmieder to RWM, 30 Aug. 1923, ZStA, RWM, Nr. 15413, Bl. 132–34; Geh. Sanitätsrat Dr. Grittnem to RK, 12 Dec. 1923, BAK, R43 I/2454, Bl. 3.

36. Wilhelm Koch to Erkelenz, 15 Dec. 1923, NL Erkelenz, #29, Bl. 176; HGSV, Entschliessung, 9 Dec. 1923, ZStA, RWM, Nr. 15413, Bl. 149; HGSSV, Ortsgruppe Duisburg to Reichstag, Mitte Juni 1924, ZStA, RWM, Nr. 15423, Bl. 113. For a general discussion of the impact of legal systems cf. E. P. Thompson, *Whigs and Hunters* (New York: Pantheon Books, 1975), pp. 258–69.

37. See, e.g., HGSSV to StM des Aeussern, Bayern, 22 Dec. 1923, BayHStA, MA 103775.

38. See ibid.; ZStA, RJM, Nr. 786–8; [Petition], Schutzverband der Inhaber v.

Hypotheken, Obligationen, Anleihen und Versicherungspolicien, 4 Feb. 1924, StA Hamburg, Cl. I Lit. T, No. 15b, Vol. 70, Fasc. 1, Cour. II; HGSV f. das deutsche Reich to Staatsministerium, 21 Dec. 1923, GLA Baden, Abt. 237, #29425.

39. "Posthof" GmbH to Bayerischer Handelsbank, 12 Feb. 1923, BAK, R43 I/652, Bl. 90.

40. See, e.g., A. Doctor Aktien-Gesellschaft to Reichstagabgeordneter Rektor Kopsch, 12 Jan. 1925, NL Dietrich, #295, Bl. 111; v. Amburger to Ausschuss für Aufwertung, Reichstag, 2 Feb. 1925, ZStA, RWM, Nr. 15423, Bl. 279.

41. See, e.g., Haus und Grundbesitzerverein Breslau to Reichsregierung, 29 Nov. 1923, ZStA, RJM, Nr. 786, Bl. 19; also, "Hypothekenaufwertung und Eigenhausbewohner," *Rheinisch-Westfälische Zeitung* 86 (1 Feb. 1924), ZStA, RWM, Nr. 15413, Bl. 268; Martin H. Geyer, "Wohnungsnot und Wohnungs-zwangswirtschaft in München 1917 bis 1924," in Feldman et al., eds., *Anpassung*, pp. 145, 150.

42. Handelskammer Bremen, Betr. Aufwertung von Hypotheken und sonstigen Markforderungen, 16 Jan. 1924, ZStA, RWM, Nr. 15413, Bl. 123; Central-verband des Deutschen Grosshandels to RWM, 11 Jan. 1924, ibid., Bl. 241.

43. The government feared just such a result: zu Reichskanzler durch Herrn Staatssekretär, 18 Jan. 1924, BAK, R43 I/2454, Bl. 71.

44. See, e.g., DIHT to RWM, 15 Jan. 1924, ZStA, RWM, Nr. 15413, Bl. 236; Handelskammer zu Chemnitz to RJM, 21 Feb. 1924, ZStA, RJM, Nr. 847, Bl. 243; DIHT, Handelskammer zu Berlin, 3. Steuernotverordnung, 7 Feb. 1924, ZStA, RWM, Nr. 15423, Bl. 9; Handelskammer Frankfurt a/M-Hanau to RFM, 21 Jan. 1924, Industrie- und Handelskammer zu München, XIII, 26.

45. RdI to RWM, 16 Jan. 1924, ZStA, RWM, Nr. 15413, Bl. 229.

46. See the minutes in IHK Münster: Arbeitsgemeinschaft, Rheinisch-West-fälisches Wirtschaftsarchiv, Abt. 5, #17, Fasz. 3; "Zur wirtschaftspolitischen Lage," in *Vergangene Zeit*, Buch 3, NL Funcke; and Stiftung Westfälisches Wirt-schaftsarchiv, K-2, #587; Deutscher Landwirtschaftsrat. Entschliessung, 10 Jan. 1924, BAK, R43 I/2395, Bl. 7.

47. Centralverband des deutschen Bank und Bankiergewerbes, Sonderaus-schuss für Hypothekenbankwesen, Betr. Entwurf der 3. Steuernotverordnung, 5 Feb. 1924, ZStA, RJM, Nr. 881, Bl. 4; Rheinische Hypothekenbank to Staats-kommissar der Rheinischen Hypothekenbank, 3 Jan. 1924, GLA Baden, Abt. 237, #29425; Bayerische Handelsbank Bodenkreditanstalt, Zur Aufwertung der Pfandbriefe und Deckungshypotheken der Hypothekenbanken, 15 Feb. 1924, BayHStA, MWi 491. For future savings patterns see Chapters 6 and 10 below.

48. "Aufwertung von Hypotheken und sonstigen Forderungen," *Mitteilungen des Landesverbandes Bayerischer Sparkassen*, 16 (10 Dec. 1923); "Aufwer-tung, Personalabbau und Jahresabschluss," *Die Sparkasse* #1134 (15 Dec. 1923); "Aufwertung von Spareinlagen?" *Die Sparkasse* #1135 (22 Dec. 1923).

49. See, e.g., Sitzung des Wirtschaftsausschusses des Reichsministeriums, 15 Dec. 1923, BAK, R43 I/1390, Bl. 201; Ausschnitt, *Mitteilungen des DSt*, #2, 15 Feb. 1924, StA Hamburg, Cl. I Lit. T, No. 15b, Vol. 70, Fasc. 1, Cour. II; StM der Justiz to RJM, 3 Dec. 1923, BayHStA, MJU 15503.

50. BAK, R43 I/1390 [Kabinettsprotokollen] and, for quotation, Herrn Staatssekretär gehorsamst vorgelegt, 13 Dec. 1923, BAK, R43 I/2358, Bl. 60, which is
based on a RFM memo.

51. See the series of reports on revenue and expenditures in BAK, R43 I/2358;
Sitzung des Reichsministeriums, 2 Dec. 1923, BAK, R43 I/1390, Bl. 10, and
Rhein-Ruhr Ausschuss des Reichskabinetts, 7 Feb. 1924, BAK, R43 I/1392, Bl.
186–88.

52. Luther, *Politiker*, p. 230; for a discussion of the tax situation see Krohn,
Stabilisierung, esp. pp. 38–40. For Luther, see, e.g., Sitzung des Wirtschaftsausschusses des Reichsministeriums, 15 Dec. 1923, BAK, R 43 I/1390, Bl. 201–03;
Germania also thought revaluation threatened the stabilization: "Die Aufwertung
der Hypotheken," *Germania* 53:340 (13 Dec. 1923).

53. See, e.g., zu Reichskanzler durch Herrn Staatssekretär, 18 Jan. 1924,
BAK, R43 I/2454, Bl. 71.

54. Reichswehrminister to RK, 7 Jan. 1924, BAK, R43 I/2454, Bl. 57; see
also the references in note 46 above, Chapter 6 below, and Luther, *Politiker*,
p. 239.

55. RFM to Senat, 31 Jan. [1924], StA Hamburg, Cl. I Lit. T, No. 15b, Vol.
70, Fasc. 1, Cour. I; A. Brodauf (DDP), "Aufwertung und Finanzen," *VZ* #40
(24 Jan. 1924).

Chapter 4

1. Abschrift, Hamburg, Gesandtschaft, #6073, 30 Nov. 1923, StA Hamburg,
Fin. Dep. IV (Betr.: Gesetz über die Aufwertung von Hypotheken . . .); StM der
Justiz to StM des Aeussern, 20 Dec. 1923, BayHStA, ML 1689; and this chapter
below; but cf. Luther, *Politiker*, pp. 229–33. For a more detailed discussion of the
internal government debate on the Tax Decree revaluation see Hughes, "Equity,"
pp. 123–80.

2. Sitzung des Wirtschaftsausschusses des Reichsministeriums, 15 Dec. 1923,
BAK, R43 I/1390, Bl. 201–3; Sitzung des Reichsministeriums, 17 Dec. 1923,
ibid., Bl. 217–20.

3. Hamburg Gesandtschaft, "Bericht über die Beratungen der vereinigten
Reichsratausschüsse über den Entwurf einer 3. Steuernotverordnung," 21 Dec.
1923, StA Hamburg, Cl. I Lit. T, No. 15b, Vol. 70, Fasc. 1, Cour. II.

4. RK to sämtlichen Herrn Reichsministers, 3 Jan. 1924, BAK, R43 I/2454, Bl.
29; RIM to RK, 6 Jan. 1924, ibid., Bl. 35; Reichswehrminister to RK, 7 Jan.
1924, ibid., Bl. 57; Abschrift, RWM to RK, 6 Jan. 1924, ZStA, RWM, Nr.
15413, Bl. 117–21; Reichsverkehrsminister to RK, 6 Jan. 1924, ZStA, RWM, Nr.
15414, Bl. 60–61; Abschrift, Reichsminister für Wiederaufbau to RK, 4 Jan.
1924, ibid., Bl. 62; REM to RK, 8 Jan. 1924, ibid., Bl. 63; Reichspostminister to
RK, 11 Jan. 1924, ibid., Bl. 66; RJM to RK, 7 Jan. 1924, ZStA, RJM, Nr. 846,
Bl. 140–45.

5. Zeiler, *Mitarbeit*, pp. 156–57.

6. Richterverein beim Reichsgericht to RK, 8 Jan. 1924, BAK, R43 I/2454, Bl. 81. Rüthers too argues the letter was not a direct challenge, *Auslegung*, pp. 80–81, as did a RWM official, Vermerk, 5 Feb. 1924, ZStA, RWM, Nr. 15413, Bl. 270.

7. Hedemann, *Reichsgericht*, p. 242; Eyck, *Weimar*, 1:287.

8. Cf. Hattenhauer, "Reichsjustizamt," pp. 49–51; Pirlet, *Kampf*, pp. 47–48; Eyck, *Weimar*, 1:287–88.

9. *Deutsche Richterzeitung*, 15 Jan. 1924; *JW* 53:2 (15 Jan. 1924): 90; "Die Aufwertung der Hypotheken," *VZ* #26 (16 Jan. 1924).

10. Staatssekretär in der Reichskanzlei to RK, 1/7. 24. Januar 1924 [sic], BAK, R43 I/2454, Bl. 83–86; "Gesetzgebung und Reichsgericht," *VZ* #54 (1 Feb. 1924).

11. Hattenhauer, "Reichsjustizamt," pp. 50–51.

12. "Kardinal Faulhaber über die Aufwertung," *G&S* 4:2 (7 Jan. 1928); Erzbischöfliches Ordinariat, Freiburg/Breisgau to RK, 14 Jan. 1924, BAK, R43 I/2454, Bl. 87. "Die Aufwertung der Hypothekenforderungen," *Germania* 54:12 (12 Jan. 1924); "Kirche und Aufwertungsfrage," *VZ* #21 (12 Jan. 1924).

13. "Die Aufwertung der Hypothekenforderungen," *Germania* 54:12 (12 Jan. 1924); "Kirche und Aufwertungsfrage," *VZ* #21 (12 Jan. 1924).

14. Dr. Paersch, "Zur Frage der Aufwertung," ZStA, Reichsbank, Nr. 6653, Bl. 196.

15. See, e.g., Entschliessung, Schutzverband der Hypotheken-, Pfandbrief-, und Obligationengläubiger in Bayern, 10 Feb. 1924, ZStA, RWM, Nr. 15423, Bl. 18; for speculative activity see *FZ* or *VZ* for Dec. 1923–Feb. 1924.

16. Protokoll #270b, 8 Jan. 1924, in Morsey and Ruppert, eds., *Protokolle*, p. 523; Lippmann to Bund der Innungen und fachlichen Vereine, Hamburg, 9 Jan. 1924, StA Hamburg, Cl. I Lit. T, No. 15b, Vol. 70, Fasc. 1, Cour. I.

17. Sitzung des Reichsministeriums, 17 Jan. 1924, BAK, R43 I/1391, Bl. 151.

18. Württembergischer Bevollmächtigte zum Reichsrat to Staatsministerium, 18 Jan. 1924, LA Württemberg, E 130/II, Bushel 392, Bl. 29; "Der RJM zur Aufwertungsfrage," *VZ* #31 (18 Jan. 1924).

19. See Chapter 7 below.

20. Cf. Luther's praise in his memoirs for Emminger: Luther, *Politiker*, p. 212.

21. Entwurf einer 3. Steuernotverordnung [19 Jan. 1924], BAK, R43 I/1391, Bl. 176. Sitzung des Reichsministeriums, 22 Jan. 1924, BAK, R43 I/2454, Bl. 119.

22. Sitzung des Reichsministeriums, 25 Jan. 1924, BAK, R43 I/1391, Bl. 244–47.

23. Ibid., Bl. 245; see Chapter 2 above; also, RAM to RK, 22 Dec. 1923, NL Marx, #58, Bl. 39a–39b; Protokoll #271, 8 Jan. 1924, in Morsey and Ruppert, eds., *Protokolle*, pp. 527–28; RAM Brauns to Domkapitular Prof. Thielemann, 8 Feb. 1924, NL Marx, #203.

24. Sitzung des Reichsministeriums, 25 Jan. 1924, BAK, R43 I/1391, Bl. 244–47.

25. Cf. Sitzung des Rhein-Ruhr Ausschusses des Reichskabinetts mit Vertretern

des besetzten Gebietes, 7 Feb. 1924, BAK, R43 I/1392, Bl. 186; Sitzung des Reichsministeriums, 29 Jan. 1924, BAK, R43 I/2454, Bl. 124.

26. 2. Fassung, Entwurf einer 3. Steuernotverordnung, 29 Jan. 1924, BAK, R43 I/2395, Bl. 20–22.

27. Sitzung des Reichsministeriums, 29 Jan. 1924, BAK, R43 I/2454, Bl. 124; for Justice Ministry attitudes see Abschrift, RJM to RK, 7 Jan. 1924, ZStA, RJM, Nr. 847, Bl. 25–29, and Abänderungsvorschlag des Reichsjustizministers, ZStA, Büro des Reichspräsidenten, Nr. 233, Bl. 63.

28. For bank efforts to influence policy see, e.g., Württembergische Hypothekenbank to Württembergischen Ministerium des Innern, 27 Dec. 1923, GLA Baden, Abt. 237, #29425; Prussian Welfare Minister to RWM, 18 Dec. 1923, ZStA, RWM, Nr. 15414, Bl. 56.

29. Beratungen der vereinigten Reichsratsausschüsse über den abgeänderten Entwurf der 3. Steuernotverordnung, Hamburg Gesandtschaft, 6 Feb. 1924, StA Hamburg, Cl. I Lit. T, No. 15b, Vol. 70, Fasc. 1, Cour. II.

30. Sitzung des Finanzpolitischen Ausschusses, 7 Feb. 1924, ZStA, RWR, Nr. 541, Bl. 160–62; Mitteilung für die Presse, 7 Feb. 1924, ibid., Bl. 194–97.

31. See *Vorwärts* 40. Jhrg. (1923); *Volksblatt für Lüneburg und Umgegend* 30. Jhrg. (1923); *Rheinische Zeitung* 32. Jhrg. (1923); Keil, *Erlebnisse*, 2:305; "Die neue Mietpolitik," *Vorwärts* 40:605 (29 Dec. 1923); "Das Aufwertungsmanöver," *Vorwärts* 41:24 (15 Jan. 1924), et al.; Allgemeiner Deutscher Gewerkschaftsbund to Reichsregierung, 26 Feb. 1924, BAK, R43 I/2454, Bl. 154–57.

32. Deutschnationales Rustzeug, Lieferung 51/55, NL Westarp; see *Kreuzzeitung* for Dec. 1923–Feb. 1924, esp. "Die Hypothekenaufwertung," 76:21 (13 Jan. 1924) and "Aufwertung und öffentliche Anleihen," 76:78 (15 Feb. 1924); also "Unsere Parlamentier bei der Arbeit," *Der Demokrat*, 20 Feb. 1924, p. 28, NL Koch-Weser, #88.

33. See, e.g., Fehrenbach to RK, 28 Dec. 1923, NL Marx, #227; Deermann (MdR) to RJM, 15 Dec. 1923, ZStA, RJM, Nr. 786, Bl. 54; Beamtenausschuss der Zentrumspartei (Breslau) to RK, 15 Dec. 1923, ibid., Bl. 175; "Politische und wirtschaftspolitische Besprechungen mit dem Zentrum," *Mercuria* 43:11 (1 Feb. 1924); Protokolle #269a, 269b, 271, 274, in Morsey and Ruppert, eds., *Protokolle*, pp. 526–28, 534–35; "Wie steht das Zentrum zur Aufwertungsfrage?" GStA Dahlem, ZSg XII/III, #38.

34. "Die Aufwertung der Hypotheken," *DAZ* 62:554 (29 Nov. 1923); "Die Wirtschaftswoche," *DAZ* 63:33 (20 Jan. 1924); and "Die entschleierte Aufwertung," *DAZ* 63:53 (1 Feb. 1924); Stresemann to Dr. Lünsmann, 30 Jan. 1924, NL Stresemann, 3159/171653; "Die 3. Steuernotverordnung," *DAZ* 63:74 (13 Feb. 1924).

35. Dr. H. Fischer to Dietrich, 19 Jan. 1924 [plus *Anlage*], NL Dietrich, #70, Bl. 274–75; Dr. H. Fischer, "Bericht über die 3. Steuernotverordnung," NL Dietrich, #70, Bl. 264–70; "Demokratische Fraktionssitzung" [newspaper clip], 17 Jan. 1924, NL Koch-Weser, #87.

36. Bayerischer stellvertretender Bevollmächtigte zum Reichsrat to StM der Justiz, 8 Feb. 1924, BayHStA, MJU 15135; Parteiführerbesprechung, 9 Feb. 1924, BAK, R43 I/2454, Bl. 132.

37. Parteiführerbesprechung, 9 Feb. 1924, BAK, R43 I/2454, Bl. 132–33; Dr. H. Fischer, "Bericht über die 3. Steuernotverordnung," NL Dietrich, #70, Bl. 264–66.

38. Bayerischer stellvertretender Bevollmächtigte zum Reichsrat to StM der Justiz, 14 Feb. 1924, BayHStA, MJU 15135.

39. "Die Steuernotverordnung im Ausschuss," *Vorwärts* 41:65 (8 Feb. 1924).

40. Schlegelberger and Harmening, *Gesetz*, pp. 391–96; for Paragraph 3 see ibid., p. 127, and Chapter 5 below; for retroactive revaluation cf. Wehinger, *Regelungsversuche*, p. 32.

41. Centralverband des deutschen Bank- und Bankiergewerbes to RWM, 21 Jan. 1924, ZStA, RWM, Nr. 15414, Bl. 137–39; Centralverband des deutschen Bank- und Bankiergewerbes to Schlegelberger, 6 Feb. 1924, ZStA, RJM, Nr. 847, Bl. 145–46. For the wording see Schlegelberger and Harmening, *Gesetz*, p. 395.

42. Ministerbesprechung, 12 Feb. 1924, BAK, R43 I/1392, Bl. 338; Sitzung des Reichsministeriums, 13 Feb. 1924, BAK, R43 I/2454, Bl. 139.

43. Luther, *Politiker*, p. 240.

44. "Steuernotverordnung und Gericht," *VZ* #94 (24 Feb. 1924); "Die Aufwertungsbegrenzung der 3. Steuernotverordnung rechtsungültig?" *Kreuzzeitung* 76:93 (24 Feb. 1924); "Zur Frage der Hypothekenaufwertung," *FZ* 68:148 (24 Feb. 1924).

45. Zentralverband Haus- und Grundbesitzer Vereine zur Aufwertung, [4 Feb. 1924], ZStA, RJM, Nr. 847, Bl. 108; "Die Spitzenverbände von Handel und Industrie zur Aufwertungsfrage," *VZ* #97 (26 Feb. 1924).

46. See the discussion of uncertainty in Chapter 6 below.

47. *RGZ* 107, 370–77; "Die Rechtsgültigkeit der 3. Steuernotverordnung," *Kreuzzeitung* 76:109 (5 Mar. 1924).

48. Dawson, "Effects of Inflation," p. 212, n. 126; Vorstand, Richterverein beim Reichsgericht to RJM, 31 Jan. 1924, ZStA, RJM, Nr. 846, Bl. 275.

49. See Nussbaum, *Money*, p. 281; Wunderlich, "Bedeutung des Aufwertungsgesetzes," p. 475; and Emminger, *Aufwertungsfrage*, p. 5.

50. [Memo on revaluation costs], GStA Dahlem, Rep 84a, #5889, Bl. 419.

Chapter 5

1. See the discussion in Childers, *Nazi Voter*, pp. 50–118, esp. pp. 65, 77–78, 87–88, 94–97; Kunz, *Civil Servants*, pp. 378, 381.

2. "Dunkle Aufwertungsabsichten der Regierung," *Vorwärts* 41:31 (19 Jan. 1924); "Die dritte Steuernotverordnung," *Rheinische Zeitung* 33:41 (18 Feb. 1924); "Steuerfragen," *Vorwärts* 41:87 (21 Feb. 1924); *Verh RT*, vol. 380, Anlage #6470; "Die sozialdemokratischen Forderungen," *Rheinische Zeitung* 33:45 (22 Feb. 1924); see also, Minister für Handel und Gewerbe to sämtlichen Preussischen Staatsministerien, 7 Jan. 1924, GStA Dahlem, Rep 84a, #5885, Bl. 737–43.

3. *Verh RT*, vol. 361, 401. Sitzung (26 Feb. 1924), pp. 12468–76; ibid., 402. Sitzung (27 Feb. 1924), pp. 12509–18; ibid., 403. Sitzung (28 Feb. 1924),

p. 12547; ibid., 406. Sitzung (6 Mar. 1924), pp. 12614–15; ibid., 407. Sitzung (7 Mar. 1924), p. 12666; Ministerbesprechung, 29 Feb. 1924, BAK, R43 I/1392, Bl. 521–22.

4. Besprechung mit Parteiführern, 14 Feb. 1924, BAK, R43 I/1020, Bl. 77; Parteiführerbesprechung, 3 Mar. 1924, ibid., Bl. 87; Parteiführerbesprechung, 5 Mar. 1924, ibid., Bl. 89.

5. Rede von Marx anlässlich die Ablösung des Reichstages, NL Marx, #61, Bl. 41; Childers, *Nazi Voter*, pp. 52–53; Halperin, *Germany*, p. 289.

6. B. Dernburg, "Zur Aufwertungsfrage," *Berliner Tageblatt* 53:354 (7 July 1924); also, Luther, *Politiker*, pp. 268–69; Heuss to Rechtsrat Dr. Elsass, 8 Mar. 1924, NL Heuss, #55.

7. See the daily press for March and April 1924; Childers, *Nazi Voter*, pp. 55–57; Childers, "Inflation," pp. 410, 414–18.

8. For creditor attitudes see, e.g., HGSSV, Ortsgruppe Göttingen to [v. Richthofen], 26 Apr. 1924, NL H. v. Richthofen, #20, Bl. 55; Entschliessung und Forderungen der heute gegründeten "Ortsgruppe Hamburg" des HGSSV, 14 Apr. 1924, StA Hamburg, Cl. I Lit. T, No. 15b, Vol. 70, Fasc. 7; Entschliessung, Gläubigerschutzverband Augsburg, 29 Feb. 1924, BayHStA, MA 103775.

9. See, e.g., Entschliessung, Gläubigerschutzverband Erlangen, 21 Mar. 1924, BayHStA, MA 103775; Schutzverband der Hypotheken-, Pfandbrief-, und Obligationengläubigern Bayern, Ortsgruppe Friedberg, Entschliessung, 10 Feb. 1924, ZStA, RWM, Nr. 15423, Bl. 18; Entschliessung und Forderungen der heute gegründeten "Ortsgruppe Hamburg" des HGSSV, 14 Apr. 1924, StA Hamburg, Cl. I Lit. T, No. 15b, Vol. 70, Fasc. 7.

10. See, e.g., Entschliessung, Gläubigerschutzverband Augsburg, 29 Feb. 1924, BayHStA, MA 103775.

11. See, e.g., Gläubigerschutzverband Sorau/N. Lausitz, 18 Feb. 1924, NL Marx, #203; "Audiatur et altera pars!" *Kreuzzeitung* 76:149 (28 Mar. 1924).

12. Curtius to Stresemann, 24 Apr. 1924, NL Stresemann, Reel 3159.

13. *Deutsche Mittelstands-Zeitung*, 2. Jhrg. (Mar.–May 1924); Childers, "Inflation," pp. 420–21; [newsclip attached to] Westarp to v. Brandstein, 30 May 1924, NL Westarp, 1924, A–D; *Rote Fahne*, 7. Jhrg., Mar.–May 1924; *Rheinische Zeitung*, 33. Jhrg., and *Vorwärts*, 41. Jhrg., Mar.–May 1924.

14. Childers, "Inflation," pp. 410, 422; Childers, *Nazi Voter*, pp. 50–118.

15. [Draft of Düringer speech to DVP 5th Party Convention, 29/30 Mar. 1924], BAK, R45 II/28, Bl. 39.

16. "Parteitag der DVP," *DAZ* 63:153 (30 Mar. 1924).

17. Der Wahlausfall in Baden, NL Dietrich, #217, Bl. 415; "Fragen der Kleinrentner—DVP und Aufwertung," GStA Dahlem, ZSg XII/III, #16.

18. *Verh RT*, vol. 380, Anlage #6522.

19. *Verh RT*, vol. 361, 410. Sitzung (12 Mar. 1924), p. 12698; Luther, *Politiker*, p. 241.

20. *DAZ*, 63. Jhrg. (Mar.–May 1924); "Reichstagabgeordneter Dr. Düringer," *Hannoversche Kurier*, Beilage zur #152 (29 Mar. 1924), BAK, R45 II/28, Bl. 148; also, "Entschliessungen des Reichsparteitages," *Hannoversche Kurier* #152/3 (30 Mar. 1924), NL Zapf, Wahl 1924; [DVP election pamphlet], Hoover Institute on War, Peace, and Revolution, Karl V. Loesch Collection, Box 2, Mappe 21;

Abschrift, *Hildesheimer Allgemeine Zeitung* #84 (8 Apr. 1924), NL Westarp, 1925, E–J (HGSSV).

21. The DVP local in Halle-Merseburg financed the publication of a vehemently prorevaluation pamphlet: R. Wüst, *Aufwertungsproblem*. For industry's role in the Reichstag delegation, see Lothar Döhn, *Politik und Interesse* (Meisenheim am Glan: A. Hain, 1970), pp. 110, 339–47, 396; Henry Turner, *Stresemann and the Politics of the Weimar Republic* (Princeton: Princeton University Press, 1963), pp. 69–71.

22. RWM Hamm to Verehrter Herr Kollege, 1 Apr. 1924, NL Stresemann, 3159/171812; Dietrich, "Was wird aus dem Sparguthaben?" NL Dietrich, #294, Bl. 26–32 (Bl. 31 and 30 for quotations); Dietrich and the DDP distributed this pamphlet widely: ibid., Bl. 34, 35, 36, 45, 48, 49; for DDP see [list of materials distributed], BAK, R45 III/32, Bl. 44; see also, Vermerkt am 16. Mai 1924, NL Koch-Weser, #30, Bl. 25.

23. "Bericht über die Verhandlungen des 5. ordentlichen Parteitages der Deutschen Demokratischen Partei" and "Material zum Wahlkampf," GStA Dahlem, ZSg XII/III, #21; see also, [Dietrich] to Herr Stockheim, 25 Mar. 1924, NL Dietrich, #217, Bl. 59.

24. Schreiber, *Grundfragen*, pp. 80–81; Reichsgeneralsekretariat der deutschen Zentrumspartei to [unnamed], 30 Apr. 1924 and Marx to [unnamed], ca. Apr. 1924, NL Marx, #203; *Germania*, 54. Jhrg., (Mar.–May 1924) and also *Westdeutsche Arbeiter Zeitung*, 25. Jhrg., (Mar.–May 1924).

25. Wahlbrief #4, 28 Apr. 1928, Vertraulich, NL Zapf, Deutsche Volkspartei, Reichsgeschäftsstelle; Abg. Dr. Hergt, "Hypothekenaufwertung und Mietzinssteuer," *Der Tag*, 12 Jan. 1924, NL Marx, #411; Hergt, "Taktik."

26. For the quotation, R. "Zur Frage der Aufwertung privatrechtlicher Ansprüche," NL Westarp, Politik, 1918–1933, Württembergische Bürgerpartei, Drucksache; "Reichstagwahl, 4. Mai 1924, Deutschnationale Nachrichten für das Vogtland," Hoover Institute on War, Peace, and Revolution, Weimar Republic Collection, Folder 95; Dr. A. Phillips, "Das Ende des Reichstages," [ca. Mar. 1924], GStA Dahlem, ZSg XII/III, #1.

27. Cf. "Die Aufwertung in Suspenso," *Magazin der Wirtschaft* 1:1 (12 Feb. 1925).

28. See Childers, *Nazi Voter*, pp. 50–118, esp. pp. 79–80, 86–87, and Tables 1.3, 2.1, 2.3, 2.4, and 2.5. Also, Childers, "Inflation," pp. 410–11, 430; Jones, "Dying Middle," pp. 23–54; Jones, "Inflation," pp. 143–68.

29. Childers, *Nazi Voter*, Tables 1.3 and 2.1, pp. 57–58.

30. Ibid., Tables 1.3 and 2.1, pp. 57–58; Halperin, *Germany*, p. 291.

31. Schetter, "Aufwertung, 1925," in Schreiber, *Jahrbuch, 1925*, p. 158.

32. Bruns to Westarp, 8 May 1924, NL Westarp, Briefwechsel [1924].

33. For the government's intent, see Chapter 4, above; also, Vermerk, 1 May 1924, ZStA, RWM, Nr. 15414, Bl. 106.

34. See, e.g., H. Zalewski, "Zur Aufwertungsfrage," *Der deutsche Oekonomist* 43:2103 (25 Mar. 1925): 34–35.

35. [Memo on telephone conversation with Oberregierungsrat Trapp, RFM], 19 Mar. 1924, ZStA, RJM, Nr. 847, Bl. 383. Emminger, *Aufwertungsfrage*, p. 5, his emphasis.

36. Schlegelberger and Harmening, *Gesetz*, p. 398; Sitzung des Reichsministeriums, 1 May 1924, BAK, R43 I/1394, Bl. 70–72; An dem StM Aeussern, 19 May 1924, BayHStA, MJU 15332.

37. Besprechung im Preussischen Justiz Ministerium, 6 June 1924, ZStA, RJM, Nr. 850, Bl. 118; Verband Preussischer Landkreise to Kreisausschuss im Hameln Weser, 18 Nov. 1924, LA Berlin, Rep 142, Landkreistag #408; Kunzen, "Aufwertung und Sparkassen," *Die Sparkasse* #1175 (29 Sept. 1924).

38. "Die deutsche Sparkassen und die Aufwertung," *Die Sparkasse* #1170 (21 Aug. 1924); Sparkasse Direktor H. Ziegler, "Die Aufwertungsfrage," *Die Sparkasse* #1150 (3 Apr. 1924).

39. Schetter, "Aufwertung, 1925," in Schreiber, *Jahrbuch, 1925*, p. 156; Schetter, "Abschluss?" in Schreiber, *Jahrbuch, 1926*, p. 158; "Kirchliches Vermögen und dritte Steuernotverordnung," *Germania* 54:393 (13 Sept. 1924); Dr. Best et al., *"Auf"-wertungsgesetzentwürfe*, p. 58; "Landessynode und Aufwertungsfrage," *Karlsruher Zeitung*, 21 Oct. 1924, GLA Baden, Abt. 237, #29425; Pfarrer H. Sargun, "Von den Landesverbänden," *Der Rentner*, Nov. 1924; Prof. G. Mayr, "Vorbilde Sparer-Selbsthilfe," *Der Sparerschutz* 2:1/2 (Jan. 1925); Pfarrer K. Schilcher, "Stand der Aufwertung," *Blätter für den katholischen Klerus* 5:47 (30 Nov. 1924).

40. Schetter, "Abschluss?" in Schreiber, *Jahrbuch, 1926*, p. 158; see citations in note 39.

41. Wehinger, *Regelungsversuche*, p. 13; Abschrift, Centralverband des deutschen Bank- und Bankiergewerbes to Reichsbank Direktorium, 25 Oct. 1924, ZStA, RJM, Nr. 852, Bl. 74; "Die Aufwertungsfrage," *Kreuzzeitung* 77:44 (27 Jan. 1925); see also, Hammer Richterverein to RJM, 31 Jan. 1924, ZStA, RJM, Nr. 847, Bl. 104.

42. "Aus der Rechtsprechung," *Die Sparkasse* #1184 (27 Nov. 1924); for the quotation see StM der Justiz, 16 Jan. 1925, BayHStA, MJU 15333; also, Wehinger, *Regelungsversuche*, pp. 33–34.

43. Ministerialsitzung vom 4. Apr. 1925, BayHStA, MA 103773.

Chapter 6

1. BAK, R43 I/1306 [Kabinettsbildung]; Halperin, *Germany*, pp. 292–93.

2. *Verh RT*, vol. 382, Anlagen #26, 28, 174, and 253.

3. Ibid., vol. 381, 14. Sitzung (28 June 1924), pp. 454–82, and vol. 382, Anlage #249.

4. Sitzung des Reichsministeriums, 21 July 1924, BAK, R43 I/1395, Bl. 199; Aufwertungsausschuss, 24 July 1924, ZStA, RJM, Nr. 850, Bl. 150.

5. See, e.g., #3936, 29 July 1924, LA Württemberg, E130/II, Bushel 392, Bl. 88a.

6. "Aufsicht auf einer Reparationskonferenz," *VZ* #504 (24 Oct. 1923); Zeiler and Sontag, *Frage*, p. 54.

7. Henning, *Deutschland*, p. 84; A. Knirlberger, "Aufwertungsfrage," *Das Bayerische Handwerk und Gewerbe* 38:20 (15 Dec. 1924).

8. For quotation, M. Priess, *Die Sachverständigengutachten und die "Aufwer-*

tungsfrage," BayHStA, MJU 15334; Ministerialrat Spindler, "Die öffentliche Anleihen," in Bauser, *Wahrheit*, pp. 27–29; Schutzverband der Hypothekengläubiger,
Ortsgruppe Babenhausen, Entschliessungen, 7 Sept. 1924, ZStA, RWM, Nr.
15423, Bl. 151; Vermögenschutz-Verein eV to RMW, 26 Jan. 1929, ZStA, RWM,
Nr. 15469, Bl. 447, and many other sources.

  9. For French attitude, cf., e.g., Stephen Schuker, *End of French Predominance in Europe* (Chapel Hill, N.C.: University of North Carolina Press, 1976),
p. 6 and passim; Unterhaltung des Generalagenten für die Reparationszahlungen
mit Herrn Reichskanzler Dr. Luther, 2 Feb. 1925, BAK, R43 I/274, Bl. 193;
"Revaluation is Unlikely," *New York Times* 74, #24, 402 (15 Nov. 1924), 19:6; see
also Abschrift, Deutsche Botschaft London, 14 Nov. 1924, ZStA, RWM, Nr.
15415, Bl. 32; RWM to RJM, 11 May 1926, ZStA, RWM, Nr. 15418, Bl. 322.

  10. Aufwertungsausschuss, 24 July 1924, ZStA, RJM, Nr. 850, Bl. 150; "Um
die Aufwertung," *VZ* #349 (24 July 1924); for the government's behind-the-scenes
activity see Zweckverband, Zweigstelle Berlin, Betr. Aufwertung, 15 July 1924,
Rheinisch-Westfälisches Wirtschaftsarchiv, Abt. 5, #21, Fasz. 16.

  11. "Die Verbände im Aufwertungsausschuss," *VZ* #351 (25 July 1924); Concept, 30 Sept. 1924, ZStA, RWM, Nr. 15414, Bl. 369. For a more detailed
discussion of these hearings see Hughes, "Equity," pp. 251–55.

  12. Concept, 30 Sept. 1924, ZStA, RWM, Nr. 15414, Bl. 373–75; Deutscher
Sparkassenverband to [Aufwertungs]Ausschuss, 17 Sept. 1924, ibid., Bl. 366.

  13. "Die Verbände im Aufwertungsausschuss," *VZ* #351 (25 July 1924); "Aufwertungsfrage," *RdI, Geschäftliche Mitteilungen* 6:18 (18 August 1924); "Um die
Aufwertung," *Kreuzzeitung* 76:351 (29 July 1924); "Die Sachverständigen über
die Aufwertung,". *VZ* #355 (28 July 1924); "Fortgang der Aufwertungsdebatte,"
VZ #356 (29 July 1924); Concept, 30 Sept. 1924, ZStA, RWM, Nr. 15414, Bl.
369–80. For petitions see ibid., Bl. 312, 315, 333, 364, and 366.

  14. "Die Aufwertungsfrage," *Kreuzzeitung* 76:350 (28 July 1924). See Chapter
2, above, for banks' earlier attitudes and, especially, Frhr. V. Pechmann, "Hypothekenbank und Pfandbrief unter dem Einfluss der Geldentwertung" (25 March
1923), in BayHStA, MJU 15503.

  15. R. Gates, "Von der Sozialpolitik zur Wirtschaftspolitik?" in Mommsen et
al., *Industrielles System*, pp. 206–25; Gerald Feldman, "The Political Economy of
Germany's Relative Stabilization During the 1920/21 Depression," in Feldman et
al., eds., *Inflation*, pp. 198–99; RWM to RK, 6 Jan. 1924, ZStA, RWM, Nr.
15413, Bl. 117; Luther, *Deutschlands Kraft*, passim.

  16. RWM to RK, 6 Jan. 1924, ZStA, RWM, Nr. 15413, Bl. 117–21, is an early
formulation of the antirevaluation case, and Anders, *Stand*, is its most succinct
presentation. See also Dannebaum, *Aufwertungsgesetz*.

  17. "Aufwertungsfrage," *RdI, Geschäftliche Mitteilungen* 6:18 (18 August
1924); Bund deutscher Mietervereine, "Denkschrift zur Aufwertungsfrage und zur
3. Steuernotverordnung," Aug. 1924 [hereafter, Mietervereine, "Denkschrift"],
NL Dietrich, #296, Bl. 34–35; see also the discussion in Gemeinsame Sitzung
der wirtschaftspolitischen und finanzpolitischen Ausschüsse, 2 Apr. 1925, ZStA,
RWR, Nr. 401, Bl. 281–83, 288–89, 292, 314–15; Badischer Bevollmächtigte
zum Reichsrat to Staatsministerium, 14 Feb. 1925, GLA Baden, Abt. 233/11774,
Vol. 10ad, Fasc 1, 1925.

18. Gemeinsame Sitzung der wirtschaftspolitischen und finanzpolitischen Ausschüsse, 2 Apr. 1925, ZStA, RWR, Nr. 401, Bl. 288–89, 302–3.

19. Anders, *Stand*, esp. p. 30; Dannebaum, *Aufwertungsgesetz*, p. 11.

20. RWM to RK, 6 Jan. 1924, ZStA, RWM, Nr. 15413, Bl. 119; Mietervereine, "Denkschrift," NL Dietrich, #296, Bl. 34–35.

21. RWM, 14 Feb. 1924, ZStA, RWM, Nr. 15414, Bl. 3.

22. See, e.g., Anders, *Stand*, p. 10; "Die Sachverständigen über die Aufwertung," *VZ* #355 (28 July 1924).

23. Luther, *Feste Mark*, pp. 42–45; cf. debate in Ministerialratsitzung vom 5 Feb. 1924, BayHStA, ML 1689.

24. Hans Luther, "Aus dem Werdegang der dritten Steuernotverordnung," *JW* 53:8 (15 Apr. 1924): 474; Handelskammer München to StM für Handel, Industrie und Gewerbe, 21 July 1924, Industrie und Handelskammer zu München, XIII, 26; Eppner to Bayerischen Industriellen Verband, 12 July 1924, ZStA, RWM, Nr. 15423, Bl. 127–28; Mietervereine, "Denkschrift," NL Dietrich, #296, Bl. 36; Freiherr v. Pechmann to Pfarrer Schilcher, 17/24 Dec. 1924, BayHStA, MJU 15335; see also the prorevaluation H. Wunderlich, "Aufwertung," in *Handwörterbuch der Staatswissenschaft* (Jena: G. Fisher, 1929), Ergänzungsband, p. 30.

25. "Die Aufwertung und die Sozialversicherung," *Germania* 54:276 (8 July 1924); Mietervereine, "Denkschrift," NL Dietrich, #296, Bl. 30, 39.

26. For quotation, v. Broich, Kgl. Pr. Major a.D. Oberstl. a.D. to Graf v. Westarp, 10 July 1925, NL Westarp, Briefwechsel, 1925, A–C. Paul Roscher to Hohen Senat, [Jan. 1924], StA Hamburg, Cl. I Lit. T, No. 15b, Vol. 70, Fasc. 7; A. Bauser, "Notwendigkeit, Aufgaben und Ziele der Volksrechtpartei," in Bauser, *Wahrheit*, p. 93–94; "Geldentwertung und Hypotheken," *DJZ* 29:3/4 (1 Feb. 1924): 123–24.

27. "An die Gewerkschaften," *Die Aufwertung* #18 (26 Sept. 1924).

28. See, e.g., Grossmann et al., *Kampf*, pp. 11–12, 18–19; Schutzverband der Hypotheken-, Pfandbrief-, und Obligationengläubiger in Bayern, Ortsgruppe Holzkirchen to Bayerischer Staatsregierung, 11 Feb. 1925, BayHStA, MA 103775.

29. "Zur Bewertung der Häuser," *Der Sparerschutz* 1:2 (15 May 1924); Brink, in Best et al. *"Auf"-wertungsgesetzentwürfe*, pp. 9, 16–55.

30. "Der deutsche Notbund geistiger Arbeiter in Bayern zur Aufwertungsfrage" [news clip], MA 103781; HGSSV, Landesverband Baden to Badischen Staatsministerium, 31 July 1924, GLA Baden, Abt. 237, #29425; Dr. M. Graff to Präsident der Reichsbank Dr. Schacht, 29 Nov. 1924, BAK, R43 I/2454, Bl. 309.

31. HGSSV to Marx, 6 Nov. 1924, ZStA, RWM, Nr. 15423, Bl. 188; Krohn, *Stabilisierung*, pp. 106–12; see Chapter 9 below, for reaction to Ruhr compensation.

32. Zeiler, *Mitarbeit*, p. 129 and passim; Mügel, *Geldentwertung*, pp. 9–19. See also, Pfarrer K., "Zur Aufwertungsfrage," *Germania* 55:78 (16 Feb. 1925).

33. G. Best, "Mein Gesetzentwurf," *Der Sparerschutz* 1:5/6 (Sept. 1924); Rechtsanwalt [?], für Bund der Sparer Ulm/Neu Ulm to Bay. Justiz Minister, 4 Feb. 1924, BayHStA, MJU 15503.

34. See, e.g., Grossmann et al., *Kampf*, p. 81.

35. See, e.g., Mitglieder der Bayerischen Volkspartei to Dr. Held, [July 1924], BayHStA, MA 103775; Max Priess, *Der Sachverständigengutachten und die*

"Aufwertung," BayHStA, MJU 15334; "Die Lösung der Aufwertungsfrage," *Die Aufwertung* (23 July 1924); C.B., "Zur Geldaufwertung," *Germania* 54:333 (10 Aug. 1924); Uderwald to Erkelenz, 29 June 1924, NL Erkelenz, #32, Bl. 36; G. Loeffler, "Denkschrift zur Aufwertung," ZStA, RWM, Nr. 15414, Bl. 308.

36. For quotation, HGSSV, Landesverband Baden to Badischen Staatsministerium, 31 July 1924, GLA Baden, Abt. 237, #29425; also "Die Lösung der Aufwertungsfrage," *Die Aufwertung* (23 July 1924); Concept, 30 Sept. 1924, ZStA, RWM, Nr. 15414, Bl. 369; Handelskammer zu Chemnitz to RJM, 13 June 1924, ZStA, RJM, Nr. 849, Bl. 269–71; Wüst, *Aufwertungskampf*, pp. 4–6; Grossmann et al., *Kampf*, p. 51.

37. HGSSV, Ortsgruppe Friedrichshafen to Marx, NL Marx, #411; "Wirtschaftsnot und Aufwertung," [1925], ZStA, RWM, Nr. 15469, Bl. 224; see also H. von Schimony-Schimonsky, "Aufwertung und Steuerlast," *Die Aufwertung* Jhrg. 1925, #9 (6 Mar. 1925); Justizrat Brink, "Wirtschaft und Aufwertung," in Bauser, *Wahrheit*, p. 64; and cf. [memo] to RK, 19 Feb. 1925, BAK, R43 I/2455, Bl. 109–10.

38. Bayerisches Statistisches Landesamt, *Verelendung*, p. 53.

39. For creditor quotation, J. Rose, "Wieder die Aufwertungsfrage," *Germania* 54:204 (25 May 1924); for the reaction to Luther's proposal see, e.g., the articles in *Die Aufwertung* #18 (26 Sept. 1924) and #19 (3 Oct. 1924); HGSSV to Marx, 3 Nov. 1924, BAK, R43 I/2395, Bl. 279; the DDP quotation is cited in Childers, "Inflation," p. 427; see also "Graf Posadowsky sprach in Erfurt," *G&S* 1:23 (9 Dec. 1925).

40. Parteiführerbesprechung, 18 Mar. 1925, BAK, R43 I/2455, Bl. 311–12; Emminger, *Kampf*, pp. 20–21.

41. See Chapter 10 below.

42. For Germany's postwar wealth, see Chapter 3 above; Dannebaum, *Aufwertungsgesetz*; Ministerium des Innern to Staatsministerium, 18 Jan. 1925, GLA Baden, Abt. 237, #29425; Enquete-Ausschuss, *Wohnungsbau*, pp. 5, 13, 47, 276, 297; Uebersicht über den allgemeinen Stand der Durchführung der Aufwertung, pp. 22, 25, NL Marx, #205; REM to RWM, 23 Feb. 1925, ZStA, RWM, Nr. 15416, Bl. 84–90; Schuker, "American 'Reparations' to Germany," pp. 364–71.

43. Petzina, *Deutsche Wirtschaft*, p. 84; Balderston, "Origins of Instability," pp. 490–93.

44. Cf. Krohn, " 'Oekonomische Zwangslage,' " esp. pp. 418–19, and Borchardt, "Scheitern," esp. pp. 133–35.

45. Cf. Svennilson, *Growth*; Lüke, *Stabilisierung*, pp. 43–44, 105–6, and passim; Borchardt, "Scheitern," pp. 133–35; James, "Did the Reichsbank?" p. 227.

46. Lüke, *Stabilisierung*, p. 93; Balderston, "Origins of Instability," pp. 494–98; Witt, "Auswirkungen," Table 2.

47. Deutsche Bundesbank, ed., *Bankwesen*, p. 291; for the tax structure, see chapter 3 above, and Krohn, *Stabilisierung*, passim; also, "Die Verarmung ganzer Volksklassen," *Der Arbeiter* 35:7 (14 Feb. 1924); Mietervereine, "Denkschrift," NL Dietrich, #296, Bl. 38.

48. Balderston, "Origins of Instability," pp. 494–98.

49. See Chapter 9 below.

50. Mietervereine, "Denkschrift," NL Dietrich, #296, Bl. 39; Fr. Höhne, "Mietzinswucher!" *G&S* 2:3 (20 Jan. 1926); "Hypothekenverzinsung," *Haus und Grundbesitzer Zeitung* (Regensburg) 5:3 (1 Feb. 1925); Betr. Aufwertungsvorschriften der Art. I der 3. Steuernotverordnung, Referentspreche, 17 Jan. 1925, BayHStA, MA 103773.

51. Svennilson, *Growth*, passim; Weisbrod, *Schwerindustrie*, pp. 235–45, 361–63, 455–56, passim.

52. For dividends, Brink, in Best et al., *"Auf"-wertungsgesetzentwürfe*, pp. 16–55; cf. Balderston, "Links," Table 4 and pp. 164–65, 174–75, on weakness of profits and self-financing and James, *Reichsbank*, pp. 181–85, on capital flight.

53. Lüke, *Stabilisierung*, p. xvi; but cf. the discussion in Busch and Feldman, eds., *Prozesse deutschen Inflation*, pp. 278–80, 283–84, and in Balderston, "Links," pp. 175–76.

54. Cf. Borchardt, "Scheitern," pp. 133–35.

55. Cf. Balderston, "Links," Table 4 and pp. 174–75, Balderston, "Origins of Instability," pp. 499–501, on business's weak profit position and its determination to pass on wage increases despite fears they could decrease competitiveness.

56. Bericht über die Verhandlungen des Aufwertungsausschusses des Reichstages der 2. Wahlperiode, 1924, StA Hamburg, Cl. I Lit. T, No. 15b, Vol. 70, Fasc. 4; Unterausschuss, 7 Oct. 1924, ZStA, RWM, Nr. 15414, Bl. 415; Vermerk, 17 Oct. 1924, ibid., Bl. 423.

57. Moggridge, *Monetary Policy*, esp. pp. 17–26, 41–42, 46, 63–91, 104–5, 112, 120–21; A. J. P. Taylor, *English History, 1914–1945* (New York: Oxford University Press, 1965), pp. 144–45, 222–24; Sidney Pollard, *The Development of the British Economy, 1914–1980* (Victoria: Edward Arnold, 1983 [3d ed.]), pp. 134–38.

58. Shepard B. Clough, *The Economic History of Modern Italy* (New York: Columbia University Press, 1964), pp. 226–30; Constantine McGuire, *Italy's International Economic Position* (New York: MacMillan Co., 1926), pp. 72, 77–85, 90–92, 103, 186, 196–205; William Welk, *Fascist Economic Policy* (Cambridge: Harvard University Press, 1938), pp. 160–65, 248; Eleanor Dulles, *The French Franc, 1914–1928. The Facts and their Interpretation* (New York: MacMillan Co., 1929), p. 410; Maier, *Recasting*, pp. 573–76.

59. Dulles, *French Franc*, pp. 412–46; Georges Lachapelle, *Les Finances de la IIIième République* (Paris: Flammarion, 1937), pp. 116–54; Alfred Sauvy, *Histoire Economique de la France entre les deux Guerres* (Paris: Fayard, 1965), 1:42–51, 60–69, 83–99; Maier, *Recasting*, pp. 494–95, 502, 506–8.

60. Balderston, "Origins of Instability," pp. 489–90.

61. Ibid., pp. 494–98, 506–10; Balderston, "Links," pp. 160–61; James, *Reichsbank*, pp. 181–85.

62. See Balderston, "Origins of Instability" and "Links"; Holtfrerich, "Auswirkungen," p. 203; James, "Causes of Banking Crisis," pp. 72, 78, 80–81.

63. The statistics on nominal savings and investments are in Deutsche Bundesbank, *Bankwesen*; index numbers on the cost of living from Holtfrerich, "Löhne,"

Table 5, were used to calculate real saving; see also, Enquete Ausschuss, *Zahlungsbilanz*, p. 136.

64. "Holders of Mark Bonds," *Journal of Commerce*, 18 May 1925, in ZStA, RJM, Nr. 860, Bl. 46; also, "Revaluation Critics Rapped by Bankers," *The World*, 18 May 1925, in ibid., Bl. 47. Both articles appeared after Ludwig Bendix spoke to the newspapers, but he wrote (L. Bendix to Auswärtiges Amt, 22 May 1925, ibid., Bl. 45) as though the articles in fact reflected the attitude of American banks. See also, for *New York Times* attitude, "Zur Frage der Hypothekenaufwertung," 4 Feb. 1925, ZStA, RWM Nr. 15415, Bl. 358, and for *Times* of London see Deutsche Botschaft London, 14 Nov. 1924, ibid., Bl. 32–33.

65. Besprechung mit Parteiführern, 18 Mar. 1925, BAK, R43 I/2455, Bl. 311–12; Sitzung des 18. Ausschusses (Aufwertung), 19 June 1925, ZStA, Reichsbank, Nr. 6654, Bl. 206.

66. Strong to Gates McGarrah, 24 Nov. 1924, Federal Reserve Bank of New York, Strong Papers 1012.5. See also, Herring to Commerce Department, Herbert Hoover Presidential Library, Commerce Official, Foreign Loans, Germany, 2 Jan. 1925. My thanks to Dr. William McNeil for both citations.

67. Balderston argues similarly, "Links," pp. 162, 167–68.

68. See the Maier and Weisbrod articles in *G&G* 11:275–94; 295–325; and G. Schulz, "Inflationstrauma, Finanzpolitik u. Krisenbekämpfung in den Jahren der Wirtschaftskrise, 1930–1933," in Feldman, ed., *Nachwirkungen*, pp. 261–96.

69. For discussions of ideology, cf. Georges Rudé, *Ideology and Popular Protest* (New York: Pantheon Books, 1980), pp. 7–37; Geertz, "Ideology," pp. 193–233; E. Shils, "Ideology: The Concept and Function of Ideology," in *International Encyclopedia of the Social Sciences*, 7:66–69; Eley, *German Right*, pp. 160–67.

Chapter 7

1. Sitzung des Reichsministeriums, 8 Aug. 1924, BAK, R43 I/2454, Bl. 222.

2. Hergt Kompromissvorschläge, [late July 1924], ZStA, RWM, Nr. 15414, Bl. 318; Bericht über die Verhandlungen des Aufwertungsausschusses des Reichstages der 2. Wahlperiode, 1924, StA Hamburg, Cl. I Lit. T, No. 15b, Vol. 70, Fasc. 4 [hereafter, Bericht/Aufwertungsausschusses, Hamburg]; Vermerk, 17 Oct. 1924, ZStA, RWM, Nr. 15414, Bl. 423.

3. Unterausschuss, 7 Oct. 1924, ZStA, RWM, Nr. 15414, Bl. 410; Vermerk, 17 Oct. 1924, ibid., Bl. 427; Bericht/Aufwertungsausschuss, Hamburg; Parteitag der Deutschen Volkspartei in Dortmund, BAK R45 II/29, Bl. 84–85; for Hergt's doubts, Hergt, "Taktik."

4. Unterausschuss, 7 Oct. 1924, ZStA, RWM, Nr. 15414, Bl. 410.

5. Hergt Kompromissvorschläge, ZStA, RWM, Nr. 15414, Bl. 319; Paul Fleischer, Vorschlag für einen Antrag betr. Abänderung der 3. Steuernotverordnung von 14. Feb. 1924, ibid., Bl. 348; Fleischer, Erläuterung zum Vorschlag, ibid., Bl. 351; [memo], 24 Sept. 1924, ZStA, RWM, Nr. 15414, Bl. 285–88.

6. "Die Kommunisten für die Opfer der Inflation," *Rote Fahne* 7:122 (4 Oct. 1924); "Der Aufwertungsschwindel geht schon wieder an!" *Rote Fahne* 7:126

(9 Oct. 1924); "Aufwertung und Spekulanten," *Germania* 54:413 (25 Sept. 1924); "Die Aufwertungsfrage im Ausschuss," *Germania* 54:416 (27 Sept. 1924).

7. Bericht/Aufwertungsausschuss, Hamburg; [memo], 24 Sept. 1924, ZStA, RWM, Nr. 15414, Bl. 285–88; Hergt Kompromissvorschläge, ibid., Bl. 322–23; for creditors, see e.g., HGSSV, Landesverband Hannover to Geschäftsstelle der DNVP Osnabrück, 30 Oct. 1924, Niedersächsisches Staatsarchiv, Erw Cl (DNVP), #90; Dr. G. Mayr, "Wirtschaftspolitische Tagesfragen," *Der Beamtenbund* 8:47 (1 Aug. 1924).

8. See Chapters 9 and 10 below.

9. [memo], 24 Sept. 1924, ZStA, RWM, Nr. 15414, Bl. 288–93.

10. Ibid.; [memo], 25 Sept. 1924, ZStA, RWM, Nr. 15414, Bl. 296–99; Vermerk, 17 Oct. 1924, ibid., Bl. 427.

11. In general, see Bericht/Aufwertungsausschuss, Hamburg. For the creditor attitude see Chapter 6 above.

12. Bericht/Aufwertungsausschuss, Hamburg; Unterausschuss, 7 Oct. 1924, ZStA, RWM, Nr. 15414, Bl. 413–15; Vermerk, 17 Oct. 1924, ibid., Bl. 423–26.

13. Ministerbesprechung, 15 Oct. 1924, BAK, R43 I/1396, Bl. 217; Ministerbesprechung, 20 Oct. 1924, *Akten RK, Marx*, pp. 1129–31; Halperin, *Germany*, p. 307.

14. Childers, *Nazi Voter*, pp. 59–60, 103; Halperin, *Germany*, pp. 308–9.

15. Childers, "Inflation," pp. 415–17; Childers, *Nazi Voter*, pp. 65–67, 87–88, 95–97.

16. Ministerbesprechung, 15 Oct. 1924, BAK, R43 I/1396, Bl. 217; also, Ministerbesprechung, 31 Oct. 1924, ibid., Bl. 357; Ministerbesprechung, 31 Oct. 1924, BAK, R43 I/2454, Bl. 256.

17. See *Akten RK, Marx*, pp. 1158–59 and "Die Aufwertungsbeschluss," *VZ*, #531 (7 Nov. 1924).

18. See A. Knirlberger, "Aufwertungsfragen," *Das Bayerische Handwerk und Gewerbe* 38:20 (15 Dec. 1924); Str., "Die Aufwertungsfrage im Wahlkampf," *Deutsche Sparkassezeitung* 1:5 (11 Dec. 1924) [hereafter, "Wahlkampf," *Deutsche Sparkassezeitung*]; An das Politische Büro Berlin, 14 Nov. 1924, and other material in Niedersächsisches Staatsarchiv, Erw Cl (DNVP), #104 [Dec. 1924 Election]; *Westdeutsche Arbeiterzeitung*, 26. Jhrg. (Oct.–Dec. 1924); *DAZ*, 63. Jhrg. (Oct.–Dec. 1924). Cf. two newspaper clips reporting on the same speech in NL Koch-Weser, #91, Bl. 109 and 114.

19. E. Leimkügel to Erkelenz, 13 Nov. 1924, NL Erkelenz, #33, Bl. 247; see also Dr. Quark to Stresemann, 6 Nov. 1924, NL Stresemann, 3159/172303.

20. For a contemporary estimate see Jones, "Inflation," p. 167, n. 83.

21. B—n, "Zum Streit um die Aufwertung," *Beamtenbund* 8:89 (27 Nov. 1924); Kundgebung, Schutzverband der Hypotheken-, Pfandbrief-, und Obligationengläubiger, Bayerns, 11 Nov. 1924, BayHStA, MA 103775.

22. "Der deutsche Notbund geistiger Arbeiter in Bayern zur Aufwertungsfrage," *Fränkischer Kurier* #137 (17 May 1924), in BayHStA, MA 103781; "Aeusserungen zweier Deutschnationalen Reichstagabgeordneten," *Die Aufwertung* (6 Mar. 1925).

23. See H. Kaelble, "Chancenungleichheit und akademische Ausbildung in

Deutschland, 1910–1960," *G&G* 1:1 (1975): 138, n. 17; see Chapter 6 above, for savings.

24. See, e.g., Wüst, *Beiträge zur Aufwertungsfrage* (2d ed.), p. 68.

25. See "Die Wahlkonflikt in der Aufwertungslage," *DAZ* 63:572 (4 Dec. 1924); for the vote see Statistisches Reichsamt, *Jahrbuch*, 1925, pp. 388–95. See also the later comments in Rademacher to Westarp, 19 Nov. 1926, NL Westarp, MdR Best, 1925.

26. Bauser, *Wahrheit*, p. 7; HGSSV, Landesverband Hannover to Geschäftsstelle der DNVP Osnabrück, 30 Oct. 1924, Niedersächsisches Staatsarchiv, Erw Cl (DNVP), #90; Kundgebung, Schutzverband der Hypotheken-, Pfandbrief-, und Obligationengläubiger, Bayerns, 11 Nov. 1924, BayHStA, MA 103775.

27. OLGpräsident i.R. Dr. Best, "Mein Gesetzentwurf über die Umwertung alter Geldschulden," *Der Sparerschutz* 1:5/6 (Sept. 1924).

28. "Der Aufwertungskanzler," *Vorwärts* 42:28 (17 Jan. 1925).

29. For quotations, see HGSSV, Landesverband Baden to Badischen Staatsministerium, 31 July 1924, GLA Baden, Abt. 237, #29425 and [letter], 14 Oct. [1924], NL Westarp, 1924, M–Z.

30. HGSSV Osnabrück to Osnabrücker Zeitungen, 5 Dec. 1924, Niedersächsisches Staatsarchiv, Erw Cl (DNVP), #90; *Der Rentner*, Nov. 1924, GStA Dahlem, ZSg XII/IV.

31. "P. Löbe in Lüneburg," *Volksblatt für Lüneburg und Umgegend* 31:283 (3 Dec. 1924); "Die Entscheidung ist da!" ibid., 31:286 (6 Dec. 1924); "Gerechte Aufwertung," *Vorwärts* 41:549 (21 Nov. 1924); "Die sozialdemokratischen Richtlinien für die Aufwertung," *Schwäbische Tagewacht* 44:279 (26 Nov. 1924).

32. "Wahlkampf," *Deutsche Sparkassezeitung*.

33. Bredt, *Hypothekenaufwertung*, p. 5; "Wirtschaftspartei und Aufwertung," *Deutsche Mittelstands-Zeitung* 2:26 (28 Nov. 1924).

34. Heuss to Koch, 1 Oct. 1924, NL Heuss, #58; Koch to Blanquet, 19 Nov. 1924, NL Koch-Weser, #31, Bl. 43; for quotation see "Die Demokraten und die Aufwertung," *Der Wähler* #2 (Nov. 1924), GStA Dahlem, ZSg XII/IV, #135.

35. Deutsche Demokratische Partei: Grundsätzen und Tatsachen, GStA Dahlem, ZSg XII/III, #2; "Die Demokraten und die Aufwertung," *Der Wähler* #2 (Nov. 1924), GStA Dahlem, ZSg XII/IV, #135.

36. Emminger, *Aufwertungsfrage*, pp. 10–16; Bericht über die öffentliche Sparerversammlung am Dienstag den 11. November im Kreuzbräu München, BayHStA, MJU 15334.

37. Parteitag der Deutschen Volkspartei in Dortmund, BAK, R45 II/29, Bl. 84–88. See also, "Wahlkampf," *Deutsche Sparkassezeitung*.

38. See Chapters 6 above and 8 and 9 below; see also, Dernburg to Deutsche Demokratische Partei, Karlsruhe, 28 Oct. 1924, NL Dietrich, #294, Bl. 78.

39. See, e.g., "Protestversammlung in Berlin," *Die Aufwertung* #19 (3 Oct. 1924); HGSSV Osnabrück to Osnabrücker Zeitungen, 5 Dec. 1924, Niedersächsisches Staatsarchiv, Erw Cl (DNVP), #90.

40. Vermerk, 17 Oct. 1924, ZStA, RWM, Nr. 15414, Bl. 428; Feder, *Aufwertung*, pp. 34, 42–43.

41. "Wahlkampf," *Deutsche Sparkassezeitung*; "Die Frage der Aufwertung,"

Der Arbeiter 36:1 (1 Jan. 1925).

42. For quotation, [draft of speeches], NL Marx, #61, Bl. 221–22, also 176–83; "Wahlkampf," *Deutsche Sparkassezeitung*; Vockel (General Secretary of the Center Party) to Osnabrücker HGSSV, 26 May 1925, NL Marx, #203; Schetter, "Aufwertung," in Schreiber, *Jahrbuch, 1925*, pp. 161–62.

43. See Vockel to Osnabrücker HGSSV, 26 May 1925, NL Marx, #203; "Das Zentrum und Reichstagabgeordneter Dr. Ross," *G&S* 4:22 (17 Mar. 1928).

44. "Demagogie der Rechtsparteien in der Aufwertungsfrage," *Der Demokrat* 5:38/39 (20 Nov. 1924), GStA Dahlem, ZSg XII/III, #13; Parteitag der Deutschen Volkspartei in Dortmund, BAK, R45 II/29, Bl. 88, 169.

45. [Letter], 14 Oct. [1924], NL Westarp, 1924, M–Z; Hergt, "Taktik."

46. Schreiben vom 4. November 1924 der Parteileitung an den Hypotheken und Sparerschutzverband [*sic*], NL Westarp.

47. [News clip], *Neue Dresdner Volkszeitung*, 7 Dec. 1924, NL Westarp, Aufwertung, 1925, S–Z; "Wahlkampf," *Deutsche Sparkassezeitung*; R. Issberner, "Wie die Deutschnationale regieren!" GStA Dahlem, ZSg XII/III, #8; "Deutschnationale und Aufwertung," in Deutsche Volkspartei, Reichsgeschäftsstelle, Wahlbrief #4 (28 Apr. 1928), NL Zapf; HGSSV Osnabrück to DNVP Osnabrück, 11 July 1925 [copy of letter from Abg. Hartz (DNVP) to HGSSV, 30 Nov. 1924], Niedersächsisches Staatsarchiv, Erw Cl (DNVP), #90.

48. Schreiben vom 4. November 1924 der Parteileitung an den Hypotheken und Sparerschutzverband [*sic*], NL Westarp.

49. Köhler to Westarp [copy of letter, Westarp to Köhler, 6 Dec. 1924], NL Westarp, 1925, E–J, HGSSV.

50. "Verdrehungskünste oder—ernst gemeint?" *Die Aufwertung* #23 (12 June 1925).

51. For quotation and assurances, HGSSV, Landesverband Lübeck to Westarp, 5 June 1925, NL Westarp, 1925, E–J, HGSSV, their emphasis.

52. Dr. Graf Keyserlingk to Westarp, 13 May 1925, NL Westarp, 1925, K–R Briefwechsel and W. Vogt to Westarp, 17 May 1925, NL Westarp, MdR Best; "Hergts Eingeständnis," *G&S* 4:42 (26 May 1928).

53. Cf. the comments in "Die Aufwertung in Suspenso," *Magazin der Wirtschaft* 1:1 (12 Feb. 1925).

54. v. Richthofen to Westarp, 6 Dec. 1925, NL Westarp, 1925, D, DNVP Berlin.

55. See Volkov, *Popular Antimodernism*, pp. 273–75, passim.

56. HGSSV Osnabrück to DNVP Osnabrück, 19 Mar. 1925, Niedersächsisches Staatsarchiv, Erw Cl (DNVP), #90; Childers, *Nazi Voter*, Tables 2.1, 2.2, 2.4, pp. 84–87; Halperin, *Germany*, pp. 308–9; Statistisches Reichsamt, *Jahrbuch, 1925*, pp. 388–95.

57. Childers, "Inflation," pp. 413–14, 430; Jones, "Dying Middle"; Childers, *Nazi Voter*, pp. 61–64.

Chapter 8

1. Staatssekretär in der Reichskanzlei, 29 Nov. 1924, BAK, R43 I/2454, Bl. 303.

2. Sitzung des Reichsministeriums, 3 Dec. 1924, BAK, R43 I/2454, Bl. 313. "Die Rechtsmässigkeit der 3. Steuernotverordnung," *Germania* 54:541 (10 Dec. 1924).

3. "Der Kampf um die Aufwertungsverordnung," *Germania* 55:47 (29 Jan. 1925).

4. Fragebogen, ZStA, RWM, Nr. 15415, Bl. 75–77; Niederschrift über das Ergebnis der kommissarischen Beratung vom 21. und 22. Januar 1925, StA Hamburg, Cl. I Lit. T, No. 15b, Vol. 70, Fasc. 4.

5. Prussian Finance Ministry to Minister President, 10 Jan. 1925, GStA Dahlem, Rep 84a, #5887, Bl. 911, and Prussian Finance Ministry to sämtl. Staatsministerien, 17 Jan. 1925, ibid., Bl. 1003. See also Prussian Finance Minister to Prussian Justice Minister, 29 Dec. 1923, GStA Dahlem, Rep 84a, #5885, Bl. 681.

6. For quotation see Sitzung des Staatsministeriums, 6 Apr. 1925, LA Württemberg, E130/II, Bushel 392, Bl. 247a. See also Minister der Finanzen, 7. Januar 1924, GLA Baden, Abt. 237, #29425; Minister der Finanzen to Staatsministerium, 2 Apr. 1925, GLA Baden, Abt. 233, #11774, Vol. 10ad, Fasc. 1; Ministerialratssitzung, 5 Feb. 1924, BayHStA, ML 1689; StM Finanzen to StM Justiz, 3 Apr. 1925, BayHStA, MJU 15665.

7. Ministerialsitzung vom 27. Februar 1925, BayHStA, MA 103780; Württemberg Ministry of Interior, 7 Aug. 1924, LA Württemberg, E130/II, Bushel 392, Bl. 101; Abschrift, Hamburg Gesandtschaft, Länderbesprechung im RFM, 9 Aug. 1924, StA Hamburg, Cl. I Lit. T, No. 15b, Vol. 70, Fasc. 18. For a more detailed discussion of these issues see Hughes, "Equity," pp. 347–52.

8. Mitteilung des DSt, 28. Juni 1923, Aufkundigung der lfd. Staatsanleihen, LA Berlin, Rep 142, DSt, Hauptverzug B, #2795/I; DSt, Aufwertung der städtischen Anleihen und Sparkassenguthaben, 17 Oct. 1924, StA Hamburg, Cl. I Lit. T, No. 15b, Vol. 70, Fasc. 18.

9. See, e.g., DSt to Magistrat Cassel, 24 July 1924; Potsdam to DSt, [ca. 30 Nov. 1924]; DSt to Württembergischen Städtetag, 3 May 1924; DSt to Düsseldorf, 16 July 1924, all in LA Berlin, Rep 142, DSt, Hauptgruppe B, #2528; and Landgemeindetag to DSt, 24 May 1924, LA Berlin, Rep 142, DSt, Hauptverzug B, #2795/I.

10. For quotation, DSt, Aufwertungsfrage, 18 Oct. 1924, StA Hamburg, Cl. I Lit. T, No. 15b, Vol. 70, Fasc. 18; see, e.g., Geschäftsstelle des Bayerischen Städtebundes to StM Innern, BayHStA, MJU 15333; Magistrat der Stadt Naumburg a/S to DSt, 14 Dec. 1923, LA Berlin, Rep 142, DSt, Hauptverzug B #2795/I; Zur Frage der Aufwertung der Kommunalanleihen, LA Berlin, Rep 142, DSt, Hauptverzug B, #2795/II; Wirtschaftsverband Sächsischer Gemeinden, an die Verbandsmitglieder!, LA Berlin, Rep 142, DSt, Hauptgruppe B, #2528.

11. Niederschrift, Vorstandssitzung, DSt, 14 Apr. 1924, LA Berlin, Rep 142, DSt, Hauptverzug A, #590/I.

12. Vorstand des Westfälischen Städtetages to DSt, 15 Apr. 1925, LA Berlin, Rep 142, DSt, Hauptgruppe B, #2528.

13. *Akten RK, Luther*, 1:xix–xxi; Krohn, *Stabilisierung*, pp. 146–48; "Die Kabinett Luther vor dem Reichstag," *FZ* 69:51 (20 Jan. 1925).

14. Bayerischer Stellvertreter zum Reichsrat to StM der Finanzen, 14 Jan. 1925, BayHStA, MA 103778.

15. *Verh RT*, vol. 386, 91. Sitzung (10 July 1925), p. 2981.

16. See Vorträge in Esti Ausschuss, NL Funcke; Verhandlungen des DIHT, 1924–25, Stiftung Westfälisches Wirtschaftsarchiv, K-2, #346; *Geschäftliche Mitteilungen des RdI*, VI. and VII. Jhrg. (1924–25).

17. "Von der Markstabilisierung zu Brüning," p. 6, NL Funcke.

18. See e.g., Roth, *Aufwertung*, pp. v–vii, and Bayerische Staatsbank. Direktorium to StM der Finanzen, 15 Apr. 1925, BayHStA, MJU 15664.

19. OLGrat Nerdet [?] to Präsidenten des OLG München, 31 Mar. 1925, BayHStA, MJU 15664; "Ueberspannung des Aufwertungsgedankens," *VZ* #45 (21 Feb. 1925).

20. Rademacher to Westarp, n.d., NL Westarp, 1925, Aufwertung.

21. Centralverband des deutschen Bank- und Bankiergewerbes to Schlegelberger, 6 Feb. 1925, ZStA, RJM, Nr. 855, Bl. 149.

22. RdI to RWM, 8 Jan. 1925, ZStA, RWM, Nr. 15415, Bl. 203; Centralverband des deutschen Bank- und Bankiergewerbes to RWM, 15 Jan. 1925, ibid., Bl. 205; Zentralverband des deutschen Grosshandels eV to RWM, 16 Jan. 1925, ibid., Bl. 206.

23. RWM, 24 Jan. 1925, ibid., Bl. 195.

24. RWM to 18. Ausschuss, 29 Jan. 1925, ibid., Bl. 238; Abschrift, ibid., Bl. 244.

25. Abschrift, ibid., Bl. 244.

26. RWM, 29 Jan. 1925, ibid., Bl. 251–52.

27. See, e.g., *DAZ*, 64 Jhrg. (1925); see also, e.g., [Langnamverein], 16 June 1925, to Herrn Mitglieder des Vorstandes und des Hauptausschusses, NL Silverberg, #423, Bl. 100; Sitzung des Hauptausschusses, 28 Apr. 1925, Verhandlung des DIHT, Heft 7, 1925, Stiftung Westfälisches Wirtschaftsarchiv, K-2, #346.

28. See, e.g., Dernburg and Gothein in the DDP, Vorstandssitzung der DDP, 11 June 1925, BAK, R45 III/19, Bl. 110; and Rademacher in the DNVP, Rademacher to Westarp, n.d., NL Westarp, 1925, Aufwertung; also, Stellungnahme des Arbeitsausschusses Deutschnationaler Industrieller zur Aufwertungsfrage, NL Westarp, 1925, D.

29. See, e.g., Handelskammer to Deputation für Handel, Schiffahrt und Gewerbe, 3 Apr. 1925, StA Hamburg, Cl. I Lit. T, No. 15b, Vol. 70, Fasc. 1, Cour. I; Bund Südwestdeutscher Industrieller to Badischen Minister des Innern, 17 Apr. 1925, GLA Baden, Abt. 237, #29426.

30. Dr. Lautenbach, 3 Feb. 1925, ZStA, RWM, Nr. 15415, Bl. 275–80; Referat, 5 Feb. 1925, ibid., Bl. 293–94.

31. Hamm to Schaeffer, 7 Apr. 1925, ZStA, RWM, Nr. 15417, Bl. 26–27; and, e.g., Entwurf, 8 May 1925, ibid., Bl. 86; also RWM (Reichardt) to StM Dr. Graf v. Rödern, 28 May 1925, ibid., Bl. 200–201.

32. Sitzung des Ausschusses des Reichslandbundes für die Aufwertungsfrage,

6 Jan. 1925, ZStA, Reichslandbund, Nr. 123, Bl. 56–65; "Die Deutschnationalen und die Pfandbriefe," *Berliner Börsen Courier* (8 June 1925); Sitzung des Reichsministeriums, 16 Mar. 1925, BAK, R43 I/2455, Bl. 279.

33. Reichslandbund to Landbundabgeordneten des Reichstages und Reichsrates, 4 Apr. 1925, ZStA, Reichslandbund, Nr. 123, Bl. 29.

34. REM to RWM, 23 Feb. 1925, ZStA, RWM, Nr. 15416, Bl. 83–90; Minister für Landwirtschaft, Domänen und Forsten to RWM, 17 Feb. 1925, ibid., Bl. 58; Preussische Landwirtschaftskammer to Minister für Landwirtschaft, Domänen und Forsten, 2 Apr. 1925, ibid., Bl. 359; also Minister des Innern to Landwirtschaftskammer, 14 Jan. 1925, GLA Baden, Abt. 237, #29425.

35. Reichslandbund to Landbundabgeordneten des Reichstages und Reichsrates, 4 Apr. 1925, ZStA, Reichslandbund, Nr. 123, Bl. 29; Döbrich et al. to Westarp, 13 May 1925, NL Westarp, 1925, MdR Best.

36. Reichslandbund Presseabteilung to Präsidial Abteilung, 7 Feb. 1925, ZStA, Reichslandbund, Nr. 123, Bl. 47; Rademacher, "Zur Frage der Aufwertung," 19 Nov. 1926, and W. Vogt to Westarp, 17 May 1925, NL Westarp, 1925, MdR Best.

37. RWM, 29 Jan. 1925, ZStA, RWM, Nr. 15415, Bl. 246; Sitzung des Reichsministeriums, 16 Mar. 1925, BAK, R43 I/2455, Bl. 279–81; Sitzung des 18. Ausschusses, 19 June 1925, ZStA, Reichsbank, Nr. 6654, Bl. 198–204; 25te Sitzung des 18te Reichstag Ausschusses, 16 June 1925, ibid., Bl. 211–17. See also, e.g., "Die Aufwertung der öffentlichen Anleihen," *Germania* 55:282 (20 June 1925).

38. RWM, 29 Jan. 1925, ZStA, RWM, Nr. 15415, Bl. 246–52; Centralverband des deutschen Bank- und Bankiergewerbes to Direktor Dalberg (RWM), 3 July 1925, ZStA, RWM, Nr. 15418, Bl. 138.

39. See, e.g., Verband Württembergischer Bankiers to Württembergischen Staatsministerium, 15 Apr. 1925, LA Württemberg, E130/II, Bushel 392, Bl. 269; Bayerische Staatsbank, Direktorium to StM Finanzen 15 Apr. 1925, and Die Aufwertung von Bankguthaben, Ergebnis der Anfrage bei den Justizministern von Württemberg, Baden und Hessen, BayHStA, MJU 15664; Ministerialratsitzung vom 17. April 1925 und Ministerialratsitzung vom 20. April 1925, BayHStA, MA 103773.

40. Sitzung des Bankausschusses, 28 Apr. 1925, Stiftung Westfälisches Wirtschaftsarchiv, K-2, #346.

41. Besuch der Vertreter der Banken, 11 Feb. 1925, NL Stresemann, 3114/149251.

42. Referat, 18 Dec. 1924, ZStA, RWM, Nr. 15415, Bl. 64.

43. See, e.g., Rheinische Hypothekenbank to Badischen Ministerium des Innern, 30 Mar. 1925, GLA Baden, Abt. 237, #29426; and, for quotation, Bayerische Handelsbank to Minister President Geheimrat Dr. Held, 30 May/1 June 1925, BayHStA, MA 103773.

44. Aufwertungsausschuss des Deutschen Sparkassen- und Giroverbandes, Leitsätze zur Aufwertungsfrage, 16 Jan. 1925, ZStA, RJM, Nr. 854, Bl. 249–50; cf. Deutscher Sparkassen- und Giroverband to DSt, 12 Feb. 1925, LA Berlin, Rep 142, DSt, Hauptverzug B, #2795/II, and Franz Künzer, Oberbürgermeister, a.D. "Zur Aufwertung der Sparguthaben," *Die Sparkasse* 45:9 (15 May 1925).

45. Verband Preussischer Landkreise to Landrat in Flatow, 6 May 1924, LA

Berlin, Rep 142, Landkreistag #408; the creditors recognized this conflict too: Dr. Groff, "Die öffentlichen Sparkassen," *Die Aufwertung* Jhrg. 1925, #3 (23 Jan. 1925).

46. Haus- und Grundbesitzerverein zu Breslau, Entschliessung, 6 May 1925, GStA Dahlem, Rep 84a, #5889, Bl. 798; Hausbesitzerverband des Landkreises Weissenfels, 28 Jan. 1925, BayHStA, MA 103780.

47. For quotation, see Dr. Br. "Der Kampf um die Aufwertung," *Norddeutsche Handwerks-Zeitung* 30:7 (12 Feb. 1925); see also, Dr. A. Knirlberger, "Aufwertungsfragen," *Das Bayerische Handwerk und Gewerbe* 38:20 (15 Dec. 1924); R. Wienecke, Syndikus der Hauptgemeinschaft des deutschen Einzelhandels, "Die unmögliche Aufwertung!" Industrie und Handelskammer zu München, XIII, 35.

48. See, e.g., Friederich Sisberg to RWM, 29 Jan. 1925, ZStA, RWM, Nr. 15423, Bl. 261.

49. Deutscher Gewerkschaftsbund, Hauptgeschäftsstelle to RK, 20 Mar. 1925, BAK, R43 I/2455, Bl. 334; "Aufwertungsforderungen des Deutschen Gewerkschafts-Bundes," *Zentralblatt der christlichen Gewerkschaften Deutschlands* 25:7 (30 Mar. 1925); "Das Kreuz der Aufwertung," *G.D.A.* Jhrg. 1925, #10 (16 May 1925).

50. "Art. 157 RV und die Aufwertung," *Gewerkschaftszeitung* 35:29 (18 July 1925).

51. See, e.g., *Deutsche Handelswacht* 32 (1925); *Die Handels- und Büroangestellte* 31 (1925); *Mercuria* 44–45 (1924–25); *Der Beamtenbund* 9 (1925), esp. Dr. A. Schönberg, "Aufwertungsfragen und Beamtenschaft," *Der Beamtenbund* 9:97 (25 Sept. 1925).

52. See, e.g., Schutzverband der Hypotheken-, Pfandbrief-, und Obligationengläubiger, Bayerische Sparer in Stadt und Land, Jan. 1925, BayHStA, MJU 15334.

53. "Luther vor dem Reichstag," *Der Deutsche Sparer* 2:4 (25 Jan. 1925).

54. Köhler to Westarp, 14 Jan. 1925, NL Westarp, 1925, E–J, HGSSV; Dr. Best, "Finanzminister, Aufwertung und Reichsverfassung," *Der Sparerschutz* 2:1/2 (Jan. 1925).

55. For the bill, "Der Aufwertungsausschuss," *FZ* 69:56 (22 Jan. 1925), "Der Aufwertungsausschuss des Reichstages," *FZ* 69:73 (28 Jan. 1925), and "Die Vorgänge im Aufwertungs-Ausschuss," *FZ* 69:74 (28 Jan. 1925); for creditor reaction, Köhler to Westarp, 14 Jan. 1925, and HGSSV to Westarp, 30 Jan. 1925, NL Westarp, 1925, E–J, HGSSV.

56. See the articles in *FZ*, esp. "Der Barmatausschuss," *FZ* 69:75 (29 Jan. 1925); "Der Barmatausschuss," *FZ* 69:76 (29 Jan. 1925); "Die Finanzskandale und die reaktionäre Hetze," *FZ* 69:97 (6 Feb. 1925); "Barmatausschuss des Reichstages," *FZ* 69:480 (1 July 1925); also, Lucas Trapp to Redaktion der *Frankfurter Zeitung*, 21 Jan. 1925, NL Dietrich, #296, Bl. 61. See also, Ernst Huber, *Deutsche Verfassungsgeschichte* 7:535–38.

57. See, e.g., "Die Entwicklung der Reichsfinanzen," *FZ* 69:76 (29 Jan. 1925); "Ruhr-Entschädigungen. Zweierlei Mass," *FZ* 69:78 (29 Jan. 1925); "Die Ruhrentschädigung," *FZ* 69:85 (1 Feb. 1925); "Die Ruhrschäden und die anderen," *FZ*

69:90 (3 Feb. 1925); "Enttäuschte Wähler der Deutschnationalen," *FZ* 69:124 (16 Feb. 1925).

58. G. Münch, "Das Aufwertungsproblem," *VZ* #10 (11 Jan. 1925).

59. O. Kühn to RWM, 1 Feb. 1925, ZStA, RWM, Nr. 15423, Bl. 246; HGSSV, Regierungsbezirk Gumbinnen, Entschliessung, 11 Feb. 1925, ZStA, RWM, Nr. 15424, Bl. 90; HGSSV, Südwest Mecklenburg, 11 Feb. 1925, ibid., Bl. 96; Syndikus Hindenburg to Joel, 31 Jan. 1925, ZStA, RJM, Nr. 854, Bl. 46–47.

60. Ein schwer geprüfter Kriegs- und Inflationsverlierer to RK, 10 June 1925, BAK, R43, I/2126, Bl. 50; HGSSV to RK, 22 Nov. 1924, BAK, R43 I/2454, Bl. 299.

61. See, e.g., v. Broich to Westarp, 10 July 1925, NL Westarp, 1925, A–C; O. Kühn to RWM, 30 Jan. 1925, ZStA, RWM, Nr. 15423, Bl. 235; Lucas Trapp to Redaktion der *Frankfurter Zeitung*, 21 Jan. 1925, NL Dietrich, #296, Bl. 61; Schutzverband der Hypotheken-, Pfandbrief-, und Obligationengläubiger, Bayerische Sparer in Stadt und Land, Jan. 1925, BayHStA, MJU 15334.

62. But cf. Betrifft: Reichspartei für Volksrecht und Aufwertung, ZStA, Kommissar für die Ueberwachung der öffentlichen Ordnung, Nr. 299, Bl. 245, which comments on the existence of considerable creditor anti-Semitism; and *G&S*, 1925–28 and *Das Deutsche Volksrecht*, 1928–33, which reveal no explicit anti-Semitism.

63. See, e.g., Wilhelm Linow, Gutachten zur Aufwertung der Hypotheken, Aug. 1924, ZStA, RWM, Nr. 15424, Bl. 54.

64. See, e.g., HGSSV Bad Nauheim to RWM, [ca. 12 Feb. 1925], ZStA, RWM, Nr. 15424, Bl. 45; [letter, HGSSV to bourgeois party Reichstag delegations], in *Die Aufwertung* Jhrg. 1925, #2 (16 Jan. 1925), p. 14; see also, J. Plate to Marx, 17 Mar. 1929, NL Marx, #203.

65. [Sparer und Hypothekengläubiger Schutzverband (Kreis Plauen)], in *Neue Vogtländische Zeitung*, 3 Feb. 1925, ZStA, RWM, Nr. 15423, Bl. 339.

66. HGSSV, Landesverband Mecklenburg, Die Aufwertungsfrage vom wirtschaftlichen Standpunkt aus betrachtet, 5 Feb. 1925, ibid., Bl. 342.

67. HGSSV Hamburg to Marx, 20 Apr. 1925, NL Marx, #203.

68. For the quotation see Dr. Best, "Die Denkschrift über die Aufwertung," *Die Aufwertung*, Sonderausdruck aus #6, and also, Dr. Best, "Wie sich die Regierung denkt," both in BayHStA, MJU 15335.

69. See, e.g., O. Kühn to RWM, 1 Feb. 1925, ZStA, RWM, Nr. 15423, Bl. 246; v. Amburger to Ausschuss für Aufwertung, 2 Feb. 1925, ibid., Bl. 279; HGSSV Rosenheim to RWM, 3 Feb. 1925, ibid., Bl. 327.

70. See Winkler, *Mittelstand*; Volkov, *Popular Antimodernism*, esp. pp. 310–11. See also the comments by the later creditor leader Bauser in the name of an early creditor group: Bund gegen Wucher und Teuerung to RK, 6 Feb. 1923, BAK, R43 I/1246, Bl. 348–49.

71. Mitglieder der Bayerischen Volkspartei to Dr. Held, 30 July 1924, BayHStA, MA 103775.

72. For quotation, Deutscher Rentnerbund Rastenburg to RWM, 14 Feb. 1925, ZStA, RWM, Nr. 15424, Bl. 107; also, e.g., Dr. Freiherr v. Haller to Justice Minister, 25 Apr. 1925, BayHStA, MJU 15333.

73. For the SPD quotation see "Aufwertungspropaganda," *Vorwärts* 42:111 (6 Mar. 1925); see the correspondence between Köhler and Westarp in NL Westarp, 1925, E–J, HGSSV. See also "Eine Antwort an Westarp," *Vorwärts* 42:291 (23 June 1925), and P. Köhler to Hochgeehrter Herr Reichstagabgeordneter, 22 Jan. 1925, NL Dietrich, #295, Bl. 233. For peasants see Feldman, *Army*, p. 464.

74. Schutzverband der Hypotheken-, Pfandbrief-, und Obligationengläubiger, Bayerische Sparer in Stadt und Land, Jan. 1925, BayHStA, MJU 15334.

75. Cf. Childers, *Nazi Voter*, Tables 2.4, 3.4, and 4.4. But cf. Jones, "Inflation," p. 167, n. 83.

76. I found only one creditor who mentioned them: Köhler to Westarp, 25 May 1925, NL Westarp, 1925, E–J, HGSSV.

77. Radlauer Bericht, Reichstag, 15 May 1925, BAK, R43 I/2456, Bl. 131; also, "Dr. Bests Austritt aus der Deutschnationalen Fraktion," *FZ* 69:359 (15 May 1925).

78. Merckel to Westarp, 21/22 May 1925, NL Westarp, 1925, D, DNVP Berlin.

79. See Chapter 10 below. Also, Jones, "Inflation"; Childers, "Inflation"; and esp. Childers, *Nazi Voter*, Tables 2.4, 3.4, and 4.4

80. *Verh RT*, vol. 384, 15. Sitzung (5 Feb. 1925), pp. 347–49; ibid., 39. Sitzung, (20 March 1925), p. 1206; ibid., vol. 385, 55. Sitzung (8 May 1925), pp. 1631–39.

81. Vermerk, 18 May 1925, GStA Dahlem, Rep 84a, #5889, Bl. 845; *Verh RT*, vol. 403, Anlagen #1140, 1160; "Dr. Bests Austritt aus der Deutschnationalen Fraktion," *FZ* 69:359 (15 May 1925).

82. "Kommunisten und Aufwertung," *Rote Fahne* 8:22 (27 Jan. 1925); for attacks on the DNVP etc., see *Rote Fahne* 8 (Jan.–July 1925), esp. "Volksentscheid über die Aufwertung," #160 (16 July 1925).

83. Parteiführerbesprechung, 18 Mar. 1925, BAK, R43 I/2455, Bl. 305; "Protest des deutschen Hausbesitzes gegen die Aufwertung," and "Zur Hypothekenaufwertungsfrage," *Haus- und Grundbesitzerzeitung* (Regensburg) 5:10 (15 June 1925); "Der Parteitag in Köln," *Deutsche Mittelstands-Zeitung* 3:11 (1 Nov. 1925).

84. Parteiführerbesprechung, 18 Mar. 1925, BAK, R43 I/2455, Bl. 306, 310–12, 314–15; Vermerk, 7 May 1925, BAK, R43 I/2456, Bl. 100; Vermerk, 29 June 1925, ibid., Bl. 185; Rademacher, "Zur Frage der Aufwertung," 19 Nov. 1926, NL Westarp, MdR Best.

85. Andre, "Aufwertungsdemagogen," *Schwäbische Arbeiterzeitung* 4:30 (24 July 1925).

86. Fr. Ehrhardt, "Das Kompromiss in der Aufwertungsfrage," *Germania* 55:226 (15 May 1925); Sitzung des Reichsministeriums, 20 Feb. 1925, BAK, R43 I/2455, Bl. 185.

87. For politicians, see, e.g., *Verhandlungen des Badischen Landtages*, II. Landtagsperiode, 4. Sitzungsperiode, Heft 543 b, Protokollheft, 23. Sitzung (27 Feb. 1925), pp. 951–52; Morsey and Ruppert, eds., *Protokolle*, pp. 584–86, 598–99; "Das Aufwertungskompromiss," *FZ* 69:361 (16 May 1925).

88. "Um eine gerechte Aufwertung," *Schwäbische Arbeiterzeitung* 4:25 (19 June 1925), and "Aufwertungsdemagogen," *Schwäbische Arbeiterzeitung* 4:30

(24 July 1925). For Andre's vote, *Verh RT*, vol. 386, 95. Sitzung (15 July 1925), p. 3209.

89. Hergt to Fraktionsvorsitzenden, 22 May 1925, BAK, R43 I/2456, Bl. 150; *Verh RT*, vol. 386, 95. Sitzung (15 July 1925), p. 3211.

90. Centralverband des deutschen Bank- und Bankiergewerbes to J. Goldschmidt, 9 Feb. 1925, NL Stresemann, 3114/149237; Besuch der Vertreter der Banken, 11 Feb. 1925, NL Stresemann, 3114/149251; for quotation, Stresemann to Schleswig, [spring 1925], NL Stresemann, 3113/148222.

91. Vorstandssitzung, Reichstagfraktion der DVP, 9 Mar. 1925, BAK, R45 II/66, Bl. 38–39; Parteiführerbesprechung, 18 Mar. 1925, BAK, R43 I/2455, Bl. 310.

92. See, e.g., Wunderlich, "Einigung der Parteien in der Aufwertungsfrage," *Industrie und Handel der Zeit* #209 (18 May 1925) in ZStA, RWM, Nr. 15417, Bl. 174.

93. Hergt, "Taktik."

94. See, e.g., Gräfin Westarp to HGSSV, 10 Feb. 1925, NL Westarp, 1925, E–J, HGSSV. The Gräfin spoke for the Graf in this and subsequently cited replies.

95. For quotation, Lebenserinnerungen der Reichskanzlerzeit, NL Luther, #463, Bl. 14–15; also, "Hergts Eingeständnis," *G&S* 4:42 (26 May 1928).

96. "Deutschnationaler Aufwertungsschwindel," *VZ* #26 (30 Jan. 1925); "Die grossen Verbände zur Aufwertungsfrage," *Kreuzzeitung* 77:63 (7 Feb. 1925); Gräfin Westarp to Oberinspektor Kolley, 26 Feb. 1925, NL Westarp, K–R, Briefwechsel.

97. For the meetings, Historisches Archiv der Gutehoffnungshütte, NL Reusch, #400101295/16 (my thanks to Dr. Larry Jones, for letting me see his notes on this reference); [report of telephone conversation with Joel, 18 Feb. 1925], BAK, R43 I/2455, Bl. 117; for Steiniger and Westarp see "Aeusserungen zweier Deutschnationaler Reichstagabgeordneten," *Die Aufwertung*. Jhrg. 1925, #9 (6 Mar. 1925); Gräfin Westarp to Otto Kühn, 16 Mar. 1925, NL Westarp, 1925, MdR Best.

98. "Best spricht," *Vorwärts* 42:267 (9 June 1925).

99. Ministerbesprechung, 11 Mar. 1925, BAK, R43 I/2455, Bl. 253.

100. Ministerbesprechung, 7 Mar. 1925, ibid., Bl. 231.

101. Parteiführerbesprechung, 18 Mar. 1925, ibid., Bl. 302–19; Teilbericht über die 34. Sitzung des 18. Ausschusses, 27 June 1925, NL Marx, #412; "Sturm im Aufwertungsausschuss," *FZ* 69:474 (28 June 1925).

102. See *Rote Fahne*, *Vorwärts*, *VZ*, and *Germania*, March–July 1925; Gräfin Westarp to HGSSV Osnabrück, 9 May 1925, and Gräfin Westarp to HGSSV Lüneburg, 6 June 1925, NL Westarp, 1925, E–J, HGSSV; for creditor reaction see HGSSV Lübeck to Fraktion der Deutschnationalen Volkspartei, 5 June 1925, ibid.

103. "Bazille gegen das Aufwertungskompromiss," *Volksblatt für Lüneburg und Umgegend* 32:126 (3 June 1925); Bazille, "Tragödie."

104. "Die Gegner des Aufwertungsgesetzes," *Süddeutsche Zeitung Stuttgart* #326 (17 July 1925); "Vier Jahre Württembergische Regierungspolitik, 1924–1928," NL Westarp, Politik 1918–1933, Württembergische Bürgerpartei, Drucksache; *Verh RT*, vol. 386, 95. Sitzung (15 July 1925), pp. 3209–14, and 96. Sitzung (16 July 1925), pp. 3265–70; Geheimer Regierungsrat Pfundtner to We-

starp, 10 June 1925, NL Westarp, 1925, D, DNVP Berlin.

105. Dörr, *Volkspartei*, p. 326; Döbrich et al. to Westarp, 13 May 1925, NL Westarp, MdR Best, 1925; Stellungnahme des Arbeitsausschusses Deutschnationaler Industrieller zur Aufwertungsfrage, NL Westarp, 1925, D, DNVP Berlin; Westarp to Herr v. Stegmann, 14 Dec. 1925, NL Westarp, 1925, D; "Vier Jahre Württembergische Regierungspolitik, 1924–1928," NL Westarp, Politik, 1918–1933, Württembergische Bürgerpartei, Drucksache.

106. G. Schreiber, "Innenpolitik des Reiches," in Schreiber, *Jahrbuch*, 1925, pp. 56–57; see also A. Phillip, *Mein Weg* (unpublished memoirs in NL Westarp), p. 167; "Frankfurt, 11. Juli," *FZ* 69:510 (11 July 1925).

107. Heimann, *Kampf*, pp. 17, 29; Schetter, "Aufwertung," in Schreiber, *Jahrbuch*, 1925, pp. 158–60.

108. "Bericht des 18. Ausschusses (Aufwertungsfrage) über den Entwurf eines Gesetzes über die Ablösung der öffentlichen Anleihen," *Verh RT*, Vol. 403, Anlage #1150; Keil, *Erlebnisse*, 2:305–6; "Um die Aufwertung," *Vorwärts* 42:235 (20 May 1925); Keil to Löbe, 19 Apr. 1926, NL Keil, Briefe L–M.

109. See *Volksblatt für Lüneburg und Umgegend*, 32. Jhrg. (1925) and *Vorwärts*, 42. Jhrg. (1925); for Keil, see his speech in *Verh RT*, Vol. 386, 91. Sitzung (10 July 1925), pp. 2935–41, and his article, "Um die Aufwertung," *Vorwärts* 42:235 (20 May 1925).

110. Reichstag, Sitzung des Aufwertungsausschusses, 21 Jan. 1925, BAK, R43 I/2455, Bl. 11; Vorsitz der DDP to HGSSV, 4 Feb. 1925, NL Dietrich, #295, Bl. 326; Rededisposition [presidential election], GStA Dahlem, ZSg XII/III, #21.

111. Heuss to Scheef et al., 30 June 1925, NL Heuss, #60; "Richthofens Aufwertungsvorschlag," *VZ* #148 (21 June 1925); "Schacht soll gutachten," *VZ* #160 (5 July 1925); "Aufwertungsabstimmung," *VZ* #168 (15 July 1925).

112. Heuss to Scheef et al., 30 June 1925, NL Heuss, #60; "Richthofens Aufwertungsvorschlag," *VZ* #148 (21 June 1925).

113. "Die Aufwertungsberatung," *Germania* 55:228 (16 May 1925); Erkelenz to Koch, 26 May 1925, NL Erkelenz, #36, Bl. 204–5; Präsidium des Reichsausschusses für Handel, Industrie und Gewerbe to Staatsminister a.D. Dietrich, 23 Jan. 1925, NL Dietrich, #295, Bl. 261.

114. Dietrich to Kohland, 20 May 1925, NL Dietrich, #72, Bl. 199; for Dernburg votes see, e.g., "Die Rückwirkung der Hypothekenaufwertung," *Vorwärts* 42:277 (14 June 1925).

115 Erkelenz to Koch, 26 May 1925, NL Erkelenz, #36, Bl. 204–5.

116. Vorstandssitzung der DDP, 11 June 1925, BAK, R45 III/19, Bl. 110.

117. David Blackbourn, "The Politics of Demagogy in Imperial Germany," in *Past and Present* 113:152–84.

Chapter 9

1. For Luther's attitude, see Chapter 2 above; "Industrie und Handelstag," *FZ* 69:317 (30 Apr. 1925); for creditor perception see, e.g., "Luther vor dem Reichstag," *Der deutsche Sparer* 2:4 (25 Jan. 1925), and this chapter below.

2. See "Einführung," *Akten RK, Luther*; Chapter 8 above; "Der Aufwertungs-

ausschuss des Reichstages," *FZ* 69:91 (4 Feb. 1925); "Aufwertungsausschuss des Reichstages," *FZ* 69:362 (16 May 1925).

3. Referententwurf einer Denkschrift über die Aufwertung (RFM), NL Marx, #412; for creditors see Dr. Best, "Die Denkschrift über die Aufwertung," Sonderdruck aus #6, *Die Aufwertung*; for ministers, e.g., Staatssekretär in der RK to RK, 27 Jan. 1925, BAK, R43 I/2455, Bl. 28.

4. "Aufwertungsgesetz in drei Wochen," *Germania* 55:60 (5 Feb. 1925); "Die Aufwertungsfrage," *Germania* 55:61 (6 Feb. 1925); "Enttäuschte Wähler der Deutschnationalen Volkspartei," *FZ* 69:124 (16 Feb. 1925).

5. See, e.g., *Germania, FZ*, and *Vorwärts* for Feb. 1925; Best "Mein Reichstagsmandat," *Die Aufwertung* #23 (12 June 1925) (reprinted, "Dr. Best," *FZ* 69:422 [9 June 1925]).

6. Ressortssprechung unter Vorsitz des Herrn Reichskanzlers, 6 Feb. 1925, BAK, R43 I/2455, Bl. 111–12; Sitzung des Reichsministeriums, 20. Feb. 1925, BAK, R43 I/2455, Bl. 181–88; Entwurf eines Gesetzes über die Ablösung der öffentlichen Anleihen, 27 Feb. 1925, ibid.; for Frenken's concerns, Abschrift, RJM to RK, 18 Feb. 1925, ZStA, RWM, Nr. 15416, Bl. 80. For a detailed discussion of the cabinet and party debate that eventually produced the revaluation laws, see Hughes, "Equity," pp. 419–70.

7. Ministerbesprechung, 11 Mar. 1925, BAK, R43 I/2455, Bl. 253–56; "Deutscher Reichstag," *FZ* 69:179 (7 Mar. 1925); "Die Aufwertungsfrage im Reichstag," *FZ* 69:180 (8 Mar. 1925); "Die dritte Steuernotverordnung fällt," *Vorwärts* 42:136 (21 Mar. 1925).

8. "Der deutschnationale Betrug," *Vorwärts* 42:127 (16 Mar. 1925); "Die Aufwertungs-Verschleppung," *VZ* #62 (13 Mar. 1925); "Die Verschleppung des Aufwertungsgesetzes," *FZ* 69:212 (20 Mar. 1925); even *Germania*, "Reichstag und Aufwertung," 55:113 (8 Mar. 1925); Ministerbesprechung, 11 Mar. 1925, BAK, R43 I/2455, Bl. 253–56.

9. Sitzung des Reichsministeriums, 16 Mar. 1925, BAK, R43 I/2455, Bl. 278–86.

10. Parteiführerbesprechung, 18 Mar. 1925, BAK, R43 I/2455, Bl. 302–19.

11. Sitzung des Reichsministeriums, 21 Mar. 1925, BAK, R43 I/2455, Bl. 346–47; Sitzung des Reichsministeriums, 22 Mar. 1925, ibid., Bl. 336–44; Reichstagabgeordneter. Bericht von Oberfohren. [20 Mar. 1925], NL Westarp, 1925, Aufwertung; Parteiführerbesprechung, 2 Apr. 1925, BAK, R43 I/2456, Bl. 7.

12. Bauser, *Wahrheit*, p. 7; Jarres to RK a.D. Geheimrat Dr. Cuno, 6 Apr. 1925, NL Jarres, #23; "Der mitteldeutsche Sparerbund zur Reichspräsidentenwahl," *Kreuzzeitung* 77:164 (7 Apr. 1925); for a general discussion of the election and Hindenburg's role see A. Dorpalen, *Hindenburg*, pp. 64–88, esp. 68, 79–83.

13. "Warum hat Hindenburg gesiegt?" *Germania* 55:200 (30 Apr. 1925); Bauser, *Wahrheit*, p. 8; F. Müller to Marx, 20 Apr. 1925, NL Marx, #203; Erinnerungsbericht, Das Jahr 1925, S. 28, NL Marx, #66.

14. For quotation, "Hindenburgs Osterbotschaft," *DAZ* 64:172 (12 Apr. 1925); for creditor attitude, "Die betrogene Sparer," *Vorwärts* 42:223 (13 May 1925); Arbeitsgemeinschaft der Aufwertungsorganisationen to Reichspräsident von Hindenburg, 12 June 1925, ZStA, Büro des Reichspräsidenten, Nr. 234, Bl. 55; for

Hindenburg's relative ignorance, see Auszug aus einem Brief von Gräfin Ada Westarp an ihre Tochter Frfr. Hiller von Gaertringen, 15 May 1925, NL Westarp [original in Familienarchiv Gärtringen].

15. *Verh RT* vol. 400, Anlage #851, Gutachten des vorläufigen Reichswirtschaftsrats.

16. Gemeinsame Sitzung der Wirtschaftspolitischen und Finanzpolitischen Ausschüsse, 4 Apr. 1925, ZStA, RWR, Nr. 401, Bl. 323–71; for quotation, ibid., Bl. 360–61.

17. *Verh RT* vol. 400, Anlage #851, Gutachten des vorläufigen Reichswirtschaftsrat.

18. See Georg Holtz, 14 Apr. 1925, NL Marx, #411; Dr. Best et al., *"Auf"-wertungsgesetzentwürfe*, pp. 11–13.

19. For a detailed discussion see Hughes, "Equity," pp. 438–42; "Aufwertungsstreit im Reichsrat," *VZ* #98 (24 Apr. 1925); "Korrektur der Aufwertung," *FZ* 69:301 (24 Apr. 1925); *Verh RT* vol. 400, Anlage #804, Gesetzentwurf, and *Ibid.*, Bd. 400, Anlage #805, Gesetzentwurf.

20. "Korrektur der Aufwertung," *FZ* 69:301 (24 Apr. 1925).

21. For the quotation, Ministerialratsitzung vom 17. April 1925, BayHStA, MA 103773.

22. "Zum Gesetzentwurf über die Aufwertung privatrechtlicher Ansprüche," *Bankarchiv* 24:13 (1 Apr. 1925): 258; *Verh RT*, vol. 400, Anlage #804, Gesetzentwurf.

23. "Das Bankgewerbe zum Aufwertungsgesetz-Entwurf," *FZ* 69:266 (9 Apr. 1925); "Zur Hypothekenaufwertung," *FZ* 69:316 (29 Apr. 1925); "Industrie und Handelstag," *FZ* 69:317 (30 Apr. 1925).

24. "Börsen und Aufwertung," *VZ* #96 (22 Apr. 1925); "Die deutsche Börsenvorstände gegen den Aufwertungs-Entwurf," *Germania* 55:185 (22 Apr. 1925).

25. For quotation, "Der Hypothekengläubiger und Sparer Schutzverband zur Aufwertung," *FZ* 69:317 (30 Apr. 1925), their emphasis; also, e.g., "Die Aufwertungsfrage," *FZ* 69:268 (10 Apr. 1925); "Der Kampf um die Aufwertung," *FZ* 69:328 (4 May 1925); "Aufwertungs-Ausschuss des Reichstages," *FZ* 69:362 (16 May 1925); Dr. Best et al., *"Auf"-wertungsgesetzentwürfe*.

26. Sitzung des Reichsministeriums, 4 May 1925, BAK, R43 I/2456, Bl. 98; Vermerk, 7 May 1925, ibid., Bl. 100–101.

27. Reichstagabgeordneter Hergt to Westarp, 7 May 1925, NL Westarp, 1925, MdR Best; Abänderungsvorschläge zu den Aufwertungsgesetzentwürfen, NL Westarp, 1925, MdR Best.

28. Sitzung des Reichsministeriums, 9 May 1925, BAK, R43 I/2456, Bl. 110–19; Parteiführerbesprechung, 11 May 1925, ibid., Bl. 120–21; Abschrift, 14 May 1925, ibid., Bl. 129; "Komplizierte Aufwertung," "Das Aufwertungskompromiss," and "Die Aufwertungs-Verständigung," *VZ* #117 (16 May 1925).

29. Vermerk, 15 May 1925, BAK, R43 I/2456, Bl. 133, and [copies of identical memos promising to support government draft, signed for DNVP, DVP, BVP, and Z], ibid., Bl. 142–44; [copy of memo identical to Bl. 142–44, but with reservations, signed for WP], ibid., Bl. 145.

30. "Das Aufwertungskompromiss," *FZ* 69:361 (16 May 1925); "Aufwertungsausschuss des Reichstages," *FZ* 69:362 (16 May 1925); see also, e.g., F. Ehrhardt,

"Das Kompromiss in der Aufwertungsfrage," *Germania* 55:226 (15 May 1925); also, Reichszentrale für Heimatdienst, "Die Neuregelung der Aufwertung," NL Marx, #411.

31. See the articles in *Kreuzzeitung*, May–June 1925, esp. "Die innere Politik der Woche," 77:216 (9 May 1925); "Das Kompromiss in der Aufwertungsfrage," 77:226 (15 May 1925); Graf Westarp, "Die innere Politik der Woche," 77:228 (16 May 1925); and Graf Westarp, "Unverantwortliche Krisenmacherei," 77:273 (14 June 1925).

32. Westarp to Best, 14 May 1925, and Meyer, Mitglieder des Preussischen Landtages to Best, 20 May 1925, NL Westarp, 1925, MdR Best; W. Keil "Die grosse Enttäuschung," *Vorwärts* 42:230 (16 May 1925); "Das Aufwertungskompromiss angenommen," *Vorwärts* 42:239 (22 May 1925).

33. Best to Parteileitung der DNVP, 21 May 1925, and Best to Parteivorstand der DNVP, 29 May 1925, NL Westarp, 1925, MdR Best; G. Best, "Mein Reichstagmandat," *Die Aufwertung*, #23 (12 June 1925).

34. "Dr. Best gegen die Deutschnationale Partei," *FZ* 69:410 (5 June 1925).

35. "Mein Reichstagmandat," *Die Aufwertung* #23 (12 June 1925); "Dr. Best," *FZ* 69:422 (9 June 1925); "Best spricht," *Vorwärts* 42:267 (9 June 1925).

36. "Die Deutschnationale gegen Dr. Best," *FZ* 69:424 (10 June 1925); "Dr. Best und die Deutschnationalen," *FZ* 69:433 (13 June 1925) "Westarp to Werner, 18 June 1925," NL Westarp, 1925, S-Z (Teilband).

37. *Verh RT* vol. 386, 84. Sitzung (26 June 1925), p. 2649.

38. Teilbericht über die 34. Sitzung des 18. Ausschusses, 27. Juni 1925, NL Marx, #412; Best, "Erklärung," 28 June 1925, Niedersächsisches Staatsarchiv, Erw Cl (DNVP), #90; "Dr. Best klagt an," *Vorwärts* 42:301 (28 June 1925). The *FZ* quotes Best as saying, "I do not set the swindled on the same level as the swindlers." "Sturm im Aufwertungsausschuss," 69:474 (28 June 1925).

39. "Der Fall Best," *FZ* 69:506 (10 July 1925).

40. "Gegen die Parteien des Aufwertungskompromisses," *FZ* 69:388 (27 May 1925); "Niederträchtige Verleumdung," *G&S* 1:1 (8 July 1925); see also HGSSV Osnabrück to DNVP Osnabrück, 3 July 1925, Niedersächsisches Staatsarchiv, Erw Cl (DNVP), #90.

41. See *Kreuzzeitung* for June–July 1925, esp. "Dr. Best moralisch erledigt," 77:296 (27 June 1925); "Die Unwahrheiten des Abg. Dr. Best," 77:297 (28 June 1925); "Dr. Best und die 'Kreuzzeitung,' " 77:301 (1 July 1925); "Die Hypothekenaufwertung im Reichstag," 77:321 (12 July 1925); and "Die innere Politik der Woche," 77:332 (18 July 1925).

42. Hergt, "Taktik"; "Die Aufwertungskomödie der Deutschnationalen," *FZ* 69:402 (2 June 1925).

43. "Die Aufwertungskomödie der Deutschnationalen," *FZ* 69:402 (2 June 1925); "Die Sparer sind schuld," *Vorwärts* 42:266 (8 June 1925); for creditors, e.g., *Die Aufwertung* #23 (12 June 1925).

44. "Die deutschnationale Aufwertungsschwindel," *FZ* 69:434 (13 June 1925).

45. See *Vorwärts*, *FZ*, *VZ*, also *Rote Fahne* for May–July 1925.

46. See Chapter 8 above; Childers, *Nazi Voter*, Tables 2.4 and 3.4.

47. "Aufwertungsausschuss des Reichstages," *FZ* 69:362 (16 May 1925).

48. Uebersicht über die wichtigsten sachlichen Abänderungen des Gesetzent-

wurfes über die Ablösung der öffentlichen Anleihen durch die Beschlüsse des 18. Ausschusses des Reichstages, GLA Baden, Abt. 233/11774, Vol. 10ad, Fasc. 1; *Verh RT*, vol. 403, Anlage #1150, p. 19; Katona, "Altbesitz," p. 275; Schlegelberger and Harmening, *Gesetz*, p. 299. See Chapter 10 below, for actual revaluation.

49. "Das Aufwertungsgesetz," *Vorwärts* 42:309 (3 July 1925); Abschrift, [29 May 1925], ZStA, RWM, Nr. 15417, Bl. 327; Schlegelberger and Harmening, *Gesetz*, p. 239.

50. Bayerischer stellvertretender Bevollmächtigte zum Reichsrat to StM für Handel, Industrie und Gewerbe, 8 June 1925, BayHStA, MJU 15664; Schlegelberger and Harmening, *Gesetz*, p. 213; Wunderlich, "Bedeutung des Aufwertungsgesetzes," p. 485.

51. "Schluss der Aufwertungskämpfe im Ausschuss," *Vorwärts* 42:317 (8 July 1925); *Verh RT* vol. 403, Anlage #1150, pp. 4–5; Herrn Staatssekretär zur geneigten Kenntnis, [ca. 13 July 1925], BAK, R43 I/2456, Bl. 310.

52. "Die Börse ist enttäuscht," *Vorwärts* 42:318 (8 July 1925); "Ende des Börsenstreiks," *Vorwärts* 42:334 (17 July 1925); "Börsenbericht," A. Hirschfeld & Co., [July 1925], NL Marx, #411. For bond sales see Chapter 10 below.

53. "Die Aufwertungsvorlage," *Beamtenbund* 9:40 (4 Apr. 1925); "Das Aufwertungskompromiss," *FZ* 69:361 (16 May 1925).

54. "Pfandbrief-Aufwertung," *FZ* 69:408 (4 June 1925); Wunderlich, "Bedeutung des Aufwertungsgesetzes," p. 475.

55. "Der Aufwertungskampf," *Vorwärts* 42:246 (27 May 1925).

56. "Die Aufwertungsfrage," *FZ* 69:435 (14 June 1925); "Graf Westarp zur Zoll- und Aufwertungsfragen," *FZ* 69:437 (15 June 1925); "Aufwertung der Industrie-Obligationen," *VZ* #167 (14 July 1925); *Verh RT*, vol. 386, 91. Sitzung (10 July 1925), p. 2989. See this chapter below for creditor perception of political double-dealing.

57. See *Verh RT*, vol. 386, 91.–96. Sitz. (10–16 July 1925); "Die Aufwertungsmehrheit," *VZ* #166 (12 July 1925); Vormerkbuch, 14 July 1925, NL Stockhausen, #7; *Verh RT*, vol. 386, Namentliche Abstimmungen 95. Sitzung (15 July 1925), pp. 3209–14, and 96. Sitzung (16 July 1925), pp. 3265–70.

58. *Verh RT*, Vol. 386, 95. Sitz. (15 July 1925).

59. "Der Empfang beim Reichspräsidenten," *Der Deutsche Sparer* 2:26 (28 June 1925); "Die verzögerte Verkündung," *VZ* #170 (17 July 1925).

60. Büro des Reichspräsidenten to Kempner, 11 July 1925, BAK, R43 I/2456, Bl. 315; Sitzung des Reichsministeriums, 16 July 1925, ibid., Bl. 319; [wire service report on Hindenburg's signature of law], 17 July 1925, ibid., Bl. 320.

61. Entwurf eines Gesetzes über die Ablösung der öffentlichen Anleihen, 27 Feb. 1925, BAK, R43 I/2455; Sitzung des Reichsministeriums, 16 Mar. 1925, ibid., Bl. 286; *Verh RT*, vol. 403, Anlage #1150, p. 6.

62. Katona, "Altbesitz," p. 273–75; cf. Witt, "Auswirkungen," n. 53.

63. For government drafts, my estimate based on [untitled memo on cost of revaluation under Tax Decree and revaluation drafts], GStA Dahlem, Rep 84a, #5889, Bl. 419, but assuming redemption of 40 billion PM in old holdings of government bonds; estimate of actual total based on calculations in ibid. and Deutsche Bundesbank (Hrsg.), *Bankwesen*, p. 291, and on contemporary esti-

mates of the amount added. See Katona, "Altbesitz," pp. 273–75; Deutsche Volks-partei, Reichsgeschäftsstelle, Wahlbrief #5, 30 Apr. 1928, NL Zapf, [untitled folder]; *Statistisches Jahrbuch*, 1927–1942; Statistisches Reichsamt, *Oeffentlicher Kredit*, p. 25.

64. Expenditures in Witt, "Auswirkungen," pp. 61–62 and n. 53 and passim, plus ca. 70 million RM per year for the preferential annuity.

65. See, e.g., Krohn, *Stabilisierung*, pp. 205–22.

66. "Statt Gerechtigkeit Unrecht und Entrechtung," *Der Rentner*, Juni (1925) Ausgabe; "Mietsteigerung und Hypothekenaufwertung," *G&S* 1:7 (19 Sept. 1925); "Dürfte die Aufwertung nach dem geltenden Staatsrecht überhaupt durch ein Gesetz geregelt werden?" *G&S* 1:14 (7 Oct. 1925); articles in *Die Aufwertung* #23 (12 June 1925); *Verh RT*, vol. 386, 92. Sitz. (11 July 1925), pp. 3009–10.

67. "Aufwertungsausschuss des Reichstages," *FZ* 69:362 (16 May 1925); "Der vorläufige Sieg Dr. Luthers und des Grosskapitals," *G&S* 1:2 (22 July 1925); "Dr. Luther," *G&S* 2:20 (19 May 1926); "Dr. Luther und das Grosskapital," *G&S* 2:24 (16 June 1926).

68. Entschliessung. Interessenverein der Aufwertungsgläubiger, [late May 1925), BayHStA, MJU 15334; "Das Echo des deutschnationalen Aufwertungs-schwindels," *FZ* 69:426 (11 June 1925); "Gegen die Parteien des Aufwertungs-kompromisses," *FZ* 69:388 (27 May 1925).

69. "Aufwertungsausschuss," *FZ* 69:484 (2 July 1925).

70. "Der vorläufige Sieg Dr. Luthers und des Grosskapitals," *G&S* 1:2 (22 July 1925); *Verh RT*, vol. 386, 91. Sitz. (10 July 1925), pp. 2988–90; Wunderlich in "Der Aufwertungskampf," *Vorwärts* 42:246 (27 May 1925); Kundgebung, Schutz-verband der Hypotheken-, Pfandbrief-, und Obligationengläubiger Bayerns, [late June 1925], BayHStA, MA 103775.

71. Keil to Löbe, 19 Apr. 1926, NL Keil, Briefe L–M; Rademacher, "Zur Frage der Aufwertung," 19 Nov. 1926, NL Westarp, MdR Best; "Das Aufwertungskom-promiss gefährdet?" *Vorwärts* 42:323 (11 July 1925).

72. "Bemerkungen," *FZ* 69:468 (26 June 1925); "Aufwertungs-Zwischenakt," *FZ* 69:472 (27 June 1925); "Frankfurt 11. Juli," *FZ* 69:510 (11 July 1925).

73. AM "Die Verteilung der Konkursmasse," *Rheinischer Merkur* 3:20 (15 May 1948); see also, e.g., Interzonenkonferenz der Chefs der Länder und Freien Städte in Bremen, 4./5. Okt 1946, in *Akten zur Vorgeschichte der Bundesrepublik Deutschland*, 1:932 (Munich: Oldenbourg, 1976); Ministerpräsidentenkonferenz, 7 June 1947, ibid., 2:580; Gerhard Colm, Joseph Dodge, and Raymond Gold-smith, "A Plan for the Liquidation of War Finance and the Financial Rehabilitation of Germany," *Zeitschrift für die gesamte Staatswissenschaft* 111:2 (1955): 220 (Colm and Goldsmith were German Americans who had lived through the collapse of the Weimar Republic); for economically oriented solutions, see, e.g., Ludwig Erhard cited in Wolfgang Benz, *Von der Besatzungsherrschaft zur Bundesrepublik* (Frankfurt/M: Fischer Taschenbuch Verlag, 1984), p. 124, and 48 German Univer-sity Professors, "Sanierung der deutschen Wirtschaft," in Christine Blumenberg-Lampe, ed., *Der Weg in die soziale Marktwirtschaft* (Stuttgart: Klett-Cotta, 1986), pp. 599–600.

Chapter 10

1. Kommers, *Politics*, pp. 35–36; cf. *JW*, 1916, p. 596.
2. See the discussion in H. Hattenhauer, "Zum Beamtenleitbild des 20. Jahrhunderts," in *NS-Recht*.
3. Kommers, *Politics*, p. 39; *RGZ* 102, 161, 164; *RGZ* 107, 379; W. Jellink, "Schutz des öffentlichen Rechtes," *Veröffentlichung der Vereinigung der deutschen Staatsrechts Lehrer*, 1925, Heft 2, p. 39.
4. Jellink, "Schutz," p. 39; RIM, 2 Feb. 1925, ZStA, RJM, Nr. 853, Bl. 311.
5. Reichsgerichtspräsident Dr. Simons, "Das Reichsgericht im 45. Lebensjahr," *Deutsche Richterzeitung* 16/194:8 (15 Nov. 1924), pp. 423–24; Jellink, "Schutz," p. 39.
6. Präsident des Reichsgerichts to RK, 30 May 1925, BAK, R43 I/1211, Bl. 315.
7. Schiffer, *Deutsche Justiz*, pp. 182–84; Huber, *Deutsche Verfassungsgeschichte*, 6:563.
8. Kommers, *Politics*, pp. 39–40.
9. For the quotation see Sitzung des Reichsministeriums, 2 Dec. 1923, BAK, R43 I/1390, Bl. 11; Staatssekretär in der Reichskanzlei to RJM, 24 Jan. 1924, ZStA, RJM, Nr. 846, Bl. 200; Staatssekretär in der Reichskanzlei to RK, 17/24 Jan. 1924, BAK, R43 I/2454, Bl. 83; "Gesetzgebung und Reichsgericht," *VZ*, #54 (1 Feb. 1924).
10. Kommissarische Beratung, 31 Jan. 1925, BAK, R43 I/1211, Bl. 253–54.
11. RIM to RJM et al., 21 Apr. 1925, BAK, R43 I/1211, Bl. 285, and Entwurf eines Gesetzes über die Prüfung der Verfassungsmässigkeit von Reichsgesetzen," ibid., Bl. 286; Huber, *Deutsche Verfassungsgeschichte* 6:563.
12. See Chapter 5 above.
13. See, e.g., HGSV Berlin Biesdorf to Staatsministerium, 21 Dec. 1923, and HGSV Osnabrück to RK, 27 Dec. 1923, GLA Baden, Abt. 237, #29425; Zeiler, in Grossmann et al., *Kampf*, pp. 95–100; [Düringer draft speech], BAK, R45 II/28, Bl. 67.
14. *RGZ* 111, 321–335 (for judicial review, 322–323).
15. See, e.g., E. v. Hippel, "Das richterliche Prüfungsrecht," in G. Anschütz and R. Thoma, *Staatsrechtes*, 2:557; J. Lenoir, "Judicial Review in Germany under the Weimar Constitution," *Tulane Law Review* 14 (1940), 368; Huber, *Verfassungsgeschichte* 6:565–66.
16. *RGZ* 124, 173; Apelt, *Weimarer Verfassung*, pp. 341–42; E. Friesenhahn, *Verfassungsgerichtbarkeit*, pp. 12–13, passim.
17. Dessauer, *Recht*, pp. 1, 23–24; Nussbaum, *Money*, p. 212; OLGpräsident Celle to Prussian Justice Minister, 20 July 1923, GStA Dahlem, Rep. 84a, #5904, Bl. 37.
18. See the pamphlets and flyers for various revaluation organizations and parties in GStA Dahlem, ZSg XII/IV and articles in *G&S* and *Deutsches Volksrecht*, 1925–32; see also Bauser, *Wahrheit*, passim; G. Holtz, "Wirtschaftsnot und Aufwertung," 15 Sept. 1926, NL Marx, #411; Kunze, *Bankrott*; Childers, *Nazi Voter*, pp. 160–63, 263–64. For a discussion of the political role of the revaluation forces in the Republic's final years, see Jones, "Inflation."

19. Gesetzentwurf des Sparerbundes, NL Marx, #411; Anlage VI. Versuch einer Berechnung der Belastung der Wirtschaft durch die Aufwertung sowie durch die Entwürfe des Sparerbundes und der Reichsarbeitsgemeinschaft, NL Marx, #205.

20. Aufzeichnung zur Chefbesprechung, 15 Apr. 1926, BAK, R43 I/2457, Bl. 241–46; Ministerbesprechung, 24 June 1926, BAK, R43 I/2458, Bl. 14; Sitzung des Reichsministeriums, 19 July 1926, ibid., Bl. 44.

21. U. Schüren, *Fürstenenteignung*, pp. 189–197; Childers, *Nazi Voter*, p. 161.

22. See Bauser, "Aufgaben des Sparerbundes," in Bauser, *Wahrheit; Denkschrift der Reichsarbeitsgemeinschaft der Aufwertungs-, Geschädigten- und Mieterorganisationen*; Jones, "Inflation," p. 161; "Verblendung und Irreführung," *G&S* 1:4 (29 July 1925).

23. Materialien zur demokratischen Politik, #134, "Die Aufwertungsparteien," 1 Mar. 1928, GStA Dahlem, ZSg XII/III, #8; Winnewisser, *Aufwertung*, p. 28; [memo], 30 July 1926, BAK, R43 I/2458, Bl. 57; Sitzung des Reichsministeriums, 8 Dec. 1933, BAK, R43 II/812, Bl. 109.

24. See, e.g., Vermerk, 12 Apr. 1926, BAK, R43 I/2457, Bl. 224; Sitzung des Interfraktionellen Auschusses, 21 June 1927, BAK, R43 I/2459, Bl. 29–30; Vermerk, 23 June 1927, BAK, R43 I/2459, Bl. 32–33; "Die Verzinsung aufgewerteter Hypotheken," *FZ* 71:486 (3 July 1927); "Annahmen der Aufwertungsnovelle," *FZ* 74:517–19 (15 July 1930); "Die neuen Aufwertungsvorschriften," *FZ* 74:542–44 (24 July 1930); G. Katona, "Neuregelung der Aufwertungshypotheken," *Der deutsche Volkswirt*, 1929–30, 2. Halbband, pp. 1146–49.

25. See, e.g., "Neue Entrechtung der Aufwertungshypothekengläubiger," *Deutsches Volksrecht* 7:91 (14 Nov. 1931); "Spargedanke und Notverordnung," *Deutsches Volksrecht* 7:99 (12 Dec. 1931).

26. Jones, "Inflation," pp. 143–44, 168; "Zum Ergebnis der Reichstagwahl," *Deutsches Volksrecht* 6:75 (17 Sept. 1930); "Unserer Reichsführer Bauser gewählt," *Deutsches Volksrecht* 8:63 (6 Aug. 1932); W. Simon to Marx, 19 Nov. 1931, NL Marx #203; Childers, *Nazi Voter*, esp. Tables 3.4 and 4.4; J. Falter/D. Hänisch, "Anfälligkeit von Arbeitern gegenüber der NSDAP," *Archiv für Sozialgeschichte* 26 (1986): Table 10 (*Berufslose*).

27. See, e.g., Martin Broszat, "Zur Struktur der NS-Massenbewegung," *Vierteljahreshefte für Zeitgeschichte* 31:1 (Jan. 1983): 69 and passim; Heinz-Gerhard Haupt, "Mittelstand und Kleinbürgertum in der Weimarer Republik," *Archiv für Sozialgeschichte* 26 (1986): 217–38; cf. Falter/Hänisch, "Anfälligkeit," pp. 179–216.

28. "Die Völkischen für das Volksbegehren des Sparerbundes," *G&S* 2:8 (25 Feb. 1926); Dr. jur. F. Lincke to RK, 13 Oct 1932, BAK, R43 II/812, Bl. 21; "Adolf Hitler und die Sparer-Ausraubung," *Deutsche Sparer Zeitung* 10:34 (27 Aug.–1 Sept. 1933); Childers, *Nazi Voter*, pp. 152–53, 163–64.

29. Childers, "Inflation," pp. 428–29; Childers, *Nazi Voter*, esp. pp. 66, 263; Childers, "Interest and Ideology."

30. See e.g., Paul Burmähl to Staatsanwaltschaft Hamburg, 1 Apr 1929, NL Marx, #203; Childers, *Nazi Voter*, p. 264 and passim.

31. Kabinettsvorlage, RJM, 7 July, 1933, BAK, R43 II/812, Bl. 67.

32. "Gleichschaltung der Sparer und Rentnerverbände," *Deutsches Volksrecht* 9:41 (10 June 1933); Sitzung des Reichsministeriums, 14 July 1933, ibid., Bl. 71; Staatssekretär in der Reichskanzlei to RJM, 21 Aug. 1933, ibid., Bl. 77; Sitzung des Reichsministeriums, 8 Dec. 1933, ibid., Bl. 109–10; RIM to Länderregierungen, 17 Mar. 1934, ibid., Bl. 158; RJM to Herrn Reichsministers, 23 Oct. 1935, ibid., Bl. 186; [news clip], BAK, R2/14025, Bl. 261; "Auflösung von Aufwertungsverbänden," *FZ* 83:568 (6 Nov. 1938).

33. For quotation, Vogels to Staatssekretär, 12 Mar. 1927, BAK, R43 I/2458, Bl. 239. Rademacher, "Zur Frage der Aufwertung," 19 Nov. 1926, NL Westarp, 1925, MdR Best; "Die Preussische Central-Bodenkredit AG," *G&S* 4:23 (21 Mar. 1928).

34. Statistisches Reichsamt, *Oeffentlicher Kredit*, p. 25.

35. Katona, "Altbesitz," pp. 273–75; Bericht und 1. Anlage der Deutschen Revisions- und Treuhandgesellschaft, Nachprüfung von Auslösungsrechten, R2/2169; "Denkschrift über Anleihe Ablösung," *FZ* 73:879 (24 Nov. 1928).

36. Reichskommissar für die Ablösung der Reichsanleihen des alten Besitzes, Rundverfügung an die Anleihealtbesitzstellen, 15 July 1926, BAK, R2/2226. Concerning anger at the government, see Dr. L. Haas to RFM, 1 Aug. 1926, and numerous other letters, ibid.

37. Katona, "Altbesitz," pp. 273–75; Schetter, "Aufwertungsgesetzgebung, 1927," Schreiber, *Jahrbuch*, 1927/28, p. 280; for repayment see BAK R2/3770; "Oktober-Auslösung der Kriegsanleihen," *Deutsche Sparer Zeitung* 10:40 (6.–12. Okt. 1933). See also, Witt, "Auswirkungen," n. 53.

38. "Die Vorzugsrente für Anleihe Altbesitzer," *Deutsche Sparer Zeitung* 12:12 (23–29 Mar. 1935).

39. "Um den Tageswert der Neubesitzanleihen," *Der deutsche Oekonomist* 51:3 (20 Jan. 1933); "Warum keine Arrosierung der Neubesitzanleihen?" ibid. 50:19 (13 May 1932).

40. "Reich Bond Calls Neglected Here," *New York Times* 82 (21 Jan. 1933): 21:7; "Denkschrift über Anleihe Ablösung," *FZ* 73:879 (24 Nov. 1928).

41. *Verh RT* Vol. 443, Anlage #2183, pp. 16–21.

42. *Verh RT*, vol. 443, Anlage #2183, and vol. 428, 199. Sitzung (14 July 1930), pp. 6356, 6366; "Annahme der Aufwertungsnovelle," *FZ* 74:517–19 (15 July 1930); "Die neuen Aufwertungsvorschriften," *FZ* 74:542–44 (24 July 1930); G. Katona, "Neuregelung der Aufwertungshypotheken," *Der deutsche Volkswirt*, 1929–30, 2. Halbband, pp. 1146–49.

43. "Die Verordnung über den Aufwertungstermin," *FZ* (12 Nov. 1931); "Das Notprogram," *FZ* 76:916 (9 Dec. 1931); Sitzung des Reichsministeriums, 8 June 1933, BAK, R 43 II/812, Bl. 65; "Aufwertungsnotverordnung," *RdI, Geschäftliche Mitteilungen* 13:26 (25 Nov. 1931); "Vor dem Ablauftermin des Hypothekenmoratoriums," *Bankarchiv* 37/38:25 (1 Oct. 1938): 608; Lucas, "Neuregelung der Aufwertungsfälligkeiten," *Bankarchiv* 36:9 (1 Feb. 1937): 229; "Notverordnung-Osthilfe-Hypothekenenteignung," *Deutsches Volksrecht* 7:93 (21 Nov. 1931); "Hypothekenmoratorium-Verlängerung," *Deutsche Sparer Zeitung* 10:49 (8–14 Dec. 1933); "Die privaten Aufwertungshypotheken zum 1. Jan. 1935," *Deutsche Sparer Zeitung* 11:51/52 (22 Dec. 1934–4 Jan. 1935).

44. "Die Stundung von aufgewerteten Industrie-Obligationen," *Wirtschaft und*

Statistik 12 (1932): 790; and the sources in n. 43 of this chapter; for Nazis, see this chapter above.

45. See the survey of market rates for revalued mortgage bonds, government bonds, and industrial obligations in *Statistisches Jahrbuch für das deutsche Reich* 52 (1933): 364.

46. See *Deutsches Volksrecht*, Vols. 6–9 (1930–33), esp. "Spargedanke und Notverordnung," 7:99 (12 Dec. 1931).

47. For Bavarian situation, Vertretung der Reichsregierung in München to RK, 29 June 1926, BAK, R43 I/2458, Bl. 23; for Wilhelmshaven System, G. Behrens, "Die Aufwertung von Sparguthaben," *G&S* 3:8 (23 Feb. 1927); Schlegelberger and Harmening, *Gesetz*, p. 222.

48. Professor Axt, "Ist das Wilhelmshaven System nur eine vereinfachte Berechnungsart oder eine Ungerechtigkeit?" *Deutsches Volksrecht* 4:80 (6 Oct. 1928); "Sparkasseaufwertung," *G&S* 4:5 (18 Jan. 1928).

49. Wilhelm Döring, "Die Aufwertung der Spareinlagen bei der öffentlichen Sparkassen," *Sozialökonomische Blätter* 2:12 (Oct. 1930): 91, 96; "Auszahlung der Sparguthaben," *Berliner Börsen Zeitung* #180 (18 Apr. 1934); "Die Freigabe der Preussischen Aufwertungsguthaben," *FZ* 77:198 (20 Apr. 1933); "Sparguthabenaufwertung in Bayern," *Der deutsche Oekonomist* 49:9 (6 Mar. 1931): 408–9; *Deutsches Volksrecht/Deutsche Sparer Zeitung*, 1930–35.

50. "Neue Sparkasseaufwertung in Sachsen," *G&S* 3:37 (6 Aug. 1927); "Sparkasseaufwertung in Mecklenburg," *Deutsches Volksrecht* 6:89 (5 Nov. 1930); "Vorbildliche Aufwertung in Württemberg," *Deutsches Volksrecht* 9:29 (11 Apr. 1933).

51. "Zur höheren Aufwertung bei den preussischen Sparkassen," *Der deutsche Oekonomist* 48:16 (24 Apr. 1930), p. 569.

52. Schlegelberger und Harmening, *Gesetz*, pp. 232–36, 239–40; "Die Aufwertung bei Betriebskassen," *FZ* 71:593 (11 August 1926); "Aufwertung der Werkspensionskassen," *Deutsches Volksrecht* 4:56 (14 July 1928); H. Potthoff, "Zur Aufwertung von Pensionsansprüchen," *Zentralblatt für Handelsrecht* 3:2 (Feb. 1928), pp. 55–58; articles entitled "Werksparkasse," in *G&S* 3:28 (6 July 1927), 3:31 (16 July 1927), 3:32 (20 July 1927), 3:36 (2 Aug. 1927); "Sparguthaben beim Phoenix," *Deutsches Volksrecht* 3:76 (21 Dec. 1927).

53. Franz Sauer, *Beamtenrecht des Reiches* (Berlin: Schwabachescher Verlagsbuchhandlung, 1933), pp. 184, 187; Heinrich Krüger, *Deutsches Beamtenrecht* (Berlin: Verlag für Sozialpolitik, Wirtschaft und Statistik, 1943), IV.a-13.

54. Wunderlich, "Bedeutung des Aufwertungsgesetzes," p. 489; "Aufwertung der Stahlwerk Becker-Obligationen," *Der deutsche Oekonomist* 49:2 (8 Jan. 1931): 30; DIHT, "Aufwertung Volksbegehren, Finanzielle Wirkungen," 11 June 1926, ZStA, RWM, Nr. 15418, Bl. 419; Deutsche Volkspartei, Reichsgeschäftsstelle, Wahlbrief #5, 30 Apr. 1928, NL Zapf (untitled folder); "Die Aufwertung der Industrie-Obligationen," *G&S* 3:57 (15 Oct. 1927). For delays see, e.g., "Das Agio der Aufwertungsobligationen," *Der deutsche Oekonomist* 50:2 (15 Jan. 1932): 57. Also *Statistisches Jahrbuch*, 1930, p. 368, and 1935, p. 362, and 1941/42, p. 471; O. Mügel, "Neuordnung der Genussrechte," *Bankarchiv* 34:6 (15 Dec. 1934): 129.

55. Nussbaum, *Bilanz der Aufwertungstheorie*, p. 17; Stand der Aufwertungs-

sachen am 31. Dezember 1928 and Stand der Aufwertungssachen am 31. Dezember 1934, BayHStA, MJU 12589; Arthur Starke, *Aufwertungs-Schluss-Gesetzgebung* (Berlin: Carl Salzmann Druck und Verlagsanstalt, n.d.), esp. pp. 34–35; for cost and complexity: Schutzverband der Hypotheken-, Pfandbrief-, und Obligationengläubiger in Bayern to Hohen Bayerischen StM der Justiz, 21 Oct. 1926, BayHStA, MWi 491; "Sabotage des Aufwertungsverfahrens," *G&S* 2:36 (8 Sept. 1926).

56. Starke, *Aufwertungs*, p. 35; Uebersicht über den allgemeinen Stand der Durchführung der Aufwertung, NL Marx, #205; *Statistisches Jahrbuch*, 1937, p. 405; *Vierteljahresheft zur Statistik des deutschen Reiches*, 51:2 (1942): 28. Figures on the number of mortgages and the amount repaid are perforce based on extrapolation from the available Prussian statistics.

57. Schutzverband der Lebens- und Feuerversicherten, "Beantwortung der wichtigsten Fragen bezüglich der Aufwertung von Lebens- und Rentenversicherung," [Oct. 1927], Stiftung Westfälisches Wirtschaftsarchiv, K-2, #600; *Statistisches Jahrbuch*, 1930, p. 370; "Die Aufwertungsquoten der Lebensversicherung," *Deutsches Volksrecht* 8:78 (28 Sept. 1932) and "Versicherungswesen," *Der deutsche Oekonomist* 46:6 (9 Feb. 1928): 195. "Verwaltungskostenbeitrag der Hypothekenbanken," *FZ* 79:528 (17 Oct. 1934).

58. Landtag, 1926/27, Aufwertung von Hypotheken und Pfandbriefen—8%iger Verwaltungskostenbeitrag—Sonderbeitrag zur Teilungsmasse, BayHStA, MWi 491; "Verwaltungskostenbeitrag der Hypothekenbanken," *FZ* 79:528 (17 Oct. 1934); "Verwaltungskostenbeitrag der Hypothekenbanken," *Deutsches Volksrecht* 7:40 (20 May 1931); for contributions by banks see *Deutsches Volksrecht*, 1929–32, *Deutsche Sparer Zeitung*, 1935; "Krisenfeste Teilungsmasse," *FZ* 77:201 (16 Mar. 1933); "Aufwertung der Kommunalobligationen," *Deutsche Bergwerkszeitung* #229 (29 Sept. 1929); *Statistisches Jahrbuch*, 1939/40, p. 420, and 1941/42, p. 460.

59. Witt, "Auswirkungen," n. 54; Gerhard Schulz, *Deutschland seit dem Ersten Weltkrieg. 1918–1945* (Göttingen: Vandenhoeck & Ruprecht, 1976), p. 86.

60. "Die sozialdemokratischen Sparkassen und die Sparkasseaufwertung im Preussen," *G&S* 4:3 (11 Jan. 1928); Hasselmann, *Konsumgenossenschaften*, pp. 404–5, 414. F. Steffan, *Bayerische Vereinsbank*, pp. 244–45; *100 Jahre Rheinische Hypothekenbank*, p. 48; Chapter 6 above; for private mortgages, Statistisches Reichsamt, *Volkseinkommen*, p. 42; also, Gesetzentwurf, BAK, R43 I/2460, Bl. 82; "Hypothekenbestand Ende 1934," *Deutsche Sparer-Zeitung* 11:50 (15–20 Dec. 1934).

61. Lüke, *Stabilisierung*, pp. 206–7; Balderston, "Links," and "Origins of Instability," passim; Chapter 6 above.

62. See "Deutschland noch ein Rechtsstaat?" *Deutsches Volksrecht* 9:1/2 (7 Jan. 1933); "Warum keine Arrosierung der Neubesitzanleihen?" *Der deutsche Oekonomist* 50:19 (13 May 1932): 621; Max Apt, *Verfassungswidrigkeit der Neubesitz Anleihe*. Berlin: C. Heymanns Verlag, 1932; Balderston, "Links"; Balderston, "Origins of Instability."

63. See *Statistisches Jahrbuch*, 1933, p. 364; Ministerium des Handels to Heinrich Wangemann, 22 Sept. 1926, BayHStA, MWi 491; [news clip], "Die Verzinsung der aufgewerteten Industrie Obligationen ab 1932," *FZ* [1928],

BayHStA, MWi 503; "Die Aufwertung der landschaftlichen Pfandbriefe," *Deutsches Volksrecht* 5:8 (26 Jan. 1929); "Fehlkonstruktionen bei Aufwertungspapieren," *Der deutsche Oekonomist* 50:51/52 (23 Dec. 1932): 1706–9; "Börsenchance der Liquidationspfandbriefe," ibid. 47:46 (14 Nov. 1929): 1492; "Zur Regelung der Aufwertungshypotheken," ibid. 48:8 (20 Feb. 1930): 251.

64. See Chapter 6 above.

Appendix

1. Dr. Best, "Die Denkschrift über die Aufwertung," Sonderdruck aus #6, *Die Aufwertung*. A number of authors published commentaries on the revaluation laws. See, e.g., Schlegelberger and Harmening, *Gesetz*.

2. Betr.: Hypothekenaufwertung, [Apr. 1925], BAK, R43 I/2456, Bl. 38; Schetter to Marx [on reverse of Marx to Schetter, 3 Sept. 1926], NL Marx, #205; see also Betr.: Aufwertungsvorschriften der Artikel I der 3. Steuernotverordnung, BayHStA, MA 103773.

3. Wunderlich, "Bedeutung des Aufwertungsgesetzes," pp. 488–89; Schlegelberger and Harmening, *Gesetz*, pp. 189–209.

4. Wunderlich, "Bedeutung des Aufwertungsgesetzes," pp. 488–89; DIHT to Mitglieder, 11 Apr. 1925, Industrie und Handelskammer zu München, XIII, 35.

5. Schetter to Marx [on reverse of Marx to Schetter, 3 Sept. 1926], NL Marx, #205; Schlegelberger and Harmening, *Gesetz*, pp. 19–22, 143–48.

6. See, e.g., Besprechung im Ministerium des Innern, 20 Jan. 1925, LA Berlin, Rep. 142, DSt, Hauptverzug B, #2795/II.

7. See Mügel, *Aufwertung*, pp. 13, 16; Wehinger, *Regelungsversuche*, p. 68; in Bavaria 58 percent of revaluation cases involved retroactive revaluation (Stand der Aufwertungssachen, 31 Dec. 1934, BayHStA, MJU 12589); Eingabe des Centralverbandes des deutschen Bank- und Bankiergewerbes to Reichstag Justice Committee, 6 May 1927, BayHStA, MJU 15691.

8. Schlegelberger and Harmening, *Gesetz*, pp. 126–27; Winnewisser, *Aufwertung*, p. 35.

9. See, e.g., RdI to RWM, 22 May 1925, ZStA, RWM, Nr. 15469, Bl. 263–64.

10. See Chapter 9 for conflict; also, RWM to Regierungen der Länder, 16 Apr. 1925, ZStA, RWM, Nr. 15416, Bl. 401–2; Vermerk, 17 June 1925, BAK, R43 I/2456, Bl. 177; Schlegelberger and Harmening, *Gesetz*, pp. 240–44.

11. Schlegelberger and Harmening, *Gesetz*, pp. 220–21, 229–30; see Chapter 10 above, for actual rates; Steffan, *Bayerische Vereinsbank*, p. 244.

12. Schlegelberger and Harmening, *Gesetz*, pp. 233, 239.

13. Schlegelberger and Harmening, *Gesetz*, p. 182; Wunderlich, "Einigung der Parteien in der Aufwertungsfrage," *Industrie und Handel der Zeit*, #209 (18 May 1925), in ZStA, RWM, Nr. 15417, Bl. 174.

14. Schlegelberger and Harmening, *Gesetz*, p. 25; for repayment problems, see Chapter 10 above; Vermerk, 9 June 1925, ZStA, RJM Nr. 859, Bl. 40.

15. Schlegelberger and Harmening, *Gesetz*, pp. 82–92; "Die Revision der Aufwertung," *Wirtschafts-Rundschau der Blätter für Genossenschaftswesen*, #14 (3 Apr. 1925); Bücherbesprechungen, *Die Sparkasse* #1183 (20 Nov. 1924); *Verh*

RT, vol. 386, 92. Sitz. (11 July 1925), pp. 3004–7, 3015; Begründung zur Umrechnungszahl, ZStA, RWM, Nr. 15416, Bl. 22–26.

16. *Verh RT*, vol. 400, Anlage #805, p. 14; Schlegelberger and Harmening, *Gesetz*, pp. 293–95, 299.

17. RFM, 16 Apr. 1925, ZStA, RWM, Nr. 15469, Bl. 235; *Verh RT*, vol. 400, Anlage #805, p. 3, and vol. 403, Anlage #1150, p. 11; Hauptpunkte der Anleihe Aufwertung, ZStA, Büro des Reichspräsidenten, Nr. 234, Bl. 5.

18. Schlegelberger and Harmening, *Gesetz*, p. 297–98; "Was man über die Vorzugsrente wissen muss," *G&S* 2:2 (13 Jan. 1926).

19. Schlegelberger and Harmening, *Gesetz*, p. 298; "Die Aufwertung durch Wohlfahrtsrente," *Germania* 55:314 (9 July 1925); *Verh RT*, vol. 403, Anlage #1150, p. 8.

20. Schlegelberger and Harmening, *Gesetz*, pp. 301–3.

Bibliography

Archival Materials

Bayerisches Hauptstaatsarchiv, Munich
  Ministerium des Aeussern
    Bd. 103773—Entwürfe u. Gesetzgebung, Aufwertung
    Bd. 103775—Zuschriften
    Bd. 103778—Entwürfe u. Gesetz, Ablösung öffentlicher Anleihen
    Bde. 103780–81—Vollzug, 3. Steuernotverordnung
    Bd. 103842—Sonstige Besteuerungsobjekten
  Ministerium der Wirtschaft
    Bd. 491–92—Aufwertung von Hypotheken und anderen Forderungen
    Bd. 495—Aufwertung (Gesetzes-Material)
  Ministerium der Justiz
    Bd. 12589—Geschäftsanfall in Aufwertungssachen
    Bd. 15135—3. Steuernotverordnung, Aenderung
    Bd. 15308—3. Steuernotverordnung, Vollzug, Allgemein
    Bd. 15503—Hypothekenaufwertung, 1923–24
    Bd. 15331—Paragraph 29, 3. Steuernotverordnung
    Bde. 15332–34—Vollzug, Art. I, 3. Steuernotverordnung
    Bd. 15335—Aenderung der Aufwertungsgesetzgebung
    Bd. 15664—Aufwertungsgesetz vom 16. Juli 1925
    Bd. 15665—Ablösung öffentlicher Anleihen, Gesetz vom 1. Juli 1925
    Bd. 15691—Aufwertung von Pfandbriefen
    Bd. 16587—Staatskommissar für Hypothekenbanken
  Ministerium der Landwirtschaft
    Bd. 1689—3. Steuernotverordnung, Aufwertung Allgemein
Bundesarchiv Koblenz
  Akten der Reichskanzlei (R43 I)
    Bde. 2454–60—Aufwertung von Schulden
    Bde. 1373–1403—Kabinettsprotokollen
    Bd. 1020—Besprechung mit den Parlamentariern und Fraktionführern
    Bd. 1028—Interfraktioneller Ausschuss
    Bde. 1305–6—Kabinettsbildung
    Bde. 2343–44—Wohnungsreform und Fürsorge
    Bde. 2394–97—Steuern
    Bd. 1211—Reichsgericht et al.
    Bd. 1250—Verträge
    Bd. 2126—Börsenwesen
    Bd. 2358—Finanz-, Zoll-, und Steuerpolitik, Allgemein
    Bd. 652—Spar- und Kreditwesen
    Bd. 274—Ausführung des Friedensvertrages

Akten der Reichskanzlei (R43 II)
  Bde. 811a–812—Aufwertung von Schulden
Reichsfinanzministerium (R2)
  Bd. 2148—Anleihe Ablösung
  Bde. 2160–62, 2182, 2226, 2294, 2328—Ausführung, Gesetz über die Ablösung öffentlicher Anleihen
  Bd. 2169—Betrügereien im Altbesitzverfahren
  Bd. 3770—Tilgung der Anleiheablösungsschuld . . .
  Bd. 1858—Ausgabe und Einlösung von Schuldverschreibungen . . .
  Bd. 1978—Reichsschuldbuch
  Bd. 4261—Vorzugsrente
  Bd. 4262—Aenderung des Anleihe-Ablösungsgesetz
Reichsministerium für Wiederaufbau (R38)
  Bd. 69—Wohnungswesen
Deutsche Volkspartei (R45 II)
  Bde. 28, 29—Parteitage
  Bd. 66—Reichstagfraktion, Vorstandssitzungen
Deutsche Demokratische Partei (R45 III)
  Bd. 12—Sitzungen, Parteiausschuss
  Bd. 19—Sitzungen, Parteivorstand
Nachlässe
  Hermann Dietrich
  Anton Erkelenz
  Otto Gessler
  Theodor Heuss
  Karl Jarres
  Erich Koch-Weser
  Hans Luther
  Hermann Pünder
  H. v. Richthofen
  Friedrich Saemisch
  Paul Silverberg
  Walther Simons
  Max v. Stockhausen
  Alfred Zapf
Deutsches Industrie-Institut, Cologne
  Nachlass Oskar Funcke
Familienarchiv Gärtringen, Gärtringen
  Nachlass Kuno Graf Westarp
Geheimes Staatsarchiv Preussischer Kulturbesitz, Berlin
  Hauptabteilung. Zeitgeschichtliche Sammlung (XII)
    Nr. III—Broschüren
    Nr. IV—Flugblätter und Plakate
  Justiz Ministerium (Rep 84a)
    Bde. 5885–90—Massnahmen gegen den Währungsverfall
    Bd. 5904—Gutachtliche Berichten betr. Aufwertung
  Staatsbank (Rep 109)

Bd. 1141—Aufwertungsregelung
Generallandesarchiv Baden, Karlsruhe
Finanzministerium, Abt. 237
    #29425–26—Aufwertungsgesetze
Staatsministerium-Reichssachen, Abt. 233
    #11774, Vol. 10ad, Fasc. 1 and 3—Aufwertung, Anleihe-Ablösung
Historisches Stadtsarchiv Cologne
    Nachlass Wilhelm Marx
Industrie- und Handelskammer zu München (XIII), Munich
    Bd. 26—Schutz der Hypothekengläubiger
    Bd. 35—Aufwertung
Landesarchiv Berlin
    Deutscher Städtetag (Rep 142)
        Hauptgruppe B, #2528—Anleihe Aufwertung
        Hauptverzug A, #590/I, 654—Städtetag Vorstandssitzung
        Hauptverzug B, #2795/I and II—Aufwertung von kommunaler Anleihen
    Landkreistag (Rep 142)
        #209, 391, 408—Aufwertung von Anleihen und Hypotheken
Landesarchiv Württemberg, Stuttgart
    Staatsministerium, E130/II
        Bushel 392–93—Aufwertung
Niedersächsisches Staatsarchiv, Osnabrück
    DNVP (Erw Cl)
    #90—HGSSV
    #104—December 1924 Election
Rheinisch-Westfälisches Wirtschaftsarchiv, Cologne
    Industrie- und Handelskammer Münster (Abt. 5)
        #17, Fasz 3—Arbeitsgemeinschaft
        #21, Fasz 16—Aufwertung
        #48, Fasz 7—Steuernotverordnung
Staatsarchiv Hamburg
    Senatsakten, Cl. I Lit. T, Nr. 15b
        Vol. 70, Fasc. 1 (Cour. I and II)—3. Steuernotverordnung
        Vol. 70, Fasc. 4, 5, 7, 18—betr., Aufwertung
    Finanzdeputation
        Betr.: Gesetz über die Aufwertung von Hypotheken
Stiftung Westfälisches Wirtschaftsarchiv, Dortmund
    Industrie- und Handelskammer Dortmund (K-1)
        #600—Aufwertung
    Industrie- und Handelskammer Bochum (K-2)
        #346—Deutsche Industrie- und Handelstag
        #569—Rundschreiben, DIHT
        #587—Vereinigung von Handelskammern
        #1147—3. Steuernotverordnung
        #1408—Aufwertung
        #1556—Arbeitsgemeinschaft
U.S. National Archives, Washington, D.C., Microcopy T120

Nachlass Gustav Stresemann
Zentrales Staatsarchiv Potsdam
Büro des Reichspräsidenten (06.01)
  Bde. 233–35—Aufwertung
Reichsjustizministerium (30.01)
  Bd. 773—Presseäusserungen—Hypothekenaufwertung et al.
  Bde. 781–89—Eingaben, Massnahmen: Schutz der Hypothekengläubiger
  Bde. 845–46—Massnahmen, Schutz der Hypothekengläubiger
  Bde. 847–60—Aufwertung der alten Markforderungen
  Bde. 880–81—Aufwertung, 3. Steuernotverordnung
  Bd. 884—Vorarbeitung zur 3. Steuernotverordnung
  Bd. 885—Frage der höhern Aufwertung von Industrie-Obligationen
Reichswirtschaftsministerium (31.01)
  Bde. 15413–18—Valorisierung (Aufwertung) von Hypotheken
  Bde. 15423–26—Eingaben betr. Aufwertungsverordnungen
  Bd. 15469—Aufwertung der öffentlichen Anleihen
Reichswirtschaftsrat (04.01)
  Bde. 369, 372, 397, 401—Wirtschaftspolitischer Ausschuss
  Bde. 540–41—Finanzpolitischer Ausschuss
  Bd. 934—Arbeitsausschuss für das Aufwertungsgesetz
Reichslandbund (61 Re 1)
  Bd. 123—Aufwertungsfrage
Reichskommissar für die Ueberwachung der öffentlichen Ordnung (15.07)
  Bd. 299—Reichspartei für Aufwertung und Recht
Reichsbank (25.01)
  Bde. 6653–54—Handakten

Periodicals

Der Arbeiter, 1924–25 (35.–36. Jhrg.).
Die Aufwertung, 1924–25 (1.–2. Jhrg., most issues).
Bankarchiv, 1923–42 (Vols. 23–42).
Bayerische Beamtenzeitung, 1925 (7. Jhrg.).
Das Bayerische Handwerk und Gewerbe, 1924–25 (38.–39. Jhrg.).
Der Beamtenbund, 1924–25 (8.–9. Jhrg.).
Berliner Tageblatt, Dec. 1924–Mar. 1925 (53.–54. Jhrg.).
Blätter für den Katholischen Klerus, 1924 (5. Jhrg.).
Deutsche Allgemeine Zeitung, Dec. 1923–July 1925 (62.–64. Jhrg.).
Deutsche Handelswacht, 1923–25 (30.–32. Jhrg.).
Das deutsche Handwerksblatt, 1924–25 (18.–19. Jhrg.).
Deutsche Juristen Zeitung, 1921–24 (26.–29. Jhrg.).
Deutsche Mittelstands-Zeitung, 1924–26 (4.–6. Jhrg.).
Der Deutsche Oekonomist, 1928–1933 (Vol. 46–51).
Deutsche Richterzeitung, 1922–23 (14.–15. Jhrg.).
Deutsche Sparer Zeitung, 1933–36 (10.–13. Jhrg.).
Der Deutsche Sparer, 1925 (2. Jhrg.; some issues).

Deutsche Sparkasse Zeitung, 1924–25 (1.–2. Jhrg.).
Deutsches Volksrecht, 1928–32 (5.–9. Jhrg.).
Eiserne Blätter, 1924 (5. Jhrg.).
Frankfurter Zeitung, June 1922, Dec. 1923–Mar. 1924, 1925–28, 1931–34 (66., 67.–73., 76.–79. Jhrg.).
Der freie Angestellte, 1924–25 (28.–29. Jhrg.).
G.D.A., 1924–25.
Germania, Nov. 1922–July 1925 (52.–55. Jhrg.).
Geschäftliche Mitteilungen des RdI, 1924–29 (6.–11 Jhrg.).
Gewerkschaftszeitung, 1924–25 (34.–35. Jhrg.).
Gläubiger und Sparer, 1925–28 (1.–4. Jhrg.).
Die Handels- und Büroangestellte, 1925 (31. Jhrg.).
Haus- und Grundbesitzerzeitung (Regensburg), 1924–25 (4.–5. Jhrg.).
Juristische Wochenschrift, 1922–24 (51.–53. Jhrg.).
Kölner Handwerkszeitung, 1924–25 (1.–2. Jhrg.).
Kölnische Zeitung, 1922–Feb. 1924.
Korrespondenz der Deutschnationalen Volkspartei, 1925 (8. Jhrg.).
Leipziger Zeitschrift für deutsches Recht, 1925 (Vol. 19).
Magazin der Wirtschaft, 1925 (1. Jhrg.).
Mercuria, 1924–25 (43.–44. Jhrg.).
Mitteilungen des Landesverbandes Bayerischer Sparkasse, 1923–25.
Neue Preussische Kreuzzeitung, Nov. 1923–Mar. 1924, Jan.–Feb. 1925 (75.–77. Jhrg.).
New York Times, 1924–25 (Vols. 73–74).
Norddeutsche Handwerks-Zeitung, 1925 (30. Jhrg.).
Pfälzische Handwerks und Gewerbe Zeitung, 1924–25 (14.–15. Jhrg.).
Rheinische Zeitung, 1923–24 (32.–33. Jhrg.).
Rote Fahne, Dec. 1922–July 1925 (5.–8. Jhrg.).
Schwäbische Arbeiterzeitung, 1925 (4. Jhrg.).
Der Sparerschutz, 1924–25 (1.–2. Jhrg.; some issues).
Die Sparkasse, 1920–25.
Steuer und Wirtschaft, 1924–25 (3.–4. Jhrg.).
Volksblatt für Lüneburg und Umgegend, 1923–25 (30.–32. Jhrg.).
Vorwärts, Nov. 1923–Mar. 1924, Nov. 1924–July 1925 (40.–42. Jhrg.).
Vossische Zeitung, Nov. 1923–July 1925.
Westdeutsche Arbeiterzeitung, 1923–25 (25.–27. Jhrg.).
Wirtschaft und Statistik, 1927–1941 (Vols. 7–21).
Zeitschrift des Gewerkschaftsbundes der Angestellten, 1924–25 (5.–6. Jhrg.).
Zentralblatt der christlichen Gewerkschaften Deutschlands, 1924–25 (24.–25. Jhrg.).

Published Contemporary Sources

Akten der Reichskanzlei, Kabinett Luther I u. II. Vols. 1 and 2. Boppard am Rhein: Harald Boldt Verlag, 1977.

Akten der Reichskanzlei, Kabinett Marx I u. II. Vols. 1 and 2. Boppard am Rhein: Harald Boldt Verlag, 1973.

Akten der Reichskanzlei, Kabinett Stresemann I u. II. Vols. 1 and 2. Boppard am Rhein: Harald Boldt Verlag, 1978.

Anders, Dr. Ferdinand. *Der Stand der Aufwertung.* Berlin: Verlag Hans Dohrn, 1924.

Bauser, A., ed. *Für Wahrheit und Recht.* Stuttgart: Verlag Württembergischer Sparerbund, 1927.

―――. *Vortrag.* Canstatt: Rössle und Kieser, 1925.

Bayerisches Statistisches Landesamt. *Die Verelendung des Mittelstandes.* Heft 106 der Beiträge zum Statistik Bayerns. Munich: n.p., 1925.

Bazille, Wilhelm. "Die Tragödie der Deutschnationalen Volkspartei." *Nationale Volksgemeinschaft* 1:2 (Sept. 1930).

Best, Dr. Georg et al. *Gegen die "Auf"-wertungsgesetzentwürfe der Regierung.* Berlin: Verlag "Die Aufwertung," [1925].

Beusch, Paul. *Währungszerfall und Währungsstabilisierung.* Berlin: Verlag von Julius Springer, 1928.

Bredt, Johann. *Hypothekenaufwertung.* Munich: J. F. Lehmanns Verlag, 1924.

Brink, Justizrat. *Reichsverband der deutschen Industrie und Aufwertung.* N.p., [1925].

Dannebaum, F. *Das kommende Aufwertungsgesetz.* Berlin: Verlag v. Franz Dahlen, 1925.

Denkschrift der Reichsarbeitsgemeinschaft der Aufwertung-, Geschädigten- und Mieterorganisationen. Berlin: n.p., 1927.

Dessauer, Friedrich. *Recht, Richtertum, und Ministerialbürokratie.* Mannheim: J. Bensheimer, 1928.

Dietrich, Hermann. *Was wird aus dem Sparguthaben?* N.p., 1924.

Emminger, Erich. *Die Aufwertungsfrage im aufgelösten Reichstag.* Munich: Dr. Fr. A. Pfeiffer & Co., 1924.

―――. *Der Kampf um die Aufwertung.* Munich: n.p., n.d.

Enquete Ausschuss. *Die deutsche Zahlungsbilanz.* Berlin: E. Mittler & Sohn, 1930.

―――. *Die Reichsbank.* Berlin: E. Mittler & Sohn, 1929.

―――. *Verhandlungen und Berichte des IV. Unterausschusses.* Vols. 1–9. Berlin: E. Mittler & Sohn, 1930.

―――. *Der Wohnungsbau.* Berlin: E. Mittler & Sohn, 1930.

Entscheidungen des Reichsgerichts in Zivilsachen. Vols. 88–124. Leipzig: Veit & Co., 1916–30.

Eulenberg, Franz. "Die soziale Wirkungen der Währungsverhältnisse." *Jahrbücher für Nationalökonomie und Statistik.* 3. Folge. 67:122 (1924): 748–94.

Feder, Gottfried. *Die Aufwertung.* Der völkische Sprachabend, #11. 1924.

Fraenkel, Ernst. *Soziologie der Klassenjustiz.* Berlin: Jungsozialistische Schriftenreihe, 1927.

Grossmann, Dr. H., et al. *Im Kampf um eine gerechte Aufwertung.* Stuttgart: Muthsche Verlagsbuchhandlung, 1924.

Heck, Phillipp. "Das Urteil des Reichsgerichts vom 28. November 1923 über die Aufwertung von Hypotheken und die Grenzen der Richtermacht." *Archiv für die civilistische Praxis* 122 (1924): 203–28.

Heimann, Hugo. *Der Kampf um die Aufwertung.* Berlin: Verlag J. H. W. Dietz, 1925.

Hergt, Oskar. "Taktik der HGSSV." *Korrespondenz der Deutschnationalen Volkspartei.* 8:129 (8 June 1925).

Hertz, Paul. *Sozialdemokratie und Aufwertung.* Berlin: J. H. W. Dietz, 1924.

Katona, Georg. "Altbesitz und Neubesitz." *Der deutsche Volkswirt* 3:9 (30 Nov. 1928): 273–75.

Kunze, Max. *Der betrügerische Bankrott der Reichsbank und die preussische Justiz.* Dresden: n.p., n.d.

Luther, Hans. *Feste Mark—Solide Wirtschaft.* Berlin: Otto Stollberg & Co., 1924.

———. *Vom Deutschlands eigener Kraft.* Berlin: Verlag von Georg Stilke, 1928.

Lutz, Paul. *Die öffentliche Kleinrentnerfürsorge. Unter besondere Rücksichtsnahme auf die örtlichen Verhältnisse in München.* Munich: n.p., 1927.

Morsey, Rudolf, and Karsten Ruppert, eds. *Die Protokolle der Reichstagfraktion der deutschen Zentrumspartei 1920–1925.* Mainz: Matthias Grunewald Verlag, 1981.

Mügel, Oskar. *Die Aufwertung. Ueberblick über die Entwicklung.* Berlin: Gersbach & Sohn, 1926.

———. *Geldentwertung und Hypotheken.* Berlin: Verlag von Franz Dahlen, 1924.

———. *Das gesamte Aufwertungsrecht.* Berlin: Verlag von Otto Liebmann, 1925.

Nussbaum, Arthur. *Die Bilanz der Aufwertungstheorie.* Tübingen: Verlag von J. C. B. Mohr, 1929.

Oelenheinz, Theodor, ed. *Spiegel der deutschen Inflation.* Leipzig: Verlag "Volks-Recht," 1928.

Oertmann, Paul. *Die Aufwertungsfrage bei der Geldentwertung.* Berlin: H. Sack, 1924.

Priess, Max. *Der Sachverständigengutachten und die "Aufwertungsfrage."* N.p., 1924.

Rademacher, Dr. Walther and Dr. Albrecht Philipp. *Das neue Aufwertungsrecht.* Berlin: Verlag von Georg Stilke, 1925.

Roth, Alfons. *Die Aufwertung.* Berlin: Hermann Sack Verlag, 1925.

Schiffer, Eugen. *Deutsche Justiz.* 2d ed. Munich: Verlag C. H. Beck, 1949.

Schlegelberger, Dr. Franz. *Aufwertungsfragen.* Munich: Max Huber Verlag, 1926.

Schlegelberger, Dr. Franz, and Rudolf Harmening. *Das Gesetz über die Aufwertung von Hypotheken und anderen Ansprüchen.* Berlin: Verlag von Franz Dahlen, 1925.

Schreiber, Georg. *Grundfragen der Zentrumspolitik.* Berlin: Verlag der Germania AG, 1924.

———, ed. *Politisches Jahrbuch, 1925.* Mönchen-Gladbach: Volksvereins Verlag, GmbH, 1925.

———, ed. *Politisches Jahrbuch, 1926.* Mönchen-Gladbach: Volksvereins Verlag, GmbH, 1927.

————, ed. *Politisches Jahrbuch, 1927/28.* Mönchen-Gladbach: Volksvereins Verlag, GmbH, 1928.

Sontag, Ernst. *Rechtsschutz der Hypothekengläubiger und Obligationäre gegen die Geldentwertung.* Berlin: Industrieverlag Spaeth & Linde, 1923.

Stampe, Ernst. *Das Aufwertungsurteil des Reichsgerichts.* Greifswald: Buch- und Kunstdruckerei Julius Abel, 1924.

Statistisches Reichsamt. *Das deutsche Volkseinkommen vor und nach dem Krieg.* Berlin: n.p., 1932.

————. *Oeffentlicher Kredit und Wirtschaftskrise.* Berlin: n.p., 1933.

————. *Statistisches Jahrbuch,* 1925–1940. Berlin: n.p., 1927–40.

————. *Vierteljahresheft zur Statistik des deutschen Reiches, 1941–43.* Berlin: n.p., 1941–43.

Titze, Heinrich. *Richtermacht und Vertragsinhalt.* Tübingen: J. C. B. Mohr, 1921.

Verhandlungen des Badischer Landtages. 2. Landtagsperiode, Heft 543b (1925). Karlsruhe: n.p., 1925.

Verhandlungen des Reichstages. Berlin: Reichsdruckerei, 1914, 1921–30.

Warneyer, Otto. *Die Aufwertung ausserhalb des Aufwertungsgesetzes vom 16. Juli 1925.* Berlin: Industrieverlag Spaeth & Linde, 1926.

Wehinger, Arno. *Die praktische Regelungsversuche der Aufwertungsfrage insbesondere in der Zeit nach der Markstabilisierung.* Dornbirn: Buchdruckerei G. Hofle, 1927.

Winnewisser, Georg. *Die Aufwertung von Industrie-Obligationen.* Karlsruhe: Verlag G. Braun, 1927.

Wolfsohn, John. *Die Aufwertung der Hypotheken und Wertpapiere.* Berlin: Carl Heymanns, 1924.

Wüst, Reinhard. *Das Aufwertungsproblem und die dritte Steuernotverordnung.* Halle/Saale: Karras & Koennecke, 1924.

————. *Beiträge zur Aufwertungsfrage.* Halle/Saale: Karras & Koennecke, 1924.

————. *Beiträge zur Aufwertungsfrage.* 2. Reihe. Halle/Saale: Buchdruckerei der Hallischen Nachrichten, 1924.

————. *Im Kampf für Wahrheit und Recht gegen "Luthertum" und "Marxismus."* Halle/Saale: Otto Hendel Druckerei, 1924.

Wunderlich, Hans. "Die rechtspolitische und wirtschaftliche Bedeutung des Aufwertungsgesetzes vom 16. Juli 1925," in Mügel, *Aufwertungsrecht,* pp. 471–501.

Zeiler, Alois. *Die Aufwertungsfrage nach der dritten Steuernotverordnung.* Munich: Hermann Leicht Verlag, 1924.

Zeiler, Alois, and Ernst Sontag. *Brennende Frage der Aufwertung.* Mannheim: J. Bensheimer, 1924.

Memoirs

Keil, Wilhelm. *Erlebnisse eines Sozialdemokraten.* Vol. 2. Stuttgart: Deutsche
   Verlags-Anstalt, 1948.
Luther, Hans. *Politiker ohne Partei.* Stuttgart: Deutsche Verlags-Anstalt, 1960.
Zeiler, Alois. *Meine Mitarbeit.* Braunschweig: Bieweg & Sohn, 1938.

Secondary Sources

Anschütz, Gerhard, and Richard Thomas. *Handbuch des deutschen Staatsrechtes*, Vol. 2. Tübingen: Verlag von J. C. B. Mohr, 1932.
Apelt, Willibalt. *Geschichte der Weimarer Verfassung.* Munich: Biederstein,
   1963.
Backer, John. *Priming the German Economy.* Durham: Duke University Press,
   1971.
Balderston, Theodore. "Links between Inflation and Depression: German Capital
   and Labour Markets 1924–1932." In *Nachwirkungen*, edited by Gerald Feld-
   man, pp. 157–85.
_____. "The Origins of Economic Instability in Germany 1924–1930. Market
   Forces versus Economic Policy." *Vierteljahresschrift für Sozial- und Wirt-
   schaftsgeschichte* 69 (1983): 488–514.
Bauer, Wolfram. *Wertrelativismus und Wertbestimmheit im Kampf um die Wei-
   marer Demokratie.* Berlin: Duncker & Humboldt, 1968.
Becker, Theodore. *Political Behavioralism and Modern Jurisprudence.* Chicago:
   Rand, McNally & Co., 1964.
Blackbourn, David. "Between Resignation and Volatility: The German Petite
   Bourgeoisie in the Nineteenth Century." In *Shopkeepers and Master Artisans
   in Nineteenth-Century Europe*, edited by Geoffrey Crossick and Heinz-
   Gerhard Haupt. London: Methuen, 1984.
_____. *Class, Religion, and Local Politics in Wilhelmine Germany: The Centre
   Party in Württemberg before 1914.* New Haven: Yale University Press, 1980.
Borchardt, Knut. "Das Gewicht der Inflationsangst in den wirtschaftspolitischen
   Entscheidungsprozessen während der Weltwirtschaftskrise." In *Nachwir-
   kungen*, edited by Gerald Feldman, pp. 233–60.
_____. *Wachstum, Krisen, Handlungsspielräume der Wirtschaftspolitik. Studien
   zur Wirtschaftsgeschichte des 19. und 20. Jahrhunderts* (Kritische Studien zur
   Geschichtswissenschaft, Vol. 50). Göttingen: Vandenhoeck & Ruprecht, 1982.
_____. "Zum Scheitern eines produktiven Diskurses über das Scheitern der
   Weimarer Republik: Replik auf Claus-Deiter Krohns Diskussionsbemerkun-
   gen." *Geschichte und Gesellschaft* 9 (1983): 124–37.
Bresciani-Turroni, Constantino. *The Economics of Inflation: A Study of Currency
   Depreciation in Post-War Germany.* London, 1937.
Busch, Otto, and Gerald Feldman, eds. *Historische Prozesse der deutschen In-
   flation.* Berlin: Colloquium Verlag, 1978.
Childers, Thomas. "Inflation, Stabilization, and Political Realignment in Ger-

many, 1919–1928." In *Die deutsche Inflation*, edited by Gerald Feldman, pp. 409–31. Berlin: de Gruyter, 1982.

————. "Interest and Ideology: Anti-System Politics in the Era of Stabilization 1924–1928." In *Nachwirkungen*, edited by Gerald Feldman, pp. 1–20.

————. *The Nazi Voter: The Social Foundations of Fascism in Germany, 1919–1933.* Chapel Hill: University of North Carolina Press, 1983.

————. "Who Indeed Did Vote for Hitler?" *Central European History* 17 (Mar. 1984): 45–53.

Clough, Shepard, and Charles Cole. *Economic History of Europe.* Boston: D. C. Heath & Co., 1952.

Dawson, John P. "Effects of Inflation on Private Law Contracts: Germany, 1914–1924." *Michigan Law Review* 33 (Dec. 1934): 171–238.

————. *Oracles of the Law.* Ann Arbor: University of Michigan Law School, 1968.

Deutsche Bundesbank, ed. *Deutsches Geld- und Bankwesen in Zahlen.* Frankfurt/M.: Fritz Knapp, GmbH, 1976.

Dilcher, Gerhard. "Das Gesellschaftsbild der Rechtswissenschaft und die soziale Frage." In *Das wilhelminische Bildungsbürgertum*, edited by Klaus Vondung. Göttingen: Kleine Vandenhoeck Reihe, 1976.

Dorpalen, Andreas. *Hindenburg and the Weimar Republic.* Princeton: Princeton University Press, 1964.

Dörr, Manfred. *Deutschnationale Volkspartei, 1925–1928.* Marburg/Lahn, 1964.

Eley, Geoff. *Reshaping the German Right: Radical Nationalism and Political Change after Bismarck.* New Haven: Yale University Press, 1980.

Ellis, Howard. *German Monetary Theory, 1905–1933.* Cambridge: Harvard University Press, 1934.

Eyck, Erich. *History of the Weimar Republic.* Vol. 1. Translated by Harlan P. Hanson and Robert G. L. Waite. Cambridge: Harvard University Press, 1962.

Feldman, Gerald. *Army, Industry, and Labor in Germany, 1914–1918.* Princeton: Princeton University Press, 1966.

————. *Iron and Steel in the German Inflation.* Princeton: Princeton University Press, 1977.

————. "The Political Economy of Germany's Relative Stabilization during the 1920/21 Depression." In *Die deutsche Inflation*, edited by Feldman et al., pp. 180–206.

————. "Social and Economic Policies of German Big Business, 1918–1929." *American Historical Review* 75 (1969): 47–55.

————, ed. *Die Nachwirkungen der Inflation auf die deutsche Geschichte 1924–1933.* Munich: R. Oldenbourg Verlag, 1985.

Feldman, Gerald, and Irmgard Steinisch. "Die Weimarer Republik zwischen Sozial- und Wirtschaftsstaat. Die Entscheidung gegen den Achtstundentag." *Archiv für Sozialgeschichte.* 18 (1978): 353–439.

Feldman, Gerald, et al., eds. *Die Anpassung an der Inflation.* Berlin: de Gruyter, 1986.

————. *Die deutsche Inflation/The German Inflation.* Berlin: de Gruyter, 1982.

————. *Die Erfahrung der Inflation.* Berlin: de Gruyter, 1984.

Fricke, Dieter, ed. *Die bürgerlichen Parteien in Deutschland.* Leipzig: Bibliographisches Institut, 1970.

Friesenhahn, Ernst. *Verfassungsgerichtbarkeit in der Bundesrepublik Deutschland.* Cologne: Carl Heymanns Verlag, 1963.

Gates, Robert. "Von der Sozialpolitik zur Wirtschaftspolitik?" In *Industrielles System,* edited by Mommsen et al., pp. 206–25.

Geertz, Clifford. "Ideology As a Cultural System." In *The Interpretation of Cultures,* edited by Clifford Geertz, pp. 193–233. New York: Basic Books, Inc., 1973.

Geiger, Theodor. *Die soziale Schichtung des deutschen Volkes.* Stuttgart: F. Enke, 1932.

Gellately, Robert. *Politics of Economic Despair.* Beverly Hills: Sage Publications, 1974.

Gordon, Harold. *Hitler and the Beer Hall Putsch.* Princeton: Princeton University Press, 1972.

Halperin, S. William. *Germany Tried Democracy.* New York: W. W. Norton & Co., 1965.

Hamilton, Richard. "Braunschweig 1932: Further Evidence of Support for National Socialism." *Central European History* 17 (Mar. 1984): 72–83.

———. "Reply to Commentators." *Central European History* 17 (Mar. 1984).

———. *Who Voted for Hitler?* Princeton: Princeton University Press, 1982.

Hardach, Karl. *Wirtschaftsgeschichte Deutschlands im 20. Jahrhundert.* Göttingen: Kleine Vandenhoeck Reihe, 1976.

Hasselmann, Erwin. *Geschichte der deutschen Konsumgenossenschaften.* Frankfurt/M.: F. Knapp, 1971.

Hattenhauer, Hans, ed. *Vom Reichsjustizamt zum Bundesministerium der Justiz.* Cologne: Bundesanzeiger, 1977.

———. *Zwischen Hierarchie und Demokratie.* Karlsruhe: C. F. Muller, 1971.

Hauschild, Harry. *Der vorläufige Reichswirtschaftsrat.* Berlin: E. S. Mittler & Sohn, 1926.

Hedemann, Wilhelm. *Flucht in den Generalklauseln.* Tübingen: J. C. B. Mohr, 1933.

———. *Reichsgericht und Wirtschaftsrecht.* Jena: Verlag von Gustav Fischer, 1929.

Henning, Friedrich-Wilhelm. *Das industrialisierte Deutschland.* Paderborn: Ferdinand Schoningh, 1974.

Hoffman, Walther. *Wachstum der deutschen Wirtschaft.* Berlin: Springer Verlag, 1965.

Holtfrerich, Carl-Ludwig. "Auswirkungen der Inflation auf die Struktur des deutschen Kreditgewerbes." In *Nachwirkungen,* edited by Gerald Feldman, pp. 187–209.

———. *Die deutsche Inflation, 1914–1923.* Berlin: de Gruyter, 1980.

———. "Internationale Verteilungsfolgen der deutschen Inflation." *Kyklos* 30 (1977): 271–92.

———. "Reichsbankpolitik 1918–1923 zwischen Zahlungsbilanz- und Quantitätstheorie." *Zeitschrift für Wirtschafts- und Sozialwissenschaft.* 1977, Heft 3, 193–214.

———. "Zu hohe Löhne in der Weimarer Republik? Bermerkungen zur

Borchardt-These." *Geschichte und Gesellschaft* 10 (1984): 122–41.

Huber, Ernst. *Deutsche Verfassungsgeschichte seit 1789.* Vol. 6, *Die Weimarer Reichsverfassung.* Stuttgart: Verlag W. Kohlhammer, 1981. Vol. 7, *Ausbau, Schutz und Untergang der Weimarer Republik.* Stuttgart: Verlag W. Kohlhammer, 1984.

———. *Verfassung.* Hamburg: Hanseatische Verlagsanstalt, 1937.

Hughes, Michael L. "Equity and Good Faith: Inflation, Revaluation, and the Distribution of Wealth and Power in Weimar Germany." Ph.D. dissertation, University of California, Berkeley, 1981.

James, Harold. "The Causes of the German Banking Crisis of 1931." *Economic History Review,* 2d ser., 37:1 (Feb. 1984): 68–87.

———. "Did the Reichsbank Draw the Right Conclusions from the Great Inflation?" In *Nachwirkungen,* edited by Gerald Feldman, pp. 211–31.

———. *The Reichsbank and Public Finance in Germany 1924–1933: A Study of the Politics of Economics during the Great Depression.* Frankfurt/M: Fritz Knapp Verlag, 1985.

Jastrow, Jgnaz. *Die Prinzipienfragen in den Aufwertungsdebatten.* Brünn: Verlag Rudolf Rohrer, 1937.

Jones, Larry E. " 'The Dying Middle': Weimar Germany and the Fragmentation of Bourgeois Politics." *Central European History* 5 (Mar. 1972): 23–54.

———. "Inflation, Revaluation, and the Crisis of Middle Class Politics." *Central European History* 12 (June 1979): 143–68.

———. "In the Shadow of Stabilization: German Liberalism and the Legitimacy Crisis of the Weimar Party System, 1924–1930." In *Nachwirkungen,* edited by Gerald Feldman, pp. 21–41.

Kommers, Donald. *Judicial Politics in West Germany.* Beverly Hills: Sage Publications, 1976.

Krohn, Claus-Dieter. "Helfferich contra Hilferding." *Vierteljahresschrift für Sozial- und Wirtschaftsgeschichte* 62 (1975): 62–89.

———. " 'Oekonomische Zwangslage' und das Scheitern der Weimarer Republik." *Geschichte und Gesellschaft* 8 (1982): 415–26.

———. *Stabilisierung und ökonomische Interessen.* Düsseldorf: Bertelsmann Universitätsverlag, 1974.

Kunz, Andreas. *Civil Servants and the Politics of Inflation in Germany, 1914–1924.* Berlin: de Gruyter, 1986.

Lane, Barbara, and Leila Rupp, eds. *Nazi Ideology.* Austin: University of Texas Press, 1978.

Laursen, Karsten, and Jurgen Pedersen. *The German Inflation.* Amsterdam: North Holland Publishing Co., 1964.

Lenoir, J. "Judicial Review in Germany under the Weimar Constitution." *Tulane Law Review* 14 (1940): 361–83.

Liebe, Werner. *Die DNVP, 1918–1924.* Düsseldorf: Droste Verlag, 1956.

List Gesellschaft. *Kapitalbildung und Steuersystem.* Berlin: R. Hobbing, 1930.

Lüke, Rolf. *Von der Stabilisierung zur Krise.* Zurich: Polygraphische Verlag, AG, 1958.

Maier, Charles. *Recasting Bourgeois Europe.* Princeton: Princeton University Press, 1975.

Mattern, Johannes. *Constitutional Jurisprudence in the German National Republic*. Baltimore: Johns Hopkins Press, 1928.

Mendelssohn-Bartholdy, Albrecht. *War and German Society*. New Haven: Yale University Press, 1937.

Mendershausen, Horst. *Two Postwar Recoveries in Germany*. Amsterdam: North Holland Publishing Co., 1955.

Modigliani, Franco. "The Life Cycle Hypothesis of Saving, the Demand for Wealth, and the Supply of Capital." *Social Research* 33 (1966): 160–217.

Moggridge, Donald. *British Monetary Policy, 1924–1931. The Norman Conquest of $4.86*. Cambridge: Cambridge University Press, 1974.

Mommsen, Hans, et al., eds. *Industrielles System und politische Entwicklung in der Weimarer Republik*. Düsseldorf: Droste Verlag, 1974.

Mückl, Wolfgang. *Die Wirkungen der Inflation*. Göttingen: O. Schwartz, 1975.

Netzband, Karl-Bernhard, and Hans Widmaier. *Währungs- und Finanzpolitik der Aera Luthers*. Basel: Kyklos Verlag, 1964.

Nipperdey, Hans, ed. *Die Grundrechte und Grundpflege der Reichsverfassung*. Vols. 1–3. Berlin: Reimar, 1930.

NS-Recht in historischer Perspektive. Munich: Oldenbourg, 1981.

Nussbaum, Arthur. *Money in the Law*. Brooklyn: The Foundation Press, Inc., 1950.

Petzina, Dietmar. *Die deutsche Wirtschaft in der Zwischenkriegszeit*. Wiesbaden: Franz Steiner Verlag, 1977.

Pirlet, Otto. *Der politische Kampf um die Aufwertungsgesetzgebung nach dem 1. Weltkrieg*. Cologne: Fotodruck Klaus Jansen, 1959.

Radbruch, Gustav. *Rechtsphilosophie*. Leipzig: Quelle & Meyer, 1932.

Roesler, Konrad. *Finanzpolitik des deutschen Reiches im Ersten Weltkrieg*. Berlin: Duncker & Humboldt, 1967.

Rüthers, Bernd. *Die unbegrenzte Auslegung*. Tübingen: J. C. B. Mohr, 1968.

Schacht, Hjalmar. *The Stabilization of the Mark*. London: George Allen & Unwin, Ltd., 1927.

Schuker, Stephen A. "American 'Reparations' to Germany, 1919–1933." In *Nachwirkungen*, edited by Gerald Feldman, pp. 335–84.

Schumacher, Martin. *Mittelstandsfront und Republik*. Düsseldorf: Droste Verlag, 1972.

Schüren, Ulrich. *Der Volksentscheid zur Fürstenenteignung, 1926*. Düsseldorf: Droste Verlag, 1978.

Shackle, George. *Years of High Theory*. Cambridge: Cambridge University Press, 1967.

Southern, David. "The Impact of Inflation: Inflation, the Courts and Revaluation." In *Social Change and Political Development in Weimar Germany*, edited by Richard Bessel and E. J. Feuchtwanger, pp. 55–76. Totowa, N.J.: Barnes & Noble, 1981.

———. "The Revaluation Question in the Weimar Republic." *Journal of Modern History* 52 (1979): D1029–D1053.

Steffan, Franz. *Bayerische Vereinsbank*. Würzburg: H. Stürtz, 1969.

Steinisch, Irmgard. "Die Auswirkungen inflationärer Wirtschaftsentwicklungen auf das Arbeitszeitproblem in der deutschen und amerikanischen eisen- und stahlerzeugenden Industrien." In *Erfahrung*, edited by Gerald Feldman et al., pp. 394–424.

Stolleis, Michael. *Gemeinwohlformeln im nationalsozialistischen Recht.* Berlin: J. Schweitzer Verlag, 1974.

Stürmer, Michael. *Koalition und Opposition in der Weimarer Republik.* Düsseldorf: Droste Verlag, 1967.

Svennilson, Ingvar. *Growth and Stagnation in the European Economy.* Geneva: United Nations Economic Commission for Europe, 1954.

Teubner, Gunther. "Paragraph 242." In *Reihe Alternativ Kommentäre. Kommentar zum Bürgerliches Gesetzesbuch, 2, Allgemeines Schuldrecht.* Neuwied/ Darmstadt, 1980.

Volkov, Shulamit. *The Rise of Popular Antimodernism in Germany. The Urban Master Artisans, 1873–1896.* Princeton: Princeton University Press, 1978.

von Mehren, Arthur. *The Civil Law System.* Englewood Cliffs: Prentice Hall, Inc., 1957.

Weisbrod, Bernd. *Schwerindustrie in der Weimarer Republik.* Wuppertal: P. Hammer, 1978.

Wieacker, Franz. *Industriegesellschaft und Privatrechtsordnung.* Frankfurt/ M: Athenäum Fischer Taschenbuch Verlag, 1974.

————. *Privatrechtsgeschichte der Neuzeit.* 2d ed. Göttingen: Vandenhoeck & Ruprecht, 1967.

————. *Zur rechtstheoretischen Präzisierung des Paragraphs 242 B.G.B.* Tübingen: J. C. B. Mohr, 1956.

Winkler, Heinrich-August. *Mittelstand, Demokratie und Nationalsozialismus.* Cologne: Kiepenheuer & Witsch, 1972.

————, ed. *Organisierter Kapitalismus.* Göttingen: Vandenhoeck & Ruprecht, 1974.

Witt, Peter-Christian. "Die Auswirkungen der Inflation auf die Finanzpolitik des deutschen Reiches 1924–1935." In *Nachwirkungen*, edited by Gerald Feldman, pp. 43–95.

————. "Finanzpolitik und sozialer Wandel in Krieg und Inflation." In *Industrielles System*, edited by Mommsen et al., pp. 395–425.

————. "RFM und Reichsfinanzverwaltung, 1918–1924." *Vierteljahresheft für Zeitgeschichte* 23 (1975): 1–61.

Index